Graham Bath's experience in testing spans over 25 years and has covered a wide array of domains and technologies. As a test manager, he has been responsible for the testing of mission-critical systems in spaceflight, telecommunications, and police incident control. Graham has designed tests to the highest levels of rigor within real-time aerospace systems such as the Eurofighter military aircraft.

As a principal consultant for the T-Systems Global Delivery Unit, "Testing Services", he has mastered the Quality Improvement Programs of several major companies, primarily in the financial and government sectors. In his current position, Graham is responsible for the company's training and test-consulting programs. Graham is co-author of the ISTQB Expert Level syllabus, "Improving the Test Process". He is a long-standing member of the German Testing Board and is chairman of the ISTQB Expert Level working group.

Drs. **Erik van Veenendaal**, CISA (www.erikvanveenendaal.nl), has been working as a practitioner and manager in the IT-industry since 1987. After a career in software development, he transferred to the area of software quality. As a test analyst, test manager, and test consultant, Erik has over 20 years of practical testing experience. He has also been a senior lecturer in the Technology Management department at the Eindhoven University of Technology for almost 10 years.

Erik founded Improve Quality Services BV (www.improveqs.nl) in 1998 as an independent organization that focuses on advanced high-quality services. He has been the company director for over 12 years. Under his direction, Improve Quality Services became a leading testing company in The Netherlands.

Erik is the co-author of numerous papers and a number of books on software quality and testing, including the best sellers *ISTQB Foundations of Software Testing* and *Test Maturity Model integration (TMMi)*. He is a regular speaker at both national and international testing conferences and a leading international trainer in the field of software testing.

Since its foundation in 2002, Erik has been heavily involved in the International Software Testing Qualifications Board (ISTQB). From 2005 to 2009, he was the vice president of the ISTQB organization; he has also been the lead of the ISTQB Expert Level working party for over 10 years. As a co-author, he is also involved in writing the Foundation, Advanced, and Expert Level syllabi. Erik is one of the founders of the TMMi Foundation and is the lead developer of the TMMi model. For his outstanding contribution to the field of testing, Erik received the European Testing Excellence Award in December 2007.

Graham Bath · Erik van Veenendaal

Improving the Test Process

Implementing Improvement and Change –
A Study Guide for the ISTQB Expert Level Module

Publisher: Gerhard Rossbach
Editor: Michael Barabas
Copyeditor: Judy Flynn
Proofreader: Julie Simpson
Project Manager: Matthias Rossmanith
Layout: Josef Hegele
Cover Design: Helmut Kraus, www.exclam.de
Printer: Sheridan
Printed in USA

ISBN 978-1-933952-82-6

1st Edition 2014
© 2014 by Graham Bath and Erik van Veenendaal

Rocky Nook, Inc.
802 East Cota St., 3rd Floor
Santa Barbara, CA 93103

www.rockynook.com

Library of Congress Cataloging-in-Publication Data

Bath, Graham, 1954-
Improving the test process : implementing improvement and change--a study guide for the ISTQB expert level module / by Graham Bath, Erik van Veenendaal.
    pages cm
ISBN 978-1-933952-82-6 (softcover : alk. paper)
1. Computer software--Testing--Examinations--Study guides. 2. Electronic data processing personnel--Certification. I. Veenendaal, Erik van. II. Title.
 QA76.76.T48B376 2013
 005.3028'7--dc23
                              2013035049

Distributed by O'Reilly Media
1005 Gravenstein Highway North
Sebastopol, CA 95472

All rights reserved. No part of the material protected by this copyright notice may be reproduced or utilized in any form, electronic or mechanical, including photocopying, recording, or by any information storage and retrieval system, without written permission of the publisher.

Many of the designations in this book used by manufacturers and sellers to distinguish their products are claimed as trademarks of their respective companies. Where those designations appear in this book, and Rocky Nook was aware of a trademark claim, the designations have been printed in caps or initial caps. All product names and services identified throughout this book are used in editorial fashion only and for the benefit of such companies with no intention of infringement of the trademark. They are not intended to convey endorsement or other affiliation with this book.

While reasonable care has been exercised in the preparation of this book, the publisher and author(s) assume no responsibility for errors or omissions, or for damages resulting from the use of the information contained herein or from the use of the discs or programs that may accompany it.

This book is printed on acid-free paper.

Preface

If your objective is to gain well-rounded, in-depth knowledge of how to improve testing processes, this book is for you. It is a "one-stop" study guide for the "Improving the Test Process" module of the ISTQB Certified Tester Expert Level.

This book will give you a thorough understanding of how to approach test process improvement from two fundamental viewpoints: the process itself and the people issues concerned with improving the process. It's not a book about using model XYZ or applying technique ABC; it considers test process improvement itself as a process, with a wide range of options, choices, and interactions.

Of course, you'll get in-depth information about models and techniques; we need to know the "tools of the trade" and how to use them. But there's more to test process improvement than merely applying models and techniques.

This book will also help you improve your soft skills. In particular it will allow you to appreciate the way people interact, how they respond to change and how they can be guided through the changes that lead to process improvement. Don't worry, you don't need to be a psychologist to improve testing processes, but understanding people issues is a critical success factor.

This book is aimed at anyone charged with improving processes. The focus is on test processes, so test managers and test consultants in particular will benefit, but many of the issues covered apply equally well to improving other IT processes and will benefit many IT professionals.

The book provides full coverage of the "Improving the Test Process" module of the ISTQB Certified Tester Expert Level [ISTQB-CTEL-ITP]. Two of the three core authors of this syllabus are also the authors of this book; we cover everything you will need to know to successfully sit for the examinations.

Acknowledgements

Our thanks go to co-author Isabel Evans, with whom we developed this ISTQB Expert Level Certified Tester Syllabus.

I (Erik) would especially like to acknowledge Danielle for her continuous support.

I (Graham) would especially like to acknowledge my family (Elke, Christopher, Jennifer) for their understanding and patience.

Contents

Preface v

Acknowledgements vi

1 Introduction 1
  1.1 About the Authors 1
      1.1.1 Erik van Veenendaal 1
      1.1.2 Graham Bath 3
  1.2 Purpose of the Book 3
  1.3 What Is an Expert? 5
  1.4 Expectations and Business Outcomes 6
  1.5 Career Paths for Testers 8
  1.6 Syllabus Parts 9
  1.7 The Certification Exam 10
  1.8 Certification 11

2 The Context of Improvement 13
  2.1 Why Improve Testing? 13
  2.2 What Can Be Improved? 17
  2.3 Views on Quality 20
  2.4 The Generic Improvement Process 25
      2.4.1 The Deming Cycle 25
      2.4.2 The IDEAL Improvement Framework 28
      2.4.3 Fundamental Concepts of Excellence 30
  2.5 Overview of Improvement Approaches 37
      2.5.1 Overview of Model-Based Approaches 37
      2.5.2 Overview of Analytical Approaches 39

		2.5.3	Hybrid Approaches 39
		2.5.4	Other Approaches to Improving the Test Process 39
	2.6	Exercises 56	

3 Model-Based Improvement   59

	3.1	Introduction to Test Process Improvement Models 60	
		3.1.1	Desirable Characteristics of Test Process Improvement Models 60
		3.1.2	Using Models: Benefits and Risks 63
		3.1.3	Categories of Models 67
	3.2	Software Process Improvement (SPI) Models 71	
		3.2.1	Capability Maturity Model Integration (CMMI) 71
		3.2.2	ISO/IEC 15504 84
		3.2.3	Comparing CMMI and ISO/IEC 15504 90
	3.3	Test Process Improvement Models 91	
		3.3.1	The Test Process Improvement Model (TPI NEXT) 91
		3.3.2	Test Maturity Model integration (TMMi) 106
		3.3.3	Comparing TPI NEXT to TMMi 124
		3.3.4	Systematic Test and Evaluation Process (STEP) 128
		3.3.5	Critical Testing Processes (CTP) 132
	3.4	Comparing Process Models and Content Models 137	
	3.5	Suitability of SPI Models and Test Process Improvement Models 138	
	3.6	Exercises 141	

4 Analytical-Based Improvement   145

	4.1	Introduction 145	
	4.2	Causal Analysis 146	
		4.2.1	Selecting Items for Causal Analysis 148
		4.2.2	Gathering and Organizing the Information 154
		4.2.3	Identifying Root Causes 160
		4.2.4	Drawing Conclusions 169
		4.2.5	Causal Analysis with System Diagrams 170

		4.2.6	Causal Analysis during Formal Reviews 171

		4.2.7	Causal Analysis Lessons Learned 173
4.3	GQM Approach 174		
		4.3.1	Introduction 174
		4.3.2	Paradigms 175
		4.3.3	GQM Process 178
		4.3.4	Supporting Tools and Techniques 185
		4.3.5	Bottom-Up Improvement 190
4.4	Analysis Using Measures, Metrics, and Indicators 191		
		4.4.1	Test Effectiveness Metrics 193
		4.4.2	Test Efficiency / Cost Metrics 195
		4.4.3	Lead-Time Metrics 196
		4.4.4	Predictability Metrics 197
		4.4.5	Product Quality Metrics 197
		4.4.6	Test Maturity Metrics 200
4.5	Exercises 201		

5	**Selecting Improvement Approaches**		**205**
5.1	Selecting Test Process Improvement Approaches 205		
5.2	Process Models 206		
5.3	Content Models 210		
5.4	Analytical Approaches 212		
5.5	Mixed Approaches 215		
5.6	Analytical Approaches and Improvement Models 216		
		5.6.1	Analytical-Based Improvement with CMMI 216
		5.6.2	Analytical-Based Improvement with TPI NEXT 217
		5.6.3	Analytical-Based Improvement with TMMi 219
		5.6.4	Analytical-Based Improvement with CTP and STEP 220
5.7	Exercises 221		

6 Process for Improvement 223

- 6.1 Introduction 223
  - 6.1.1 IDEAL Process Improvement Framework 223
  - 6.1.2 Test Policy 225
- 6.2 Initiating the Improvement Process 229
  - 6.2.1 Identify Stimulus for Change 230
  - 6.2.2 Set Objectives for Test Improvement 231
  - 6.2.3 Set Context 237
  - 6.2.4 Build Sponsorship 237
  - 6.2.5 Charter Infrastructure 238
- 6.3 Diagnosing the Current Situation 238
  - 6.3.1 Planning the Assessment 240
  - 6.3.2 Assessment Preparation 241
  - 6.3.3 Performing Interviews 242
  - 6.3.4 Giving Feedback 243
  - 6.3.5 Analyzing Results 243
  - 6.3.6 Performing Solution Analysis 244
  - 6.3.7 Recommending Improvement Actions 247
- 6.4 Establishing a Test Improvement Plan 249
  - 6.4.1 Set Priorities 250
  - 6.4.2 Develop an Implementation Approach 250
  - 6.4.3 Planning the Improvements 251
- 6.5 Acting to Implement Improvement 252
  - 6.5.1 Selecting and Executing a Pilot 254
  - 6.5.2 Manage and Control the Implementation 254
- 6.6 Learning from the Improvement Program 255
- 6.7 Exercises 256

7	**Organization, Roles, and Skills**		**259**
7.1	Organization		259
	7.1.1	The Test Process Group (TPG)	260
	7.1.2	Test Improvement with Remote, Offshore, and Outsourced Teams	266
7.2	Individual Roles and Staffing		268
	7.2.1	The Test Process Improver	268
	7.2.2	The Lead Assessor	270
	7.2.3	The Co-Assessor	271
7.3	Skills of the Test Process Improver/Assessor		272
	7.3.1	Interviewing Skills	273
	7.3.2	Listening Skills	283
	7.3.3	Presentation and Reporting Skills	286
	7.3.4	Analytical Skills	292
	7.3.5	Note-Taking Skills	293
	7.3.6	Skills of Persuasion	295
	7.3.7	Management Skills	297
	7.3.8	Summary	298
7.4	Exercises		298
8	**Managing Change**		**301**
8.1	Introduction		302
8.2	Overview		303
	8.2.1	The Fundamental Change Process	303
	8.2.2	The Satir Model	304
	8.2.3	Tipping Points and Change	306
8.3	Prepare for Change		308
	8.3.1	Establish the Need for Improvement	308
	8.3.2	Create a Sense of Urgency	311
	8.3.3	Establish the Improvement Team	312
8.4	Decide What to Change		313
	8.4.1	Establish a Vision of the Future	314

	8.4.2	Set Specific Objectives and Align to Business Goals	314
	8.4.3	Decide on an Implementation Strategy	314
	8.4.4	Balance Short-Term and Longer-Term Benefits	315
8.5	Making Change Happen		316
	8.5.1	Communicating for Buy-In and Understanding	316
	8.5.2	Anticipating Chaos	317
	8.5.3	Managing the Chaos	318
	8.5.4	Handling Resistance to Change	319
	8.5.5	Climbing Out of Chaos: Developing Transforming Ideas	321
8.6	Making Change Stick		322
	8.6.1	Rollout of New Ideas and Practices	323
	8.6.2	Provide Lasting Support	326
	8.6.3	Create a New Culture of Improvement	327
	8.6.4	Practice Continuous Improvement Principles	327
8.7	Data Privacy		328
8.8	Exercises		328

9 Critical Success Factors 331

9.1	Critical Success Factors		331
	9.1.1	Getting Started	332
	9.1.2	Getting the Job Done	334
	9.1.3	Critical Success Factors: A Case Study	337
9.2	Setting a Culture for Improvement		340
	9.2.1	Defining "Improvement Culture"	340
	9.2.2	Aspects of Improvement Culture	341
	9.2.3	Test Process Improvement Manifesto	345
9.3	Exercises		347

10 Adapting to Different Life Cycle Models 351

10.1	Test Process Improvement with Different Life Cycles	351
10.2	Exercises	357

Appendix A: Glossary   **359**

Appendix B: Literature and References   **385**

B.1   Books/Journals 385
B.2   ISTQB Publications 388
B.3   Standards 389
B.4   Web References 390

Appendix C: The Syllabus Parts   **391**

Appendix D: The Exam   **393**

D.1   General Exam Aspects 393
D.2   Part 1 Exam: "Assessing Test Processes" 395
D.3   Part 2 Exam: "Implementing Test Process Improvement" 397
D.4   Tips 399
D.5   Common Problems 400

Appendix E: Summary of Cognitive Levels (K-Levels)   **403**

Appendix F: Answers   **405**

Index   **411**

1 Introduction

In this chapter we introduce ourselves and the Expert Level syllabus "Improving the Test Process", which forms the basis for this book.

Concerning the Expert Level in general, we will ask the fundamental question, What is an expert? and describe the expectations that can be placed on becoming an expert in test process improvement.

We show the overall ISTQB Certified Tester scheme and explain the importance of the Expert Level in enabling the definition of career paths for testers.

The "Improving the Test Process" syllabus is divided into two separately examinable parts. Each part is briefly described and issues concerning the certification exam are explained.

1.1 About the Authors

1.1.1 Erik van Veenendaal

Dr. Erik van Veenendaal, CISA, has been working as a practitioner and manager in the IT-industry since 1987. After a career in software development, he transferred to the area of software quality. As a test analyst, test manager and test consultant, Erik has over 20 years of practical testing experience. He has implemented structured testing, formal reviews and requirements processes and has carried out test process improvement activities based on Testing Maturity Model integration (TMMi) in a large number of organizations in different industries. Erik has also been a senior lecturer at the Eindhoven University of Technology, Faculty of Technology Management, for almost 10 years.

Erik founded Improve Quality Services BV (www.improveqs.nl) back in 1998 as an independent organization that focuses on advanced high-quality services. He has been the company director for over 12 years. Under his direction, Improve Quality Services became a leading testing company in The Netherlands. Customers are especially to be found in the area of embedded software (e.g., Philips, Océ en Assembléon) and in the finance domain (e.g., Rabobank, ING, and Triodos Bank). Improve Quality Services offers international consultancy and training services with respect to testing (e.g., test process improvement using the TMMi framework), quality management, and requirements engineering. Improve Quality Services BV was the second worldwide company to become accredited to perform TMMi assessments. It is a market leader for ISTQB Foundation Level and ISTQB Advanced Level training courses and a member of the International Requirements Engineering Board (IREB).

Erik is the (co-)author of numerous papers and a number of books on software quality and testing, including the bestsellers *ISTQB Foundations of Software Testing*, *Test Maturity Model integration (TMMi)*, *The Testing Practitioner*, and *Testing according to TMap*. Erik was the first person to receive the ISEB Practitioner certificate with distinction and is also a Certified Information Systems Auditor (CISA) and accredited TMMi lead assessor. He is a regular speaker at both national and international testing conferences and a leading international trainer (ISTQB accredited) in the field of software testing. He holds the EuroSTAR record, winning the best tutorial award three times.

Since its foundation in 2002, Erik has been strongly involved in the International Software Testing Qualifications Board (ISTQB). From 2005 to 2009, he was the vice president of the ISTQB organization, and he is the founder of the local Belgium and The Netherlands board, the Belgium Netherlands Testing Qualifications Board (BNTQB). He is the editor of the ISTQB *Standard Glossary of Terms Used in Software Testing*. As a working party chair, he has been the lead of the ISTQB Expert Level working party for over 10 years. As a co-author, he is also involved in writing in the syllabi at the Foundation, Advanced, and Expert Levels. Erik is one of the founders of the TMMi Foundation and is currently its vice chair. He is the lead developer of the TMMi model. Erik is actively involved in various working parties of the International Requirements Engineering Board (IREB). For his outstanding contribution to the field of testing, Erik received the European Testing Excellence Award in December 2007.

After having provided leadership to Improve Quality Services BV for over 12 years, Erik stepped down from that role in July 2010. Since that time he has been living in Bonaire, where he is involved in international test consultancy, training, international organizations (e.g., ISTQB, TMMi, and IREB), publications, and presentations.

Erik can be contacted via email at eve@improveqs.nl and through his website, www.erikvanveenendaal.nl. You can also follow Erik on Twitter; his username is @ErikvVeenendaal.

1.1.2 Graham Bath

Graham Bath's experience in testing spans over 30 years and has covered a wide array of domains and technologies. As a test manager, he has been responsible for the testing of mission-critical systems in spaceflight, telecommunications, and police incident control. Graham has designed tests to the highest levels of rigor within real-time aerospace systems such as the Tornado and Eurofighter military aircraft.

As a principal consultant for the T-Systems Global Delivery Center, Testing Services, he has mastered the quality improvement programs of several major companies, primarily in the financial, government, and automotive sectors. In his current position, Graham is responsible for developing the testing skills of T-Systems' professional testing staff and for its range of test improvement offerings.

Graham is a regular speaker at testing conferences and has given tutorials on test improvement throughout the world. He is co-author (together with Judy McKay) of *The Software Test Engineer's Handbook*, which is a study guide for the ISTQB Test Analyst and Technical Test Analyst Advanced Level certificates.

Graham chairs the ISTQB Expert Level Working Group and is co-author (together with Erik van Veenendaal and Isabel Evans) of the ISTQB Expert Level Certified Tester syllabus "Improving the Test Process."

As a longstanding member of the German Testing Board, Graham chairs the GTB's Advanced Level and Expert Level working groups.

Graham was born and raised in England but now lives and works in Munich, Germany. You can contact him via email at graham.bath@t-systems.com.

1.2 Purpose of the Book

We set ourselves some fairly tough requirements for this book. After all, it is intended for those aspiring to become "experts" in the field of test process improvement. Before we launch into the actual content, we'd like to give you a brief overview of the basic requirements we set ourselves. This will help you understand the general approach we have taken in structuring and writing the book.

First and foremost we, the authors, require that the book provides a thorough coverage of the subject matter and is readable.

Overview

Each chapter includes a brief introduction to summarize content.

Completeness and Structure

This book is based on the ISTQB Expert Level syllabus "Improving the Test Process" [ISTQB-CTEL-ITP] and covers everything you will need to know to successfully sit for the examinations. You can also use the information in this book to become a competent and employable test process improver.

We have maintained the structure of the syllabus throughout this book. Chapter and section numbers map closely to each other.

Readability

When writing a book that is based on a predefined syllabus, it's all too easy to focus on syllabus coverage alone. Of course, syllabus coverage is essential, but the result is often a rather "dry" reading experience, which we don't want. We want you to have a book that gives you syllabus coverage and is readable.

We intend to make this book readable by adopting a particular style and standardized approach to each chapter:

- Learning objectives

  These are the specific learning objectives provided in the syllabus and will be of particular use for those of you studying for the certification exam.

- Technical content

  Within each chapter, we deal with the actual technical content of a particular subject. The learning objectives of the ISTQB Expert Level syllabus are not just focused on learning and repeating, they are designed so that you can apply what you have learned and justify your choices. To help you achieve this we go beyond the information provided in the syllabus and add more descriptive material to give you a "well-rounded" level of knowledge.

- Exercises

  The exercises help develop your ability to apply the material provided in the book. These are not intended as formal multiple-choice exam practice questions written against learning objectives. Note that the ISTQB Expert Level exam also includes essay-type questions, which require a written answer. Appendix D provides a detailed overview of the exam that will help candidates to prepare.

- Appendices

    Useful information has been grouped together into the appendices listed in table 1–1.

Table 1–1 Overview of appendices

Appendix	Description
A	Glossary of terms used in the book. The definitions of these terms are in line with the ISTQB glossary and are included for ease of reference.
B	Literature and references. This appendix is divided into separate sections for books, ISTQB publications, websites, and standards.
C	Syllabus parts. This appendix summarizes the two syllabus parts.
D	The certification exam. Section 1.7 describes broadly the exam. Further details and tips are provided in this appendix.
E	K-levels. Each learning objective is assigned a specific cognitive level (K-level). A summary of these K-levels is provided.
F	Answers to exercises Solutions to the multiple-choice exercises for each chapter are provided.

1.3   What Is an Expert?

Regrettably, the word *expert* is probably one of the most overused terms in our industry. In a competitive world it has become all too popular to label ourselves or others as "experts." In fact, if you were to ask 10 people to define the term *expert*, you would likely get 10 different answers. When the ISTQB set up the Expert Level qualification, it therefore came as no surprise that there was some considerable debate about what *expert* should actually mean. Should it be some kind of "super guru," should it be anyone with a bit more experience than average, or should it simply be left open to interpretation? The definition of a testing expert used by ISTQB is "a person with the special skills and knowledge representing mastery of a particular testing subject. Being an expert means possessing and displaying special skills and knowledge derived from training and experience."

The approach taken by ISTQB is to consider "expert" as an integral part of a career path in testing (see section 1.5). Each Expert Level module defines its own specific expectations and business outcomes (these are covered in section 1.4).

The Expert Level program can be characterized by the following key attributes:

- "Higher level" learning objectives are included that emphasize the ability to evaluate, make judgments, and bring together different elements to form a coherent whole (please refer to appendix E for details).
- Subjects are given in-depth consideration.
- High levels of experience are expected to achieve certification.
- "Continuous learning" is expected. Unlike the Foundation and Advanced Level certificates, an Expert Level certificate is not for life; it is valid for five years. Certification renewal can be achieved either by retaking the exam or by collecting sufficient credits in the Certification Extension scheme [ISTQB-CEP] (see section 1.8).

1.4 Expectations and Business Outcomes

It is not intended that candidates who qualify at the Expert Level should immediately be considered "world experts" in test process improvement. The expectation is that the qualified ISTQB CTEL in "Improving the Test Process" will be able to provide expert support within their organization or project to initiate, implement, and support improvements to testing in that organization or project.

Business outcomes describe the value obtained from acquiring the Expert Level certificate, principally from the perspective of an employer or sponsor. These are the people who ask the fundamental question, What can I expect an expert in test process improvement to do for me and my organization?

The Expert Level Overview document [ISTQB-EL-OVIEW] describes the business outcomes for each Expert Level module. The business outcomes for the "Improving the Test Process" syllabus are allocated to the two syllabus parts (see section 1.6 and appendix C) as follows:

Part 1: Assessing test processes

The expert test process improver is able to perform each of the following tasks:

TP1.1   Lead programs for improving the test process within an organization or project and can identify and manage critical success factors.

TP2   Take appropriate business-driven decisions on how to approach improvement to the test process.

TP3   Assess the current status of a test process, propose step-wise improvements, and show how these are linked to achieving business goals.

TP5   Analyze specific problems with the test process and propose effective solutions.

Part 2: Implementing test process improvement

The expert test process improver is able to perform each of the following tasks:

TP1.2   Lead programs for implementing test process improvements within an organization or project and identify and manage critical success factors.

TP4   Set up a strategic policy for improving the test process and implement that policy.

TP6   Create a test improvement plan that meets business objectives.

TP7   Develop organizational concepts for improvement of the test process that include required roles, skills, and organizational structure.

TP8   Establish a standard process for implementing improvement to the test process within an organization.

TP9   Manage the introduction of changes to the test process, including cooperation with the sponsors of improvements.

TP10   Understand and effectively manage the human issues associated with assessing the test process and implementing necessary changes.

1.5 Career Paths for Testers

Introduction of the Expert Level establishes the core structure of the ISTQB Certified Tester program, which starts with Foundation Level and progresses via the Advanced Level up to Expert Level. The syllabi within each level are carefully scoped to ensure that testing themes are introduced at an appropriate level and to ensure that specific subjects, such as test process improvement, are developed in increasing detail. The result is a structure that supports the development of career paths for professional testers. The arrows in the following diagram show the current paths within the ISTQB Certified Tester structure.

Career paths not only indicate an individual's progression in terms of their experience and knowledge of a particular subject (e.g., test process improvement), they also indicate the certifications required to progress from one level to another. The Expert Level Overview document [ISTQB-EL-OVIEW] defines the amount of experience and the certifications required to achieve the different Expert Level certifications.

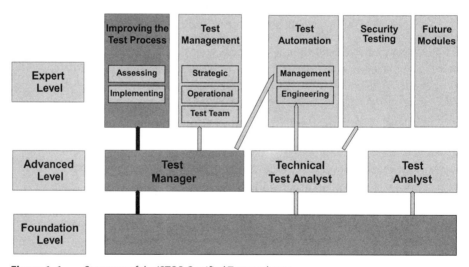

Figure 1-1   *Structure of the ISTQB Certified Tester scheme*

Figure 1-1 shows that the Expert Level syllabi are generally divided into parts. A candidate will be required to pass both examinations to achieve full certification and to formally become a Certified Expert Level Tester (CTEL) on the subject of improving the test process. Syllabus parts are discussed further in section 1.6 and in appendix C. Note that further career paths will be defined as more modules become available.

The career path for test process improvers is shown in table 1–2.

Table 1–2 Career path for test process improvers

Certification level – Cognitive levels	Relevant subjects for the expert test process improver
Foundation – Understand	• The fundamental test process

Advanced:
Test Manager
– Understand
– Apply
	• Test improvement process:
	  Basic steps in the IDEAL model
	• Introduction to test process improvement models:
	  TMMi, TPI NEXT, CTP, and STEP

Expert: Improving the Test Process – Apply – Analyze – Evaluate – Create	• The context of improvement • Analytical approaches • Model-based approaches • Selecting improvement approaches • Process for improvement • Organization, roles, and skills • Managing change • Critical success factors • Adapting to different life-cycle models

Refer to appendix E for a brief description of the cognitive levels (K-levels) mentioned in table 1–2.

1.6 Syllabus Parts

The ISTQB Expert syllabus "Improving the Test Process" [ISTQB-CTEL-ITP] covers material that requires a minimum of 8.5 days of study. The overall syllabus is therefore divided into two parts, which allows separate courses to be provided, each with a specific focus, as shown in table 1–3:

Table 1–3 *Parts of the "Improving the Test Process" module of the ISTQB Certified Tester Expert Level syllabus*

Syllabus part	Principal focus
Part 1: Assessing the Test Process	• Different approaches to test process improvement • Assessing test processes using models • Analytical approaches to test process assessment • Creating improvement recommendations
Part 2: Implementing Test Process Improvement	• Creating and implementing a test improvement plan • Organizing the test process improvement effort (roles, organizational forms) • Required skills • Managing change

Note that a candidate will be required to take both examinations in order to achieve full certification. Please refer to the following section and appendix D for further details of the exam.

1.7 The Certification Exam

The examination is introduced in this section. For further details, please refer to the document *Expert Level Exam Structure and Rules* issued by ISTQB [ISTQB-EL-EXAM] and appendix D.

A separate exam is provided for each part of the "Improving the Test Process" syllabus (see the preceding section). Each exam is made up of two components:

- Multiple-choice questions
- Essay questions

Before taking the exam, you must meet the following entry conditions:

- A participant must have an ISTQB Advanced Level Test Manager certificate (or equivalent, such as, for example, ISEB Practitioner, Version 1.1 – September 4, 2001).
- Examinees who wish to take a nonpublic exam, scheduled at the end of an accredited training course, must first produce evidence to the Examination Body that they have attended all days of that course (the training provider will normally provide this at the end of the course).

Before taking the exam, it is recommended that:

- participants have at least seven years of practical testing experience
- participants have attended a training course, although, as with other ISTQB levels, this is not formally required to take a (public) exam (i.e., an exam not provided at the end of a course).

Pass Mark

The pass mark for each exam is 65 %.

1.8 Certification

To receive full certification at the Expert Level (CTEL), you must pass both exams (see section 1.7) and provide proof of the following practical working experience:

- At least five years of general testing experience in the industry
- At least two years of industry experience in test process improvement

Written proof of this experience and two verifiable references need to be submitted.

The Expert Level certificate is initially valid for five years. After the initial five years, individuals may extend their current level of certification for another five-year period. There is no limit to the number of times a certification can be extended.

Extension is achieved by retaking the exam for the Expert Level certificate or by completing activities to accumulate a minimum of 200 certification extension credits (CECs) before the current certification expires. The activities, renewal process, and CECs that may be awarded are defined in the ISTQB Certified Tester Expert Level, Certification Extension Process document [ISTQB-CEP].

2 The Context of Improvement

If your intention is to improve the test process in your project or organization, you will need to convince managers, business owners, and fellow testers of the necessity for this and explain to them how to you intend to proceed.

This chapter addresses these fundamental issues and sets the overall context for test process improvement. It starts by asking the basic questions "Why improve testing?" and "What things can I improve?" and then goes on to consider the subject of (product) quality, both in general terms and with regard to different stakeholders. Following this, an overview is provided of the systematic methods and approaches available that can help to achieve the quality objectives in your project or organization by improving the testing process. This chapter introduces some of the concepts and approaches that will be expanded upon in other chapters.

2.1 Why Improve Testing?

Syllabus Learning Objectives

LO 2.1.1 (K2) Give examples of the typical reasons for test improvement.
LO 2.1.2 (K2) Contrast test improvement with other improvement goals and initiatives.
LO 2.1.3 (K6) Formulate to all stakeholders the reasons for proposed test process improvements, show how they are linked to business goals and explain them in the context of other process improvements.

This is an exciting time to be a test professional. Systems in which software is a dominant factor are becoming more and more challenging to build. They are playing an increasingly important role in society. New methods, techniques, and tools are becoming available to support development and maintenance tasks. Because systems play such an important role in our lives, both economically and socially, there is pressure for the software engineering discipline to focus on quality issues. Poor-quality software is no longer acceptable to society. Software failures can result in catastrophic losses. In this context the importance of the testing discipline, as one of the quality measures that can be taken, is growing rapidly. Often 50% of the budget for a project is spent on testing. Testing has truly become a profession and should be treated as such.

Many product development organizations face tougher business objectives every day, such as, for example, decreased time to market, higher quality and reliability, and reduced costs. Many of them develop and manufacture products that consist of over 60 percent software, and this figure is still growing. At the same time, software development is sometimes an outsourced activity or is codeveloped with other sites. Together with the trend toward more reuse and platform architecture, testing has become a key activity that directly influences not only the product quality but also the "performance" of the entire development and manufacturing process.

In addition to these concerns is the increasing importance and amount of software in our everyday world. Software in consumer products doubles in size every 24 months; for example, TVs now have around 300,000 lines of code, and even electric razors now have some software in them. In the safety-critical area, there are around 400,000 lines of code in a car, and planes have become totally dependent on software. The growing amount of software has been accompanied by rapid growth in complexity. If we consider the number of defects per "unit" of software, research has shown that this number has, unfortunately, hardly decreased in the last two decades. As the market demands better and more reliable products that are developed and produced in shorter time periods and with less money, higher test performance is not an option; it is an essential ingredient for success.

The scope of testing is not necessarily limited to the software system. People who buy and use software are not really interested in the code; they need services and products that include a good user experience, business processes, training, user guides, and support. Improvements to testing must be carried out in the context of these wider quality goals, whether they relate to an organization, the customer, or IT teams.

For the past decades, the software industry has invested substantial effort to improve the quality of its products. Despite encouraging results from various quality improvement approaches, the software industry is still far from achieving the ultimate goal of zero defects. To improve product quality, the software industry has often focused on improving its development processes. A guideline that has been widely used to improve the development processes is Capability Maturity Model Integration (CMMI), which is often regarded as the industry standard for software process improvement.

Despite the fact that testing often accounts for at least 30 to 40 percent of the total project costs, only limited attention is given to testing in the various software process improvement models such as CMMI. As an answer, the testing community has created its own improvement models, such as TMMi and TPI NEXT, and is making a substantial effort on its own to improve the test performance and its process. Of course, "on its own" does not mean independent and without context. Test improvement always goes hand in hand with software development and the business objectives.

As stated earlier, the context within which test process improvement takes place includes any business or organizational process improvement and any IT or software process improvement. The following list includes some typical reasons for business improvements that influence testing:

- Improve product quality
- Reduce time to market but maintain quality levels
- Save money, improve efficiency
- Improve predictability
- Meet customer requirements
- Be at a capability level; e.g., for outsourcing companies
- Ensure compliance to standards; e.g., FDA in the medical domain (see section 2.5.4)

The fishbone diagram in figure 2–1 was the result of a retrospective session in a large embedded software organization and shows some of the causes of poor test performance and possible remedies. It also shows that test performance improvement is not the same as test process improvement because there are many other aspects that are of importance in improving test performance. The conclusions are also that improving test performance is not an easy and straightforward task; it is a challenge that covers many aspects.

2 The Context of Improvement

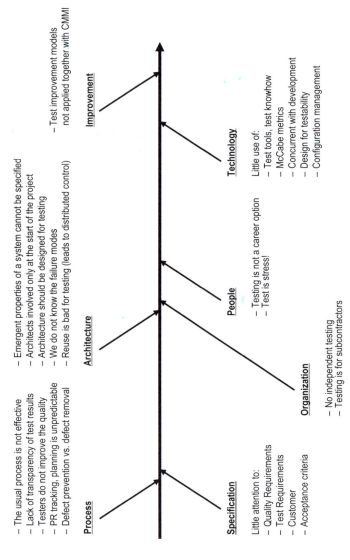

Figure 2-1 Fishbone diagram for test performance

2.2 What Can Be Improved?

> **Syllabus Learning Objectives**
>
> LO 2.2.1 (K2) Understand the different aspects of testing, and related aspects, that can be improved.

Software process improvement (SPI) is the continuous improvement of product quality, process effectiveness, and process efficiency leading to improved quality of the software product.

Test improvement is the continuous improvement of the effectiveness and/or the efficiency of the testing process within the context of the overall software process. This context means that improvements to testing may go beyond just the process itself; for example, extending to the infrastructure, organization, and testers' skills. Most test improvement models, as you will see later in this book, also address to a certain extent infrastructure, organizational, and people issues. For example, the TMMi model has dedicated process areas for test environment, test organization, and test training. Although the term most commonly used is *test process improvement*, in fact a more accurate term would be *test improvement* since multiple aspects are addressed in addition to the process.

Whereas some models for test process improvement focus mainly on higher test levels, or address only one aspect of structured testing—e.g., the test organization—it is important to initially consider all test levels (including static testing) and aspects of structured testing. With respect to dynamic testing, both lower test levels (e.g., component test, integration test) and higher test levels (e.g., system test, acceptance test) should ultimately be within the scope of the test improvement process.

The four cornerstones for structured testing (life cycle, techniques, infrastructure, and organization) [Pol, Teunnissen, and van Veenendaal 2002] should ultimately be addressed in any improvement. Priorities are based on business objectives and related test improvement objectives. Practical experiences have shown that balanced test improvement programs (e.g., between process, people, and infrastructure) are typically the most successful.

Preconditions

Test process improvements may indicate that associated or complementary improvements are needed for requirements management and other parts of the development process. Not every organization is able to carry out test process improvement in an effective and efficient manner. For an organization to be able to start, fundamental project management should preferably be available. This means, for example, that requirements are documented and managed in a planned and controlled manner (otherwise how can we perform test design?). Configurations should be planned and controlled (otherwise how do we know what to test?), and project planning should exist at an adequate level (otherwise how can we do test planning?). There are many other examples of how improvements to software development can support test improvements. This topic will be discussed in more detail in chapter 3 when test improvement models like TPI NEXT and TMMi are described.

If the aspects just described are missing, or are only partially in place, test process improvement is still possible and can function as a reverse and bottom-up quality push. Generally, the business drives (pushes) the improvement process, the business objectives then drive the software improvement process, and the software development improvement objectives then drive the test improvement process (see figure 2–2). However, with the reverse quality push, testing takes the driver's seat. As an example, if there are no or poor requirements, test designs become the requirements. If there is poor estimation at the project level, test estimation will dictate the project estimate. Of course, this will not be easily accepted, and much resistance can be expected. However, this reverse quality push is often used as a wake-up call to show how poor software development processes are. This approach is less efficient and perhaps even less effective, but if the involved test process improvement members are fit for the job, the push can be strong enough to have a positive impact on the surrounding improvement "domains."

Context

As a result, test process improvement cannot be considered a separate activity (see figure 2–2). It is part of software improvement activities, which in turn should be part of a total quality management program. Progress made in these areas is an indication of how effective the test process investment can be. Test process improvements may also be driven by overall SPI efforts. As previously mentioned, testing goals must always be aligned to business goals, so it is not necessarily the best option for an organization or project to achieve the highest level of test maturity.

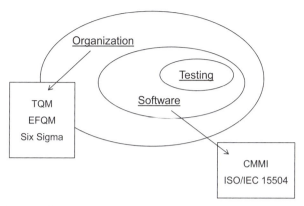

Figure 2-2   Context of test process improvement

From figure 2–2, you can see that test process improvement takes place within the context of organizational and business improvement. This may, for example, be managed via one of the following:

- Total Quality Management (TQM)

> **Total Quality Management**   An organization-wide management approach centered on quality, based on the participation of all members of the organization, and aiming at long-term success through customer satisfaction and benefits to all members of the organization and to society. Total Quality Management consists of planning, organizing, directing, control, and assurance. [After ISO 8402]

- ISO 9000:2000
- An excellence framework such as the EFQM Excellence Model (see section 2.4.3)
- Six Sigma (see section 2.4.3)

Test process improvement will most often also take place in the context of software process improvement.

> **Software Process Improvement (SPI)**   A program of activities designed to improve the performance and maturity of an organization's software processes and the results of such a program. [After Chrissis, Konrad, and Shrum, 2004]

This may be managed via one of the following:

- Capability Maturity Model Integration, or CMMI (see section 3.2.1)
- ISO/IEC 15504 (see section 3.2.2)
- ITIL [ITIL]
- Personal Software Process [PSP] (see section 2.5.4) and Team Software Process [TSP]

2.3 Views on Quality

> **Syllabus Learning Objectives**
>
> LO 2.3.1 (K2) Compare the different views of quality.
> LO 2.3.2 (K2) Map the different views of quality to testing.

Before starting quality improvement activities, there must be consensus about what quality really means in a specific business context. Only then can wrong expectations, unclear promises, and misunderstandings be avoided. In a single organization or project, we may come across several definitions of quality, perhaps used inadvertently and unacknowledged by all the people in the project. It is important to realize that there is no "right" definition of quality. Garvin showed that in practice, generally five distinct definitions of quality can be recognized [Garvin 1984], [Trienekens and van Veenendaal 1997]. We will describe these definitions briefly from the perspective of software development and testing. Improvement of the test process should consider which of the quality views discussed in this section are most applicable to the organization. The five distinct views on quality are as follows:

- Product-based
- User-based
- Manufacturing-based
- Value-based
- Transcendent-based

The Product-Based Definition

For testing, this view of quality relates strongly to non-functional testing. Product quality is determined by characteristics such as reliability, maintainability, and portability. When the product-based definition of quality is important, we

> **Product-based quality** A view of quality, wherein quality is based on a well-defined set of quality attributes. These attributes must be measured in an objective and quantitative way. Differences in the quality of products of the same type can be traced back to the way the specific quality attributes have been implemented. [After Garvin]

should evaluate which non-functional characteristics are of major importance and start improving non-functional testing based on this. The product-based view is common in the safety critical industry, where reliability, availability, maintainability, and safety (RAMS) are often key areas that determine product quality. For some products, usability is of extreme importance. The products can come from many industries and be used by individuals for activities such as, for example, gaming and entertainment, or are delivered to the public at large (i.e., via ATM). For these types of products, giving the appropriate amount of attention to usability (a non-functional characteristic) during development and testing is essential.

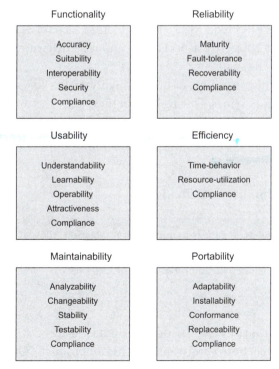

Figure 2–3   The ISO 9126 quality model

A typical quality approach is software development and testing based on the ISO 9126 standard (or the ISO 25000 series, which has superseded ISO 9126). The standard defines six quality characteristics and proposes the subdivision of each quality characteristic into a number of subcharacteristics (see figure 2–3). This ISO 9126 set reflects a huge step toward consensus in the software industry and addresses the general notion of software product quality. The ISO 9126 standard also provides metrics for each of the characteristics and subcharacteristics.

The User-Based Definition

> **User-based quality**   A view of quality wherein quality is the capacity to satisfy the needs, wants, and desires of the user(s). A product or service that does not fulfill user needs is unlikely to find any users. This is a context-dependent, contingent approach to quality since different business characteristics require different qualities of a product. [After Garvin]

Quality is fitness for use. This definition says that software quality should be determined by the user(s) of a product in a specific business situation. Different business characteristics require different "qualities" of a software product. Quality can have many subjective aspects and cannot be determined on the basis of only quantitative and mathematical metrics.

For testing, this definition of quality highly relates to validation and user acceptance testing activities. During both of these activities, we try to determine whether the product is fit for use. If the main focus of an improvement is on user-based quality, the validation-oriented activities and user acceptance testing should be a primary focus.

The Manufacturing-Based Definition

> **Manufacturing-based quality**   A view of quality whereby quality is measured by the degree to which a product or service conforms to its intended design and requirements. Quality arises from the process(es) used.
> [After Garvin]

This definition of quality points to the manufacturing—i.e., the specification, design, and construction—processes of software products. Quality depends on the extent to which requirements have been implemented in a software product in conformance with the original requirements. Quality is based on inspection, reviews, and (statistical) analysis of defects and failures in (intermediate) products. The manufacturing-based view on quality is also represented implicitly in many standards for safety-critical products, where the standards prescribe a thorough development and testing process.

For testing, this definition of quality strongly relates to verification and system testing activities. During both of these activities we try to determine whether the product is compliant with requirements. If the main focus of an improvement is on manufacturing-based quality, then verification-oriented activities and system testing should be a primary focus. This view of quality also has the strongest process improvement component. By following a strict process from requirement to test, we can deliver quality.

The Value-Based Definition

> **Value-based quality** A view of quality wherein quality is defined by price. A quality product or service is one that provides desired performance at an acceptable cost. Quality is determined by means of a decision process with stakeholders with trade-offs between time, effort, and cost aspects. [After Garvin]

This definition states that software quality should always be determined by means of a decision process involving trade-offs between time, effort, and cost. The value-based definition emphasizes the need to make trade-offs, which is often achieved by means of communication between all parties involved, such as sponsors, customers, developers, and producers. Software or systems being launched as an (innovative) new product apply the value-based definition of quality because if we spend more time to get a better product, we may miss the market window and a competitor might beat us by being first to market.

This definition of testing relates strongly to risk-based testing. We cannot test everything but should focus on the most important areas to test. Testing is always a balancing act: a decision process conducted with stakeholders with trade-offs between time, effort, and cost aspects. This view also means giving priority to business value and doing the things that really matter.

The Transcendent-Based Definition

This "esoteric" definition states that quality can in principle be recognized easily depending on the perceptions and feelings of an individual or group of individuals toward a type of software product. Although this one is the least operational of the definitions, it should not be neglected in practice. Frequently, a transcendent statement about quality can be a first step toward the explicit definition and measurement of quality. The entertainment and game industry may use this view on quality, thereby giving testing a difficult task. Often user panels and beta testing is performed to get feedback from the market on the excitement factor of the new product. Highly innovative product development is another area where one may encounter this view of quality.

As testers or test process improvers, we typically do not like the transcendent-based view of quality. It is very intangible and almost impossible to target. It can probably best be used to start a conversation with stakeholders about a different view of quality and assist them in making their view more explicit.

> **Transcendent-based quality** A view of quality wherein quality cannot be precisely defined but we know it when we see it or are aware of its absence when it is missing. Quality depends on the perception and affective feelings of an individual or group of individuals toward a product. [After Garvin]

The existence of the various quality definitions demonstrates the difficulty of determining the real meaning and relevance of software quality and quality improvement activities. Practitioners have to deal with this variety of definitions, interpretations, and approaches. How we define "quality" for a particular product, service, or project depends on context. Different industries will have different quality views. For most software products and systems, there is not just one view of quality.

The stakeholders are best served by balancing the quality aspects. For these products, we should ask ourselves, What is the greatest number or level of characteristics (product-based) that we can deliver to support the users' tasks (user-based) while giving best cost benefit (value-based) and following repeatable, quality-assured processes within a managed project (manufacturing-based)? Starting a test process improvement program means we start by having a clear understanding of what product quality means. The five distinct views on quality are usually a great way to start the discussion with stakeholders and achieve some consensus and common understanding of what type of product quality is being targeted.

2.4 The Generic Improvement Process

> **Syllabus Learning Objectives**
>
> LO 2.4.1 (K2) Understand the steps in the Deming Cycle.
> LO 2.4.2 (K2) Compare two generic methods (Deming Cycle and IDEAL framework) for improving processes.
> LO 2.4.3 (K2) Give examples for each of the Fundamental Concepts of Excellence with regard to test process improvement.

Process improvements are relevant to the software development process as well as to the testing process. Learning from one's own mistakes makes it possible to improve the process that organizations are using to develop and test software. The Deming improvement cycle—Plan, Do, Check, Act—has been used for many decades and is still relevant when testers need to improve the process in use today.

The following sections provide three generic improvement processes that have been around for many years and have been used as a basis for many (test) improvement approaches or models that exists today. Understanding the background and essentials of the generic improvement processes implies that one understands a number of the underlying principles of test improvement approaches and models discussed later in this book.

2.4.1 The Deming Cycle

Continuous improvement involves setting improvement objectives, taking measures to achieve them, and once they have been achieved, setting new improvement objectives. Continuous improvement models have been established to support this concept. One of the most common tools for continuous improvement is the Deming cycle. This simple yet practical improvement model, initially called the Shewhart cycle, was popularized by Edwards and Deming as Plan, Do, Check, Act (PDCA) [Edwards 1986]. The PDCA method is well suited for many improvement projects.

> **Deming cycle** An iterative four-step problem-solving process (Plan, Do, Check, Act), typically used in process improvement. [After Deming]

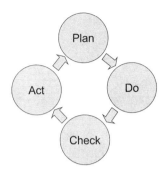

Figure 2–4   *Deming cycle*

Plan

Figure 2–4 shows how the Deming cycle operates. The Plan stage is where it all begins. Targets are defined for quality characteristics, costs, and service levels. The targets may initially be formulated by management as business improvement goals and successively broken down into individual *control points* that should be checked (see the following list) to see that the activities have been carried out. An analysis of current practices and skills is performed, after which improvement plans are set up for improving the test process. Prior to implementing a change, you must understand both the nature of your current problem and how your process failed to meet a stakeholder requirement. You and/or your problem-solving team determine the following:

- Which process needs to be improved
- How much improvement is required
- The change to be implemented
- When the change is to be implemented
- How you plan to measure the effect of the change
- What will be affected by this change (documents, procedures, etc.)

Once you have this plan, it's time to move to the Do stage.

Do

The Do stage is the implementation of the change. After the plans have been made, the activities are performed. Included in this step is an investment in human resources (e.g., training and coaching). Identify the people affected by the change and inform them that you're adapting their process for specific reasons like customer complaints, multiple failures, and continual improvement opportunity. Whatever the reason, it is important to let them know about the change. You'll need their buy-in to help ensure the effectiveness of the change. Then implement the change, including the measurements you'll need in the Check stage. Monitor the change after implementation to make sure no backsliding occurs. You wouldn't want people to return to the old methods of operation. Those methods were causing your company pain to begin with!

Check

The control points identified in the Plan stage are tracked using specific metrics, and deviations are observed. The variations in each metric may be predicted for a specific time interval and compared with the actual observations to provide information on deviations between the actual and expected. At the Check stage is where you'll perform analysis of the data you collected during the Do stage. Considerations include the following questions:

- Did the process improve?
- By how much?
- Did we meet the objective for the improvement?
- Was the process more difficult to use with the new methods?

Act

Using the information gathered, opportunities for performance improvement are identified and prioritized. The answers from the Check stage define your tasks for the Act stage. For example, if the process didn't improve, there's no point in asking additional questions during the Check stage. But action can be taken. In fact, action must be taken! The problem hasn't been solved. The action you'd take is to eliminate the change you implemented in the Do stage and return to the Plan stage to consider new options to implement. If the process did improve, you'd want to know if there was enough improvement. More simply, if the improvement was to speed up the process, is the process now fast enough to meet requirements? If not, consider additional methods to tweak the process so that you do meet improvement objectives. Again, you're back at the Plan stage of the Deming cycle.

Suppose you met the improvement objectives. Interview the process owner and some process participants to determine their thoughts regarding the change you implemented. They are your immediate customer. You want their feedback. If you didn't make the process harder (read "more costly or time consuming") your action in this case would be to standardize your improvement by changing any required documentation and to conduct training regarding the change.

Keep in mind that sometimes you will make the process more time consuming. But if the savings from the change more than offset the additional cost, you're likely to have implemented an appropriate change.

Sustainment

You're not done yet. You want to sustain the gain as visualized in figure 2–5; know that the change is still in place, and still effective. A review of the process and measures should give you this information. Watch the process to view for yourself whether the process operators are performing the process using the improvements you've implemented. Analyze the metrics to ensure effectiveness of your Deming cycle improvements.

Note that in the first two steps (Plan and Do), the sense of what is important plays the central role. In the last two steps (Check and Act), statistical methods and systems analysis techniques are most often used to help pinpoint statistical significance, dependencies, and further areas for improvement.

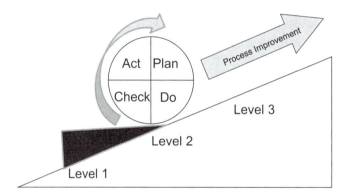

Figure 2–5 *The Deming cycle in context, sustaining the improvements*

2.4.2 The IDEAL Improvement Framework

The IDEAL framework [McFeeley/SEI 1996] is basically a more detailed implementation of the previously described Deming cycle specifically developed for software process improvement. The PDCA cycle can easily be recognized within IDEAL, but the model is enriched with a full description of phases and activities to be performed. The IDEAL model is the Software Engineering Institute's (SEI's) organizational improvement model that serves as a road map for initiating, planning, and implementing improvement actions. The IDEAL model offers a very pragmatic approach for software process improvement; it

2.4 The Generic Improvement Process

> **IDEAL** An organizational improvement model that serves as a roadmap for initiating, planning, and implementing improvement actions. The IDEAL model is named for the five phases it describes: initiating, diagnosing, establishing, acting, and learning.

also emphasizes the management perspective and commitment. It provides a road map for executing improvement programs using a life cycle composed of sequential phases containing activities (see figure 2–6). It is named for its five phases (initiating, diagnosing, establishing, acting, and learning). IDEAL originally focused on software process improvement; however, as the SEI recognized that the model could be applied beyond software process improvement, it revised the model so that it may be more broadly applied. Again, while the IDEAL model may be broadly applied to organizational improvement, the emphasis herein is on software process improvement.

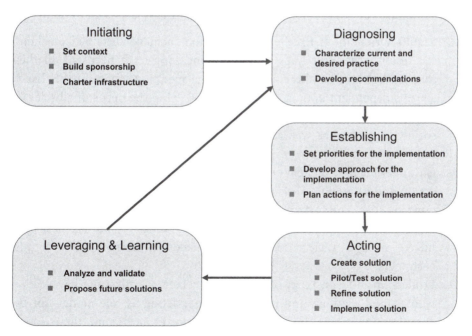

Figure 2–6   Phases of an improvement program according to IDEAL

The IDEAL improvement framework is described in detail in chapter 6 with a special bias toward test process improvement.

2.4.3 Fundamental Concepts of Excellence

A set of Fundamental Concepts of Excellence has been developed by the European Foundation for Quality Management (EFQM) and serves both as a basis for improvement and as a quality management model. These concepts can also be used to compare models. Many models have since been built using these concepts either explicitly or implicitly, including the EFQM Excellence Model, Malcom Baldrige model, and Six Sigma. Such models are often combined with the balanced scorecard (see section 6.2.2). The balanced scorecard provides a way of discussing the business goals for an organization and deciding how to achieve and measure those goals.

The set of concepts can be used as the basis to describe an excellent organizational culture. They also serve as a common language for senior management. The Fundamental Concepts of Excellence are used in organizational excellence models globally to measure organizations against the nine criteria (see figure 2–7).

The Fundamental Concepts of Excellence [URL: EFQM] are as follows:

- Results Orientation: Excellent organizations achieve sustained outstanding results that meet both the short- and long-term needs of all their stakeholders, within the context of their operating environment. Excellence is dependent upon balancing and satisfying the needs of all relevant stakeholders (this includes the people employed, customers, suppliers, and society in general as well as those with financial interests in the organization).
- Customer Focus: Excellent organizations consistently add value for customers by understanding, anticipating, and fulfilling needs, expectations, and opportunities. The customer is the final arbiter of product and service quality, and customer loyalty, retention, and market share gain are best optimized through a clear focus on the needs of current and potential customers.
- Leadership and Constancy of Purpose: Excellent organizations have leaders who shape the future and make it happen, acting as role models for the organization's values and ethics. The behavior of an organization's leaders creates a clarity and unity of purpose within the organization and an environment in which the organization and its people can excel.

- Management by Processes and Facts: Excellent organizations are widely recognized for their ability to identify and respond effectively and efficiently to opportunities and threats. Organizations perform more effectively when all interrelated activities are understood and systematically managed and decisions concerning current operations are planned. Improvements are made using reliable information that includes stakeholder perceptions.
- People Development and Involvement: Excellent organizations value their people and create a culture of empowerment for the achievement of both organizational and personal goals. The full potential of an organization's people is best realized through shared values and a culture of trust and empowerment, which encourages the involvement of everyone.
- Continuous Learning, Innovation, and Improvement: Excellent organizations generate increased value and levels of performance through continual improvement and systematic innovation by harnessing the creativity of their stakeholders. Organizational performance is maximized when it is based on the management and sharing of knowledge within a culture of continuous learning, innovation, and improvement.
- Partnership Development: Excellent organizations enhance their capabilities by effectively managing change within and beyond the organizational boundaries. An organization works more effectively when it has mutually beneficial relationships, built on trust, sharing of knowledge, and integration with its partners.
- Corporate Social Responsibility: Excellent organizations have a positive impact on the world around them by enhancing their performance while simultaneously advancing the economic, environmental, and social conditions within the communities they touch. The long-term interests of the organization and its people are best served by adopting an ethical approach and exceeding the expectations and regulations of the community at large.

European Foundation for Quality Management (EFQM)

The European Foundation for Quality Management (EFQM) has developed a model (figure 2–7) that was introduced in 1992 and has since been widely adopted by thousands of organizations across Europe. As you might expect, the EFQM Excellence Model meets the Fundamental Concepts of Excellence well. There are many approaches for achieving excellence in performance, but this model is based on the principle that "outstanding results are achieved with respect to People, Customers, Society and Performance with the help of Leader-

> **EFQM (European Foundation for Quality Management) Excellence Model**
> A non-prescriptive framework for an organization's quality management system, defined and owned by the European Foundation for Quality Management and based on five "Enabling" criteria (covering what an organization does) and four "Results" criteria (covering what an organization achieves).

ship Policy and Strategy that is carried through Resources, People, Processes and Partnerships." [URL: EFQM]

The EFQM Excellence Model can be used in different ways:

- It can be used to compare your organization with other organizations.
- It can be used as a guide to identify areas of weakness so that they can be improved.
- It can be used as a basic structure for an organization's management system.
- It can be used as a tool for self-assessment where a set of detailed criteria are given and organizations grade themselves under different headings.

On a yearly basis the EFQM Excellence Award is given to recognize Europe's best-performing organizations, whether private, public or non-profit. To win the EFQM Excellence Award, an applicant must be able to demonstrate that its performance not only exceeds that of its peers but also that it will maintain this advantage into the future.

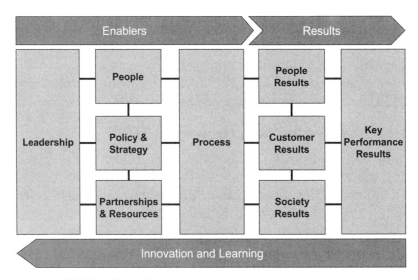

Figure 2–7 *EFQM Excellence Model*

The model's nine boxes represent the criteria against which to assess an organization's progress toward excellence (see figure 2–7). Each of the nine criteria has a definition, which explains its high-level meaning. To develop the high-level meaning further, each criterion is supported by a number of sub-criteria. These pose a number of questions that should be considered in the course of an assessment. Five of these criteria are so-called "enablers" for excellence and four are measures of "results."

Enablers – How We Do Things

- Leadership: How leaders develop and facilitate the achievement of the mission and vision, develop values required for long-term success and implement them via appropriate actions and behaviors, and are personally involved in ensuring that the organization's management system is developed and implemented.
- Policy and strategy: How the organization implements its mission and vision via a clear stakeholder-focused strategy, supported by relevant policies, plans, objectives, targets, and processes.
- People: How the organization manages, develops, and releases the knowledge and full potential of its people at an individual, team-based, and organization-wide level and plans these activities to support its policy and strategy and the effective operation of its processes.
- Partnership and resources: How the organization plans and manages its external partnerships and internal resources to support its policy and strategy and the effective operation of its processes.
- Process: How the organization designs, manages, and improves its processes to support its policy and strategy and fully satisfy, and generate increasing value for, its customers and other stakeholders.

Results – What We Target, Measure, and Achieve

- Customer results: What the organization is achieving in relation to its external customers
- People results: What the organization is achieving in relation to its people
- Society results: What the organization is achieving in relation to local and international society as appropriate
- Key performance results: What the organization is achieving in relation to its planned performance

The nine criteria of the EFQM Excellence model are interlinked with a continuous improvement loop known as RADAR (Results, Approach, Deployment, Assessment, and Review). RADAR is also the method for scoring when using the EFQM model:

- Results: Covers what an organization has achieved and what has to be achieved
- Approach: Covers what an organization plans to do to achieve target goals
- Deployment: Covers the extent to which the organization uses the approach and in what parts
- Assessment and Review: Covers the assessment and review of both approach and deployment of the approach

Malcolm Baldrige Model

The Baldrige Criteria for Performance Excellence is another leading model to provide a systems perspective for understanding performance management [URL: Baldrige]. The American model of the Baldrige Award for Quality is a contrast to the European Excellence Award. However, the Baldrige model is very similar to the European EFQM model in many aspects. The model is widely respected in the United States where its criteria are also the basis for the process. Most US states have quality award programs based on the Baldrige criteria.

The Baldrige Model criteria are divided into seven key categories:

1. Leadership
2. Strategic Planning
3. Customer Focus
4. Measurement, Analysis, and Knowledge Management
5. Workforce Focus
6. Process Management
7. Results

Each category is scored based on the approach used to address it, how well it is deployed throughout the organization, the cycles of learning generated, and its level of integration within the organization. An excellent way to improve your maturity is to use the criteria as a self-assessment and then compare your organization's methods and processes with winners of the Baldrige Award. An integral part of the Baldrige process is for winners to share nonproprietary information from their applications so there is a ready-made benchmark for your organization's maturity.

Six Sigma

Many organizations are using the concepts of Six Sigma to improve their business processes [Pyzdek and Keller 2009]. While the name Six Sigma has taken on a broader meaning, the fundamental purpose of Six Sigma is to improve processes such that there are at least six standard deviations between the worst-case specification limit and the mean of process variation. For those of us who are challenged by statistics, that means the process is essentially defect free!

The DMAIC process, used by Six Sigma, is a variation of the PDCA cycle introduced by Deming that many people find helpful. The Six Sigma methodology is basically a structured approach to improvement and problem solving using measurable data to make decisions using the five-step DMAIC project flow: Define, Measure, Analyze, Improve, and Control (see figure 2–8). Six Sigma can help organizations improve processes. The best approach is to align Six Sigma projects with the organization's strategic business plan by using, for example, the balanced scorecard. When Six Sigma projects are aligned with the organization's strategic direction, good results can be achieved.

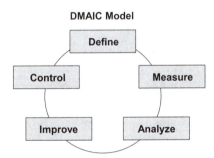

Figure 2–8   *Six Sigma DMAIC model*

Define

The Six Sigma team, usually consisting of an expert and apprentices, meets with the resource champion, such as the organizational president, to define what project is to be worked on, based on goals. The Define phase is where the problem statement and scope of project are defined and put down in writing. This process usually starts as a top-down approach where the senior managers have certain gaps that they see in their critical metrics and want to close those gaps. Those metrics and gaps need to then be broken down into manageable pieces for them to become projects.

Measure

Process parameters are used to measure progress and to determine that the experiments are having the right effects. This is where you actually start to put all the numbers together. Once you have defined the problem in the Define phase, you should have an output or outputs that you are interested in optimizing. The main focus of the Measure phase is to confirm that the data you are collecting is accurate.

Analyze

Using Design of Experiments (a structured approach to identifying the factors within a process that contribute to particular effects, then creating meaningful tests that verify possible improvement ideas or theories), brainstorming, process mapping, and other tools, the team collects data and analyzes it for clues to the root cause. In this phase, you collect data on all your inputs and outputs and then use one or more of the statistical tools to analyze them. The first thing you are trying to find out from your analysis is if there is a statistically significant relationship between each of the inputs and the outputs.

Improve

The champion and Six Sigma team meet with other stakeholders to find the best way to implement the fix that makes sense for the company. This is the phase where all the work you have done so far in your project can come together and start to show some success. All the data mining and analysis that has been done will give you the right improvements to define your processes. The phase starts with the creation of an improvement implementation plan. In order to create the implementation plan, you need to gather up all the conclusions that have been formed through the analysis that you have done. Now that you know what improvements need to be made, you have to figure out what you need to do in order to implement them.

Control

This phase is where you make sure that the improvements that you have made stay in place and are tightly controlled. The last part of DMAIC, Control, also means getting people trained in the new procedures so that the problem does not return.

2.5 Overview of Improvement Approaches

Syllabus Learning Objectives

LO 2.5.1 (K2) Compare the characteristics of a model-based approach with analytical and hybrid approaches.

LO 2.5.2 (K2) Understand that a hybrid approach may be necessary.

LO 2.5.3 (K2) Understand the need for improved people skills and explain improvements in staffing, training, consulting and coaching of test personnel.

LO 2.5.4 (K2) Understand how the introduction of test tools can improve different parts of the test process.

LO 2.5.5 (K2) Understand how improvements may be approached in other ways, for example, by the use of periodic reviews during the software life cycle, by the use of test approaches that include improvement cycles (e.g., project retrospectives in SCRUM), by the adoption of standards, and by focusing on resources such as test environments and test data.

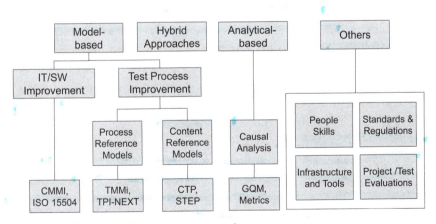

Figure 2–9   Overview of improvement approaches

2.5.1 Overview of Model-Based Approaches

Using a model to support process improvement is a tried and trusted approach that has acquired considerable acceptance in the software and testing industry. The underlying principle and philosophy of using process improvement models is that there is a correlation between an organization's process maturity and capability in terms of the predictability of the result of functionality, effort, throughput time, and quality of the software process. Practical experiences have shown that excellent results can be achieved using a model-based approach, although many stories from failed process improvement projects are available as well.

Guidelines that have been widely used to improve the system and software development processes are Capability Maturity Model Integration, or CMMI (section 3.2.1) and ISO/IEC 15504 (section 3.2.2). These are often regarded as the industry standard for system and software process improvement. Despite the fact that testing can account for substantial parts of project costs, only limited attention is given to testing in the various software process improvement models such as the CMMI. As an answer, the testing community has created complementary improvement models.

Models for test process improvement can be broadly divided in two groups:

- Process reference models
- Content reference models

The primary difference between process reference models and content reference models lies in the way in which this core of test process information is leveraged by the model. Process reference models define generic bodies of testing best practices and how to improve different aspects of testing in a prescribed step-by-step manner. Different maturity levels are defined that range from an initial level up to an optimizing maturity level, depending both on the actual testing tasks performed and how well they are performed. The process reference models discussed in this book are Test Maturity Model integration (TMMi) and the Test Process Improvement model TPI NEXT.

Content reference models also have a core body of best testing practices, but they do not implement the concept of different process maturity levels and do not prescribe the path to be taken for improving test processes. The principal emphasis is placed on the judgment of the user to decide on where the test process is and where it should be improved. The content reference models discussed in this book are the Critical Testing Process (CTP), in section 3.3.5, and the Systematic Test and Evaluation Process (STEP), in section 3.3.4.

Chapter 3 covers model-based approaches in detail.

2.5.2 Overview of Analytical Approaches

Analytical approaches are used to identify problem areas in our processes and set specific improvement goals. Achievement of these goals is measured using predefined parameters. Whereas model-based approaches are most often applied top down, analytical approaches are very much bottom up; that is, the focus is on the problems that happen today in our projects.

By using techniques such as causal analysis, possible links between things that happen (causes) and the consequences they may have (effects) are made clear. Causal analysis techniques (section 4.2) are used as a means of identifying the root causes of defects. Analytical approaches also involve the analysis of specific measures and metrics in order to assess the current situation in a test process and then decide on what improvement steps to take and how to measure their impact. The Goal-Question-Metric (GQM) approach (section 4.3) is a typical example of such an analytical approach.

Chapter 4 covers analytical approaches in more detail.

2.5.3 Hybrid Approaches

Most organizations, or perhaps even all, use a hybrid approach. In some cases this is explicit, but in most case it happens implicitly. In the process improvement models CMMI and TMMi, process areas exist that specifically address causal analysis of problem areas. Most process improvement models also emphasize the need to gather, analyze, and report on metrics. However, within process improvement models the analytical techniques and aspects are largely introduced at higher maturity levels. A hybrid approach is therefore usually most successful when organizations and projects have already taken their initial steps toward higher maturity; for example, introducing a full-scale measurement system when test planning, monitoring, and control are not yet in place does not make much sense.

It is rather uncommon to find an organization practicing analytical techniques for a longer period of time without having some kind of overall (model-based) framework in place. Thus, in practice, most often model-based and analytical-based approaches are combined in some way.

2.5.4 Other Approaches to Improving the Test Process

Improvements to the test process can be achieved by focusing on certain individual test improvement aspects described next (see figure 2–9). Note that most of these aspects are also covered within the context of the process improvement models mentioned earlier in section 2.5.1.

Test Process Improvement by Developing People's Skills

Improvements to testing may be supported by providing increased understanding, knowledge, and skills to people and teams who are carrying out tests, managing testing, or making decisions based on testing. These may be testers, test managers, developers and other IT team members, other managers, users, customers, auditors, and other stakeholders. In addition to having a mature process, people still and often make the difference.

Increases in skills and competence may be provided by training, awareness sessions, mentoring, coaching, networking with peer groups, using knowledge management repositories, reading, and other educational activities. Beware though, it is almost never "just" training, and especially coaching (training on the job) often makes the difference.

Skill levels may be associated with career paths and professional progression. An example of test career paths is the so-called test career cube [van Veenendaal 2010] (see figure 2–10). The test career cube allows testing professionals to grow from tester to test manager (first dimension). Not every tester has the same interests and strong points: the second dimension of the test career cube allows testers to differentiate between technical, methodical, and managerial skills. The final dimension is the backbone for each successful career: the theoretical background that comes from training, coaching, and development of technical and social skills. The cube is a tool for career guidance by the human resource manager to match the ambitions, knowledge, and skills of the professional testers to the requirements of the organization. The test career cube was initially developed as part of the Test Management Approach [Pol, Teunnissen, and van Veenendaal 2002], and is now also part of TMap NEXT [Koomen, et al. 2006].

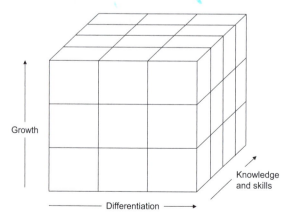

Figure 2–10   *The test career cube*

Skills and competencies that need to be improved may be testing skills, other IT technical skills, management skills, soft skills, or domain skills, as in the following examples:

- Test knowledge – test principles, techniques, tools, etc.
- Software engineering knowledge – software, requirements, development tooling, etc.
- Domain knowledge – business process, user characteristics, etc.
- Soft skills – communication, effective way of working, reporting, etc.

Knowledge and skills are rapidly becoming a challenge for many testers. It is just not good enough anymore to understand testing and hold an ISTQB certificate. Many of us will no longer work in our "safe" independent test team. We will work more closely together with business representatives and developers, helping each other when needed and as a team trying to build a quality product. It is expected from testers to have domain knowledge, requirements engineering skills, development scripting skills, and strong soft skills, for example, for communication and negotiation. As products are becoming more and more complex and have interfaces to many other systems both inside and outside the organization, many non-functional testing issues will become extremely challenging. At the same time, businesses, users, and customers do not want to compromise on quality. To be able to still test non-functional aspects such as security, interoperability, performance, and reliability, highly specialized testers will be needed. Even more so than today, these experts will be full-time test professionals with in-depth knowledge and skills in one non-functional testing area only.

Skills for test process improvers are covered further in section 7.3. However, the skills described are needed not just in the improvement team but across the entire test team, especially for senior testers and test managers.

The "people" aspect may well be managed and coordinated by the test improvement team most often (and preferred) in cooperation with human resources departments. Their main tasks and responsibilities in the context of people would then be as follows:

- Increase knowledge and skill levels of testers to support activities in the existing or improved test processes.
- Increase competencies of individual testers to enable them to carry out the activities.
- Establish clearly defined testing roles and responsibilities.

- Improve the correlation between increasing competence and rewards, recognition, and career progression.
- Motivate test staff.

Both TPI NEXT and TMMi have coverage of people aspects (e.g., training, career path) in their model. However, they are far from being people-oriented improvement models. In the following sections, two dedicated people improvement models are briefly discussed. Although not specific to testing, many practices and elements can easily be reused to improve the test workforce.

Personal Software Process (PSP)

An important step in software process improvement was taken with the Personal Software Process (PSP) [Humphrey 97], recognizing that the people factor was of utmost important in achieving quality. The PSP extends the improvement process to the people who actually do the work—the practicing (software) engineers. The PSP concentrates on the work practices of the individual software professionals. The principle behind the PSP is that to produce quality software systems, every software professional who works on the system must do quality work. The PSP is designed to help software professionals consistently use sound engineering practices. It shows them how to plan and track their work, use a defined and measured process, establish measurable goals, and track performance against these goals. The PSP shows software professionals how to manage quality from the beginning of the job, how to analyze the results of each job, and how to use the results to improve the process for the next project. Although not specifically targeted toward testers, many of the defined PSP practices can also be applied by those involved in testing.

The goal of the PSP is to help software professionals produce zero-defect, quality products on schedule. The PSP aims to provide software engineers with disciplined methods for improving personal software development processes. The PSP helps (software) engineers to do the following:

- Improve their estimating and planning skills
- Make commitments they can keep
- Manage the quality of their projects
- Reduce the number of defects in their work

People CMM

The People Capability Maturity Model, or People CMM [Curtis, Hefley, and Miller 2009], has been developed and is being maintained by the Software Engineering Institute (SEI). It aims at helping organizations to develop the maturity of their workforce and address their critical people issues. It is based on current best practices in fields such as human resources, knowledge management, and organizational development. It guides organizations in improving their processes for managing and developing their workforces. It helps organizations to do the following:

- Characterize the maturity of their workforce practices
- Establish a program for continuous workforce improvement
- Set priorities for people-oriented improvement actions
- Integrate workforce development with process improvement
- Establish a culture of excellence

People CMM provides a road map for implementing workforce practices that continuously improve an organization's workforce capability. Since an organization cannot implement all of the best workforce practices at once, a step-by-step approach is taken. Each progressive level of the model (see figure 2–11) produces a unique transformation in the culture of an organization. In order to achieve this, organizations are equipped with practices to attract, develop, organize, and motivate their workforce. Thus People CMM established an integrated system of workforce practices that matures through increasing alignment with the organization's business objectives, performance, and changing needs.

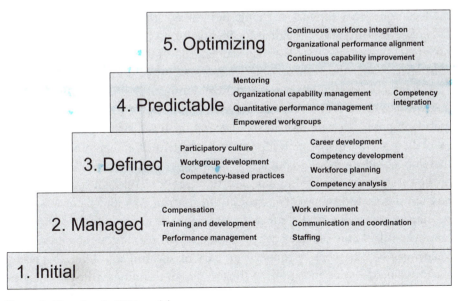

Figure 2–11   People CMM model

The People CMM consists of five maturity levels, each of which is a well-defined evolutionary plateau that institutionalizes new capabilities for developing the organization's workforce.

Test Process Improvement by Using Tools

The quality of test tools has matured during the past number of years. Their scope, diversity, and application have increased enormously. (Refer to *Foundations of Software Testing – ISTQB Certification* [Black, van Veenendaal, and D. Graham 2012] for an overview of tools available.) The use of such tools may often bring about a considerable improvement in the productivity of the test process. At a time when time to market is more critical than ever, and applying the latest development methods and tools has shortened the time it takes to develop new systems, it is clear that testing is on the critical path of software development and that having an efficient test process is necessary to ensure that deadlines are met. Faced with these challenges, we need tools to provide the necessary support. In the past, tools have grown to maturity and can, if implemented correctly, provide support in raising the efficiency, quality, and control of the test process.

The critical success factor for the use of test tools is the existence of a standard process for testing and the organization of that process. The implementation of one or more test tools should be based on the standard test process and the techniques that support it. Herein lies a major problem, because test tools do not always fit well enough into an organization's test process. Within a mature test process, tools will provide added value, but in an immature test process environment they can become counterproductive. Automation requires a certain level of repeatability and standardization regarding the activities carried out. An immature process does not comply with these conditions. Since automation imposes a certain level of standardization, it can also support the implementation of a more mature test process. Improvement and automation should therefore go side by side—to put it briefly, "Improve and Tool." For example, one of the authors was involved in a project to improve test design by using black-box test design techniques. The project did not run well and there was much resistance, partly due to the effort that was needed to apply these techniques. However, all of this changed when some easy-to-use test design tools [van Veenendaal 2012] were introduced as part of the project. After the testers started using the tools and applying the test design techniques, the effectiveness of testing was improved (in an efficient way).

> **Test tool** A software product that supports one or more test activities, such as planning and control, specification, building initial files and data, test execution, and test analysis. [Pol, Teunnissen, and van Veenendaal 2002]

Test improvements may be gained by the successful introduction of tools. These may be efficiency improvements, effectiveness improvements, quality improvements, or all of these, as in the following examples:

- A large number of tests can be carried out unattended and automatically (e.g., overnight).
- Automation of routine and often boring test activities leads to greater reliability of the activities and to a higher degree of work satisfaction in the test team than when they are carried out manually. This results in higher productivity in testing.
- Regression testing can, to a large extent, be carried out automatically. Automating the process of regression testing makes it possible to efficiently perform a full regression test so that it can be determined whether the unchanged areas still function according to the specification.
- Test tools ensure that the test data is the same for consecutive tests so that there is a certainty about the reliability of the initial situation with respect to the data.
- Some tools—e.g., static analysis—can detect defects that are difficult to detect manually. Using such tools, it is in principle possible to find all incidences of these types of faults.
- Test and defect management tools align working practices regarding the documentation of test cases and logging defects.
- Code coverage tools support the implementation of exit criteria at the component level.

Specifically, the process improver can use tools to aid in gathering, analyzing, and reporting data, including performing statistical analysis and process modeling. Note that these are not necessarily testing tools.

Testing tools are implemented with the intention of increasing test efficiency, increasing control over testing, or increasing the quality of deliverables. Implementation of testing tools is not trivial, and the success of the implementation depends on the selected tool addressing the required improvement and the implementation process. A structured selection and implementation is needed and is a critical success factor for achieving the expected improvement to the testing process. In summary, the following activities need to be performed as part of a tool selection process [van Veenendaal 2010]:

- Identify and quantify the problem. Is the problem in the area of control, efficiency, or product quality?
- Consider alternative solutions. Are tools the only possible solution? For example, look for alternatives in both the test and development process.
- Prepare an overall business case with measurable business objectives. Consider costs (see table 2–1) in the short and long term, expected benefits, and pay-back period.

Table 2–1 Overview of tool costs categories

Initial tool costs	Recurring tool costs
Knowledge acquisition	Tool ownership (maintenance, license fees, support fees, sustaining knowledge levels)
Selection process	Portability
Integration with other tools	Availability and dependencies
Costs for purchase, adaptation, or development	Maintaining and updating test scripts

- Identify and document tool requirements; include constraints and prioritize the requirements. In addition to tool features, consider requirements for hardware, software, supplier, integration, and information exchange.
- Perform market research and compile a short list. At this point you may also consider developing your own tools, but watch for becoming too people dependent and allow for a long-term solution.
- Organize supplier presentations. Let them use your application and prepare an agenda: What do you expect to see?
- Formally evaluate the tool; use it on a real project but allow for additional resources.
- Write an evaluation report and make a formal decision on the tool(s).

Once the selection has been completed, the tool needs to be deployed in the organization. The following list includes some critical success factors for the deployments of the tools:

- Treat it as a project. Formal testing may be needed during the pilot, such as, for example, integration testing with other tools and environments.

- Roll out the tool incrementally. Remember, if you don't know what you're doing, don't do it on a large scale.
- Adapt and improve the testing processes based on the tool.
- Provide training and coaching.
- Define tool usage guidelines.
- Perform a retrospective meeting and be open to lessons learned during its application. (This may even result in improvements to the tool selection and deployment process—for example, following the causal analysis for problems during the first large-scale applications of the tool.)
- Monitor the tool's use and its benefits.
- Beware that deployment is a change management process (see chapter 8).

The tool selection and deployment may well be carried out by the test improvement team with the support of tool specialists. Once a thorough selection and implementation process has been carried out, an adequate test tool (suite) will support the test improvement process! In today's test improvement projects, tools should always be considered. After all, we are living and working in an IT society.

Note that the process reference models covered in chapter 3 approach the issue of test tools slightly differently. In the TPI NEXT model (see section 3.3.1), a dedicated key area is defined on test tools. Within the TMMi model (see section 3.3.2), no process area is dedicated to test tools and test automation. Within TMMi, test tools are treated as a supporting resource (practices) and are therefore part of the process area where they provide support; for example, applying a test design tool is a supporting test practice within the process area Test Design and Execution at TMMi level 2 and applying a performance testing tool is a supporting test practice within the process area Non-functional Testing at TMMi level 3.

Test Process Improvement in Different Test Approaches

When we consider test process improvement, most often we think of a full-blown test improvement program or project. Yet many software life cycles already have an activity related to learning and improvement defined as part of their life cycle model. Thus, even without a full test improvement program, some focused and bottom-up improvements could well take place. Of course, the optimal situation is where these life-cycle-based improvement activities are facilitated and coordinated by an overall test improvement program. We then have almost continuous improvement cycles embedded in daily routines, which is at the heart of many improvement methods.

> **Software life cycle** The period of time that begins when a software product is conceived and ends when the software is no longer available for use. The software life cycle typically includes a concept phase, requirements phase, design phase, implementation phase, test phase, installation and checkout phase, operation and maintenance phase, and sometimes, retirement phase. Note that these phases may overlap or be performed iteratively.

In the following sections, we discuss briefly the most common improvement activities that are already an integral part of a life cycle, approach, technique, or method.

Sequential Life Cycle

In more mature organizations, both sequential and iterative life cycles will typically include post implementation reviews, phase end reviews, lessons learned meetings, and other opportunities to gather feedback and implement improvements. All of these methods and techniques are typically covered under the general heading of retrospective meeting. With sequential life cycles applied to longer projects, the retrospective meeting may also take place at the end of each milestone and not just at the end of the project.

Retrospective meetings are a great chance to recap how the work went and what lessons were learned. In general, a project retrospective helps to optimize teamwork and communication and creates more fun and better results during a project. By means of a retrospective, the team gets new insights into what went well and what to do better. At the end there are always lessons to be learned. Best results from a retrospective meeting are achieved by including management and not just limiting the attendees to the developers and testers.

A retrospective is an open discussion. Attendees are invited to share thoughts and experiences and come up with lessons learned. So the general form is pretty open. Normally a facilitator provides a short introduction: why a retrospective is being done and what it is about. To get the ball rolling, the concept is explained and a wide selection of topics are put on the table, such as the following:

- Implementation
- Team communication
- Customer communication
- Budget and resources

> **Retrospective meeting** A meeting at the end of a project during which the project team members evaluate the project and learn lessons that can be applied to the next project.

- Product quality
- Tools

The wide range of retrospective topics will help draw all participants into the conversation and encourage them to start sharing their thoughts. After that, the team needs to start talking about their project experience by using standard questions like these:

- What worked well?
- What did we learn from this project?
- What should we do differently next time?
- What don't we understand that needs to be clarified for the future?

It is usually amazing how much one can learn for the next project in a retrospective meeting.

Iterative Life Cycle

In iterative methodologies with short iterations (for example, agile methodologies), the feedback loops will happen more frequently, and therefore the opportunities to implement improvements are more frequent. For example, agile development life cycle models such as scrum expect a continuous improvement loop as part of the normal project process input, with a project retrospective and improvement of processes (including the test process) at the end of each iteration (*sprint*). After the sprint end review and prior to the next sprint planning meeting, a scrum team has a sprint retrospective meeting. This is typically a two- to three-hour, time-boxed meeting. At this meeting, the so-called "scrum master" encourages the team to challenge their process framework and practices to make them more effective and enjoyable for the next sprint. The purpose of the retrospective is to review and evaluate how the last sprint went in regard to people, relationships, process, and tools. The evaluation should identify and prioritize the major items that went well and those items that, if done differently, could make things even better. By the end of the sprint retrospective, the team should have identified actionable improvement measures that it implements in the next sprint. These changes become the adaptation to the empirical review.

Test Closure Phase

The test closure phase of a test life cycle is one of the principal phases in which a test retrospective or lessons learned review should take place. A good example of a test life cycle approach where the test closure is described in detail is in TMap [Pol, Teunnissen, and van Veenendaal 2002]. During the test closure phase, the test process is evaluated and an analysis takes place to identify lessons learned and determine changes to the test approach needed for future releases and projects. This is most often a brainstorming session with all team members involved. The data gathered and intermediate reports are combined with the results into a final test report. Both the test process and the quality of the product are being evaluated. It is recommended that an overview of costs and benefits of the test process is drawn up, a difficult but also very engaging and necessary activity. The often large quantities of data that are available are essential to improve future planning (estimation) and improvement of the test processes, the development processes, and the quality system. The data that is gathered can be used as a basis to identify possible improvements and enhance test maturity.

Exploratory Testing

In exploratory testing, each test session is followed by an assessment of where best to focus the next testing. This allows for an improvement cycle at the end of each session. On the basis of test charters, test sessions are performed, during which the tester becomes acquainted with the new product and at the same time designs and executes test cases. A session is an uninterrupted period of time of between two hours and one day in which the tester can perform testing based on one or more test charters. When the test session has ended, a debriefing takes place involving fellow testers and other interested parties. Experiences with the product (e.g., new product risks identified) are discussed, and test ideas and defects found are exchanged. In the context of exchanging ideas, you may ask the question, What is the most important defect you have encountered today?

Risk-Based Testing

In scripted, structured approaches to testing, the effort made to draw up the strategy, plan, and scripts may mitigate against a desire to implement improvements during the test project. However, it is possible to undertake a lessons learned retrospective or other process review at more frequent intervals and then use this to refocus and improve testing. In particular, when you're following a risk-based approach, the risk-based tests will need to be changed (improved) to address the new or changed risks as the business, product, and project risks change during the life cycle of the system. A good example of a risk-based testing method that describes this learning curve is PRISMA [van Veenendaal 2012]. (The PRISMA method is also part of the ISTQB Advanced Test Manager syllabus.)

Testers have the responsibility to ensure that the test coverage for any identified risk is in line with the priority of that risk. It is essential that the coverage is monitored as testing progresses. It is not easy to agree on the perceived levels of risk and the appropriate coverage levels needed to mitigate those risks. It is even harder to ensure that as risks change, the corresponding testing changes as well. You must bear in mind that test coverage can be reduced as well as increased. If there are multiple test cycles, future test cycles should be adapted to an updated product risk assessment. The product risk assessment may be updated to accommodate any totally new or changed product risks, unstable or defect-prone areas discovered during testing, risks introduced from fixed defects, testing's concentration on typical defects found during testing, and potentially, undertested areas (low test coverage). Any new or additional test cycles should be planned using an analysis of such risks as an input.

Unfortunately, many testers still perform one product risk assessment at the beginning of a project and then act as though risks do not change throughout the project. Product risk identification and analysis are based on stakeholders' perceptions and expectations. These will almost always change over time. Early testing will reveal some new risks while mitigating others. Evolving requirements usually mean evolving product risks. It pays to revisit the risk assessment on a periodic basis, at least at every major milestone. This will make testing more effective by addressing the newly identified product risks and more efficient by not wasting precious time testing for risks that have become less important.

Test Process Improvement Related to Adoption of Standards and Regulations

Process improvement may be dictated by standards and regulations. For example, the requirements of domain-dictated standards such as the American Food and Drug Administration (FDA) can mean that specific improvements are required to enable work to be performed in that domain. Compliance to standards may be required for legal, regulatory, or commercial reasons or for

> **Standard** A formal, possibly mandatory set of requirements developed and used to prescribe consistent approaches to the way of working or to provide guidelines (e.g., ISO/IEC standards, IEEE standards, and organizational standards). [After CMMI]

improving communication across teams, organizations, or national borders. Standards may also be used to set or measure in-house processes and improvements against benchmarks set by other organizations.

Many of us (including the authors) have experienced that a test document, e.g., a test plan, wasn't accepted by QA because it wasn't according to the standard. We might say, "Who cares, as long as it does the job!" However, the real question to ask ourselves here is "Who's to blame: the standard, or those who apply the standard?" Having worked in many industries with many different standards over the years, we probably have to state that it is down to those applying the standards to use them effectively. Following a standard for the sake of following a standard will not help. Of course, it makes a difference whether it's a mandatory external standard, e.g., FDA, or "just" a company-internal standard.

Unfortunately, there is no single software testing standard yet (the ISO/IEC 29119 standard may address this when released). There are many standards that touch upon software testing, but many of these standards overlap and contain what appear to be contradictory requirements. Perhaps worse, there are large gaps in the coverage of software testing by standards, such as integration testing, where no useful standard exists at all. Where standards related to software and system testing do exist, we would like to point to a number of recommended standards as examples of how they can be used for both building confidence between supplier and consumer, and providing information on good practice to the new or even experienced tester.

IEEE 829 – Software and System Test Documentation standard

One of the most popular and well-known testing standards is IEEE 829. IEEE 829 is referenced in many testing books and lectures as part of the ISTQB certification scheme. The updated version from 2008 [IEEE 829-08] has many benefits over the "old" version of 1998 [IEEE 829]. Among other improvements, it now provides dedicated templates for a master test plan and a level test plan in addition to various instances of test reports. Of course, IEEE 829 should not be used as a restrictive harness but rather as a source of inspiration. In fact, there are three main ways you can use this standard effectively:

1. If you do not yet have templates in your organization or project for test documentation, do not start reinventing the wheel! IEEE 829 can be a great source to use when defining your own customized test documentation standards.
2. If you do already have a set of templates in use, it can be used as a checklist. A review of your own set of documentation standards against IEEE 829 can lead to some improvement ideas and is a verification of completeness of your own test documentation standards.
3. Many of us now work with third parties (e.g., outsourcing) and try to make agreements on the test processes to be used and documentation to be produced. However, what is a "good" test log or test plan? This question often leads to a never-ending discussion. Our recommendation would be to use the well-known and internationally accepted IEEE 829 as part of the test agreements and state that test documents to be delivered have to comply with IEEE 829—an easy but effective way out of an on-going discussion.

IEEE 1028 – Reviews

When discussing reviews, we always wonder why we are not all using such an effective and relatively low-cost technique. Surveys show that only 50 percent of projects use reviews and only 25 percent use them in the way they are meant to be used. Yet the technique has been around since 1976, when Michael Fagan published his famous paper "Design and Code Inspections to Reduce Errors in Program Development" [Fagan 1976]. One of the things that strikes us as very strange is that many companies define their own review processes. Most often they end up with at least 90 percent of what has already been defined by IEEE 1028 [IEEE 1028] but somehow succeed in mixing up terms and renaming the review types. This is confusing and a waste of effort to say the least (it's probably only great for consultancy companies that provide the service). IEEE 1028 is a very straightforward standard that provides the processes for different types of review, such as, for example, inspection, walkthrough, technical review, and management review. We recommend not wasting effort in defining what is already provided and trying to gain added value from that 10 percent difference but rather focus on getting reviews implemented using IEEE 1028 as a common reference process framework.

BS7925-2 Software Component Testing

Although the BS7925-2 standard [BS-7925-2] was originally targeted toward component testing, it can be used by all testers at whatever test level they work.

The standard not only provides a test process framework that is intended specifically for component testing, but much more important, provides great detailed descriptions for both structure-based and specification-based test design techniques. The standard provides a description in the annex together with detailed examples for all test design techniques, which is really helpful. This gives a highly usable and complete overview of test design techniques that should be used when introducing or improving test design within your company or project. We recommend that you download this standard and start using it. It's totally independent of any testing method or process.

In summary, test process improvement organizations may bring about improvements by selecting appropriate standards and specifying how they are to be used. A standard may be used for the following purposes:

- To achieve compliance and consequently to meet the requirements of the standard
- As a source of ideas and examples to aid choices in improvements
- As a source of standardized practices that may provide better interoperability of systems and processes within a changing network of partner companies
- As a measurement benchmark for comparison with other organizations

Finally, we strongly recommend not reinventing the wheel but instead using the testing standards available, which can give a test improvement program an effective boost. But remember, use standards with common sense. A detailed overview of testing standards can be found in the book *The Testing Practitioner* [van Veenendaal 2010]. Test improvement models, especially TMMi, often recommend specific standards that can support the implementation of a new or changed testing practice.

Test Process Improvement Focused on Specific Resources

A managed and controlled test environment is indispensable for any testing. It is also needed to obtain test results under conditions that are as close as possible to a "real-life" situation. This is especially true for higher-level testing; for example, at system and acceptance test levels. Furthermore, at any test level the reproducibility of test results should not be endangered by undesired or unknown changes in the test environment. Test environment management includes managing availability and access to the test environment by providing log-in details, managing test data, providing and enforcing configuration management, and providing technical support on issues that arise during test execution and may disturb progress. Test data, including its creation and management, is another aspect of vital importance to being able to perform structured testing effectively and efficiently.

However, the management of the test environment, test data, and other technical resources is often outside the test team's or test organization's control. If these areas are seen as a focus for improvement, the teams and departments controlling these resources will need to be engaged in the test improvement process. Both TPI NEXT (section 3.3.1) and TMMi (see section 3.3.2) address test environment, test data control and management, and required resources within their test improvement model by means of a specific key area or process area. However, if an analytical approach such as root cause analysis is used (see chapter 4), these resources need to be explicitly added as factors to be considered. Whereas the previously mentioned models take these issues (including resources) already into account, this is not the case for analytical approaches.

The following processes are required to set up and manage the test environment:

- Requirements definition for the environment
- Designing, building, and verification/testing of the environment
- Acceptance of the environment
- Deployment process
- Capacity planning
- Configuration and change management for the environment
- Accessing control processes
- Booking and scheduling of environments within and between teams
- Retirement and dismantling of environments

The following processes are required to support the design, acquisition, and management of test data:

- Test analysis and design activities
- Test implementation activities
- Backup, restore, and archive processes
- Configuration and change management on specific data sets
- Applicable data security procedures (possibly required by law)

Improvements required at an organizational level for resources such as environments and data may include requests for savings in costs and energy usage reductions to meet the social responsibility and environmental targets for the organization. These may be addressed by efficiencies in the deployment and use of the environments and by, for example, the virtualization of environments.

The focus for improvement teams regarding resources covers the following:

- Identifying improvement areas outside the test team's control
- Engaging with the controlling teams, if necessary by escalation through management
- Engaging with improvement teams outside testing to coordinate improvements
- Identifying and implementing improvements within the test team and across test teams for provision and management of resources

2.6 Exercises

The following multiple-choice questions will give you some feedback on your understanding of this chapter. Appendix F lists the answers.

2-1 To which view on product quality does risk-based testing most strongly relate?

   A: Product-based

   B: Manufacturing-based

   C: User-based

   D: Value-based

2-2 The test strategy of an embedded software company in a safety-critical industry states that testing of reliability, availability, maintainability, and safety is essential to all products being developed. To which view on product quality does this test strategy statement relate?

   A: Product-based

   B: Manufacturing-based

   C: User-based

   D: Transcendent-based

2-3 Which of the following is an example of a typical business reason for starting a test improvement program?

A: Implement formal test design techniques

B: Optimize usage of test tools

C: Achieve a higher level of product quality

D: Obtain commitment to the test policy and test strategy

2-4 Which of the following is an example of an organization/business improvement model?

A: Capability Maturity Model Integration (CMMI)

B: Six Sigma

C: ISO/IEC 15504

D: TPI NEXT

2-5 In which phase of the Deming cycle will one determine what will be affected by a change?

A: Plan

B: Do

C: Check

D: Act

2-6 What is not a typical precondition for a successful test improvement program?

A: Requirements are documented and managed.

B: Configurations are planned and controlled.

C: A measurement program is defined and deployed.

D: Project planning exists at an adequate level.

2-7 Which of the following is an enabler for excellence defined by the EFQM model?

A: Society

B: Leadership

C: Customer

D: Continuous Learning

2-8 In focusing on the people aspect within test process improvement, which of the following skills are typically, in addition to testing, needed by test analysts?

A: Requirements engineering

B: Project management

C: Communication skills

D: A and C

2-9 During a tool selection process, an overall business case needs to be prepared with measurable business objectives: costs, expected benefits and pay-back period. Which of the following is not a typical cost associated with test tools?

A: Integration

B: Maintenance

C: Usability

D: Knowledge acquisition

2-10 Which of the following activities and methods has a short feedback and improvement cycle always embedded?

A: Exploratory testing

B: Test closure phase

C: Risk-based testing

D: Sequential lifecyle

3 Model-Based Improvement

Using a model to support test process improvement is a tried and trusted approach that has acquired considerable acceptance in the testing industry. In fact, the success of this approach has unfortunately led some people to believe that this is the only way to approach test process improvement. Not so. As you will see in other chapters of this book, using models is just one way to approach test process improvement, and models are certainly not a substitute for experience when it comes to recommending test process improvements. However, models do offer a structured and systematic way of showing where a test process currently stands, where it might be improved, and what steps can be taken to achieve a better, more mature test process. The success and acceptance of using models calls for a thorough consideration of the options available to test process improvers when they are choosing a model-based approach.

The objective of this chapter is to help test process improvers make the right choices when it comes to test process improvement models, give them a thorough overview of the issues concerning model use, and provide an overview of the most commonly used models: TMMi, TPI NEXT, CTP, and STEP. We will also be looking at what the software process improvement models CMMI and ISO/IEC 15504 can offer the test process improver. Of course, it would not be practical for this chapter to consider these models right down to the last detail; that would add around 500 pages to the book! The reader is kindly requested to consult the referenced works for more detailed coverage.

This chapter first looks at model-based approaches in general and asks the fundamental questions, What would we ideally expect to see in a model used for test process improvement? and, What assumptions are we taking when using a model?

Test process improvement models are not all the same; they adopt different approaches, they are structured differently, and they each have their own strengths and weaknesses. The remainder of the chapter focuses on these aspects with regard to the models previously mentioned.

3.1 Introduction to Test Process Improvement Models

Syllabus Learning Objectives

LO 3.1.1 (K2) Understand the attributes of a test process improvement model with essential generic attributes.

LO 3.1.2 (K2) Compare the continuous and staged approaches including their strengths and weaknesses.

LO 3.1.3 (K2) Summarize the assumptions made in using models in general.

LO 3.1.4 (K2) Compare the specific advantages of using a model-based approach with their disadvantages.

3.1.1 Desirable Characteristics of Test Process Improvement Models

Fundamentally, a test process improvement model should provide three essential benefits:

- Clearly show the current status of the test process in a thorough, structured, and understandable manner
- Help to identify where improvements to that test process should take place
- Provide guidance on how to progress from the current to the desired state

Let's be honest. A first look at the available models for test process improvement can be confusing; there are so many styles, approaches, and formal issues to consider. With all this, it can be difficult to appreciate the fundamental attributes we should be looking for in such a model. This section describes a number of specific areas that can help us understand the aspects of a test process improvement model that can generally be considered as "desirable." The areas are covered under the following headings:

- Model Content
- Model Design
- Formal Considerations

Model Content

- Practicality and ease of use are high on the list of desirable model characteristics. A model that is overcomplicated, difficult to use, and impractical will struggle to achieve a general level of acceptability from both its users and the stakeholders who should be benefitting from its use. Convincing others to adopt an impractical model will be difficult and may even place a question mark over the use of a model-based approach.
- A well-researched, empirical basis is essential. Models must be representative of a justified "best practice" approach to testing. Without any solid basis for this justification, models may be seen as simply a collection of notions and ideas put forward by a limited number of individuals. Because such models have unproven validity, the test process improver must look for examples where value has been demonstrated in actual practice.
- Details are important. A strong mover behind the development of test process improvement models was the low level of testing detail provided by software development models (e.g., CMMI). This was often considered inadequate for thorough and practical test process improvement. A model for test process improvement must therefore provide sufficient detail to allow in-depth information about test processes to be obtained and permit a wide range of specific testing issues to be adequately covered. Models that deal only in generalities will be difficult to apply in practice and may need considerable subjective interpretation when used for test process assessment purposes.
- The user must be supported by the model in identifying, proposing, and quantifying improvements that are specific to identified test process weaknesses. A variety of improvement suggestions for specific testing problems is desirable. A model that proposes only a single solution to a problem or only focuses on the assessment part of test process improvement will be of only limited value.

Model Design

- Models should help us achieve test process improvements in small, manageable steps rather than great leaps. By providing a mechanism for small, evolutionary improvements, models for test process improvement should support a wide range of improvement scopes (e.g., minor adjustments or major programs) and ensure that those improvements are clearly defined in the model.

- The prioritization of improvements is an essential aspect in determining an acceptable test improvement plan. Models should support the definition of priorities and enable businesses to understand the reasons for those priorities.
- Models must support the different activities found in a test process improvement program (the IDEAL approach discussed in chapter 6 identifies, for example, five principal activities). The model should be considered as a tool with which to support the implementation of a test process improvement program. The model itself should not demand major changes to the chosen approach to test process improvement.
- Flexibility is a highly desirable characteristic of test process improvement models. Within a given organization, a variety of different project types may be found, such as large projects, projects using standard software, and projects using a particular software development life cycle. The model must be flexible enough to deal with all of these project types. In addition, the model must cater to the different business objectives being followed by an organization. This calls for a high level of model flexibility, including the possibility to apply tailoring.
- Suggestions for test process improvement may be given (prescribed) by the model or depend on the judgment of the user. These approaches have their advantages and disadvantages, so a decision on which is considered desirable has to be made by the model user within their own project and organizational context.
- As discussed in section 3.1.3, some models represent improvements to test process maturity in predefined steps, or *stages*, and others consider improvement of particular test process aspects in a nonstaged, or *continuous*, manner. Together with the "degree of prescription" aspect mentioned in the preceding point, this is perhaps the most significant characteristic that defines test process improvement models. The user must determine which is most desirable in their specific project and organizational context.

Formal Considerations

- To provide value for projects and organizations, a test improvement model must be publicly known, supported (e.g., by external consultants and/or websites), and available to all potential users (e.g., via the Internet and/or as a book). "Home-made," unpublished models that have little or no support may be useful within a very limited scope, but generally speaking they are limited in value compared to publicly available models that are supported (e.g., by consultants or user groups).

- The merits of a model may be judged by the level of acceptance, recognition, and "take up" shown by both professional bodies and the software testing industry in general. Using a model that is not tried and tested presents an avoidable risk.
- Models that are simply promoted as a marketing vehicle for commercial organization may not exhibit the degree of independence required when suggesting test process improvements. Models must show strong independence from undesired commercial influences and be clearly unbiased.
- The use of a model may require the formal accreditation of assessors. This level of formality may be considered as beneficial to organizations seeking a formal certification of their test process maturity. The level of formal accreditation required for assessors and the ability to certify an organization distinguishes some models from others.

3.1.2 Using Models: Benefits and Risks

Using a model for test process improvement can be highly beneficial, but the user must be aware of particular risks in order to achieve those benefits. As you will see, many of the risks are associated with the assumptions that are frequently made when using a model. Just as with any risk, lack of awareness and failure to take the necessary mitigation actions may result in failure of the overall test process improvement program.

In this section, the benefits associated with using models are covered, followed by a description of individual risk factors and how they might be mitigated.

Benefit: Structured Approach

As mentioned in the introduction to this chapter, models permit the adoption of a structured approach to test process improvement. This not only benefits the users of the model, it also helps to communicate the test process improvement approach to stakeholders. Managers benefit from the ease with which test process improvements can be planned and controlled. Resources (people, time, money) can be clearly allocated and prioritized, progress can be transparently communicated, and return on investment can be more easily demonstrated. Business owners benefit from a structured, model-based approach by having clearly established objectives that can be prioritized, monitored, and where necessary, adjusted. This is not to say that test improvements that are not model-based are unplanned, difficult to manage, and hard to communicate; models do, however, provide an valuable instrument with which these issues can be effectively addressed.

Benefit: Leveraging of Testing Best Practices

At the heart of all models for test process improvement is the concept of *best practices* in testing, as proposed by the model's developers. Aligning a project's test process to a particular model will leverage these best practices and, it is assumed, benefit the project. This is one of the fundamental benefits of adopting a model-based approach to test process improvement, but it needs to be balanced with the risks associated with ignoring issues of project or organizational context, which are discussed later.

Benefit: Thorough Coverage

Testing processes have many facets, and a wide range of individual aspects (e.g., test techniques, test organization, test life cycle, test environment, test tools) need to be considered if broad-based test process improvement is established as the overall objective. Such objectives can be achieved only if all relevant aspects of the test process are covered. Test process improvement models should provide this thorough coverage; they identify and describe individual testing aspects, and they give stakeholders confidence that important aspects have not been missed. Note that some test improvement models (e.g., TOM) do not provide full coverage, making this a desirable characteristic of a test improvement model.

Of course, if the objective of test process improvement is highly focused on a particular problem area (e.g., test team skills), this benefit will fully apply and a decision to use a model-based approach would need careful consideration.

Benefit: Objectivity

Models provide the test process improver with an objective body of knowledge from which to identify weaknesses in the test process and propose appropriate recommendations. This objectivity can be a decisive factor in deciding on an approach to test process improvement. An approach that is not model-based and relies on particular people will be perceived as less objective by stakeholders (especially management), even if this is not justified.

Objectivity can be an important benefit when conducting assessment interviews; it reduces the risk that particular questions are challenged by the interviewee, especially where the interviewee is more experienced than the interviewer in particular areas of testing. Similarly, the backing of an objective model can be of use when "selling" improvement proposals to stakeholders. Objectivity cannot, of course, be total. Models are developed by people and organizations. If all of those people come from the same organization, the model will be less objective than one developed by many people from different organizations and countries.

Benefit: Comparability

Consistently using a test process improvement model allows organizations to compare the maturity levels achieved by different projects in their organization. Within an organization, this enables particular projects to be defined as reference points for other projects and provides a convenient, company-specific baseline.

Industry-wide baselines are a potential benefit of using models, but only a few such baselines have been established [van Veenendaal and Cannegieter 2013], [van Veenendaal 2011].

Risk: Failure to Consider Project Context

Models are, by definition, a representation of reality. They help us to understand complexities more easily by creating a generic view that can then be applied to a specific situation. The risk with any model is that the generic representation may not always fit the specific situations in your project or organization. All projects have their own particular context, and there is no way to define a "standard" project, except at a (very) high level. Because of this, the model you are using for test process improvement must match the specific project context as closely as possible. The less precise this match is, the higher the risk that the best practices are no longer appropriate for the specific project.

Mitigating these risks is a question of judgment by the model user. What is best for the specific project? Where should I make adjustments to the model? Where do I need to make interpretations when assessing test process maturity? These are the questions the test process improver needs to answer when applying a particular test improvement model. Some of the typical areas to be considered are listed here:

- Project criticality. Projects with a high level of criticality often need to show compliance with standards. Any aspects of the model that would prevent this compliance need to be filtered out.
- Technology and architecture used. Certain technologies and architectures may favor particular best practices over others. Applications that are imple-

mented using, for example, multisystem architectures may place relatively more emphasis on non-functional testing than simple web-based applications. Similarly, the importance of a representative test environment may be different for the two architectures. The model used must reflect these different project contexts. If the model used suggests that a fully representative test environment should be available, this may be "over the top" in the context of a simple application needing just functional testing.

- Development using a sequential software development life cycle (SDLC) places a different emphasis on testing compared to software developed according to agile practices. Test improvement models may be used in both contexts, but considerably more interpretation and tailoring will be required for the agile context (more on this in chapter 10).

TPI NEXT and TMMi permit aspects of the test process assessment to be filtered out as "not applicable" without affecting the achieved maturity level. This goes some way toward eliminating aspects that do not conform to the project or organizational context.

Risk: "Model Blindness"

This is a very common risk that we have observerd on many occasions. An inexperienced user might believe that a test process improvement model does the thinking for them and relieves them of the need to apply their own judgment. This false assumption presents a substantial risk to gaining approvals and recognition for improvement recommendations. If test process improvers are questioned by stakeholders about improvement proposals or assessment results, weak responses such as "because the model says so" show a degree of "model blindness" that reveals their inexperience in improving test processes. Stakeholders generally want to hear what the test process improver thinks and not simply what the model prescribes as a result of a mechanical checklist-based assessment.

A model cannot replace common sense, experience, and judgment, and users of models should remember the famous quote by W.E. Deming and G. Box: "All models are wrong: some are useful." The models described in this book are considered "useful," but if the user cannot explain the reasoning behind results and recommendations, the level of confidence in the results and proposals they present may erode to an extent that they are not adopted.

Mitigating the risks of model blindness means validating the results and recommendations suggested by the model and making the appropriate adjustments if these do not make sense within the context of the project or organization. Does it make sense, for example, to propose the introduction of weekly test status reporting when the project has a web-based dashboard showing all the relevant information "on demand"? Users of models should consider them as valuable instruments to support their judgments and recommendations.

Risk: Wrong Approach

This book examines a number approaches to test process improvement, one of which involves using a test process improvement model. Risks arise when a model-based approach becomes "automatic" and is applied without due consideration for the particular objectives to be achieved. This could fundamentally result in an inappropriate approach being adopted and resources being ineffectively allocated. As discussed in chapter 5, a combination of a model-based and analytical-based approach is often preferred.

Mitigating this risk requires awareness. Test process improvers must be aware that models sometimes oversimplify complex issues of cause and effect and, indeed, that improvements may not be required in testing but in other processes, such as software development. These issues to be considered when choosing the most appropriate approach to test process improvement are described in chapter 5.

Risk: Lack of Skills

A general lack of skills in performing test process improvements and in applying a specific model may lead to one or more of the risks mentioned previously.

Mitigation of this risk is not just simply an issue of training (although that is surely one measure to be considered). Roles and responsibilities for those involved in test process improvements must include a description of required experience and qualifications (see section 7.2). Any deviations from these requirements must be balanced by the potential impact of the risks mentioned previously on the project or organization (e.g., setting inappropriate priorities, failure to take project context into account).

3.1.3 Categories of Models

Models for test process improvement can be broadly categorized as shown in figure 3–1. The diagram also indicates the four models considered in this book.

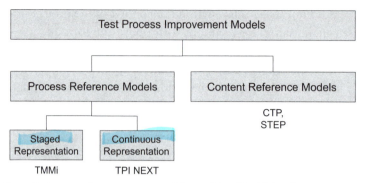

Figure 3–1   Test process improvement models considered in this book

Process Reference Models and Content Reference Models

Reference models in general provide a body of information and testing best practices that form the core of the model. The primary difference between process reference models and content reference models lies in the way in which this core of test process information is leveraged by the model, although content reference models tend to provide more details on the various testing practices.

In the case of process reference models, a predefined scale of test process maturity is mapped onto the core body of test process information. Different maturity levels are defined, which range from an initial level up to an optimizing maturity level, depending both on the actual testing tasks performed and on how well they are performed. The progression from one maturity level to another is an integral feature of the model, which gives process reference models their predefined "prescribed" character. The process reference models discussed in this book are the Test Maturity Model integration (TMMi) model and the Test Process Improvement model TPI NEXT.

Content reference models also have a core body of best testing practices, but they do not implement the concept of different process maturity levels and do not prescribe the path to be taken for improving test processes. The principal emphasis is placed on the judgment of the user to decide on where the test process is and where it should be improved. The content reference models discussed in this book are the Critical Testing Process (CTP) model [Black 2003] and the Systematic Test and Evaluation Process (STEP) model [Craig and Jaskiel 2002].

Continuous and Staged Representations

As noted, process reference models define a scale of test process maturity. This is of practical use in showing the achieved test process maturity, in comparing the maturity levels of different projects or organizations, and in showing improvements required or achieved.

The method chosen to represent test process maturity can be classified as either staged or continuous. With a staged representation, the model describes sucessive maturity levels. Test Maturity Model integration (TMMi), which is described in section 3.3.2, defines five such maturity levels. Achieving a given maturity level (stage) requires that specific testing activities (TMMi refers to these as *process areas*) are performed as prescribed by the model. For example, test planning is one of the testing activities that must be perfomed to achieve the TMMi maturity level 2. Test process improvement is represented by progressing from one maturity level to the next highest level (assuming there is one).

Staged representations are easy to understand and show a clear step-by-step path toward achieving a given level of test process maturity. This simplicity can also be beneficial when discussing test process maturity with senior management or where a simple demonstration of achieved test process maturity is required, such as with tendering for testing projects. It is probably this simplicity that makes staged models popular. A recent survey showed that 90 percent of the CMMI implemenations were stage based and only 10 percent were using continuous representation.

When a model is used that implements a staged representation of test process maturity, the user should be aware of certain aspects that may be seen as limiting. One of these aspects is the relatively course-grained definition of the maturity levels. As noted, each maturity level requires that capability be demonstrated for several testing activities and that all of those activities must be present for the overall maturity level to be achieved. If a test process can demonstrate, for example, that only one of the required testing activities assigned to maturity level 2 is performed and compliant, the overall test process maturity is still rated as level 1. This is reasonable. However, when all but one of the matu-

> **Staged representation**   A model structure wherein attaining the goals of a set of process areas establishes a maturity level; each level builds a foundation for subsequent levels. [Chrissis, Konrad, and Shrum 2004]

rity level 2 activities are performed, the model still places the test process at maturity level 1. This "all or nothing" approach can result in a negative impression of the test process maturity.

Continuous representations of process maturity (such as used in the TPI NEXT model) are generally more flexible and finer grained than staged representations. Unlike with the staged approach, there are no prescribed maturity levels through which the entire test process is required to proceed, which makes it easier to target the particular areas for improvement needed to achieve particular business goals.

The word *continuous* is applied to this representation because the models that use this approach define not only the various key areas of a testing process (e.g., defect management) but also the (continuous) scale of maturity that can be applied to each key area (e.g., basic *managed* defect management, *efficient* defect management using metrics, and *optimizing* defect management featuring root-cause analysis for defect prevention).

Assessing the maturity of a particular key area is achieved by answering specific questions that are assigned to a given maturity level. There might be, for example, four questions assigned to the *managed* maturity level for defect management. If all questions can be answered positively, the defect management aspect of the test process is assessed as *managed*. Other key areas may be assessed at different levels of maturity; for example, reporting may be at an *efficient* level and test case design at an *optimizing* maturity level.

Clearly, the continuous representation provides a more detailed and differentiated view of test process maturity compared to the staged representation, but the simplicity offered by a staged approach cannot be easily matched. Using a continuous representation model can easily lead to a complex assessment of a test process, where stakeholders may find it hard to "see the forest, and not all the trees." Models that use a continuous representation, such as TPI NEXT (and particularly its earlier version, TPI) suffer from the perception of being too technical and difficult to communicate to non-testers.

Continuous representation   A capability maturity model structure wherein capability levels provide a recommended order for approaching process improvement within specified process areas. [Chrissis, Konrad, and Shrum 2004]

3.2 Software Process Improvement (SPI) Models

Syllabus Learning Objectives

LO 3.2.1 (K2) Understand the aspects of the CMMI model with testing-specific relevance.

LO 3.2.2 (K2) Compare the suitability of CMMI and ISO/IEC 15504-5 for test process improvement to models developed specifically for test process improvement.

3.2.1 Capability Maturity Model Integration (CMMI)

Introduction

In this section, we'll consider the CMMI model. The official book on CMMI provides a full description of the framework and its use (see *CMMI, Guidelines for Process Integration and Product Improvement* [Chrissis, Konrad, and Shrum 2004]). Users will gain additional insights into the framework by consulting this publication and the other sources of information available at [URL: SEI].

Capability Maturity Model Integration (CMMI) is a process improvement approach that provides organizations with the essential elements of effective processes. It is an approach that helps organizations improve their processes. The model provides a clear definition of what an organization should do to promote behaviors that lead to improved performance.

With five *maturity levels* (for the staged representation) and four *capability levels* (for the continous representation), CMMI defines the most important elements that are required to build better product quality, or deliver greater services, and wraps them all up in a comprehensive model. The goal of the CMMI project is to improve the usability of maturity models for software engineering and other disciplines by integrating many different models into one overall framework of best practices. It describes best practices in managing, measuring, and monitoring software development processes. The CMMI model does not

> **Capability Maturity Model Integration (CMMI)**   A framework that describes the key elements of an effective product development and maintenance process. The Capability Maturity Model Integration covers best practices for planning, engineering and managing product development and maintenance. [Chrissis, Konrad, and Shrum 2004]

describe the processes themselves; it describes the characteristics of good processes, thus providing guidelines for companies developing or honing their own sets of processes.

The CMMI helps us understand the answer to the question, How do we know?

- How do we know what we are good at?
- How do we know if we're improving?
- How do we know if the process we use is working well?
- How do we know if our requirements change process is useful?
- How do we know if our products are as good as they can be?

CMMI helps you to focus on your processes as well as on the products and services you produce. This is important because many people who are working in a position such as program manager, project manager, or a similar product creation role are paid bonuses and given promotions based on whether they achieve deadlines, not whether they follow or improve processes. Essentially, using CMMI reminds us to focus on process improvement.

Commercial and government organizations use the CMMI models to assist in defining process improvements for systems engineering, software engineering, and integrated product and process development.

Structure

CMMI comes with two different representations: staged and continuous (see section 3.1.3). The staged version of the CMMI model identifies five levels of process maturity for an organization (figure 3-2):

1. Initial (chaotic, ad hoc, heroic): The starting point for use of a new process.
2. Managed (project management, process discipline): The process is used repeatedly.
3. Defined (institutionalized): The process is defined and confirmed as a standard business process.
4. Quantitatively Managed (quantified): Process management and measurement take place.
5. Optimizing (process improvement): Process management includes deliberate process optimization and improvement.

3.2 Software Process Improvement (SPI) Models

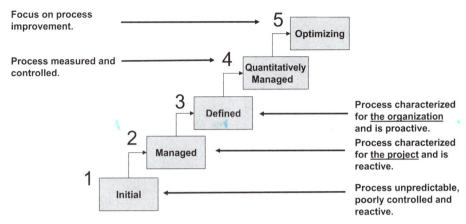

Figure 3–2   CMMI staged model: five maturity levels with their characteristics

There are process areas (PAs) within each of these maturity levels that characterize that level (more about process areas later). Organizations are supported with the CMMI to improve the maturity of their software process through an evolutionary path of the five maturity levels, from "ad-hoc and chaotic" to "mature and disciplined" management. As organizations become more mature, risks are expected to decrease and productivity and quality are expected to increase. The staged representation provides more focus for the organization and has by far the largest uptake in the industry.

Using the continuous representation, an organization can also pick and choose the process areas that make the most sense for them to work on. The continuous representation defines capability levels within each process area (see figure 3–3). In the continuous representation, the organization is thus allowed to concentrate its improvement efforts on its own primary areas of need without regard to other areas and is therefore generally considered to be more flexible but more difficult to use.

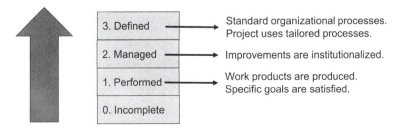

Figure 3–3   CMMI continuous model: four capability levels per process area

The differences in the CMMI representations are solely organizational; the content is equivalent. When choosing the staged representation, an organization follows a predefined pattern of process areas that are organized by maturity level. When choosing the continuous representation, organizations pick process areas based on their interest in improving only specific areas.

There are multiple "flavors" of the CMMI, called *constellations*, that include CMMI for Development (CMMI-DEV), CMMI for Services (CMMI-SVC), and CMMI for Acquisition (CMMI-ACQ). The three constellations share a core set of 16 process areas. CMMI-DEV commands the largest market share, followed by CMMI-SVC and then CMMI-ACQ. CMMI for Development has 22 *process areas*, or *PAs* (see table 3–1). Each process area is intended be adapted to the culture and behaviors of your own company.

Table 3–1 Process areas in CMMI-DEV for each maturity level

Level	Focus	Process areas
5 Optimizing	Continuous Process Improvement	• Organizational Innovation and Deployment • Causal Analysis and Resolution
4 Quantitatively Managed	Quantitative Management	• Organizational Process Performance • Quantitative Project Management
3 Defined	Process Standardization	• Requirements Development • Technical Solution • Product Integration • Verification • Validation • Organizational Process Focus • Organizational Process Definition • Organizational Training • Integrated Project Management • Risk Management • Decision Analysis and Resolution
2 Managed	Basic Project Management	• Requirements Management • Project Planning • Project Monitoring and Control • Supplier Agreement Management • Measurement and Analysis • Process and Product Quality Assurance • Configuration Management

CMMI uses a common structure (set of components) to describe each of the process areas. The process area components are grouped into three types: required, expected, and informative.

- **Required components** describe what an organization must achieve to satisfy a process area. This achievement must be visibly implemented in an organization's processes. The required components in CMMI are the specific and generic goals. Goal satisfaction is used in assessments as the basis for deciding if a process area has been achieved and satisfied.
- **Expected components** describe what an organization will typically implement to achieve a required component. Expected components guide those who implement improvements or perform assessments. Expected components include both specific and generic practices. Either the practices as described or acceptable alternatives to the practices must be present in the planned and implemented processes of the organization before goals can be considered satisfied.
- **Informative components** provide details that help organizations get started in thinking about how to approach the required and expected components. Sub-practices, example work products, notes, examples, and references are all informative model components.

A process area has several different components (see figure 3–4 and table 3–2).

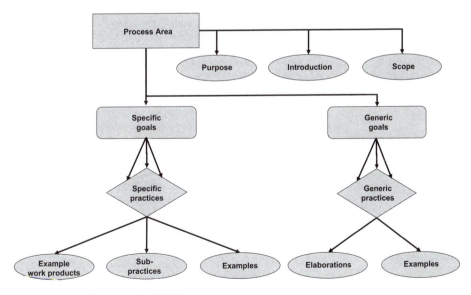

Figure 3–4   *Structure of a CMMI process area*

Each PA has one to four goals, and each goal is made up of practices. Within each of the PAs, these are called specific goals and practices because they describe activities that are specific to a single PA. There is one additional set of goals and practices that apply in common across all of the PAs; these are called generic goals and practices. There are 12 *generic practices (GPs)* that provide guidance for organizational excellence and institutionalization, including behaviors such as setting expectations, training, measuring quality, monitoring process performance, and evaluating compliance. Organizations can be *rated* at a capability level (continuous representation) or maturity level (staged representation) based on over 300 discreet *specific* and *generic* practices.

Table 3–2 Components of CMMI Process Areas

Component name	Description
Introductory notes	The introductory notes section of the process area describes the major concepts covered in the process area and is an informative component.
Scope	The scope section of the process area specifically identifies the test practices that are addressed by the process area and, if necessary, test practices that are explicitly outside the scope of this process area.
Specific goals	A specific goal describes the unique characteristic that must be present to satisfy the process area. A specific goal is a required model component and is used in assessments to help determine whether a process area is satisfied.
Generic goals	Generic goals appear near the end of a process area and are called generic because the same goal statement appears in multiple process areas. A generic goal describes the characteristics that must be present to institutionalize the processes that implement a process area. A generic goal is a required model component and is used in assessments to help determine whether a process area is satisfied.
Specific practices	A specific practice is the description of an activity that is considered important in achieving the associated specific goal. The specific practice describes the activities expected to result in achievement of the specific goals of a process area. A specific practice is an expected model component.
Example work products	The example work products section lists sample outputs from a specific practice. These examples are called example work products because there are often work products that are just as effective but are not listed. An example work product is an informative model component.
Sub-practices	A sub-practice is a detailed description that provides guidance for interpreting and implementing a specific practice. Sub-practices may be worded as if prescriptive but are actually an informative component meant only to provide ideas that may be useful for test process improvement.

Component name	Description
Generic practices	Generic practices appear near the end of a process area and are called generic because the same practice appears in multiple process areas. A generic practice is the description of an activity that is considered important in achieving the associated generic goal. A generic practice is an expected model component.
Generic practices elaboration	A generic practices elaboration appears after a generic practice in a process area to provide guidance on how the generic practice should be applied uniquely to the process area. A generic practice elaboration is an informative model component.
Supporting informative components	There are many places where further information is needed to describe a concept. This information is provided in terms of the following components: ***Notes*** A note is text that can accompany any other model component. It may provide detail, background, or rationale. A note is an informative model component. ***Examples*** An example is a component comprising text and often a list of items, usually in a box, that can accompany nearly any other component and provides one or more examples to clarify a concept or described activity. An example is an informative model component. ***References*** A reference is a pointer to additional or more detailed information in related process areas and can accompany nearly any other model component. A reference is an informative model component.

With CMMI-DEV, process areas are organized by so-called categories: Process Management, Project Management, Engineering, and Support. The grouping into categories is a way to discuss their interactions and is especially used with a continuous approach (see figure 3–5). For example, a common business objective is to reduce the time it takes to get a product to market. The process improvement objective derived from that could be to improve the project management processes to ensure on-time delivery.

The following two diagrams summarize the structural components of CMMI described so far. The first diagram (figure 3–4) shows how the structural elements are organized with the staged representation.

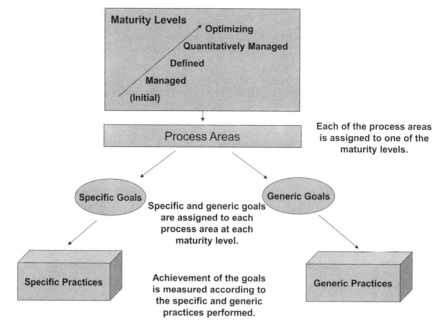

Figure 3-5   *CMMI staged model: structural elements*

The diagram in figure 3-6 shows how the structural elements of CMMI are organized in the continuous representation.

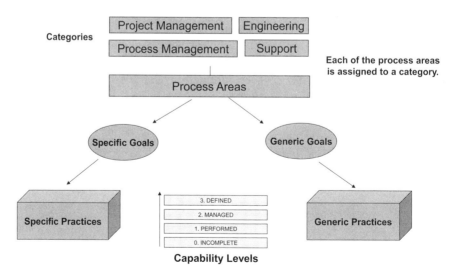

Figure 3-6   *CMMI continuous model: structural elements*

To conclude the description of the CMMI structure, the allocation of CMMI-DEV process areas to each category is shown in table 3–3. Note that the process areas shown in italic are particularly relevant for testing. Some of these will be discussed in more detail in the following pages.

Table 3–3 Process areas of CMMI-DEV grouped by category

Category	Process area
Process Management	• Organizational Process Definition • Organizational Process Focus • Organizational Performance Management • Organizational Process Performance • Organizational Training
Engineering	• *Product Integration* • Requirements Development • *Technical Solution* • *Validation* • *Verification*
Project Management	• Integrated Project Management • *Project Monitoring and Control* • *Project Planning* • Quantitative Project Management • Requirements Management • *Risk Management* • Supplier Agreement Management
Support	• *Causal Analysis and Resolution* • *Configuration Management* • Decision Analysis and Resolution • *Measurement and Analysis* • Process and Product Quality Assurance

Testing-Related Process Areas

The two principal process areas with testing relevance shown in table 3–3 are Validation and Verification. These process areas specifically reference both static and dynamic test processes.

Although still considered "not much" and "too high-level" by many testers, having these two dedicated process areas does make a difference. It means that process improvement initiatives using the CMMI shall also address testing.

However, the number of pages dedicated by CMMI to testing is approximately 20 pages out of 400!

The Validation process area addresses testing to demonstrate that a product or product component fulfills its intended use when placed in its intended environments. Table 3–4 shows the specific goals and specific practices that make up this process area.

Table 3–4 *CMMI Process Area: Validation*

CMMI: Process Area: Validation	
Specific goals	Specific practices
SG1: Prepare for Validation	• Select Product for Validation • Establish the Validation Environment • Establish Validation Procedures and Criteria
SG2: Validate Product or Product Components	• Perform Validation • Analyze Validation Results

The purpose of the Verification process area is to ensure that selected work products meet their specific requirements. It also includes static testing, that is, peer reviews. Table 3–5 shows the specific goals and specific practices that make up this process area.

Table 3–5 *CMMI Process Area: Verification*

CMMI: Process Area: Verification	
Specific goals	Specific practices
SG1: Prepare for Verification	• Select Work Products for Verification • Establish the Verification Environment • Establish Verification Procedures and Criteria
SG2: Perform Peer Reviews	• Prepare for Peer Reviews • Conduct Peer Reviews • Analyze Peer Review Data
SG3: Verify Selected Work Products	• Perform Verification • Analyze Verification Results • Identify Corrective Action

The process areas Technical Solution and Product Integration also deal with some testing issues, although again this is very lightweight.

The Technical Solution process area mentions peer reviews of code and some details on performing unit testing (in total, four sentences). The specific practices identified by the CMMI are as follows:

- Conduct peer reviews on the selected components
- Perform unit testing of the product components as appropriate

The Product Integration process area includes several practices in which peer reviews are mentioned (e.g., on interface documentation), and there are several implicit references to integration testing. However, none of this is specific and explicit.

In addition to the specific testing-related process areas, some process areas also provide support toward a more structured testing process, although the support provided is generic and does not address any of the specific testing issues.

Test planning can be addressed as part of the CMMI Project Planning process area. The goals and practices for test planning can often be reused for the implementation of the test planning process. Project management practices can be reused for test management.

Test monitoring and control can be addressed as part of the CMMI process area Project Monitoring and Control. The goals and practices for project planning and control can often be reused for the test monitoring and control process. Project management practices can be reused for test management.

Performing product risk assessments within testing to define a test approach and test strategy can partly be implemented based on goals and practices provided by the CMMI process area Risk Management.

The goals and practices of the CMMI process area Configuration Management can support the implementation of configuration management for test deliverables. Testing will also benefit if configuration management is well implemented during development (e.g., for the test object).

Having the CMMI process area Measurement and Analysis in place will support the task of getting accurate and reliable data for test reporting. It will also support testing if you're setting up a measurement process on testing-related data, such as, for example, defects and the testing process itself.

The goals and practices of the Causal Analysis and Resolution CMMI process area provide support for the implementation of defect prevention, a typical test improvement objective at higher maturity levels.

Assessments

An assessment can give an organization an idea of the maturity of its processes and help it create a road map toward improvement. After all, you can't plan a route to a destination if you don't know where you currently are. The SEI does not offer certification of any form. It simply licenses and authorizes lead appraisers to conduct appraisals (commonly called assessments).

There are three different types of appraisals: Class A, B, and C (see table 3–6). The requirements for CMMI appraisal methods are described in *Appraisal Requirements for CMMI (ARC)*. The Standard CMMI Assessment Method for Process Improvement (SCAMPI) is the only appraisal method that meets all of the ARC requirements for a Class A appraisal method. Only the Class A appraisal can result in a formal CMMI rating. A SCAMPI Class C appraisal is typically used as a gap analysis and data collection tool, and the SCAMPI Class B appraisal is often employed as a user acceptance or "test" appraisal.

The SEI certifies so-called lead appraisers. Only a Certified SCAMPI Lead Appraiser can conduct a SCAMPI A appraisal. Especially the staged representation is used to achieve a CMMI Level Rating from a SCAMPI appraisal. The results of the appraisal can then be published on the SEI website [URL: SEI].

Table 3-6 Characteristics of CMMI appraisals

Characteristics	Class A	Class B	Class C
Amount of objective evidence gathered	High	Medium	Low
Rating generated	Yes	No	No
Resource needs	High	Medium	Low
Team size	Large	Medium	Small
Appraisal team leader requirements	Lead appraiser	Lead appraiser or team leader	Lead appraiser or team leader

Benefits

To understand what the benefit of CMMI might be to your organization, you need to think about what improved processes might mean for you. What would be the impact to your organization if project predictability was improved by 10 percent? What would be the impact if the cost of finding and fixing defects was reduced by 10 percent? By benchmarking before beginning process improvement, you can compare any process improvements to the benchmark to ensure a positive impact on the bottom line.

Turning to a real-world example of the benefits of CMMI, Lockheed Martin, between 1996 and 2002, was able to increase software productivity by 30 percent while decreasing the unit software cost by 20 percent [Weska 2004]. Another organization reported that achieving CMMI maturity level 3 allowed it to reduce its costs from rework by 42 percent over several years, and yet another described a 5:1 return on investment for quality activities in a CMMI maturity level 3 organization.

The SEI states that it measured increases of performances in the categories cost, schedule, productivity, quality, and customer satisfaction for 25 organizations (see table 3–7). The median increase in performance varied between 14 percent (customer satisfaction) and 62 percent (productivity).

However, the CMMI model mostly deals with what processes should be implemented and not so much with how they can be implemented. SEI thus also mentions that these results do not guarantee that applying CMMI will increase performance in every organization. A small company with few resources may be less likely to benefit from CMMI.

Table 3–7 Results reported by 25 organizations in terms of performance change over time

Performance category	Median	Number of data points	Low	High
Cost	20%	21	3%	87%
Schedule	37%	19	2%	90%
Productivity	62%	17	9%	255%
Quality	50%	20	7%	132%
Customer satisfaction	14%	6	-4%	55%
Return on investment	4.7:1	16	2:1	27.7:1

Summary

CMMI is not a process, it is a book of "whats," not a book of "hows," and it does not define how your company should behave. More accurately, it defines what behaviors need to be defined. In this way, CMMI is a behavioral model as well as a process model.

Like any framework, CMMI is not a quick fix for all that is wrong with a development organization. SEI cautions that improvement projects will likely be measured in months and years, not days and weeks. Because they usually have more knowledge and resources, larger organizations may find they get better results, but CMMI process changes can also help smaller companies.

3.2.2 ISO/IEC 15504

Just like CMMI, the ISO/IEC 15504 standard [ISO/IEC 15504] (which was known in its pre-standard days as SPICE) is a model for software process improvement that includes specific testing processes. The standard comprises several parts, as shown in figure 3–7.

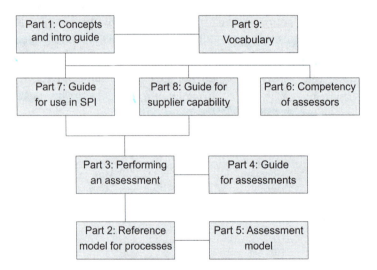

Figure 3-7   Parts of ISO/IEC 15504

Several parts of the standard have relevance for test process improvers. Part 5 is of particular relevance because it describes a process assessment model that is made up of two specific *dimensions*:

- The process dimension describes the various software processes to be assessed.
- The capability dimension enables us to measure how well processes are being performed.

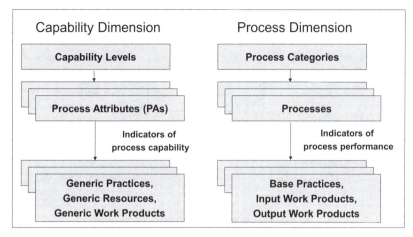

Figure 3-8   ISO/IEC 15504-5: Process and Capability dimensions

To understand how ISO/IEC 15504 can be used for test process improvement, the two dimensions are summarized in the following sections with particular focus on the testing-specific aspects. Further details can be obtained from *Process Assessment and ISO/IEC 15504: A Reference Book* [van Loon 2007] or, of course, from the standard itself.

Process Dimension

The process dimension identifies, describes, and organizes the individual processes within the overall software life cycle. The activities (*base practices*) and the work products used by and created by the processes are the *indicators* of process performance that an assessor evaluates.

ISO/IEC 15504 allows any compliant process model to be used for the process dimension, which makes it easy for specific schemes to adopt. For example, the assessment processes and schemes of CMMI (SCAMPI) and TMMi (TAMAR) are ISO 15504 Part 4 compliant. To provide the assessor with a usable "out of the box" standard, part 5 of ISO/IEC 15504 also describes an "exemplar" process model, which is principally based on the ISO/IEC 12207 standard "Software Life Cycle Processes" [ISO/IEC 12207]. The process categories and groups defined by the exemplar process model are shown in figure 3–9; this is the process model that assessors use most often.

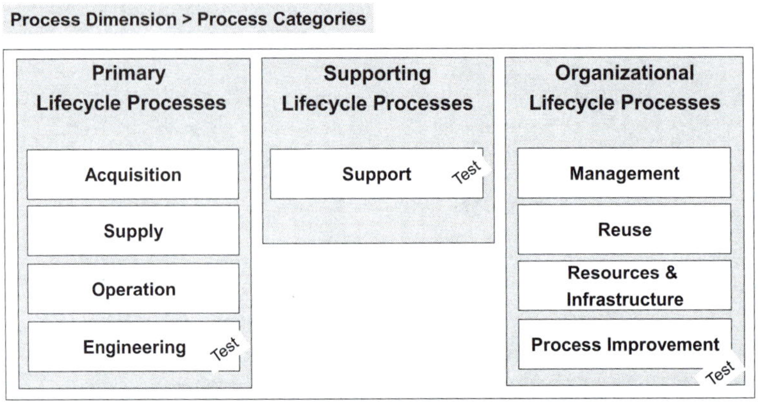

3 Model-Based Improvement

Figure 3-9   ISO/IEC 15504-5: Process categories and groups

The ISO/IEC 15504-5 Process Assessment Model shown in figure 3–9 contains a process dimension with three process categories and nine process groups, three of which (marked "test" in the figure) are of particular relevance for the test process improver. Let's now take a closer look at those testing-specific process groups, starting with Engineering (see figure 3–10).

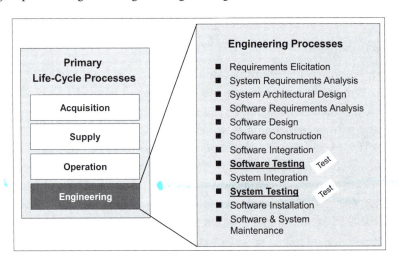

Figure 3-10   ISO/IEC 15504-5: Engineering processes

The software testing and system testing processes relate to testing the integrated software and integrated system (hardware and software). Testing activities are focused on showing compliance to software and system requirements prior to installation and productive use.

The process category Supporting Life-Cycle Processes contains only a single group of processes (see figure 3–11). These may be employed by any other processes from any other process category.

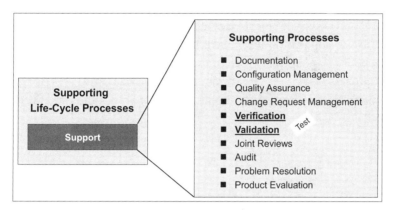

Figure 3–11 *ISO/IEC 15504-5: Supporting processes*

The processes Verification and Validation are very similar to the CMMI process areas with the same names covered in section 3.2.1. Verification, according to the ISTQB definition, is "confirmation by examination and through provision of objective evidence that specified requirements have been fulfilled. This process area checks that work products such as requirements, design, code, and documentation reflect the specified requirements.

A closer look at the verification of designs shows the level of detail provided in ISO/IEC 12207. A list of criteria is defined for the verification of designs:

- The design is correct and consistent with and traceable to requirements.
- The design implements proper sequence of events, inputs, outputs, interfaces, logic flow, allocation of timing and sizing budgets, and error definition, isolation, and recovery.
- The selected design can be derived from requirements.
- The design implements safety, security, and other critical requirements correctly as shown by suitably rigorous methods.

The standard also defines the following list of outcomes:

- A verification strategy is developed and implemented.
- Criteria for verification of all required software work products is identified.
- Required verification activities are performed.

- Defects are identified and recorded.
- Results of the verification activities are made available to the customer and other involved parties.

Validation, according to the ISTQB definition, is "confirmation by examination and through provision of objective evidence that the requirements for a specific intended use or application have been fulfilled." The validation process focuses on the tasks of test planning, creation of test cases, and execution of tests.

The process category Organizational Life-Cycle Processes is aimed at developing processes (including the test process) across the organization (see figure 3–12).

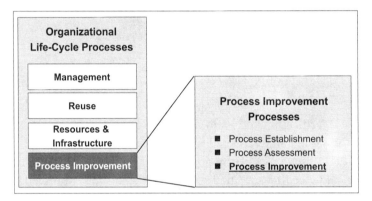

Figure 3–12 ISO/IEC 15504-5: Organizational processes

These processes emphasize the organizational policies and procedures used for establishing and improving life cycle models and processes. Test process improvers should take note of these processes in ISO/IEC 15504, Part 5, although the overall process of test process improvement is covered more thoroughly in the IDEAL model described in chapter 6.

Capability Dimension

ISO/IEC 15504 defines a system for evaluating the maturity level (capability) achieved by the processes being assessed. This is the "how well" dimension of the model. It applies a continuous representation approach (see section 3.1.3).

The overall structure of the capability dimension is shown in figure 3–8 earlier in this chapter. The diagram in figure 3–13 shows the specific capability levels and the process attributes assigned to those levels.

3.2 Software Process Improvement (SPI) Models

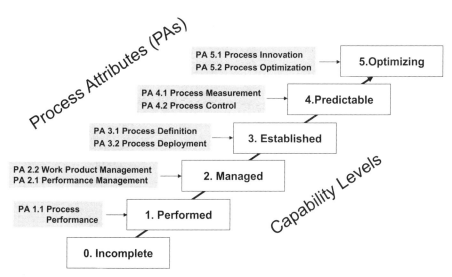

Figure 3-13 ISO/IEC 15504-5: Capability levels and process attributes

The capability of any process defined in the process dimension can be evaluated according to the capability scheme shown in figure 3–13. This is similar but (regrettably) not identical to the scheme defined by CMMI. Process attributes guide the assessor by describing generic indicators of process capability; these include generic descriptions of practices, resources, and work products. Further details can be obtained. Please refer to *Process Assessment and ISO/IEC 15504: A Reference Book* [van Loon 2007] or the ISO/IEC 15504 standard for further details.

Using ISO/IEC 15504-5 for Assessing Test Processes

Test process improvers will tend to focus on the processes just described. The assessment provides results regarding the achieved capability for each assessed process and features a graded scale with four levels: fully achieved, largely achieved, partially achieved, and not achieved (per capability level). The diagram shown in figure 3–14 is an example of the assessment results for two testing-related processes that also describes the rules to be applied when grading the capability of a process.

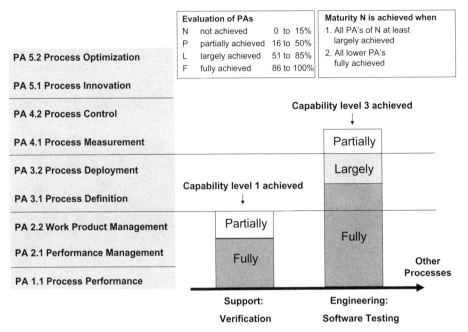

Figure 3–14 ISO/IEC 15504-5: Assessment of capability (example)

3.2.3 Comparing CMMI and ISO/IEC 15504

A full evaluation of the differences between these two software process improvement models is beyond the scope of our book on test process improvement. Some of the comparisons shown in table 3–8 may be useful background information, especially if you are involved in an overall decision on software process improvement models.

Table 3–8 Comparison between CMMI and ISO/IEC 15504-5

Aspect	Description
Level of detail	CMMI is more detailed than ISO/IEC 15504. CMMI includes sub-practices that serve as direct support for implementing the specific practices. This can result in more effort being required for assessments.
Scope	The CMMI staged representation model is generally better suited to larger organizations. ISO/IEC 15504 permits single processes to be assessed for a single project or all processes to be assessed across the entire organization.
Flexibility	ISO/IEC 15504-5 allows various process assessment models to be used. This permits tailoring to specific industries such as the space and automotive industries. CMMI offers *only* one generic process model to be used.

Aspect	Description
Uptake	CMMI is almost a de facto standard. ISO/IEC 15504 is not heavily used but often used as a standard to build on; e.g., the assessment processes and schemes of CMMI (SCAMPI) and TMMi (TAMAR) are ISO/IEC 15504 compliant
Assessment process	ISO/IEC 15504 encompasses an assessment process. CMMI does not. The CMMI assessment process is described in a separate guideline (SCAMPI)

The suitability of using software process improvement models compared to those dedicated to test process improvement is discussed in section 3.5.

3.3 Test Process Improvement Models

3.3.1 The Test Process Improvement Model (TPI NEXT)

Syllabus Learning Objectives

LO 3.3.1 (K2) Summarize the background and structure of the TPI NEXT test process improvement model.

LO 3.3.2 (K2) Summarize the key areas of the TPI NEXT test process improvement model.

LO 3.3.8 (K3) Carry out an informal assessment using the TPI NEXT test process improvement model.

LO 3.3.10 (K5) Assess a test organization using either the TPI NEXT or TMMi model.

Introduction

We will now consider two principal areas of the TPI NEXT model. First we'll describe the structure of the model and its various components. Then we'll consider some of the issues involved in using the model to complete typical test process improvement tasks.

The official book on TPI NEXT provides a full description of the model and its use (see *TPI NEXT – Business Driven Test Process Improvement* [van Ewijk, et al. 2009]). Users will gain additional insights into the model by consulting this publication and the other sources of information avilable at the website for the TPI NEXT model [URL: TPI NEXT].

TPI NEXT A continuous business-driven framework for test process improvement that describes the key elements of an effective and efficient test process.

Overview of Model Structure

The TPI NEXT model is based upon the elements shown in figure 3–15. Users of the previous version of the model (called simply TPI) will recognize a basic structural similarity between the models, although "clusters" (described in the next paragraph) are a new addition to the structure. Different aspects of the test process are represented in TPI NEXT by 16 key areas (e.g., reporting), each of which can be evaluated at a given maturity level (e.g., managed).

Achieving a particular maturity level for a given key area (e.g., managed test reporting) requires that the specific checkpoints (questions) are *all* answered positively (including those of any previous maturity levels). The checkpoints are also grouped into clusters, which are made up of a number of checkpoints from different key areas. Clusters are like the "stepping stones" along the path of test process improvement. We will be looking at all these model elements in more detail in the sections that follow.

TPI NEXT uses a continuous representation to show test process maturity. This can be shown on the test maturity matrix, which visualizes the achieved test process maturity for each key area. Again, some examples of the test maturity matrix are shown in the following sections.

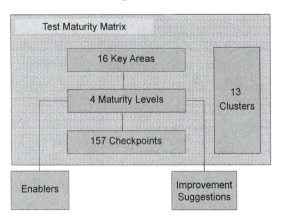

Figure 3–15   *Structure of the TPI NEXT model*

Maturity Levels

The TPI NEXT model defines the following maturity levels per key area:

- Initial: No process. Ad-hoc activities
- Controlled: Performing the right test process activities
- Efficient: Performing the test process efficiently
- Optimizing: Continuously adapting to ever-changing circumstances

The continuous representation used by the TPI NEXT model means that each key area (see the following section) can achieve a particular maturity level. Note that key areas are what other improvement models refer to as process areas.

If all key areas have achieved a specific maturity level, then the test process as a whole is said to have achieved that maturity level. Note that this permits staged objectives to be set for test process improvement if this is desired (e.g., the test process shall achieve the efficient maturity level). In practice, many organizations use TPI NEXT in this staged way as well.

Key Areas

The body of testing best practices provided by the TPI NEXT model is based on the TMap NEXT methodology [Koomen, et al. 2006] and the previous version of the methodology simply called TMap [Pol, Teunnissen, and van Veenendaal 2002]. They are organized into 16 key areas, each of which covers a particular aspect of the test process (e.g., test environment). The key areas are further organized into three groups: stakeholder relations, test management, and test profession. This organization is particularly useful when reporting at a high level about assessment results and improvement suggestions (e.g., "the testing profession is only weakly practiced within small projects" or "stakeholder relations must be improved by organizing the test team more efficiently").

Figure 3–16 shows the key areas and their groups.

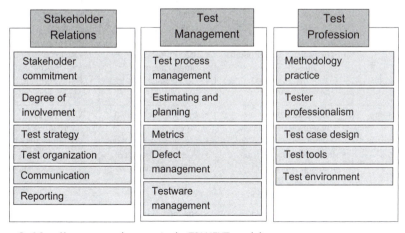

Figure 3–16   *Key areas and groups in the TPI NEXT model*

Table 3–9, table 3–10, and table 3–11 provide an overview of the principal areas considered by the key areas in the controlled, efficient, and optimizing maturity levels for the three groups shown in figure 3–16. More detailed information is available in the book *TPI NEXT – Business-Driven Test Process Improvement* [van Ewijk, et al. 2009].

Table 3–9 Summary of key areas in the stakeholder relations group

Stakeholder relations	Aspects covered at different maturity levels		
Key area	Controlled	Efficient	Optimizing
1: Stakeholder commitment	• Identity of principal stakeholder • Budget availability • Stakeholder reliability • Product risk analysis	• Identity of all other stakeholders • Level of stakeholder involvement	• Line management commitment • Stakeholder adaptability
2: Degree of involvement (of testing)	• Test assignments • When testing starts • Involvement in project planning and risk analysis	• Involvement in defect analysis, evaluating change requests, and improving test basis	• Standing of the test team within the organization • Involvement in lessons learned
3: Test strategy	• Agreements with principal stakeholder • Relationship of test strategy to risks • Retest and regression test strategies	• Agreements with all stakeholders • Coverage of test levels and test types • Adequacy of test design techniques used	• Process of test strategy creation • Effectiveness of test strategy based on production defect metrics
4: Test organization (TO)	• People, tasks, and responsibilities • Structure of accountability of TO • TO services and products	• Coordination and delivery of testing activities and services • TO in the overall organization • Compliance with test policy	• Optimization of TO services and products • Accountability of TO for success/failure of test assignment • Benchmarking of TO capability
5: Communication	• Awareness and traceability of decisions, actions, and status • Interaction of test team and stakeholders in exchanging information and decision-making	• Specific information flows • Meeting participation • Adequate means of communication	• Continuous improvement of communications
6: Reporting	• Basic information in written reports • Frequency and suitability of reporting for stakeholder needs	• Balance of needs and costs • Trends and recommendations (progress, goals, risks)	• Used for continuous test process improvement • Used for continuous software process improvement in organization

Table 3-10 Summary of key areas in the test management group

Test management	Aspects covered at different maturity levels		
Key area	Controlled	Efficient	Optimizing
7: Test process management	• Test plan and contents • Agreement between principal stakeholder and other stakeholders • Monitoring and controlling	• Handling of test plan deviations • Adjustment of test plan and resource reallocation	• Continuous improvement of test process management
8: Estimating and planning	• Estimating techniques used • Planning information created • Agreement with principal stakeholder	• Accuracy of estimating and planning for all test activities • Testability of test basis	• Reuse of testware for improved test planning • Estimating techniques, principles, and metrics at organization level
9: Metrics	• Metrics for estimating and controlling project • Systematic recording and storage • Accuracy of metrics	• Balance of needs and costs • Impact of collection on test process • Test process efficiency metrics • Interpreting and acting on metrics	• Contribution made by metrics to test process improvement
10: Defect management (DM)	• Defect life cycle and responsibilities • Basic defect items recorded • Accessibility of DM tool	• DM tool support for DM life cycle • Further defect items recorded • Commonality of DM tool • Reporting capability of DM tool • Use of defect trends	• Availability of DM guidelines for projects • Organizational support for DM • Root cause analysis and defect prevention
11: Testware management	• Identifying by name and version • Test case relationship to test basis • Accessibility • Procedures used	• Referencing by name and version • Traceability of test cases to requirements • Storage, roles, and responsibilities	• Conservation of testware for reuse (items, guidelines, handover)

Table 3–11 Summary of key areas in the test profession group

Test profession	Aspects covered at different maturity levels		
Key area	Controlled	Efficient	Optimizing
12: Methodology practice	• Documented test method used • Applicability to project context • Usefulness of test method	• Recorded information • Conditional, optional, and mandatory aspects • Use of templates	• Continuous improvement of test method
13: Tester professionalism	• Training and experience of testing staff • Familiarity with test method • Availability of all expertise needed • Evaluation of testing staff skills	• Available certifications • Justification of chosen techniques • Performance of tasks • Job satisfaction of testing staff	• Participation in skills development activities • Career paths for testers • Accountability and responsibility for own work • Continuous improvement of own work process
14: Test case design	• Level at which test cases are recorded • Type of test case information documented	• Understandability of test cases by peers • Coverage of test basis • Techniques used • Use of checklists	• Improvement of test case design using defect analysis • Test case validity and maintainability • Future use of techniques
15: Test tools	• Availability, usage, and benefits gained • Knowledge levels present	• Selection criteria and creation of business case • Integration into the test process	• Consistency of tools policy and test policy • Reuse of expertise and tools best practices • Achievement of business case
16: Test environment	• Requirements • Supplier agreements • Availability • Change procedures	• Design and acceptance of test environment • Service-level agreements	• Ownership • Contractual agreements • Services provided

Checkpoints

The maturity level of a particular key area is assessed by answering checkpoints. These are closed yes/no-type questions that should enable a clear judgment to be made by the interviewer.

Table 3–12, from *TPI NEXT – Business-Driven Test Process Improvement* [van Ewijk, et al. 2009], shows the four checkpoints that must all be answered yes for the key area stakeholder commitment to achieve the controlled maturity level. Note that checkpoints are identified using a format that contains the number of the key area (01 to 16), a single letter representing the maturity level (*c*, *e*, or *o*), and the number of the checkpoint within the key area (1 to 4).

Table 3–12 Examples of checkpoints

Checkpoint number	Checkpoint description: Key area: Stakeholder commitment. Maturity Level: Controlled
01.c.1	The principal stakeholder is defined (not necessarily documented) and known to the testers.
01.c.2	Budget for test resources is granted by and negotiable with the principal stakeholder.
01.c.3	Stakeholders actually deliver the committed resources.
01.c.4	The principal stakeholder is responsible for a documented product risk analysis (the input for the test strategy).

When interviewing a test manager, for example, we may pose the question, "What kind of information do you receive from your principal stakeholder?" (Note that it is not recommended to use checkpoints directly for interviewing purposes; see section 7.3.1 regarding interviewing skills). If the words *product risk analysis* do not occur in the answer, we might mention this explicitly in a follow-up question, and if the answer is negative, the result is a clear "no" to the fourth checkpoint (01.c.4) shown in table 3–12. The stakeholder commitment key area has not been achieved at the controlled maturity level (or indeed the other higher-level maturity levels, efficient and optimizing) since *all* checkpoints need to be addressed positively.

Evaluating checkpoints is not always as straightforward as this. Take, for example, the third checkpoint (01.c.3). To evaluate this checkpoint, we need the following information:

- A list of stakeholders
- A list of the resources they have committed to testing (e.g., staff, infrastructure, budget, documents)
- Some form of proof that these resources were delivered

Let's assume we have eight stakeholders and, in total, 20 individual resources they have committed to. It has been established that all resources except for one were delivered, but one (e.g., a document) was delivered late. How might an assessor evaluate this checkpoint? A strict assessor would simply evaluate the checkpoint as no. A pragmatic assessor would check on the significance of the late item, whether this was a one-off or recurring incident, and what the impact was on the test process. A pragmatic assessment may well be yes, if a minor item was slightly late and the stakeholder has otherwise been reliable. This calls for judgment and a particular attitude on the part of the assessor. As these typical examples show, some checkpoints are easy and clear to assess, but some need more work, experience, and judgment to enable an appropriate conclusion to be reached.

Test Maturity Matrix

The test maturity matrix is a visual representation of the overall test process that combines key areas, test maturity, and checkpoints. Figure 3–17 shows the test maturity matrix.

Key Area	Initial	Controlled				Efficient				Optimizing		
1 Stakeholder commitment		1	2	3	4	1	2	3		1	2	3
2 Degree of involvement		1	2	3	4	1	2	3		1		2
3 Test strategy		1	2	3	4	1	2	3		1		2
4 Test organization		1	2	3	4	1	2	3	4	1	2	3
5 Communication		1	2	3	4	1	2	3		1		2
6 Reporting		1		2	3	1	2	3		1		2
7 Test process management		1	2	3	4	1	2	3		1		2
8 Estimating and planning		1	2	3	4	1	2	3	4	1	2	3
9 Metrics		1		2	3	1	2	3	4	1		2
10 Defect management		1	2	3	4	1	2	3	4	1	2	3
11 Testware management		1	2	3	4	1		2	3	1	2	3
12 Methodological practice		1		2	3	1	2	3	4	1		2
13 Tester professionalism		1	2	3	4	1	2	3	4	1	2	3
14 Test case design		1		2	3	1	2	3	4	1	2	3
15 Test tools		1		2	3	1	2	3	4	1	2	3
16 Test environment		1	2	3	4	1	2	3	4	1	2	3

Figure 3–17   Test maturity matrix: checkpoint view

The individual numbered cells in the matrix represent the checkpoints for specific key areas and maturity levels. As shown earlier in table 3–12, for example, the key area stakeholder commitment has four checkpoints at the controlled level of test process maturity.

The test maturity matrix is a useful instrument for showing the "big picture" of current and desired test process maturity across all key areas. This is discussed later in "Using TPI NEXT: Overview."

There are two ways to show the test maturity matrix. The checkpoint view is shown in figure 3–17. The cluster view is shown in figure 3–18, after the concept of clusters is introduced.

Clusters

The purpose of clusters is to ensure that a sensible, step-by-step approach is adopted to test process improvement. It makes no sense, for example, to focus all our efforts on achieving an optimizing maturity level in the key area of metrics when defect management is way back at the initial stage.

Clusters are collections of individual checkpoints taken from different key areas. The TPI NEXT model defines 13 clusters, which are identified with a single letter; A is the very first cluster and M the final cluster. Figure 3–18 shows clusters on the test maturity matrix (the cluster view).

Key Area	Initial	Controlled			Efficient			Optimizing		
1 Stakeholder commitment		A	B	B	C	F	H	H	K	M	M
2 Degree of involvement		A	B	C	E	H	H	J	L		L
3 Test strategy		A	A	B	E	F	F	H	K		L
4 Test organization		A	D	D	E	I	I	J	J	K	L	L
5 Communication		B	C	C	D	F	F	J	M		M
6 Reporting		A		C		C	F	G	G	K		K
7 Test process management		A	A	B	B	G	H	J	K		M
8 Estimating and planning		B	B	C	C	G	H	I	I	K	L	L
9 Metrics		C		C		D	G	H	H	I	K		K
10 Defect management		A	A	B	D	F	F	H	J	K	L	L
11 Testware management		B	B	D	E	I			J	L	L	L
12 Methodological practice		C		D		E	F	H	J	J	M		M
13 Tester professionalism		D	D	E	E	G	G	I	I	K	K	M
14 Test case design		A		A		E	F	I	I	J	K	K	M
15 Test tools		E		E		E	F	G	G	I	L	M	M
16 Test environment		C	D	D	E	G	H	J	J	L	M	M

Figure 3–18   Test maturity matrix: cluster view

In the cluster view, the checkpoints associated with a particular base cluster are represented by the letter of the cluster to which they belong (table 3–13 shows the checkpoints in base cluster A).

The path from cluster A to M represents the recommended progression of the test process and assists the test process improver in setting improvement priorities. The highest-priority recommendation would typically be assigned to fulfilling a checkpoint in the earliest cluster not yet fully completed.

Note that base clusters are allocated to a specific overall test process maturity level. Completing base clusters A thru E achieves an overall "controlled" test process maturity, for "efficient" the base clusters F thru J are required, and for "optimizing" the base clusters K, L, and M must be completed.

The TPI NEXT model permits specific business objectives (e.g., cost reduction) to be followed in test process improvement. The mechanism for applying this is to adjust the checkpoints contained in a given cluster using a procedure described later (see "Using TPI NEXT: Overview"). The predefined, unchanged clusters in TPI NEXT are referred to as *base* clusters to distinguish them from clusters that may have been modified to meet specific business objectives.

Base cluster A is shown in table 3–13 as an example (from *TPI NEXT – Business-Driven Test Process Improvement* [van Ewijk, et al. 2009]).

Table 3–13 Example of a cluster

Base cluster A	
Checkpoint number	**Checkpoint description**
01.c.1	The principal stakeholder is defined (not necessarily documented) and known to the testers.
02.c.1	The test assignment, scope, and approach are negotiated early with the principal stakeholder as one of the first test activities.
03.c.1	The principal stakeholder agrees with the documented test strategy.
03.c.2	The test strategy is based on a product risk analysis.
04.c.1	People involved know where to find the persons (or department) responsible for test services.
06.c.1	The reporting contains aspects of time and/or costs, results, and risks.
07.c.1	At the start of the test project, a test plan is created. The test plan includes <content items>.
07.c.2	The test plan is agreed upon with the principal stakeholder.
10.c.1	The defect life cycle is defined (including a retest) and applied.
10.c.2	The following items are recorded for each defect: <the model provides a list of items to be checked>.
14.c.1	The test cases are recorded on a logical level.
14 c.2	The test cases consist of a description of <the model provides a list of items to be checked>.

As can be seen, base cluster A consists of 12 checkpoints drawn from eight different key areas. The locations of the 12 checkpoints that belong to base cluster A can be clearly identified in the test maturity matrix shown below in figure 3–19. The checkpoints in this cluster will be the first items to be implemented if our test process needs to be built up from the initial level of maturity and if no adjustment of the cluster contents has been performed to address specific business objectives.

Enablers

In section 3.1.2, "Using Models: Benefits and Risks," a particular risk was discussed that highlighted the possibility of choosing the "wrong approach" when adopting a model-based solution to test process improvement. The risk originates from a failure to recognize the strong interrelationships between the testing process and other processes involved in software development. By focusing only on the test process, there is a risk that problems that are not within the test process itself get scoped out of the analysis. We end up treating symptoms (i.e., effects) instead of the root causes.

The idea behind *enablers* is to provide a link between the test process and other relevant processes within the software development life cycle to clarify how they can both benefit from exchanging best practices and working closely together. In some instances, enablers also provide links to software process improvement models such as CMMI and ISO/IEC 15504.

The following example applies to the key area "test strategy" at the controlled maturity level. This includes the following two checkpoints (from *TPI NEXT – Business-Driven Test Process Improvement* [van Ewijk, et al. 2009]) with relevance to product risk analysis:

- Checkpoint 03.c.2: The test strategy is based on product risk analysis.
- Checkpoint 03.c.3: There is a differentiation in test levels, test types, test coverage and test depth, depending on the analyzed risks.

Performing product risk analysis within TPI NEXT is not a part of the test process, so the TPI NEXT model simply suggests "use risk management for product risks" as an enabler to achieving the two checkpoints. The test process improver can check up on risk management practices by considering any source of information they choose. This may be the implementation of a software process improvement model, such as CMMI (risk management is a specific process area with CMMI), or it could be a knowledgeable person in their department.

Note that the TPI NEXT model does not consider enablers formally in the same way as checkpoints. Enablers are simply high-level hints and links that increase awareness and help to mitigate the risks mentioned previously.

Improvement Suggestions

There are two principal sources of test process improvements supported by the TPI NEXT model. The first source is to simply consider any checkpoints that have not yet been achieved in order to reach the desired test process maturity. This source of information covers the direct "what needs to be achieved" aspect of required improvements.

Test improvement plans (see section 6.4) should not focus entirely on listing unachieved checkpoints; there must be an indication of how particular business objectives can be achieved through test process improvements. The TPI NEXT model supports this by providing a second source of test process improvements. These are *improvement suggestions*, which are described for the three maturity levels of each key area. They give advice on how particular maturity levels might be achieved by implementing the suggestions.

The following example taken from TPI NEXT shows the four improvement suggestions for achieving controlled test process maturity for the stakeholder commitment key area:

- Locate the person who orders test activities or is heavily dependant on test results.
- Research the effect of poor testing on production and make this visible to stakeholders. Show which defects could have been found earlier by testing. Indicate what the stakeholders could have done to avoid the problems.
- Keep to simple, practical examples.
- Focus on "quick wins."

Using TPI NEXT: Overview

We will now describe some of the frequently performed activities in test process improvement with regard to using the TPI NEXT model. The following activities are described:

- Representing business objectives
- Evaluating assessment results
- Setting improvement priorities

Representing Business Objectives

If the objective followed by test process improvement is a general improvement in maturity across the entire range of key areas, then the base clusters defined in the TPI NEXT model can be used as a guide for planning step-by-step improvements. This is also the case for an organization that obviously has a low test process maturity where it is probably better to initially start improving right away using the base clusters. Generally speaking, however, there is more benefit to be gained for an organization by defining business objectives and not relying entirely on the default base clusters.

If more specific business objectives have been established (e.g., as part of a test policy), then a more focused approach to test process improvement is required. This is achieved with the TPI NEXT model by prioritizing key areas according to their impact on the business objective(s) and then reallocating checkpoints to clusters according to a defined procedure. The actual procedure is described in detail in *TPI NEXT – Business-Driven Test Process Improvement* [van Ewijk, et al. 2009] and can be applied either manually or (recommended) by using the "scoring tool" provided as a free download from the TPI NEXT website [URL: TPI NEXT]. This Microsoft Excel–based tool provides a mechanism for setting key area priorities to high, neutral, or low and adjusting clusters as shown in figure 3–19.

Assigning key area priorities according to business objectives requires careful consideration and much expertise, especially where more than one objective is to be followed and potential for conflicting priorities exists. Support for this task is provided in the previously mentioned book [van Ewijk, et al. 2009] by describing some typical business objectives (e.g., reduce the cost of testing) and indicating which key area priorities should be set. Figure 3–19 shows the test maturity matrix (cluster view) with all priorities set to their default neutral priority. Figure 3–20 shows the test maturity matrix with key area priorities set according to the recommendations given in the book [van Ewijk, et al. 2009] for reducing the cost of testing.

Key Area	H	N	L	Initial	Controlled				Efficient			Optimizing		
1 Stakeholder commitment		x			A	B	B	C	F	H	H	K	M	M
2 Degree of involvement		x			A	B	C	E	H	H	J	L		L
3 Test strategy		x			A	A	B	E	F	F	H	K		L
4 Test organization		x			A	D	D	E	I	I	J	K	L	L
5 Communication		x			B	C	C	D	F	F	J	M		M
6 Reporting		x			A		C	C	F	G	G	K		K
7 Test process management		x			A	A	B	B	G	H	J	K		M
8 Estimating and planning		x			B	B	C	C	G	H	I	K	L	L
9 Metrics		x			C		C	D	G	H	H	K		K
10 Defect management		x			A	A	B	D	F	F	H	K	L	L
11 Testware management		x			B	B	D	E	I		J	L	L	L
12 Methodological practice		x			C		D	E	F	H	J	M		M
13 Tester professionalism		x			D	D	E	E	G	G	I	K	K	M
14 Test case design		x			A		A	E	F	I	J	K	K	M
15 Test tools		x			E		E	E	F	G	G	L	M	M
16 Test environment		x			C	D	D	E	G	H	J	L	M	M

Figure 3–19 Unprioritized test maturity matrix

Key Area	H	N	L	Initial	Controlled			Efficient			Optimizing		
1 Stakeholder commitment			x	A	C	C	D	G	I	I	L	M	M
2 Degree of involvement	x			A	A	B	D	G	G	I	K		K
3 Test strategy	x			A	A	A	D	E	E	G	J		K
4 Test organization	x			A	C	C	D	H	H	I	J	K	K
5 Communication		x		B	C	C	D	F	F	J	M		M
6 Reporting			x	B		D		D	G	H	H	L		L
7 Test process management	x			A	A	B	B	G	H	J	K		M
8 Estimating and planning	x			B	B	C	C	G	H	I	I	K	L	L
9 Metrics			x	D		D		E	H	I	I	J	L		L
10 Defect management	x			A	A	A	C	E	E	G	I	J	K	K
11 Testware management		x		B	B	D	E	I		I	J	L	L	L
12 Methodological practice		x		C		D		E	F	H	J	J	M		M
13 Tester professionalism		x		D	D	E	E	G	G	I	I	K	K	M
14 Test case design		x		A	A		E	F	I	I	J	K	K	M
15 Test tools	x			D	D	D	D	E	F	F	H	K	L	L
16 Test environment			x	D	E	E	F	H	I	K	K	M	M	M

Figure 3-20 *Prioritized test maturity matrix: Reduce costs of testing*

Comparing the two diagrams reveals the mechanism used by TPI NEXT when setting priorities:

- The priority for each key area is assigned by placing an X in one of the priority columns marked H (high), N (neutral). and L (low).
- The clusters assigned to checkpoints in high-priority key areas are shifted forward by one cluster. Cluster C becomes B, cluster D becomes C, and so on. Cluster A cannot be shifted forward and therefore remains unchanged. Since TPI NEXT assumes a sequential implementation of clusters (i.e., from A to M), a higher priority is achieved for those checkpoints that have been reassigned to an earlier cluster.
- The clusters assigned to checkpoints in low-priority key areas are shifted backwards by one cluster. Cluster B becomes C, cluster C becomes D, and so on. Cluster M cannot be shifted backwards and therefore remains unchanged.

Note that the reallocation of clusters does not influence the allocation of individual checkpoints to key areas and maturity levels. They remain unchanged. Prioritization is accomplished by reassigning checkpoints to particular clusters.

A manual adjustment may be performed to take into account any logical inconsistencies introduced by the reallocation procedure and to balance the number of checkpoints in clusters if a particular cluster should have a disproportionately large number of checkpoints assigned (detailed information on this subject is in section B.3.3 in *TPI NEXT – Business-Driven Test Process Improvement* [van Ewijk, et al. 2009]).

A set of clusters is available for organizations that want to comply to a certain CMMI level. These four clusters (see *TPI NEXT – Business-Driven Test Process Improvement* [van Ewijk, et al. 2009] and "TPI NEXT Clusters for CMMI" [Marselis and van der Ven 2009]) indicate which checkpoints must be satisfied to make sure that the testing activities, as part of all SDLC activities, comply with the requirements to meet CMMI levels 2, 3, 4, or 5.

Evaluating Assessment Results

Individual checkpoints are evaluated after the test process assessment has been completed and the results are presented on the test maturity matrix. If the TPI NEXT scoring tool is used, the assessor simply enters the yes/no result for each checkpoint and this is automatically shown in the overall test maturity matrix. It is good practice to also enter a comment that supports the rationale for choosing yes or no. This is especially useful if there is any discussion about whether the checkpoint is met or not.

The diagram in figure 3–21 shows the achieved test process maturity (i.e., the checkpoints answered with yes) in black and the required but not achieved maturity (i.e., the checkpoints answered with no) in gray. Checkpoints that are not required (in this example, those assigned to the optimizing maturity level) are shown in white.

Key Area	H	N	L	Initial	Controlled			Efficient			Optimizing		
1 Stakeholder commitment			x	A	C	C	D	G	I	I	L	M	M
2 Degree of involvement	x			A	A	B	D	G	G	I	K		K
3 Test strategy	x			A	A	A	D	E	E	G	J		K
4 Test organization	x			A	C	C	D	H	H	I	J	K	K
5 Communication		x		B	C	C	D	F	F	J	M		M
6 Reporting			x	B	D		D	G	H	H	L		L
7 Test process management	x			A	A	B	B	G	H	J	K		M
8 Estimating and planning	x			B	B	C	C	G	H	I	K	L	L
9 Metrics			x	D	D		E	H	I	I	J	L	L
10 Defect management	x			A	A	A	C	E	E	G	J	K	K
11 Testware management		x		B	B	D	E	I	I	J	L	L	L
12 Methodological practice		x		C	D		E	F	H	J	J	M	M
13 Tester professionalism		x		D	D	E	E	G	G	I	K	K	M
14 Test case design		x		A	A		E	F	I	I	J	K	M
15 Test tools	x			D	D		D	E	F	F	H	K	L	L
16 Test environment			x	D	E	E	F	H	I	K	K	M	M

Figure 3–21   *Assessment results: Reduce costs of testing*

Presenting results on the test maturity matrix provides a visual overview of achieved and required test maturity levels and enables high-level statements such as the following examples to be made:

- Only four key areas have achieved a controlled process maturity level.
- Fundamental aspects of the test strategy and test process management are not implemented (a reference to the unachieved checkpoints in clusters A and B).
- Achieving the required "efficient" test process maturity is likely to need significant investment and several improvement stages.

Setting Improvement Priorities

Once the results have been entered on the test maturity matrix, improvement priorities can be quickly identified. As a rule, the earliest cluster that has not yet been completed represents the highest priority. In the case of figure 3-21 two checkpoints in cluster A have not been achieved (these are shown in table 3-14).

Table 3-14 Required improvements with highest priority

Checkpoint number	Required improvements with highest priority
03.c.2	The test strategy must be based on a product risk analysis.
07.c.2	The test plan must be agreed upon with the principal stakeholder.

Any further improvements proposed would be aligned to the cluster sequence and assigned successively lower priorities.

3.3.2 Test Maturity Model integration (TMMi)

Syllabus Learning Objectives

LO 3.3.3 (K2) Summarize the background and structure of the TMMi test process improvement models.
LO 3.3.4 (K2) Summarize the TMMi level 2 process areas and goals.
LO 3.3.5 (K2) Summarize the TMMi level 3 process areas and goals.
LO 3.3.6 (K2) Summarize the relationship between TMMi and CMMI.
LO 3.3.9 (K3) Carry out an informal assessment using the TMMi test process improvement model.
LO 3.3.10 (K5) Assess a test organization using either the TPI NEXT or TMMi model.

Introduction

We will now consider the TMMi model. We'll first describe the background to the model and the TMMi maturity levels. Thereafter, the structure of the model, the relationship with CMMI, and TMMi assessments are discussed. The official book on TMMi provides a full description of the model and its use (see *Test Maturity Model integration (TMMi) – Guidelines for Test Process Improvement* [van Veenendaal and Wells 2012]). Users will gain additional insights into the

> **Test Maturity Model integration (TMMi)** A five-level staged framework for test process improvement (related to the Capability Maturity Model Integration [CMMI] model) that describes the key elements of an effective test process.

model by consulting this publication and the other sources of information available at the TMMi Foundation's website [URL: TMMi].

TMMi is a noncommercial, organization-independent test maturity model. With TMMi, organizations can have their test processes objectively evaluated by certified assessors, improve their test processes, and even have their test processes and test organizations formally accredited if they comply with the requirements. Many organizations worldwide are already using TMMi for their internal test improvement process. Other organizations already have formally achieved TMMi level 2, level 3, and even level 4. TMMi has been developed by the TMMi Foundation, a nonprofit organization based in Dublin (Ireland) that has as main objectives to develop and maintain the TMMi model, create a benchmark database, and facilitate formal assessment by accredited lead assessors. Testers can (free of charge) become members of the TMMi Foundation, and from that membership a board is being elected.

TMMi is aligned with international testing standards such as IEEE and the syllabi and terminology of the International Software Testing Qualifications Board (ISTQB). The TMMi Foundation has consciously not introduced new or their own terminology but reuses the ISTQB terminology. This is an advantage for all those test professionals who are ISTQB certified (approximately 300,000 worldwide at the time of this writing). TMMi is also an objective- and business-driven model. Testing is never an activity on its own. By introducing the process area Test Policy and Goals already at TMMi level 2, testing becomes aligned with organizational and quality objectives early in the improvement model. It should be clear to all stakeholders why there is a need to improve as well as an understanding of the business case.

A difference between TMMi and other test improvement models is the strict conformity of TMMi to the CMMI framework (see section 3.2.1). The structure and the generic components of CMMI have been reused within TMMi. This has two main advantages: first, the structure already has been shown in practice to be successful, and second, organizations that use CMMI are already familiar with the structure and terminology, which makes it easier to accept TMMi and simplifies the application of TMMi in these organizations. TMMi is positioned as a complementary model to CMMI version 1.3 [Chrissis, Konrad, and Shrum

2004], addressing those issues important to test managers, test engineers, and software quality professionals. Testing as defined in the TMMi is applied in its broadest sense to encompass all software product quality-related activities. Just like the CMMI staged representation, the TMMi uses the concept of maturity levels for process evaluation and improvement. The staged model uses predefined sets of process areas to define an improvement path for an organization. This improvement path is with TMMi described by a model component called a maturity level. A maturity level is a well-defined evolutionary plateau toward achieving improved organizational processes. Furthermore, process areas, goals, and practices are identified. Applying the TMMi maturity criteria will improve the test process and have a positive impact on product quality, test engineering productivity, and cycle-time effort [van Veenendaal and Cannegieter 2011]. The TMMi has been developed to support organizations in evaluating and improving their test process. Within the TMMi, testing evolves from a chaotic, ill-defined process with a lack of resources, tools, and well-educated testers to a mature and controlled process that has defect prevention as its main objective.

Practical experiences are positive and show that TMMi supports the process of establishing a more effective and efficient test process. Testing becomes a profession and a fully integrated part of the development process. The focus of testing will ultimately change from defect detection to defect prevention.

TMMi Maturity Levels

TMMi has a staged architecture for process improvement. It contains stages, or levels, through which an organization passes as its testing process evolves from one that is ad hoc and unmanaged to one that is managed, defined, measured, and optimized. Achieving each stage ensures that an adequate improvement has been laid as a foundation for the next stage. The internal structure of the TMMi is rich in testing practices that can be learned and applied in a systematic way to support a quality testing process that improves in incremental steps.

There are five levels in the TMMi that prescribe a maturity hierarchy and an evolutionary path to test process improvement (see figure 3–22). Each level has a set of process areas that an organization needs to implement to achieve maturity at that level.

Experience has shown that organizations do their best when they focus their test process improvement efforts on a manageable number of process areas at a time and that those areas require increasing sophistication as the organization improves. Because each maturity level forms a necessary foundation for the next level, trying to skip a maturity level is usually counterproductive. At the

> **Maturity level** Degree of process improvement across a predefined set of process areas in which all goals in the set are attained. [van Veenendaal and Wells 2012]

same time, you must recognize that test process improvement efforts should focus on the needs of the organization in the context of its business environment and the process areas at higher maturity levels may address the current needs of an organization or project. For example, organizations seeking to move from maturity level 1 to maturity level 2 are frequently encouraged to establish a test department that is addressed by the Test Organization process area that resides at maturity level 3. Although the test department is not a necessary characteristic of a TMMi level 2 organization, it can be a useful part of the organization's approach to achieve TMMi maturity level 2.

Figure 3–22 shows the maturity levels and the process areas for each level.

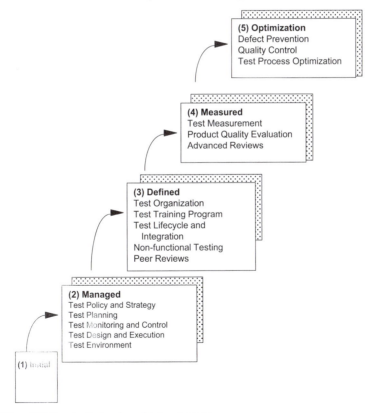

Figure 3–22   *TMMi maturity levels and process areas*

The process areas for each maturity level of the TMMi as shown in figure 3–22 are also listed in the sections that follow, along with a brief description of the characteristics of an organization at each TMMi level. The description will introduce the reader to the evolutionary path prescribed in the TMMi for test process improvement.

Note that the TMMi does not have a specific process area dedicated to test tools and/or test automation. Within TMMi, test tools are treated as a supporting resource (practices) and are therefore part of the process area where they provide support; for example, applying a test design tool is a supporting test practice within the process area Test Design and Execution at TMMi level 2 and applying a performance testing tool is a supporting test practice within the process area Non-functional Testing at TMMi level 3.

For each process area, improvement goals have been defined that in turn are supported by testing practices as shown in figure 3–23. Two types of improvement goals are distinguished within the TMMi: specific goals and generic goals. Specific goals describe the unique characteristics that must be present to satisfy the process area; for example, "establish test estimates" is a specific goal for the Test Planning process area. The specific practices describe the activities expected to result in achievement of the specific goals for a process area. The generic goals describe the characteristics that must be present to institutionalize the processes

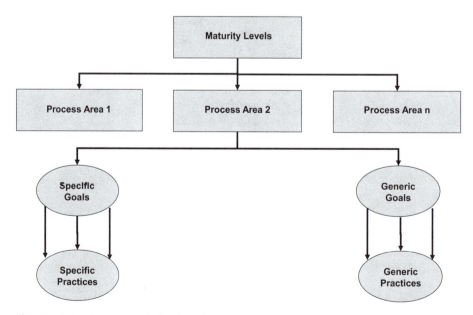

Figure 3–23   *TMMi maturity levels and process areas*

that implement a process area; for example, "institutionalize a managed process" is an example of a generic goal applicable to all TMMi process areas. The generic practices in turn describe the activities expected to result in achievement of the generic goals.

A more detailed description of the TMMi structure is provided later.

Level 1 – Initial

At TMMi level 1, testing is a chaotic, undefined process and is often considered a part of debugging. The organization usually does not provide a stable environment to support the processes. Success in these organizations depends on the competence and heroism of the people in the organization and not the use of proven processes. Tests are developed in an ad hoc way after coding is completed. Testing and debugging are interleaved to get the bugs out of the system. The objective of testing at this level is to show that the software runs without major failures. Products are released without adequate visibility regarding quality and risks. In the field, the product often does not fulfill its needs, is not stable, and/or is too slow. Within testing there is a lack of resources, tools, and well-educated staff. At TMMi level 1 there are no defined process areas. Maturity level 1 organizations are characterized by a tendency to overcommit, abandonment of processes in a time of crisis, and an inability to repeat their successes. In addition, products tend not to be released on time, budgets are overrun, and delivered quality is not according to expectations.

Level 2 – Managed

At TMMi level 2, testing becomes a managed process and is clearly separated from debugging. The process discipline reflected by maturity level 2 helps to ensure that existing practices are retained during times of stress. However, testing is still perceived by many stakeholders as being a project phase that follows coding.

In the context of improving the test process, a company-wide or program-wide test strategy is established. Test plans are also developed. Within the test plan a test approach is defined, whereby the approach is based on the result of a product risk assessment. Risk management techniques are used to identify the product risks based on documented requirements. The test plan defines what testing is required and when, how, and by whom. Commitments are established with stakeholders and revised as needed. Testing is monitored and controlled to ensure that it is going according to plan and actions can be taken if deviations occur. The status of the work products and the delivery of testing services are visible to management. Test design techniques are applied for deriving and selecting test cases from specifications. However, testing may still start relatively late in the development life cycle, such as, for example, during the design or even during the coding phase.

In TMMi level 2, multilevel testing exists: there are component, integration, system, and acceptance test levels. For each identified test level there are specific testing objectives defined in the organization-wide or program-wide test strategy. The processes of testing and debugging are differentiated. The main objective of testing in a TMMi level 2 organization is to verify that the product satisfies the specified requirements. Many quality problems at this TMMi level occur because testing occurs late in the development life cycle. Defects are propagated from the requirements and designed into code. There are no formal review programs as yet to address this important issue. Post code, execution-based testing is still considered by many stakeholders as the primary testing activity.

The process areas and their specific goals at TMMi level 2 are listed in table 3–15.

Table 3–15 TMMi Level 2

TMMi Level 2 – Managed	
Process Area	**Specific Goals**
2.1 Test Policy and Strategy	SG 1 Establish a Test Policy SG 2 Establish a Test Strategy SG 3 Establish Test Performance Indicators
2.2 Test Planning	SG 1 Establish a Product Risk Assessment SG 2 Establish a Test Approach SG 3 Establish Test Estimates SG 4 Develop a Test Plan SG 5 Obtain Commitment to the Test Plan
2.3 Test Monitoring and Control	SG 1 Monitor Test Progress and Plan SG 2 Monitor Product Quality against Plan and Expectations SG 3 Manage Corrective Action to Closure
2.4 Test Design and Execution	SG 1 Perform Test Analysis and Design using Test Design Techniques SG 2 Perform Test Implementation SG 3 Perform Test Execution SG 4 Manage Test Incidents to Closure
2.5 Test Environment	SG 1 Develop Test Environment Requirements SG 2 Perform Test Environment Implementation SG 3 Manage and Control Test Environments

Level 3 – Defined

At TMMi level 3, testing is no longer confined to a phase that follows coding. It is fully integrated into the development life cycle and the associated milestones. Test planning is done at an early project stage (e.g., during the requirements phase) and is documented in a master test plan. The development of a master test plan builds on the test planning skills and commitments acquired at TMMi level 2. The organization's set of standard test processes, which is the basis for maturity level 3, is established and improved over time. A test organization and a specific test training program exist, and testing is perceived as being a profession. Test process improvement is fully institutionalized as part of the test organization's accepted practices.

Organizations at level 3 understand the importance of reviews in quality control; a formal review program is implemented although not yet fully linked to the dynamic testing process. Reviews take place across the life cycle. Test professionals are involved in reviews of requirements specifications.

Whereas the test designs at TMMi level 2 focus mainly on functional testing, test designs and test techniques are expanded at level 3 to include non-functional testing, e.g., usability and/or reliability, depending the business objectives.

A critical distinction between TMMi maturity levels 2 and 3 is the scope of the standards, process descriptions, and procedures. At maturity level 2, these may be quite different in each specific instance—for example, on a particular project. At maturity level 3, these are tailored from the organization's set of standard processes to suit a particular project or organizational unit and therefore are more consistent except for the differences allowed by the tailoring guidelines. Another critical distinction is that at maturity level 3, processes are typically described more rigorously than at maturity level 2. As a consequence, at maturity level 3, the organization must revisit the maturity level 2 process areas.

The process areas and their specific goals at TMMi level 3 are listed in table 3–16.

Table 3-16 TMMi level 3

TMMi Level 3 – Defined		
Process Area	**Specific Goals**	
3.1 Test Organization	SG 1	Establish a Test Organization
	SG 2	Establish Test Functions for Test Specialists
	SG 3	Establish Test Career Paths
	SG 4	Determine, Plan, and Implement Test Process Improvements
	SG 5	Deploy the Organizational Test Process and Incorporate Lessons Learned
3.2 Test Training Program	SG 1	Establish an Organizational Test Training Capability
	SG 2	Provide Test Training
3.3 Test Lifecycle and Integration	SG 1	Establish Organizational Test Process Assets
	SG 2	Integrate the Test Lifecycle Models with the Development Models
	SG 3	Establish a Master Test Plan
3.4 Non-functional Testing	SG 1	Establish a Non-Functional Product Risk Assessment
	SG 2	Establish a Non-Functional Test Approach
	SG 3	Perform Non-Functional Test Analysis and Design
	SG 4	Perform Non-Functional Test Implementation
	SG 5	Perform Non-Functional Test Execution
3.5 Peer Reviews	SG 1	Establish a Peer Review Approach
	SG 2	Perform Peer Reviews

Level 4 – Measured

Achieving the goals of TMMi levels 2 and 3 has the benefits of putting into place a technical, managerial, and staffing infrastructure capable of thorough testing and providing support for test process improvement. With this infrastructure in place, testing can become a measured process to encourage further growth and accomplishment. In TMMi level 4 organizations, testing is a thoroughly defined, well-founded, and measurable process. Testing is perceived as evaluation; it consists of all life cycle activities concerned with checking products and related work products.

An organization-wide test measurement program will be put into place that can be used to evaluate the quality of the testing process, to assess productivity, and to monitor improvements. Measures are incorporated into the organization's measurement repository to support fact-based decision-making. A test measurement program also supports predictions relating to test performance and cost. With respect to product quality, the presence of a measurement program allows an organization to implement a product quality evaluation process by defining quality needs, quality attributes, and quality metrics. (Work) products are evaluated using quantitative criteria for quality attributes such as reliability, usability, and maintainability. Product quality is understood in quantitative terms and is managed to the defined objectives throughout the life cycle.

Reviews and inspections are considered to be part of the test process and are used to measure product quality early in the life cycle and to formally control quality gates. Peer reviews as a defect detection technique are transformed into a product quality measurement technique in line with the process area Product Quality Evaluation. TMMi level 4 also covers establishing a coordinated test approach between peer reviews (static testing) and dynamic testing and the use of peer review results and data to optimize the test approach, aiming to make the testing both more effective and more efficient. Peer reviews are now fully integrated with the dynamic testing process—for example, as part of the test strategy, test plan, and test approach.

The process areas and their specific goals at TMMi level 4 are listed in table 3–17.

Table 3–17 TMMi level 4

TMMi Level 4 – Measured	
Process Area	**Specific Goals**
4.1 Test Measurement	SG 1 Align Test Measurements and Analysis Activities SG 2 Provide Test Measurement Results
4.2 Product Quality Evaluation	SG 1 Project Goals for Product Quality and Their Priorities Are Established SG 2 Actual Progress Toward Achieving the Project's Product Quality Goals Is Quantified and Managed
4.3 Advanced Reviews	SG 1 Coordinate the Peer Review Approach with the Dynamic Test Approach SG 2 Measure Product Quality Early in the Lifecycle by Means of Peer Reviews SG 3 Adjust the Test Approach Based on Review Results Early in the Lifecycle

Level 5 – Optimization

The achievement of all previous test improvement goals at levels 1 through 4 of TMMi has created an organizational infrastructure for testing that supports a completely defined and measured process. At TMMi maturity level 5, an organization is capable of continually improving its processes based on a quantitative understanding of statistically controlled processes. Improving test process performance is carried out through incremental and innovative process and technological improvements. The testing methods and techniques are optimized and there is a continuous focus on fine-tuning and process improvement. An optimized test process, as defined by the TMMi, is one that has the following characteristics:

- Managed, defined, measured, efficient, and effective
- Statistically controlled and predictable
- Focused on defect prevention
- Supported by automation as much as is deemed an effective use of resources
- Able to support technology transfer from the industry to the organization
- Able to support reuse of test assets
- Focused on process change to achieve continuous improvement

To support the continuous improvement of the test process infrastructure, and to identify, plan, and implement test improvements, a permanent test process improvement group is formally established and is staffed by members who have received specialized training to increase the level of skills and knowledge required for the success of the group. In many organizations this group is called a Test Process Group. Support for a Test Process Group formally begins at TMMi level 3 when the test organization is introduced. At TMMi levels 4 and 5, the responsibilities grow as more high-level practices are introduced, such as, for example, identifying reusable test (process) assets and developing and maintaining the test (process) asset library.

The Defect Prevention process area is established to identify and analyze common causes of defects across the development life cycle and define actions to prevent similar defects from occurring in the future. Outliers to test process performance, as identified as part of process quality control, are analyzed to address their causes as part of Defect Prevention. The test process is now statistically managed by means of the Quality Control process area. Statistical sampling, measurements of confidence levels, trustworthiness, and reliability drive the test process. The test process is characterized by sampling-based quality measurements.

At TMMi level 5, the Test Process Optimization process area introduces mechanisms to fine-tune and continuously improve testing. There is an established procedure to identify process enhancements as well as to select and evaluate new testing technologies. Tools support the test process as much as is effective during test design, test execution, regression testing, test case management, defect collection and analysis, and so on. Process and testware reuse across the organization is also common practice and is supported by a test (process) asset library.

The three TMMi level 5 process areas—Defect Prevention, Quality Control, and Test Process Optimization—all provide support for continuous process improvement. In fact, the three process areas are highly interrelated. For example, Defect Prevention supports Quality Control by analyzing outliers to process performance and by implementing practices for defect causal analysis and prevention of defect reoccurrence. Quality Control contributes to Test Process Optimization, and Test Process Optimization supports both Defect Prevention and Quality Control, for example, by implementing the test improvement proposals. All of these process areas are, in turn, supported by the practices that were acquired when the lower-level process areas were implemented. At TMMi level 5, testing is a process with the objective of preventing defects.

The process areas and their specific goals at TMMi level 5 are listed in table 3–18.

Table 3–18 TMMi level 5

TMMi Level 5 – Optimization	
Process Area	**Specific Goals**
5.1 Defect Prevention	SG 1 Determine Common Causes of Defects SG 2 Prioritize and Define Actions to Systematically Eliminate Root Causes of Defects
5.2 Quality Control	SG 1 Establish a Statistically Controlled Process SG 2 Testing Is Performed Using Statistical Methods
5.3 Test Process Optimization	SG 1 Select Test Process Improvements SG 2 New Testing Technologies Are Evaluated to Determine Their Impact on the Testing Process SG 3 Deploy Test Improvements SG 4 Establish Re-use of High Quality Test Process Assets

Structure of the TMMi

The structure of the TMMi is largely based on the structure of the CMMI. This is a major benefit because many people/organizations are already familiar with the CMMI structure. Like the CMMI structure, TMMi makes a clear distinction between practices that are required (goals) and those that are recommended (specific practices, example work products, etc.). The TMMi model required and expected components are summarized to illustrate their relationship in figure 3–24. For a full description of this structure and its components, see section 3.2.1, which describes the structure of CMMI; the structure and components for the staged version of CMMI also apply to TMMi.

To provide the reader with some understanding of how all of these components are put together within the TMMi, a small part of the actual TMMi model is provided here (text box next page). The example provided comes from the TMMi level 3 process area Peer Reviews and shows the components related to the specific goals.

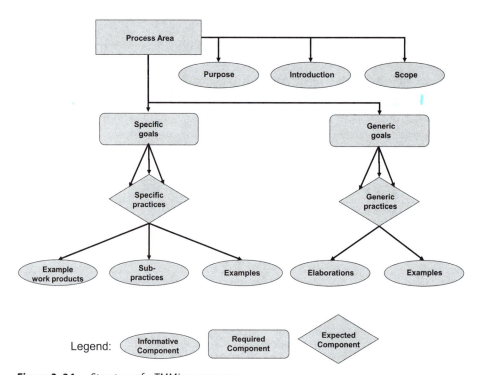

Figure 3–24   Structure of a TMMi process area

Specific Practices by Goals

SG 1   Establish a Peer Review Approach   ← *Specific goal*

A review approach is established and agreed upon.

SP 1.1   Identify work products to be reviewed   ← *Specific practice*

The work products to be reviewed are identified, including the type of review and critical participants (stakeholders) to involve.

Example work products   ← *Example work products*

List of work products to be reviewed

1. Review approach
2. Review log
3. Peer review schedule

Sub-practices   ← *Sub-practices*

1. Select work products that will undergo a peer review based on the peer review policy and the identified product risks
2. Determine what type(s) of peer review will be conducted for the selected work products

Examples of types of peer reviews include the following (IEEE 1028):

- *Inspection*
- *Walkthrough*
- *Technical Review*   ← *Example*
- *Informal Review*

Note, it is possible that multiple types of reviews are selected for the same work product, e.g., for work products related to critical product risks.

← *Sub-practices*

3. Identify key participants who shall be involved in a peer review
4. Review the defined review approach with stakeholders
5. Develop a detailed peer review schedule, including the dates for peer review training and when material for peer reviews will be available
6. Obtain commitments to undertake the review approach and schedule from key stakeholders

TMMi and CMMI

Although TMMi can be also used in isolation, it was initially positioned and developed as a complementary model to the CMMI. As a result, in many cases a given TMMi level needs specific support from process areas at its corresponding CMMI level or at higher CMMI levels. Process areas and practices that are elaborated within CMMI generally are not repeated within TMMi; they are only referenced. For example, the process area Configuration Management, which is also applicable to test (work) products/testware, is not elaborated upon in detail within the TMMi; the practices from CMMI are referenced and implicitly reused.

Table 3-19 and table 3-20 summarize the CMMI process areas that complement and/or overlap with the TMMi process areas required for TMMi level 2 and TMMi level 3. Note that, as shown in the tables, supporting process areas (S) and parallel process areas (P) are denoted. Supporting process areas (S) encompass those process areas and related practices that should ideally be in place to support achievement of the TMMi goals. Parallel process areas (P) are those that are similar in nature in TMMi and CMMI and can be simultaneously pursued. Further details and background regarding these relationships can be found in *Test Maturity Model integration (TMMi) – Guidelines for Test Process Improvement* [van Veenendaal and Wells 2012].

Table 3-19 Support for TMMi maturity level 2 from CMMI process areas

TMMi	CMMI	Supporting CMMI process areas for TMMi level 2
2	2	• Configuration Management (S) • Process and Product Quality Assurance (S) • Project Monitoring and Control (S) • Project Planning (S) • Measurement and Analysis (S) • Requirements Management (S)
2	3	• Requirements Development (S) • Risk Management (S)

Table 3–20 Support for TMMi maturity level 3 from CMMI process areas

TMMi	CMMI	Supporting CMMI process areas for TMMi level 3
3	2	• Configuration Management (S) • Measurement and Analysis (S) • Process and Product Quality Assurance (S) • Project Planning (S)
3	3	• Organizational Process Definition (P) • Organizational Process Focus (P) • Organizational Training (S) • Verification (P) (for TMMi process area Peer Reviews)

Note that the test-specific Verification and Validation process areas of the CMMI are not listed as supporting or parallel process areas for the dynamic testing processes within TMMi. For these CMMI process areas, the relationship is complementary. The TMMi process areas provide support and a more detailed specification of what is required to establish a defined verification and validation process. Practical experiences have shown that an organization that complies with the TMMi level 2 requirements will, at the same time, largely or fully fulfill the requirements for the CMMI process areas Verification and Validation (with the exception of the peer review specific goal and related practices within the Verification process area). This is a good example of how satisfying the goals and implementation of the practices in one model (TMMi) may lead to satisfactory implementation in the other (CMMI). It is also a good example of how the TMMi test-specific improvement model complements the more generic software and system development improvement models (e.g., CMMI).

TMMi Assessments

Many organizations find value in benchmarking their progress in test process improvement both for internal purposes and for external customers and suppliers. Test process assessments focus on identifying improvement opportunities and understanding the organization's position relative to the selected model or standard. The TMMi provides a reference model to be used during such assessments. Assessment teams use TMMi to guide their identification and prioritization of findings. These findings, along with the guidance of TMMi practices, are used to plan improvements for the organization. The assessment framework itself is not part of the TMMi. Requirements for TMMi assessments are described by the TMMi Foundation in the document "TMMi Assessment Method Application Requirements" (TAMAR) [TMMi Foundation 2009]. These requirements are based upon the ISO/IEC 15504 standard and SCAMPI (see section 3.2.2). (Note that formal TMMi assessments follow the requirements for SCAMPI class B appraisals.) The achievement of a specific maturity level must mean the same thing for different assessed organizations. Rules for ensuring this consistency are contained in the TMMi assessment method requirements. The TMMi assessment method requirements contain guidelines for various classes of assessments (e.g., formal assessments, quick scans, and self-assessments).

Because the TMMi can be used in conjunction with the CMMI (staged version), TMMi and CMMI assessments are often combined, evaluating both the development process and the testing process. Since the models are of similar structure, and the model vocabularies and goals overlap, parallel training and parallel assessments can be accomplished by an assessment team. The TMMi can also be used to address testing issues in conjunction with continuous models. Overlapping process areas that relate to testing can be assessed and improved using the TMMi, while other process areas fall under the umbrella of the broader-scope model.

During the assessment, the evidence is gathered to determine the process maturity of the organization or project being assessed. To be able to draw conclusions, a sufficient amount of evidence is needed, and that evidence must be of sufficient depth. Whether the amount and depth of evidence is sufficient depends on the goal of the assessment.

The objective evidence is used to determine to what extent a certain goal has been reached. To be able to classify a specific or generic goal, the classification of the underlying specific and generic practices needs to be determined. A process area as a whole is classified in accordance with the lowest classified goal that is met. The maturity level is determined in accordance with the lowest classified process area within that maturity level.

The level to which an organization achieves a particular process area is within TMMi measured using a scale that consists of the following levels:

- N – Not Achieved
- P – Partially Achieved
- L – Largely Achieved
- F – Fully Achieved

To score N (Not Achieved), there should be little or no evidence found of compliance with the goals of the process area. The percentage of process achievement that would score N would be from 0 percent to 15 percent. To score P (Partially Achieved), there should be some evidence found of compliance, but the process may be incomplete, not widespread, or inconsistently applied. The percentage of process achievement for processes that would score P would be over 15 percent and up to 50 percent. To score L (Largely Achieved), there should be significant evidence found of compliance, but there may still be some minor weaknesses in implementation, application, or results of this process. The percentage of process achievement for processes that would score L would be 50 percent and up to 85 percent. To score F (Fully Achieved), there should be consistent evidence found of compliance. The process has been implemented both systematically and completely and there should be no obvious weaknesses in implementation, application, or results of this process. The percentage of process achievement for processes that would score F would be over 85 percent and up to 100 percent. Note that "only" 85 percent is needed to be rated Fully Satisfied; this implies that practices with little or no added value for the project or organization can be discarded and nevertheless an F rating can be achieved.

There are two additional ratings that can be utilized:

- Not Applicable: This classification is used if a process area is not applicable to the organization and is therefore excluded from the results. As long as at least two-thirds of the process areas at a maturity level are applicable, an organization can nevertheless formally achieve a TMMi level despite the fact that one or more process areas are not applicable.
- Not Rated: This classification is used if the process area is not ratable due to insufficient evidence.

More information on assessments in general can be found is section 6.3.

Improvement Approach

The TMMi provides a full framework to be used as a reference model during test process improvement. It does not provide an approach for test process improvement such as IDEAL (see chapter 6). Practical experiences with TMMi have shown that the most powerful initial step to test process improvement is to build strong organizational sponsorship before investing in test process assessments. Given sufficient senior management sponsorship, establishing a specific, technically competent Test Process Group that represents relevant stakeholders to guide test process improvement efforts has proven to be an effective approach. Some other ideas and guidelines regarding an approach for test process improvement can be found in *The Little TMMi* [van Veenendaal and Cannegieter 2011].

3.3.3 Comparing TPI NEXT to TMMi

Syllabus Learning Objectives

LO 3.3.7   (K5) Recommend which is appropriate in a given scenario, either the TPI NEXT or the TMMi model

Making choices about the approach to take for assessing test processes and implementing improvements is one of the fundamental tasks for a test process improver. In section 2.5, the following overall approaches were introduced:

- Model-based
- Analytical-based (see chapter 4)
- Hybrid approaches
- Other approaches (e.g., skills, tools; see chapter 2)

In chapter 5 we will consider the overall issue of choosing the most appropriate of these test improvement approaches for a particular project or organization.

In this section the two principal test process reference models described in the previous sections are compared according to the following attributes:

- Representation
- Main focus
- Overall approach
- Test methods
- Terminology
- Relationship to SPI models

Representation

Section 3.1.3 describes the two representations used by process reference models: continuous and staged.

TMMi uses a staged representation:

- Five successive maturity levels are defined, each of which requires that specific testing activities (process areas) are performed.

- The sequence to follow for improving test process maturity is simple to understand.
- An "all or nothing" approach is followed, meaning that all the items within a particular maturity level (stage) must be achieved before the next one can be reached.

TPI NEXT uses a continuous representation:

- Sixteen key areas of a testing process are defined, each of which can be assessed at a managed, efficient, or optimizing level of maturity.
- A differentiated view of test process maturity can be achieved, but this may be more difficult to communicate to certain non-testers (e.g., management).
- Steps to follow for implementing process improvement are represented by clusters. These are logical groups of checkpoints from more than one key area.

Main Focus

TMMi:

- The improvement focus is on detailed coverage of a limited number of process areas per maturity level. This supports the organization in having a clear focus during the improvement program.
- Each process area can be assessed at a detailed level based on scoring the specific and generic practices.
- The interactions from TMMi to CMMI are covered in detail. This enables testing to be considered within the context of the software development process.
- At higher maturity levels, testing issues such as testability reviews, quality control, defect prevention, and test measurement programs are covered in detail.

TPI NEXT:

- An overview across the entire test process is achieved with the 16 key areas.
- Interactions with other processes are covered. This enables testing to be considered within the context of the entire software development process.
- Each key area can be assessed at a detailed level with specific checkpoints.

Overall Approach

TMMi:

- There is a strong focus on obtaining management commitment and defining business objectives upfront to drive the test improvement program.
- The formal assessment approach is described in a separate guideline: the TMMi Assessment Method Application Requirements (TAMAR).
- Assessments may be conducted formally with certified TMMi assessors or informally.
- Conducting an assessment requires that performance of all process areas that are applicable and practices at a certain maturity level are evaluated. Depending on the formality of the TMMi assessment, this can result in substantial effort being required. A formal assessment can result in certifying a specific organization at a certain TMMi maturity level.

TPI NEXT:

- A thorough, business-driven and test engineering approach is adopted.
- The model is occasionally perceived as emphasizing the technical test engineering aspects too much and therefore appealing principally to experienced testers. To a large degree, this is a legacy from the previous version of the model (TPI). The TPI NEXT model takes a more business-driven approach than its predecessor and achieves this by enabling key areas to be prioritized according to particular business goals.
- Conducting an assessment requires that the answers to specific questions (checkpoints) are evaluated. The checkpoints may be for particular key areas and maturity levels or for a defined group (cluster) of checkpoints. The number of checkpoints per key area and maturity level is between two and four, making the evaluation task relatively quick.

Test Methods

TMMi:

- The model is based on independent research and is not aligned to a specific testing methodology. The model is aligned with international testing standards such as, for example, IEEE.

TPI NEXT:

- Generic testing practices described in the TMap NEXT methodology form the terms of reference for the model. This does not mean that TMap NEXT must be used for test process improvements.

Terminology

TMMi:

- Standard testing terminology is used that is strongly aligned to the ISTQB glossary of testing terms.

TPI NEXT:

- The terminology used is based on the TMap methodology [Pol, Teunnissen, and van Veenendaal 2002] and its successor TMap NEXT.

Relationship to SPI Models

TMMi:

- The model structure and maturity levels are highly correlated to the CMMI model.

TPI NEXT:

- No formal relationship to a specific SPI model exists.
- Mappings are described to the SPI models CMMI and ISO/IEC 15504.

Other Issues Not Covered in the Syllabus

Tool support:

- TMMi: A full assessment tool and workbench is available through the TMMi assessment training.
- TPI NEXT: A free scoring tool is available.

Published benchmark:

- TMMi: Yes [van Veenendaal and Cannegieter 2013]
- TPI NEXT: No

Take-up:

- TMMi: Rapidly increasing, strong in Europe, India, Korea, China, and Brazil
- TPI NEXT: Strong European base but also international (especially in United States, India, and China)

3.3.4 Systematic Test and Evaluation Process (STEP)

Syllabus Learning Objectives

LO 3.4.1 (K2) Summarize the background and structure of the STEP content-based model.

LO 3.4.2 (K2) Summarize the activities, work products and roles of the STEP model.

Overview of Structure

Systematic Test and Evaluation Process (STEP) is a content-based test improvement model introduced in 2002 in a book written by Rick Craig and Stefan Jaskiel, *Systematic Software Testing* [Craig and Jaskiel 2002]. In this section, we'll refer to that book as the principal source of information.

> **Systematic Test and Evaluation Process** A structured testing methodology, also used as a content-based model for improving the testing process. Systematic Test and Evaluation Process (STEP) does not require that improvements occur in a specific order.

The structure of the STEP model is shown in figure 3–25.

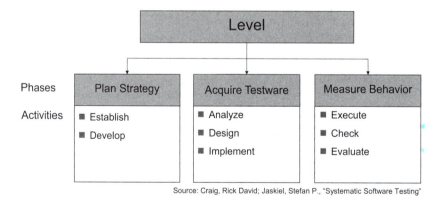

Figure 3–26 Systematic Test and Evaluation Process (STEP) structure

Figure 3–25 shows the hierarchical structure of the STEP model with the components listed in table 3–21.

3.3 Test Process Improvement Models

Table 3-21 STEP structural elements

Element of the STEP structure	Description
Level	A (test) level is a group of test activities that are organized and managed together. Examples include component test, integration test, system test, and acceptance test.
Phase	Phases represent the principal steps performed in each level. These are "plan the strategy," "acquire the testware," and "measure the behavior."
Activity	An activity represents a specific task within a phase.

Summary of STEP Content

In general, STEP takes a requirements-based life cycle approach to testing, in which testing activities add value to the overall software development effort. The early design of test cases in the development life cycle enables early verification of requirements and benefits software design by providing models of intended software usage. STEP places strong emphasis on early defect detection and the use of systematic defect analysis to prevent defects from entering life cycle products. Being developed back in 2002, STEP is a rather traditional model mainly related to the V-model SDLC.

Table 3–22 summarizes the structure of a test level. Note that STEP expects the user to adapt this structure to meet project needs.

Table 3-22 Structure of a test level in STEP

Structure of a test level (e.g., integration test)			
Phase	Major activity	Tasks	Typical work products
Plan strategy	Establish the master test plan at the start of project (covers all levels)	• Process for product (software) risk analysis • Project (planning) risks, assumptions, and contingencies • Master test planning	• Risk list • Master test plan (content based on IEEE 829-1998)
	Develop detailed plans	• Development of the detailed plans for each test level, based on the master test plan	• Level test plan; content may be specific to a level (e.g., integration test: which modules to be assembled as a group)

Structure of a test level (e.g., integration test)			
Phase	Major activity	Tasks	Typical work products
Acquire testware	List test objectives	• Performing test analysis to create a list of prioritized test objectives (further details provided after this table) • Process for creating a list of test objectives and coverage of requirements	• Inventory tracking matrix
	Design the tests	• Test design techniques (black-box, white-box, experience-based)	• IEEE 829-1998 documents • Specifications for test design, test cases, and test procedure
	Implement the plans and designs	• Setting up test environment • Test teams • Tooling • Evaluating testware	• Results of testware evaluation
Measure behavior	Execute tests	• Execute test cases • Log incidents • Report on test status	• Test incident reports • Test log • Testing status and results
	Check adequacy of test set	• Measure test effectiveness (defect measures and coverage measures)	• Defect measures • Coverage measures
	Evaluate software and testing processes	• Improving the test process (see "Using STEP for Test Process Improvement" below for further details)	• Improvement plan

The STEP model provides detailed support for performing the tasks and defines the work products created. It basically provides a full test process model description. For example, the following actions support the "perform test analysis to create a list of prioritized test objectives" task shown in table 3–22 (part of the major activity "list test objectives" within the "acquire testware" phase):

1. Gather reference materials
2. Form a brainstorming team
3. Determine test objectives
4. Prioritize objectives
5. Parse objectives into lists

6. Create an inventory tracking matrix
7. Identify tests for unaddressed conditions
8. Evaluate each inventory item
9. Maintain the testing matrix

Roles

STEP describes four roles, which are summarized in figure 3–26.

Test Manager	Test Analyst	Tester	Reviewer
■ Plan ■ Coordinate ■ Communicate to stakeholders	■ Detailed planning ■ List test objectives ■ Analyze ■ Test design & specification	■ Implement test case ■ Execute tests ■ Check results ■ Log tests ■ Report problems	■ Examine and evaluate work products

Figure 3–27 *Roles described in STEP*

STEP includes detailed descriptions of the test manager and the software tester roles (in fact, *Systematic Software Testing* [Craig and Jaskiel 2002] devotes an entire chapter to each role).

Using STEP for Test Process Improvement

As shown earlier in table 3–22, the STEP model explicitly identifies test process improvement as one of the activities within the "measure behavior" phase. The description of the generic steps to apply that is provided in STEP is similar to the IDEAL approach described in chapter 6.

STEP does not require that improvements occur in a specific order, but high-level descriptions of the CMM and TPI process assessment models are given to enable STEP to be blended with these models (note that these two models have since been superceded by CMMI and TPI NEXT but no update has taken place for STEP).

3.3.5 Critical Testing Processes (CTP)

Syllabus Learning Objectives

LO 3.4.3 (K2) Summarize the CTP content-based model.
LO 3.4.4 (K2) Summarize the critical test processes within the CTP content-based model.
LO 3.4.5 (K2) Summarize the role of metrics within the CTP content-based model.

Overview of Structure

Critical Testing Processes (CTP) is a content-based test improvement model introduced in 2003 in a book written by Rex Black [Black 2003]. This book is the principal source of information regarding CTP and serves as the basis for the description in this section.

At the highest level, CTP defines a test process with the following four principal steps (see figure 3–27):

- Plan   Understand the testing effort
- Prepare   Understand the people and tests
- Perform   Do the testing and gather the results
- Perfect   Guide adaption and improvement

Figure 3–28   *Critical Testing Processes (CTP) test process steps*

Even though the CTP steps are presented in a logical sequence, their execution may overlap. In the "classic" style of the Deming improvement cycle, they are linked together to form an iterative process.

> **Critical Testing Processes (CTP)**   A content-based model for test process improvement built around 12 critical processes. These include highly visible processes, by which peers and management judge competence, and mission-critical processes, in which performance affects the company's profits and reputation.

The basic concept of CTP is that certain activities within the test process can be classified as "critical" to performing effective and efficient testing. A test process becomes critical when it has the following characteristics:

- Repeated frequently → affects efficiency
- Highly cooperative → affects team cohesion
- Visible to peers and superiors → affects creditability
- Linked to project success → affects effectiveness

In other words, it becomes critical when it directly and significantly affects the test team's ability to find bugs and reduce risks. These critical testing processes are each associated with a particular step, as shown in figure 3–28.

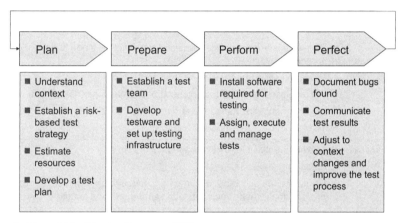

Figure 3–29 *Critical Testing Processes (CTP)*

Figure 3–28 shows 11 critical testing processes. In addition, the test process itself is also considered to be an overarching critical testing process. Each of the critical testing processes is described in the CTP model together with examples and a description of the steps and sub-steps to be performed, from which checklists can be constructed.

The checklists may be tailored to suit a particular project context and then used to assess the status of a test process. CTP does not implement the highly structured approach to assessing test process maturity used in process models such as TMMi and TPI NEXT. The user of CTP must combine their own experience with guidance from the model to make statements about test process maturity and where improvements should be made.

Summary of Critical Testing Processes

The 11 initial critical testing processes are summarized in table 3-23 through table 3-26 according to the test process steps defined in CTP. Please note that the text used in the tables is based on *Critical Testing Processes* [Black 2003]. Readers requiring more in-depth information should consult the referenced book.

Table 3-23 CTP activities in planning the testing

CTP: Test process step: Plan	
Critical testing process	**Aspects covered by the critical testing process**
Understand context	• Life cycles used (e.g., for software development) • Current or planned process improvements • Testware created (specific items and the value they add to the project and/or organization) • Existing testing practices • Stakeholders relationships (expectations, areas for improvement) • Management expectations regarding value added by testing • The role of QA as compared to testing
Establish a risk-based test strategy	• Current practices for risk management • Identifying stakeholders • Identifying, categorizing, documenting, and agreeing with stakeholders on product quality risks, their mitigation strategies, and priorities
Estimate resources	• Developing a work breakdown structure (WBS) considering all test process activities • Project criticality • Scheduling the testing based on the WBS • Estimating budget needs based on the WBS and schedule • Costs and benefits of testing (return on investment) • Obtaining buy-in and support from line management
Develop a test plan	• Test planning process (create, distribute, review, negotiate, agree, adjust) • Good planning practices to apply (e.g., for outsourcing, for setting completion criteria, etc.)

Table 3-24 CTP activities in preparing the tests

CTP: Test process step: Prepare	
Critical testing process	**Aspects covered by the critical testing process**
Establish a test team	• Required skills, attitudes, and motivation • Hiring and staffing strategies • Career paths for testers • Skills development
Develop testware and set up testing infrastructure	• Required testware (e.g., test cases) • Test coverage • Test conditions • Test techniques to be used • Design of test cases • Use of test oracles • Combinatorial challenges • Elements of a test environment • Design, implementation, and verification of test environment • Configuration control • Updating risk management information

Table 3-25 CTP activities in performing the tests

CTP: Test process step: Perform	
Critical testing process	**Aspects covered by the critical testing process**
Install software required for testing	• Identifying and installing software under test • Managing the test release • Smoke testing
Assign, execute, and manage tests	• Test case selection • Assignment of test cases for execution • Execution of test cases • Recording results • Adjusting priorities and plans

Table 3-26 *CTP activities in perfecting the test process*

CTP: Test process step: Perfect	
Critical testing process	**Aspects covered by the critical testing process**
Document bugs found	• Defect reporting process • Testing and debugging • Communication of defects • Defect tracking tool selection
Communicate results	• Test results reporting process (steps and good practices) • Handling the presentation of results
Adjust to context changes and improve the test process	• Change management process (gather, select, review, plan, present, decide) • Attributes of a mature test process • Sources of formal test processes • Overview of testing strategies • Incremental process improvement • Issues in implementing improvements

The Role of Metrics within CTP

CTP describes a number of metrics relevant to the critical testing processes. These may be applied to test management or for improving the test process. Some examples are provided in table 3-27.

Table 3-27 *Examples of metrics used in CTP*

Critical testing process	Examples of metrics used
Plan: Understand context	Understanding the current project status • Defects found • Test cases executed
Plan: Estimate resources	Estimating testing return on investment • Cost of testing • Cost of failure
Perfect: Communicate results	Showing current status • Test coverage for each quality risk category • Defects found per severity level
Perfect: Document defects found	Measuring the quality of the bug reports • Re-open rate (i.e., presumed fixed but actually not) • Average time from opening to closing a bug report

Using CTP for Test Process Improvement

In general, each critical testing process has a dedicated section, "Implement Improvements," that can be used as a guide.

The critical testing process "adjust to context changes and improve the test process" suggests the following high-level approach to test process improvement:

- Identify the three or four critical testing processes that account for approximately two-thirds of resource usage.
- Gather detailed metrics on these critical testing processes.
- Propose improvements based on these metrics and develop an improvement plan.

3.4 Comparing Process Models and Content Models

Adopting a model-based approach presents the user with options that need careful consideration. Table 3–28 identifies some of the principal aspects that distinguish process models from content models.

> **Process-based model**   A framework wherein processes of the same nature are classified into a overall model; e.g., a test improvement model.

> **Content-based model**   A process model providing a detailed description of good engineering practices; e.g., test practices.

Table 3–28 Aspects of process models and content models

Aspect	Process models (TPI NEXT, TMMi)	Content models (CTP, STEP)
Approach	Detailed, predefined ("prescribed") improvement approach based on a strong model structure.	Provides general guidance within a basic model structure.
Basic assumption	"Do this and your test process will improve." "A more mature process will result in testing with better results."	"Applying these practices properly and in the right context can benefit a test process."

Aspect	Process models (TPI NEXT, TMMi)	Content models (CTP, STEP)
Identifying improvements	Improvements are proposed in the model. User experience is required to formulate context-specific improvement suggestions.	User combines guidance from the model with own experience and knowledge of project context.
Sequence of improvement	Follow defined paths within the overall model definition.	Decisions are taken by the test process improver using the content model as a source of knowledge and good practices.
Support for the user	Open: Model descriptions and supporting information available free of charge from websites. Models are maintained and updated. Independent training is available.	Proprietary: Books published by model authors. No updates since publication.
Level of exposure	Expanding worldwide application with principal user base in Europe. Frequently discussed in articles and presentations. Generally more popular than content models.	Data currently not available.

As mentioned in chapter 2, model-based and analytical approaches may be combined to achieve the objectives placed on the test process. By combining particular aspects of process- and content-based models, this form of hybrid approach can also be considered when performing model-based test process improvement. For example, the TPI NEXT process model may be used for obtaining an assessment of the test process maturity and the CTP content model can then be consulted to gain further insights in formulating improvement suggestions. Similarly, TMMi may be used to perform an informal test process assessment and the templates suggested in STEP used to support particular improvement suggestions regarding, for example, test documentation.

3.5 Suitability of SPI Models and Test Process Improvement Models

The previous sections of this chapter have considered the use of software process improvement (SPI) models and those dedicated entirely to test process improvement. Comparing the suitability of the two for conducting test process improvement depends on a careful consideration of the factors described in the following sections.

Level of Detail

Using SPI models can be advantageous if only a relatively high-level consideration of the testing process is desired. If details are important, a test process improvement model is more appropriate. By way of example, let's just consider the way that CMMI (an SPI model) and TMMi (a test process improvement) consider test planning.

CMMI describes two process areas with direct relevance for testing (section 3.2.1): Validation (VAL) and Verification (VER). The Validation process area contains two specific goals, one of which, "prepare for validation (SG1)," is where we might expect to find test planning. This is not the case. The generic practice "plan the process (GP 2.2)" is where planning in the context of verification is described, and here we find a general statement that a plan has to be established for verification. This high-level statement may be sufficient for some assessments, but for a detailed view of test planning we need to consult a dedicated model for test process improvement, such as TMMi.

TMMi describes test planning as a specifc process area (PA2.2) within the Managed maturity level (level 2). The Test Planning process area describes five specific goals (e.g., SG4, "Develop a test plan"), each with between three and five specific practices (e.g., SG4.5, "Establish the test plan"). These specific practices define work products and provide detailed descriptions of sub-practices (refer to *Test Maturity Model integration (TMMi) – Guidelines for Test Process Improvement* [van Veenendaal and Wells 2012] for further details). Assessing test planning using the TMMi model will require more effort than with CMMI. The level of detail provided by TMMi enables a much more precise evaluation of test planning to take place and, perhaps even more important, provides a more solid basis for making specific improvement recommendations.

The example just described illustrates why the need for test process improvement models arose. SPI models are simply not detailed enough for a thorough consideration of the test process. If a detailed consideration is required, using a test process improvement model is essential. If you are happy with a high-level view and don't want to dive into the details, an SPI model may be more appropriate.

Scope of Improvement

The scope of an improvement initiative strongly influences the type of model to be used (assuming a model-based approach is to be followed). If the purpose of the initiative is to consider the software process as a whole, then clearly an SPI model will be more suitable. Under these circumstances the test process will most likely be considerd at a relatively high level.

Improvements initiatives with a testing scope will gain better insights into the test process by using a specific model for test process improvement. Care has to be taken here not to consider the test process as an "island" and ignore other processes such as development and release management. This is why test process improvement models also consider non-testing subjects (e.g., TPI NEXT includes enablers; see section 3.3.1)

Consistency of Approach

Organizations that have adopted an SPI model as part an overall process improvement policy may also favor using this model for test process improvement. In this sense, the "suitability" of the SPI model is driven by considerations such as availability of skills in using the SPI model and in having a common, consistent approach to process improvements.

Organizations may be encouraged to use dedicated test process improvement models that address this consistency issue. The TMMi model, for example, allows organizations that apply CMMI to perform test process improvement with a dedicated test process improvement model, without losing consistency.

Marketing Considerations

Like it or not, marketing plays a role in deciding whether to use an SPI or a test process improvement model. In particular, in countries where test process improvement models are not yet widely used, or in countries with a large user base for a particular SPI (e.g., CMMI in India and the United States), the desire or requirement to market an organization at a particular level of maturity cannot be overlooked. In some cases, an organization may be required to demonstrate a given capability based on a certain SPI's process maturity scale. These are powerful marketing arguments that cannot be ignored and may even take priority over more technical considerations.

Organizations that are offering test outsourcing may therefore choose TMMi since they want to become formally certified and use this certification (also) as a marketing vehicle.

3.6 Exercises

The following multiple-choice questions will give you some feedback on your understanding of this chapter. Appendix F lists the answers.

3-1: Which of the following is *not* a desirable characteristic of models?
    A: Identify where improvements should take place
    B: Show the current status
    C: Gather test process metrics
    D: Provide guidance on how to progress

3-2: Which of the following is a benefit of using models?
    A: Ability to capture project best practices
    B: Provide an industry benchmark
    C: Show solutions to testing problems
    D: Compare the maturity status between projects

3-3: Which of the following is a risk of using models?
    A: Belief that the model is always correct
    B: Time taken for the assessment
    C: Prevents real root causes from being identified
    D: Results difficult to discuss with business owners

3-4: Which of the following models cannot be used for test process improvement?
    A: Process reference model
    B: Continuous reference model
    C: Content reference model
    D: Software process improvement model

3-5: Which CMMI first process maturity level is *not* in the correct place in the following sequence?

A: Initial

B: Defined

C: Managed

D: Optimizing

E: Quantitatively Managed

3-6: Which process area is found at the CMMI process maturity level Managed?

A: Measurement and Analysis

B: Verification

C: Risk Management

D: Validation

3-7: Which process category in ISO/IEC 15504 contains the process "process improvement"?

A: Primary Life-Cycle Processes

B: Supporting Life-Cycle Processes

C: Organizational Life-Cycle Processes

D: Secondary Life-Cycle Processes

3-8: Which statement is true regarding the process dimension in ISO/IEC 15504 ?

A: The process dimension enables us to measure how well processes are being performed.

B: The process dimension defines generic practices for each process.

C: The process dimension identifies, describes, and organizes the individual processes within the overall software life cycle.

D: The process dimension provides indicators of process capability.

3-9: Which statement is true regarding clusters in the TPI NEXT model?

　　A: Clusters are used only in the staged representation.

　　B: A cluster combines improvement suggestions with enablers.

　　C: A cluster contains several checkpoints from a specific key area.

　　D: Clusters help show the required sequence of improvements.

3.10: Which of the following specific goals would you be targeting during the implementation of the Test Policy and Strategy process area of the TMMi model?

　　A: Perform a product risk assessment

　　B: Establish test performance indicators

　　C: Establish a test approach

　　D: Establish a test organization

3-11: Which of the following is not an element of the STEP model structure?

　　A: Phase

　　B: Step

　　C: Activity

　　D: Level

3-12: Which of the following activities is not defined in the CTP planning stage?

　　A: Establish a test team

　　B: Understand context

　　C: Estimate resources

　　D: Establish a risk-based test strategy

4 Analytical-Based Improvement

Analytical approaches are used to identify problem areas in our test processes and set project-specific improvement goals. Achievement of these goals is measured using predefined parameters.

Specifically, we'll first be looking at causal analysis techniques as a means of identifying the root causes of defects. After describing a framework for determining and analyzing data to be analyzed (the GQM approach), we'll take a good look at the specific data items that can provide insights into our test process when analyzed.

In addition to the task of test process improvement, project-level problems normally dealt with by the test manager may also benefit from the analytical approaches described in this chapter.

As frequently occurs when several potential options are available for achieving a particular objective, a mix of model-based and analytical approaches might be appropriate. We'll discuss this in more detail in chapter 5, "Selecting Improvement Approaches."

4.1 Introduction

As you saw in chapter 3, using models for test process improvement can be an effective approach if you need to improve systematically and want the benefit of a strong body of knowledge behind you. But this isn't always the most appropriate approach. Sometimes specific testing problems are the main focus of improvement efforts. Just imagine a typical status meeting or retrospective in the testing project. These might be some of the common issues that are mentioned:

- "Our requirements are so unstable; we need too much effort for creating test cases."
- "Our test results have too many false passes."
- "It takes forever to get these defects turned around!"

In general, it's ineffective trying to solve such specific problems by just using a model-based approach. Sure, you'll get some benefit from using a model to solve a specific problem, but this is a bit like trying to crack a nut with a sledgehammer; models can sometimes be simply too generic for solving specific problems.

This is where using analytical techniques can be helpful. They provide a more focused approach for helping to solve specific problems like these. They help us get a handle on the root causes for specific problems and they enable us to set up a systematic framework for gathering and analyzing the relevant data. In the following sections, we will examine what root causes are, outline a systematic framework, and consider how to select the data to analyze.

4.2 Causal Analysis

Syllabus Learning Objectives

LO 4.2.1 (K2) Understand causal analysis using cause/effect diagrams.

LO 4.2.2 (K2) Understand causal analysis during an inspection process.

LO 4.2.3 (K2) Understand the use of standard anomaly classification for causal analysis.

LO 4.2.4 (K2) Compare the causal analysis methods.

LO 4.2.5 (K3) Apply a causal analysis method on a given problem description.

LO 4.2.6 (K5) Recommend and select test process improvement actions based on the results of a causal analysis.

LO 4.2.7 (K4) Select defects for causal analysis using a structured approach.

When problems arise and we want to find the cause, we frequently start off with a mass of information; we simply can't see the forest for the trees. As test process improvers and test managers, we might have a wealth of different sources of information available to us (e.g., meetings, status reports, defect reports, informal discussions, tools). However, it's not just the sources of information that are many and varied; we also receive the information in a number of different forms. Take as an example the problem of long defect turnaround time. We might receive information about this in one or more of the following forms:

> **Causal analysis**   The analysis of defects to determine their root cause.
> [Chrissis, Konrad, and Shrum 2004]

- Verbal communication (a discussion at a project meeting, a chat in the coffee room, a tip from a colleague, a word of warning from a customer). The information might be received as a statement like, "Hey, it takes forever to get these defects turned around."
- Written communication (emails, informal notes, formal reports sent to a stakeholder, a user complaint received via the defect management system). The information might be received as a sentence like, "I've noticed lately that the defects in the payroll system are taking a long time to fix—what's going on?"
- We may also have metrics and measures at our disposal that we are monitoring to ensure that defect turnaround time does not exceed an agreed-upon limit. We may, for example, be monitoring the time taken between setting the status "new" and the status "closed" for defects logged in our defect management system.

Now let's add to this the different views and prejudices sometimes held by relevant stakeholders:

- Testers: It's the developers.
- Developers: It's the testers.
- Users: I don't care what the cause is, I just want working software.

All of this makes for a hard time in getting a handle on the problem of establishing causality. The methods that we will now describe help us to capture and organize information about particular problems and, in so doing, help us to focus on causality.

By using causal analysis, we can visualize possible links between things that happen (causes) and the consequences they may have (effects). As a result, we have a better chance of identifying the key root causes. In other words, we start to see the forest instead of all those trees.

Having an effective defect and/or incident management process that records defect information is an important precondition for performing causal analysis. The procedure of conducting causal analysis is conducted in the following steps:

- Selecting items for causal analysis
- Gathering and organizing the information

- Identifying root causes
- Drawing conclusions (e.g., looking for common causes)

Each of these basic steps will now be described, after which we'll take a look at how some of the improvement models you met in chapter 3 incorporate the concept of causal analysis.

4.2.1 Selecting Items for Causal Analysis

In the context of improving the test process, the items chosen for causal analysis typically belong to one of the following categories:

- Defects and failures:
  - A defect that resulted in an operational failure (e.g., loss of a rocket launcher on takeoff).
  - A defect found during testing (e.g., an exposed security vulnerability).
  - An incident that occurred when using an application (e.g., users report to the help desk that they can't make secure money transactions from a web-based banking application).
- Process issues reported by stakeholders:
  - An issue raised by one of the stakeholders (e.g., the project leader mentions that test status reports have too little information about product risks covered by the tests performed).
  - A problem area identified by a team member during a project meeting or retrospective (e.g., low availability of required testing environments).
- Issues detected by performing analysis:
  - Low levels of defect detection in particular parts of an application or in particular test levels.
  - Elapsed time between reporting defects and receiving corrected software steadily increasing.

If you get the initial selection of items for causal analysis wrong, you'll probably end up using your analysis effort inefficiently. You'll wind up finding the root causes of unimportant items or analyzing "one-off" items that don't lend themselves so easily to a general improvement to the test process. Faced with these risks, it's essential that we extract the maximum benefit from our analysis by finding the root cause(s) of items with the highest impact, such as recurring defects that are costly to fix, are damaging to reputations, or endanger safety.

It will be helpful to involve relevant stakeholders in the defect selection process and to establish defect selection parameters (such as those explained later in the section "Defect Categorizations"). This reduces the chance of unintentional bias in the selection and has the added benefit of helping to develop trust regarding the motives for performing causal analysis.

One or more of the following approaches can assist in selecting the right items for causal analysis:

- The Pareto Principle (80/20 rule)
- Defect categorizations
- Analysis of statistics
- Holding project retrospective meetings

Let's look at each of these approaches in turn.

Use of the Pareto Principle

The Pareto Principle is sometimes referred to simply as the 80/20 rule and is often used in testing where selections need to be made of particular items from a larger whole (e.g., test data, test cases).

When the Pareto Principle is used to select defects for causal analysis, we are making the assumption that 20 percent of defects can be considered as representative of all. The use of the word *representative* gives us a clue on how to identify the 20 percent we are after: equivalence partitioning.

Applying equivalence partitioning techniques to a collection of defects will help identify equivalence classes from which a single representative defect may be selected. We start by taking a high-level view of all defects and by grouping them. The groups (partitions) are then divided successively in a top-down manner until we have the 20 percent of total defects we are going to analyze. If you're a bit rusty in using equivalence partitioning, take a look at the ISTQB Foundation Level syllabus [ISTQB_FL], pick up a good book on test design techniques, or ask an experienced test analyst to help you out.

Generally speaking, use of the Pareto Principle is best combined with other approaches to make more informed defect selections.

> **Pareto analysis**   A statistical technique in decision-making that is used for selection of a limited number of factors that produce significant overall effect. In terms of quality improvement, a large majority of problems (80 percent) are produced by a few key causes.

Defect Categorizations

The problem with using the Pareto Principle in the way mentioned previously is that we have to spend time defining the groups of defects from which to select a representative defect. Using defect categorizations, we don't have to do that; the groups are predefined. This gives us the following advantages:

- We can capture recurring defect root causes that apply to our particular domain, project, or organization. These are the defects we might be especially interested in if improvement activities have been implemented to reduce their occurrence. (Have the measures worked?)
- We can be on the alert for specific types of defects that are of particular significance to us (see the list in table 4–1 for examples).
- We can run through the list relatively quickly, making it a useful approach for use in project retrospectives.

Table 4–1 lists some typical categorizations that will help identify defects for causal analysis.

Table 4–1   *Defect categorizations for causal analysis selection*

Defect category	Description
High impact	These defects are a prime source for causal analysis. Impact (severity) may be based on a classification scheme, such as IEEE 1044 (see below) or be determined from the defect description as part of the analysis. The availability of a risk assessment for individual functional and non-functional aspects of the software under test can also be highly beneficial to the assessment of a defect's impact.
High frequency	Finding (and correcting) the root cause of frequently occurring defects will give more benefit compared to finding the root cause of low-frequency "one-off" defects.
Production failures	Defects that result in failures in production are prime candidates for selection, especially if the expectation was that testing should have prevented this failure. Any root causes detected within the testing strategy used would be particularly beneficial for test process improvement.
Method of detection	Defects that are detected using static analysis and reviews may give clues regarding their root cause (e.g., incorrectly specified requirements, poor coding style) compared to those detected by dynamic testing. Defects found by regression testing may point to problems with the configuration management of source code or poor software design (e.g., highly coupled code modules).
Associated quality attribute	Defects normally relate to a particular quality attribute, such as functionality, performance, security, and reliability. We would want to select defects for analysis from each quality attribute to determine whether the testing strategy used was "missing" particular kinds of defects.

Defect category	Description
Level of information available	In general, we can expect to find the root cause of well-documented defects more easily than defects with little or no information available. This defect category is entirely focused on the return on investment aspect of performing causal analysis.
Domain-specific defects	This category may be subdivided to cover a wide range of domain-specific aspects.
Standards-related defects	Any defect that indicates nonconformity with applicable standards is a candidate for causal analysis.
Defects that failed at retest	Selection of defects in this category might, for example, reveal process problems within the development organization or inconsistencies in setting up the testing infrastructure (e.g., test data, test environment, automated test scripts).
Defects rejected by development	Analysis of these defects could, for example, highlight problems in the defect descriptions submitted by testers or inconsistencies in the interpretation of requirements by testers and developers.
Defects with excessive fix times	Selection of such defects for causal analysis could reveal root causes similar to those mentioned in the previous point. They might also expose communications problems within the project (in particular, between the development and the testing organization). The definition of "excessive" could be based on agreed service levels or a defined maximum number of days.

When selecting defects, we can also make use of the categorizations provided in standards such as IEEE 1044 [IEEE 1044]. The standard provides a useful scheme for categorizing the sources of software anomalies and lists the following principal sources (see table 3b in IEEE 1044 "Investigation classification scheme – Sources"):

- Specification
- Code
- Database
- Manual and guides
- Plans and procedures
- Reports
- Standards/policies

Analysis of Statistics

A variety of statistical information may be used to help select defects for causal analysis. This information may be in the form of tests for statistical significance, comparisons of parameters (often plotted against time), or simple diagrams (e.g., scatter diagrams). Remember, the main objective here is to enable defects to be selected. We are not engaging in the root-cause analysis itself.

The following examples illustrate how the analysis of statistics can be used in defect selection.

Identifying clusters of defects

Clusters may be identified by showing distributions of defects within a particular defect category. Adding a time dimension to this data may further help identify candidates for causal analysis. Figure 4–1 shows the defect category "rejected by development" plotted over a 30-day test phase.

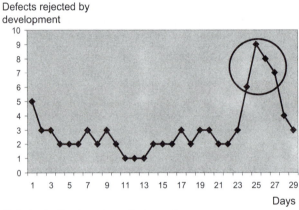

Figure 4–1   *Defect selection based on rejects per day*

The diagram shows a sudden peak in the number of defects rejected by development toward the end of the test phase. One or more defects taken from the group of 30 defects within the circle would be good candidates for causal analysis. Further selection criteria may be applied to reduce the number of defects selected (e.g., only those with high severity).

Using statistical distributions

Distributions can be useful in identifying "abnormal" defects for causal analysis. As an example, the diagram in figure 4–2 shows a distribution of times to fix a defect (elapsed days between defect status "new" and defect status "ready to retest"). In this example, defect fix times are assumed to follow a normal distribution between "fast" and "lengthy." As shown in the diagram, we would select defects for causal analysis if their fix time exceeds two standard deviations above the mean (i.e., the top 2.5 percent), which in this case equates to a period of 10 days or more.

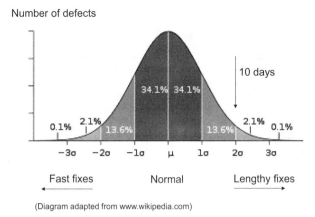

Figure 4-2   *Defect selection based on defect resolution time*

In the diagram, the central shaded area is less than one standard deviation (sigma) from the mean. For the normal distribution, this accounts for about 68 percent of the defects. Extending to two standard deviations on either side of the mean accounts for a total of about 95 percent of defects. Three standard deviations account for about 99.7 percent of defects.

Logical combinations

Combinations of defect factors can be evaluated (e.g., using filters in a spreadsheet) to enable us to focus on specific defects. For example, we may wish to place emphasis on security defects with high severity that occurred in production (i.e., a combination of three factors).

Holding Project Retrospective Meetings

Selection and/or verification of defects for causal analysis is an activity well suited to being performed as part of a project retrospective meeting.

If selection has taken place before the meeting, the candidate defects may be verified during the meeting. This involves not only a technical verification of the selected defect(s), but also an evaluation of the costs and benefits to be expected from performing the root-cause analysis.

If defect selection has not been performed before the meeting, and if sufficient time is allocated, the actual selection process itself may be conducted. Use of a checklist such as shown in table 4-1 can be an efficient and effective way to do this.

4.2.2 Gathering and Organizing the Information

Earlier we talked about how a clear, well-structured view of the complete picture is important to enable the root causes to be identified for the issues we have selected for analysis. In this section, we'll look at some initial tasks to perform and then some of the ways to structure information using the following types of diagram:

- Cause-effect (Ishikawa) diagrams
- Mind maps
- System models

For those of you studying for the ISTQB Expert Level certification, the last two are not part of the syllabus, but they do offer valuable insights into possible alternatives to using Ishikawa cause-effect diagrams.

Getting Started: Select a Suitable Approach

The task of performing causal analysis is both analytic and creative. To get satisfactory results, an approach needs to be set up that provides a supportive framework for the participants.

Inevitably, causal analysis will involve differences of opinion. A person needs to be nominated who can lead a work group through the various steps in causal analysis and keep them focused on the objective; that is, find the root cause(s) of the problem.

The leader sets up a work group and agrees with them on the following issues regarding the approach:

- The method(s) to be used
  Different methods may be applied to gather and analyze information. The actual choice made may depend on factors such as company standards, own best practices, geographic location of participants, and the required degree of formality. Here are some of the most commonly used methods:
  - Workshops
  - Brainstorming sessions
  - Reviews
- Structuring of information (refer to the diagram types described later)
- Required participants
  The work group should consist of those stakeholders who are affected by the problem. Where necessary, people with particular skills can be added to the work group so that a good balance of specialists and generalists is achieved.

Before starting, it is recommended that the leader performs the following tasks:

- Provide members of the work group with an introduction to the methods and diagrams to be used.
- Install a sense of group ownership for the results. Remember, ownership of the information is with the group rather than with management [Robson 1995].

Cause-Effect (Ishikawa) Diagrams

These diagrams enable us to focus on a particular defect and structure the potential causes. You'll also hear these diagrams referred to as Ishikawa diagrams (after the Japanese quality engineer Kaoru Ishikawa, who first developed them) or as "fishbone" diagrams (the reason for which will become obvious). Figure 4–3 shows the basic structure of the diagram.

The basic form portrays the defect as the fish's head, usually on the right side of the diagram. The backbone provides the main path to the defect, and the possible causes are grouped around the backbone. Each cause is shown using an arrow symbol. These are the fishbones, which are arranged in a tree-like hierarchy of increasingly smaller, finer bones (causes). The depth to which the hierarchy of causes goes is left to your judgment; you just keep adding and regrouping until you have a structure that you feel is sufficiently detailed and well organized.

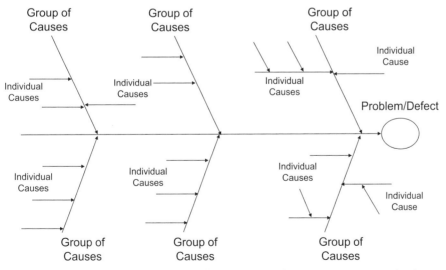

Figure 4–3 *Generic structure of cause-effect (Ishikawa) diagrams. You can see why they are also called fishbone diagrams.*

> **Cause-effect diagram** A graphical representation used to organize and display the interrelationships of various possible root causes of a problem. Possible causes of a real or potential defect or failure are organized in categories and subcategories in a horizontal tree structure, with the (potential) defect or failure as the root node. [After Juran and Godfrey 2000]

You need to take care when using these diagrams not to think of the finer bones further down the hierarchy as in some way less important than the major bones. This is not the case. Causes that are further down the hierarchy (fine bones) are simply further removed from the defect and depend on a sequence of other factors to get there. These "fine bones" may be the actual root causes you are looking for!

Standard categories can be used to group the information. They give us a good starting point for defining the main bones and support us just like a checklist. Using standard categories helps us to avoid forgetting things ("blind spots") and can get the ball rolling when creating cause-effect diagrams from scratch. This can be particularly helpful where groups of people perform cause-effect analysis in a workshop situation and where an initial "mental block" may be experienced. Figure 4–4 shows an example.

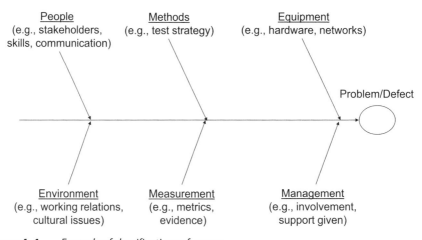

Figure 4–4 *Example of classifications of causes*

This example is taken from Ishikawa's website [URL: Ishikawa], which also describes other useful classifications covering, for example, specific types of application or business areas.

Now let's take a look at an example applied to a fictitious in-flight emergency situation for an aircraft (see figure 4–5). Remember, at this stage it's all about gathering and organizing the information so that we can later identify root causes.

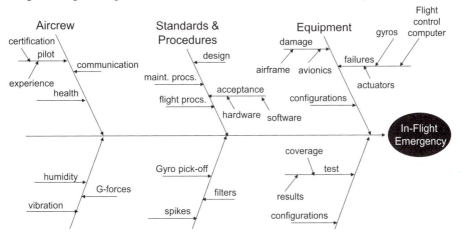

Figure 4–5   Example: Fishbone diagram for an in-flight emergency

What can we observe from this example? Well, perhaps the most obvious point is that the subject of the analysis is an incident in an overall system (in this case, an aircraft), consisisting of hardware, software, people, procedures, and environmental factors. This is typical of many complex systems we find today, where software is just one part of the whole. Indeed, the software may be distributed across many individual applications, each performing different functions within the whole system (this is why the term *system of systems* or *multi-system* is often used in this context). If we are performing root-cause analysis of incidents in systems like this, it is quite possible that the suggested improvements do not impact the software testing process. The emergency situation could, for example, have been the result of pilot inexperience or equipment malfunction.

If we take a look at the classifications used in the example shown in figure 4–5, it also becomes apparent that effective cause-effect analysis requires the gathering together of expertise from a wide range of subject areas. This applies not just to multi-systems like aircraft; it also applies to software defects where we might want to involve different stakeholders and people with specific software development or testing expertise (e.g., in evaluating security threats).

Note that in figure 4–5 the standard classifications we looked at earlier have served us well in the initial structuring of the cause-effect diagram. Taking the generic classifications as a starting point, the first step has been to replace some of them with more appropriate groupings. In this example, the generic classification "people" has been renamed "aircrew" and the generic "methods" classification has been replaced by "standards & procedures." As a next step in structuring the information, the generic classification "management" has been removed and the "software" grouping has been added. We have identified the aspects "configurations," "test results," and "test coverage" as potential root causes worthy of analysis, and these have been added to the software "bone" on the diagram.

These are typical decisions that might be made in the initial rounds of gathering information. Remember, these are all just initial steps in the iterative process of gathering, structuring, and analyzing information with a view to finding root causes. At this stage, the fishbone diagram is still high-level.

Mind Maps

As we noted earlier, gathering and organizing information are important steps that allow root-cause analysis to be conducted effectively. The strength of mind maps is the relative ease with which associations between different potential causes can be developed and shown diagrammatically. Mind maps are especially useful for showing the "big picture" and for supporting workshops and brainstorming sessions, especially if tools are used. The following diagram shows a mind map for the in-flight emergency example. It was created using the MindManager tool [URL: MMP].

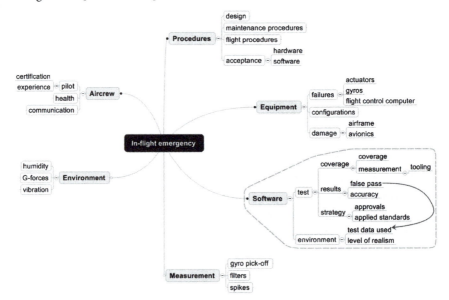

Figure 4–6   Cause-effect analysis using mind maps

Generally speaking, mind maps place the subject (i.e., defect or incident) in a central position and show the main subject areas as branches radiating away from the subject with increasing levels of detail. Used this way, they essentially provide the same information as an Ishikawa diagram but just capture it differently. Mind maps are generally easy to use and several tools (including freeware) are available.

System Models

Any model of the system or parts of the system can be of use in performing causal analysis and identifying test process improvements. Some of these models will be familiar to test analysts; they are often created when designing test cases and frequently detect defects in the specification being used (e.g., requirements). The models developed or used by the test analyst when applying specification-based test design techniques can also be of use when considering the root causes of defects. Why did particular defects get through the net? Where could we tighten up the test design process in order to avoid failures like this in the future? These are among the questions that the system models used in test design can help us to answer. The following models are the most useful to consider here:

- State transition diagrams
- Decision tables

Developers may also create models that can be used for causal analysis, such as, for example, the following:

- Use-case descriptions
- UML diagrams (e.g., activity diagrams, sequence diagrams)
- Data-flow diagrams

Note that the models referred to here will help mainly in the root-cause analysis of particular failures. To enable test process improvements to be identified, it will generally be required to consider several of these individual evaluations and then form a consolidated conclusion.

In addition the the models mentioned, the creation of systems diagrams (see *Quality Software Management, Volume 1* [Weinberg 1992]) can be useful in helping to identify process problems, including those relating to testing. The construction of these diagrams involves the identification of system elements and the flow of information between them (see section 4.2.5).

Responsibilities

Remember, in this book we are focusing mainly on the causes of defects with a view to identifying possible test process improvements. Depending on the nature of the defect, the task of conducting root-cause analysis may be either our own responsibility as test process improvers or allocated to another person (e.g., a line manager) who might take a different focus. This is particularly the case, for example, where the consequences of the defect have been catastrophic and/or when legal or contractual issues are involved.

Other Uses

The types of diagram discussed in this section may also be used for other purposes than test process improvement. In risk management, for example, Ishikawa diagrams may be used to analyze the potential risks of high-impact failures. In this case, the individual risks that may lead to the failure are grouped and the likelihood of them occurring added to the diagram. We can then multiply the individual likelihoods in a potential chain of events to get the total likelihood of the failure occurring for that chain. In addition to showing risk likelihood, the diagrams may show whether a path can actually be defined that leads to the failure (i.e., "can this failure actually occur?"). This can be a particularly useful approach when analyzing safety-critical systems.

Organizing the Information: Summary of Benefits

The diagrams we have covered provide the following general benefits:

- They allow information to be gathered and communicated relating to the potential causes of specific defects.
- Standard classifications of causes can help to structure the information and support the thorough consideration of defect causes.
- Different forms of visualization help to show potentially complex cause-effect interactions.

4.2.3 Identifying Root Causes

Once the information about defects has been gathered and organized, you can proceed with the next activity, the task of identifying the root causes. Now, you may be thinking that you can do the information gathering and analysis simultaneously. Certainly, when you gather information about possible root causes you unavoidably start to think about the root causes. You should note these initial thoughts down for later. At this stage, though, it's better not to focus on root-cause identification straight away. If you try to gather information and analyze simultaneously, you run the risks discussed in the following paragraphs.

The work group gets swamped with premature discussions about root causes before all the relevant information is gathered. Good moderation skills will be needed to guide the discussions in the work group and prevent the group from going off into detailed analysis before the big picture is available.

The information gathered may be incomplete, especially where a fixed amount of time is allocated to the task. You really don't want to complete your only scheduled information-gathering workshop having drilled down on some areas but having left other areas untouched.

By considering root-causes before finishing the information gathering, there is a natural tendency to jump to conclusions. This may lead to the wrong conclusions being reached regarding root causes, which is precisely the result we are trying to avoid. A good approach is therefore to separate the information-gathering task from the analysis task as much as possible. This allows ideas about the gathered information to mature for a period of time before the analysis takes place, and reduces the risks previously mentioned.

Let's now consider how to use the information you have gathered to identify root causes using Ishikawa diagrams. The ISTQB syllabus refers to the following six-step approach proposed by Mike Robson [Robson 1995] regarding the use of Ishikawa diagrams:.

- Step 1: Write the effect on the right-hand side of the diagram.
- Step 2: Draw in the ribs and label them according to their context.
- Step 3: Remind the work group of the rules of brainstorming.
- Step 4: Use the brainstorming method to identify possible causes.
- Step 5: Incubate the ideas for a period of time.
- Step 6: Analyze the diagram to look for clusters of causes and symptoms.

These steps will be explicitly identified when considering the following four generic tasks.

- Task 1: Set up the Ishikawa diagram.
- Task 2: Identify individual "mostly likely" causes.
- Task 3: Add information to assist the analysis.
- Task 4: Work top-down through the hierarchy of causes.

Each of the four generic tasks for using Ishikawa diagrams will now be explained by developing the "in-flight emergency" example.

Task 1: Set Up the Ishikawa Diagram

Preliminary activities are straightforward since the Ishikawa diagram has a simple structure. Some organizations that use Ishikawa diagrams frequently may have standard templates available. Otherwise, the initial form of the diagram is relatively easy to create.

First, write the effect on the right-hand side of the diagram (step 1 in Robson's approach). After that, the areas to be analyzed are identified. As you saw earlier, the information you gather may cover a large number of individual areas (as represented, for example, by the bones on an Ishikawa diagram). A good approach is to consider each of these areas in turn. This will keep the work group focused on a particular area and enable particular subject matter experts (SMEs) to participate more easily (there's nothing worse than having SMEs waiting around for their turn to participate).

Once the areas to be analyzed have been identified, they are drawn onto the diagram as ribs and labeled (Robson's step 2). If particular areas of the overall diagram are to be considered, they are clearly marked on the diagram. The result is a diagram like the one shown in figure 4–7, which shows the "in-flight emergency" example with the "software" area to be considered shaded.

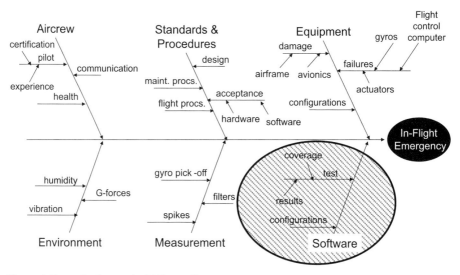

Figure 4–7   Setting up the Ishikawa diagram

Task 2: Identify Individual "Mostly Likely" Causes

With the area to be analyzed in focus, the most likely root causes are identified. These might be the ones that are "shouting" at you from the diagram or that your instinct and experience tells you are a good bet. You need to make a definite statement on these causes; they need to be either ruled out or confirmed as requiring further analysis.

A typical start to this activity is a short brainstorming session (Robson's step 3). The leader of the work group first reminds the participants of the general rules to be applied:

- No criticism is allowed; all ideas are accepted in the brainstorming stage.
- Random, crazy ideas are welcome, as are ideas that extend other people's ideas.
- The objective is to gather a large number of ideas where possible.
- All ideas will be recorded, including random, crazy, and repeating ideas.
- We will not evaluate during the session; we will take a break before doing that.

Checklists are useful to support the brainstorming or the discussions that follow. The checklist shown in table 4–2 lists some common root causes for software failures in flight control software. (Note that this is only a brief example; in reality the list would be much longer!)

Table 4–2 Example checklist of common root causes

ID	Description
T1	The test environment used has not been adequately updated to reflect production standards.
T2	Failure to update test environments linked to poor communication between the configuration management departments responsible for software and hardware configuration items.
T3	Results from dynamic tests were reported as "pass" when the software contained defects.
T4	Type of structural coverage required misunderstood by testers and therefore incorrectly reported.
T5	Developers supporting the module tests have insufficient skills in using the structural coverage tools. Some results data incorrectly reported.

Task 3: Add Information to Assist the Analysis

As the discussion develops, the next step is to refine the diagram by adding any further possible causes to it, linking different items of information, and appending any other information that might be of assistance to the analysis (Robson's step 4). To do this, the work group is often gathered around a white board or sharing diagrams via a conferencing facility or a web-based tool.

Figure 4–8 shows how our Ishikawa diagram could look after we have been through this step. These are the additions made to the "software" area of the diagram:

- Some more detailed potential root causes have been identified in the software area and added as "finer" bones to the structure.
- Any potential root causes that are associated with checklist points are identified using their checklist identifier. This is useful because it indicates where the root causes from previous problems might apply.
- An association has been identified between "test data used" and "false pass" and a link has been drawn (remember, a false pass is a test that passes but fails to identify the presence of a defect in the test object. We also call them false negatives).
- Some probability information has been added. Remember, "certainty" between a particular cause and an effect is frequently not possible. Adding a probability value will help guide the further analysis. In the example, high and low probability are shown. The remaining are considered to have negligible probability.

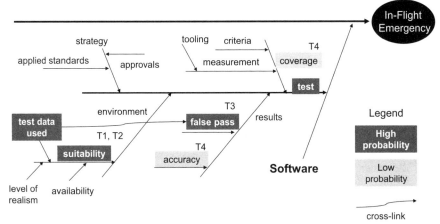

Figure 4–8   Extending the cause-effect analysis in the software test area

The process of adding more detail and information continues until we are satisfied that there is enough material to support the identification of root causes. The decision when to stop is one that requires judgment by the work group. Not enough information may lead to us missing an important root cause ("the devil is in the details"), and adding too much information, apart from consuming resources, may obscure the very thing we are looking for. Let's assume for the moment that this is enough detail. Note that the ownership of the Ishikawa diagram remains with the work group rather than with management.

- Adding information using Tipping-Point theory: To appreciate how Tipping Point theory can help in causal analysis, a brief introduction to the concept is needed. Tipping Point theory [Gladwell 2000] is concerned with the way in which changes take place very quickly by spreading like epidemics to an ever-increasing number of people. It can be useful to apply Tipping Point theory to initiate and orchestrate the rapid spread of desired changes, and this is an important aspect we will be looking at later, in chapter 7. However, you can also use certain concepts from Tipping Point theory to look back on why undesirable epidemic-like changes took place. These are the concepts you can use in performing causal analysis on problems involving several people. Clearly this is not the case for our in-flight emergency; we don't have a situation where an ever-increasing number of emergencies has spread to many aircraft. However, an awareness of Tipping Point concepts will certainly be useful when you are adding information to your causal analysis diagrams.

The observation from Tipping Point theory that is particularly useful to causal analysis is that the start of epidemic-like change is sensitive to the particular conditions and circumstances in which they occur (i.e., their context). The study of these conditions and circumstances is captured in the "broken windows" concept, which observes that if a window is broken and left unrepaired, people will conclude that no one cares and nobody is in control. This can spiral out of control; more and more windows get broken and whole neighborhoods can fall into disrepair.

When we perform causal analysis in the area of software testing, we can start to look for "broken windows" as the potential triggers for the incidents, failures, and problems that are the focus of the analysis. Take, for example, test case design practices. If several test analysts are engaged in designing test cases in a project, a standard methodology may be required to ensure that the test cases can be shared between all test analysts and to enable a particular test strategy to be implemented. For individual test analysts, applying the standard methodology may place an overhead on their work (e.g., by requiring more formal documentation). A single test analyst who chooses not to apply the standard methodology may "infect" others if the standard practice is not enforced. They ask themselves, "Why should I bother when others don't apply the methodology and nobody cares?" What could happen as a result? When the standard methodology is not applied, misunderstandings between test analysts might become more frequent. They might mistakenly believe that a test condition has been covered by one analyst. Software failures might then result, where gaps in the test case coverage fail to detect software faults. If we were to be analyzing the root causes of these failures we would identify the initial noncompliance to the standard test design methodolgy as a "broken window" in the test process that spread to some or all test analysts. Awareness of typical broken windows in testing processes and how they can spread if they are not corrected is valuable knowledge when applying causal analysis. We may choose to add this information to an Ishikawa diagram or create a checklist of typical broken windows in testing to support the analysis.

Task 4: Work Top-Down through the Hierarchy of Causes

At this stage we have a good insight into the potential root causes and our diagram(s) have been steadily refined and supplemented with details. Depending on time available, it may be advisable to let the information and ideas "incubate" for some time before continuing (Robson's step 5).

It's possible that the "most likely" root causes we selected in step 2 have now become firm favorites, or we may have revealed other candidates when adding the information in step 3. The best way to approach the identification of root causes with Ishikawa diagrams is to work from the top (i.e., near the head of the fish) and trace paths through the hieracrchy of bones. We stop when going down a further level of detail has no added value. At each level of detail we ask, "Where could the path take us now?" in pursuit of a root cause.

In Robson's six-step approach to using Ishikawa diagrams, he suggests that we may also use the Pareto idea (80 percent of the benefit for 20 percent of the effort) to identify clusters of problems that are candidates to solve (Robson's step 6). Our example would benefit greatly from this last step because of the relatively low amount of detail described.

The outcome of this step in seldom a surprised shout of "Eureka, we've found it!" By now we have a fairly good idea of where the root cause might be. Working top-down this way through the hierarchy of causes enables us to either identifiy the most likely root cause or narrow down the search sufficiently to allow more detailed investigation to be started.

Figure 4–9 shows the Ishikawa diagram of the software area for the in-flight emergency problem.

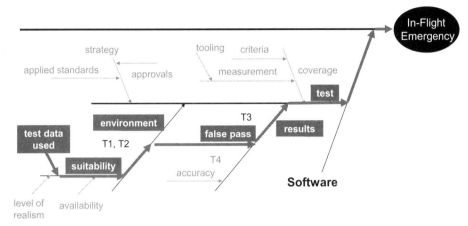

Figure 4–9 Locating the root cause in the software test area

The figure shows the path we have identified from analyzing the information in the diagram (thick arrows). Areas of the diagram that have been discounted as root causes are now shown in grey. Working top-down, we recognized "software test" as a potential root cause and noted that the "false pass" aspect of the results "bone" was an aspect where previous problems had been detected (hence the checklist item T3). From there we noted that we had identified a possible link to the "test data used" item in the "environment" area of the diagram. Note that these items of interest were identified as "high probability."

After discussion in the work group, the conclusion, in this instance, was that the in-flight emergency had been the result of the following sequence: Test data used in the test environment was unsuitable, leading to false passes being recorded after executing test cases. The software faults that were not detected in these test cases subsequently led to a software failure and the in-flight emergency.

Of course, we would also need to indicate which specific area of the software failed and which specific test cases had been supplied with unsuitable test data and explain why that test data was unsuitable (e.g., taken from a previous project where the data related to a different aircraft type). This would be the additional data to be supplied to enable the root cause of the problem to be really pinpointed.

> **Cause-effect graph** A graphical representation of inputs and/or stimuli (causes) with their associated outputs (effects), which can be used to design test cases.

Our discussion of cause-effect diagrams has so far focused on the principal task of finding the causes of actual problems (effects). Two further uses for these versatile diagrams can also be identified.

The first of these relates to the cause-effect graphing test design technique, which captures the causes and effects using a specific notation. This enables test cases to be defined that cover the causes (test inputs) and their effects (test outputs). The example shown in figure 4–10 is based on the following specification.

When a person takes a train after 9 a.m., they can buy a return ticket at the Super-Saver price. When a person takes a train before 6 a.m., they can buy a return ticket at the Saver price. At other times, a standard return ticket must be purchased. People with a Rail-Card25 receive a 25 percent discount on all tickets except the Super-Saver.

The causes and effects are identified from the specification and shown on a cause-effect graph.

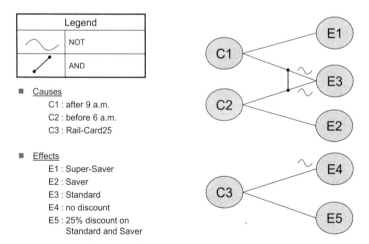

Figure 4–10   *Example of a cause-effect graph*

As a further step, the cause-effect graph may be represented as a table and test cases defined that cover combinations of inputs (causes). Refer to *A Practitioner's Guide to Software Test Design* [Copeland 2003] and the Software Component Testing standard [BS 7925-2] for further details.

Cause-effect diagrams may also be used in the analysis of potential (rather than actual) failures. This can be particularly useful when analyzing safety-critical systems. It involves working back from the "failure mode" order to detect whether any potential paths could be leading to the failure.

4.2.4 Drawing Conclusions

After completing the steps, we should first decide whether conclusions can be drawn or not. Maybe we need more information, maybe we ran out of time, maybe the problem is simply too complex for the work group to consider. There are many reasons why the work group is unable to draw specific conclusions, and these should be clearly communicated to relevant stakeholders.

If the work group is confident that root cause(s) can be identified with reasonable certainty, it must then consider the following questions:

- Was this a "one-off" event?
- Have we detected something wrong in part(s) of the test process which might lead to the same or similar failures in the future?
- Do we need to suggest changes to other processes?
- Can we identify any common causes?

Root causes that are considered to be one-off events can be problematic for test process improvers. Does "one-off" imply "not important"? Not always. This may be the first of many similar or related software failures if we don't make changes to the test process. The impact of the one-off event may be severe enough to warrant immediate action.

If we are performing causal analysis regularly, then we should research previous cases for similarities (remember, a single root cause may reveal itself in a number of different ways). We may identify associations with other problems or we might find it useful to revisit a previously conducted causal analysis using any new information available (e.g., about unsuitable test data). Take care with one-offs; it's not advisable to change the test process for each and every problem that raises its ugly head. This might result in too many small process changes, and you could end up tinkering unnecessarily with the test process. As you will see in chapter 7, introducing too many process changes at the same time is not a good idea.

As test process improvers we are, of course, interested in any root causes that have implications on the test process. We will give this aspect more detailed consideration in chapter 6. Causal analysis may, however, point to root causes in IT processes other than testing. This is frequently the case for those IT processes on which the test process depends. For example, a flawed configuration management process may result in too many regression faults being found (i.e., things that used to work no longer work). The root cause here lies within the configuration management process; we cannot effectively resolve the root cause of the problem by proposing test process improvements. Where conclusions are drawn outside of the test process, we should inform the appropriate stakeholder and provide support as required.

After conclusions have been drawn about the individual issues considered in the causal analysis, a check needs to be made to see if other, similar causes have been identified in the past. When identifying root causes (see section 4.2.3, task 2, "Identify individual most likely causes"), this kind of information can be particularly useful and is often held as a checklist (see table 4–1 for an example). At this stage we may be updating the checklist with additional information, or we may be identifying new common causes to add to the list.

If you are using a defect classification scheme, such as the IEEE 1044, Standard Classification for Software Anomalies [IEEE 1044], the cause will be allocated according to a predefined categorization scheme. For example, IEEE 1044 provides a table with the following principal categories of causes (Table 3a Investigation classification scheme – Actual cause):

- Product
- Test system
- Platform
- Outside vendor/Third party
- User

Recording information about defects using a common classification scheme such as IEEE 1044 allows an organization to gather statistics about improvement areas to be analyzed (see section 4.2.1) and to monitor the success of improvement initiatives (see section 4.4). However, schemes like this require an organization-wide approach with tools support, training, and tailoring. The introduction of a classification scheme such as IEEE 1044 may even be considered a test process improvement in its own right.

4.2.5 Causal Analysis with System Diagrams

System diagrams [Weinberg 1992] are a useful way of showing interactions between different elements of a system. The main benefit of system diagrams is their ability to reveal different types of feedback loops within the system and its components. Feedback loops are divided into the following two principal categories:

- Balancing
- Reinforcing

Systems with balancing feedback loops are stable in nature. A system that contains such loops will reduce any difference between a current and a desired system state until a balanced state is achieved.

Systems with reinforcing feedback loops exhibit unstable characteristics. A system that contains such loops will increase any difference between a current and a desired system state in either a positive or negative sense. With positive reinforcing feedback (sometimes called *virtuous circles*), a continually improving state is achieved by the system. Negatively reinforcing feedback results in a continuously deteriorating system state and is often referred to as a *vicious circle*.

Full coverage of this subject is out of scope for the Expert Level syllabus, but test process improvers may benefit by taking a closer look at Weinberg's interesting analytical approaches.

Benefits and Limitations

Creating system diagrams can be particularly useful when gathering and organizing information (see section 4.2.5). They enable us to identify vicious circles and can therefore make an important contribution to the overall process of problem analysis. The ability to represent the interaction between different elements of a system gives us a "big picture" view of a system as a whole and enables us to investigate particular system aspects that would otherwise be difficult to visualize. The only real "limitation" of creating system diagrams lies in the very nature of the approach to be applied and the notation to be used. This is not highly intuitive; you need training and experience to master it. As a result, difficulties may arise when applying systems thinking in a work group with varying degrees of experience in using the approach. Used in the context of software testing, it is advisable to involve people with the experience of system architectures and development to get the best results for causal analysis.

4.2.6 Causal Analysis during Formal Reviews

An alternative approach to causal analysis involves adaption of the formal review (inspection) process described in the ISTQB Foundation and Advanced syllabi. As you might expect from a formal procedure (see *Software Inspection*

> **Inspection** A type of review that relies on visual examination of documents to detect defects, such as, for example, violations of development standards and nonconformance to higher-level documentation. It is the most formal review technique and therefore always based on a documented procedure [After IEEE 610, IEEE 1028].

[Gilb and Graham 1993]), using the software inspection process for causal analysis also involves the performance of specific, controlled steps.

The following principal activities take place within a two-hour facilitated meeting with two main parts:

- Part 1: 90 minutes
  - Defect selection
  - Analysis of specific defects
- Part 2: 30 minutes
  - Analysis of generic defects

In part 1 of the meeting, the defects may be preselected for discussion by the inspection leader or they may be the outcome of a project retrospective meeting. Clearly, the approaches covered in section 4.2.1 will be of use in selecting these defects so that the most important defects are considered. The first part of the analysis then looks at the specific defects and their root causes. This will involve any of the approaches discussed in this chapter and produces the following results:

- Defect description
- Cause category (see figure 4–4 for an example)
- Cause description, including any chain of events leading to the defect
- The process step when the defect was created
- Specific actions to eliminate the cause

In part 2 of the meeting the focus is placed on finding patterns, trends, and overall aspects of the defects. The work group considers aspects that have shown recent improvement as well as those areas of the test process that have gone well or badly. The work group may also support the test manager by proposing areas to be tested in a risk-based test strategy.

Benefits and Limitations

Considering causal analysis as an extension of inspections is a good idea if an organization already performs formal reviews. The formalism of the approach may restrict some of the more interactive and creative activities found in other approaches.

4.2.7 Causal Analysis Lessons Learned

Now that causal analysis has been considered, it's a good idea to reflect on some lessons learned.

The "Causes-Effect Fallacy"

Gerald Weinberg, in his book about systems thinking [Weinberg 1992], discusses this frequently occurring fallacy. The basis for his observation is the incorrect belief held by some that for each problem a cause can *always* be shown and that cause and problem are directly related to one another. Unless we have a trivial system, these "rules" simply don't hold up. Sometimes the link from root cause to problem is far from direct.

Saying "We Don't Know" Is Better Than Guessing

Sometimes we can't find the root cause to a problem or we are uncertain of our conclusions. It may also be that the underlying root causes are on a different part of the diagram that is not within our responsibility. We may have invested significant resources to analyze a problem and there is pressure to come up with "the cause." Despite the pressure, we must be honest enough to say, "We don't know" rather than lead a project or organization in potentially the wrong direction through guesswork.

"Lean and Mean" Work Groups

Occasionally it can be useful to invite people to a workshop or brainstorming session just to give them insight into these activities and increase their sense of involvement. Where causal analysis is concerned, this is not always a good idea. The work is intensive, there may be many proposals put forward for consideration, and there will be much (sometimes heated) debate. What we want in such situations are the people who can contribute directly to the task of finding root causes, and no others. The larger the work group, the greater the potential for unproductive contributions and unhelpful group dynamics. Keep the group "lean and mean."

Encourage Analytical Thinkers

Group dynamics often play a significant role in causal analysis. Work group participants will inevitably have different ideas about root causes; they may have their own "pet theory," or they may simply want to impress their peers by being the first ones to find the problem. Good moderation skills will be needed to manage these group dynamics and get the best out of the work group. Don't forget, the members of the group with strong analytical skills and good intuition may not always be the ones who can communicate them most effectively. They will need encouragement and the space in which to express themselves. They could give you the key to the puzzle.

Step Back and Think

When intensive discussion is taking place and lots of ideas are being proposed, it's occasionally a good idea to step back, think, and then return to the diagram. This is recommended as a separate step ("incubate ideas") in *Problem Solving in Groups* [Robson 1995] before the detailed analysis takes place. However, this is a practice that can be useful at most stages in causal analysis.

4.3 GQM Approach

Syllabus Learning Objectives

LO 4.3.1 (K2) Describe the Goal-Question-Metric (GQM) approach.
LO 4.3.2 (K3) Apply the Goal-Question-Metric (GQM) approach to derive appropriate metrics from a testing improvement goal.
LO 4.3.3 (K3) Define metrics for a testing improvement goal.
LO 4.3.4 (K2) Understand the steps and challenges of the data collection phase.
LO 4.3.5 (K2) Understand the steps and challenges of the interpretation phase.

4.3.1 Introduction

A well-known and popular software measurement approach is the Goal-Question-Metric (GQM) approach. Measurement is an important aid to test improvement. *Measurement* is performing data collection and analysis on the processes

4.3 GQM Approach

> **Goal-Question-Metric (GQM)** An approach to software measurement using a three-level model: conceptual level (goal), operational level (question), and quantitative level (metric).

and products to identify empirical relations. Bottom-up improvement approaches typically include some kind of measurement approach, of which the Goal-Question-Metric approach [Basili 1984] is the most well known. It is a widely accepted approach and much applied in industry. It's a goal-oriented approach, which makes it especially popular in goal-driven business environments.

The GQM method provides a systematic approach for tailoring and integrating goals, based upon the specific needs of the project and the organization, to models of the test process. The approach includes product and quality perspectives of interest [Basili and Caldiera 1994]. The result of the application of the GQM method is the specification of a measurement system targeting a particular set of issues and a set of rules for the interpretation of the measurement data.

We will now present available techniques for GQM measurement. The emphasis of the method is focused on the interpretation of measurement data. Organizations should recognize that an improved understanding is an essential part of continuous improvement. Bottom-up approaches, such as GQM, provide this understanding. It is recommended to apply top-down improvement approaches, as described, for example, in the Testing Maturity Model integration (TMMi) model, in parallel with software measurement.

Even though the GQM approach is mostly considered to be a (test) process measurement approach, it can also be used to measure product quality.

4.3.2 Paradigms

The Goal-Question-Metric (GQM) approach originates from Professor Victor Basili of the University of Maryland. During his involvement at the Software Engineering Laboratory (SEL) at NASA, he developed this approach to study the characteristics of software development. Two important paradigms are important when considering GQM measurement: the GQM paradigm and the Quality Improvement Paradigm (QIP). Both will be introduced briefly.

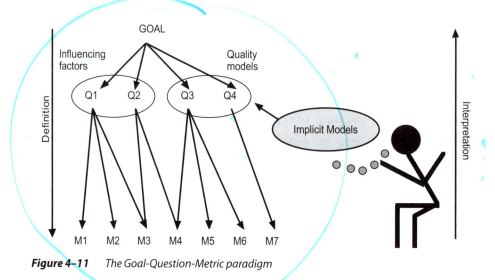

Figure 4–11 The Goal-Question-Metric paradigm

GQM Paradigm

The Goal-Question-Metric (GQM) paradigm represents a systematic approach to tailor and integrate goals with software process and products models. It is based on the specific needs of a project and organization. Within GQM, measurement goals are derived from high-level corporate goals and then refined into measurable values (metrics). GQM defines a certain goal, refines this goal into questions, and defines metrics that must provide the information to answer these questions. When the questions are answered, the measured data can be analyzed to identify whether the goals are attained. Thus, by using GQM, metrics are defined from a top-down perspective and analyzed and interpreted bottom-up, as shown in figure 4–11. As the metrics are defined with an explicit goal in mind, the information provided by the metrics should be interpreted and analyzed with respect to this goal to conclude whether or not it is attained [Van Solingen 2000].

GQM trees of goals, questions, and metrics are built on the knowledge of the testing experts in the organizations. Knowledge acquisition techniques are used to capture the implicit models of those involved in testing built up during many years of experience. Those implicit models give valuable input to the measurement program and will often be more important than the available explicit process models.

Quality Improvement Paradigm

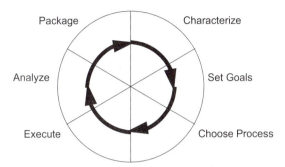

Figure 4–12 *The Quality Improvement Paradigm*

The general framework defined for continuous bottom-up improvement is the Quality Improvement Paradigm (QIP). QIP stresses the importance of seeing the development and testing of software as an immature process. So that more knowledge can be gained about that process, each project is regarded as an application of methods and techniques, providing an opportunity to increase the insight of the development process. By closely monitoring every project that is carried out, the process by which the software is developed and tested can be analyzed, evaluated, and improved. In theory, QIP is an approach that develops and packages models of software development and testing. The availability of such models is regarded as a major source for improvement because knowledge is made explicit. The steps that QIP describes are characterization, goal setting, process selection, execution, analysis, and packaging (see figure 4–12).

Improvement according to QIP is continuous: the packaged experience forms the basis for a new characterization step, which in turn is followed by the other steps. Process performance is monitored by measurement. QIP is the result of applying scientific method to the problem of software quality improvement and is therefore related to the Shewart-Deming cycle Plan, Do, Check, Act (PDCA). The major difference is that QIP develops a series of models that contain the experience related to the environmental context, while Plan, Do, Check, Act incorporates the experience into the standard process.

Measurement must be applied to evaluate goals defined within the second step of QIP. These goals must be measurable, driven by the models, and defined from various perspectives, such as user, customer, project, or organization. QIP makes use of the GQM approach for defining and evaluating these goals.

For those of you studying for the ISTQB Expert Level certification, QIP is not part of the syllabus, but it does offer valuable insights to ideas behind GQM.

4.3.3 GQM Process

We will now describe the GQM process steps, followed by the two basic GQM activities: definition and interpretation.

GQM Process Steps

The GQM paradigm, as presented in figure 4–11, does not define a process for applying the GQM approach. However, a GQM process model has been developed that reflects the continuous cycle of QIP. The steps to take are applicable when introducing measurement in practice. What follows is a description of the steps defined within the GQM process model. Figure 4–13 shows these steps.

Figure 4–13   *The activities for goal-oriented measurement*

Step 1: Organization and Project Characterization

Defining the measurement program starts with a characterization of the organization and the project. The results of the characterization are used in the definition, ranking, and selection of the goals and also in establishing the GQM plan.

Step 2: Goal Definition

The second step in the GQM process is defining measurement goals. Measurement goals can directly reflect business goals but also specific project goals or even personal goals. Measurement goals must be carefully selected using criteria such as priority to the project or organization, risk, and time in which a goal can be reached.

Clear and realistic goals must be defined. Two types of goals can be distinguished:

- Knowledge goals ("knowing where we are today") are expressed in terms such as *evaluate*, *predict*, and *monitor*. Examples are evaluating how many hours are actually spent on retesting or monitoring the test coverage. The goal is to gain insight and understanding.
- Improvement goals ("what do we want to achieve?") are expressed in terms such as *increase*, *decrease*, *improve*, and *achieve*. Setting such goals means that we already know that there are shortcomings in the current test process or environment and that we want to overcome them.

An example of an improvement goal is "decrease the number of testing hours by 20 percent and at the same time maintain a constant level of test coverage." In order to ascertain this, the following two knowledge goals can be defined:

- Evaluate the total number of testing hours per project.
- Evaluate the achieved levels of coverage per project.

It is important to investigate whether the goals and the (test) maturity of the organization match. It is pointless to set a goal (i.e., to try to achieve a certain level of coverage) when the necessary resources (knowledge, time, tools) are not (yet) available.

Step 3: Developing the Measurement Program

A major activity when developing a measurement program is refining the selected goals into questions and metrics. It is important to check whether metrics answer questions and that answers to such questions provide a contribution toward reaching the defined goals.

An essential characteristic of a well-defined measurement program is good documentation. Three documents should be developed:

- GQM plan
- Measurement plan
- Analysis plan

GQM Plan

A GQM plan describes in a top-down way what has to be measured. It describes the measurement goals and how they are refined into questions and metrics.

For each goal, several questions should be derived. They are basically questions that need answers in order to know whether the goals have been met. The questions have to be formulated in such a way that they almost act as a specification for a metric. In addition, it is also recommended that you define responsibilities for supplying the data from which metric values can be calculated. As an example, we'll use the knowledge goal "provide insight into the effectiveness of testing" [Pol, Teunnissen, and van Veenendaal 2002]. From this goal several questions come to mind. Here, we will limit the number of question to three.

> Goal
> G1: Provide insight into the effectiveness of testing
>
> *Questions:*
> Q1.1: How many defects have been found during testing?
> Q1.2: How many defects have been reported in the first three months of production?
> Q1.3: What level of test coverage has been achieved?

From the questions, the metrics are derived. The data needed for the metrics will later be gathered during testing. By asking the right questions, one almost automatically arrives at the right set of metrics for the measurement goal. It is important to specify each metric in detail—for example, what is a defect?

> G1: Provide insight into the effectiveness of testing
> Q1.1: How many defects have been found during testing?
> M1.1: Total number of defects found per severity category?
> Q1.2: How many defects have been reported in the first three months of production?
> M1.2: Number of defects reported by users in the first three months of production
> Q1.3: What level of test coverage has been achieved?
> M1.3.1: Statement coverage achieved
> M1.3.2: Requirements coverage achieved

Here are some hints for defining the metrics:

- Start with a limited set of metrics and build them up slowly
- Keep the metrics easy to understand. The definition must appeal to the intuition of those involved. For example, try to avoid using lots of formulas. The more complicated the formulas, the more difficult they are to interpret.
- Choose metrics that are relatively easy to collect. The more effort it takes to collect the data, the greater the chance that they will not be accepted.
- Automate data collection as much as possible. In addition to being more efficient, it prevents the introduction of manual input errors in the data set.

Measurement Plan

A measurement plan describes how the measurements shall be conducted. It describes metrics, procedures, and tools to report, collect, and check data. Describing metrics is not the same as identifying them as part of the GQM tree. Typically, a metric is defined by using the following attributes:

- Formal definition, including the measurement formula
- Textual explanation
- Analysis procedure, including hypothesis (possible outcomes) and influencing factors
- Person that collects the metric
- Point of time when the data is measured, such as, for example, which life cycle phase

Analysis Plan

An analysis plan defines how to provide verified and validated measurement results to the project team at the right abstraction level. It is the basic guideline to support the feedback of measurement information to the project team.

Step 4: Execution of the Measurement Program

In the execution step of the measurement program, the measurement data is collected according to the procedures defined in the measurement plan and the feedback material is prepared as described by the analysis plan. During the test process, a wide variety of data can be collected. This can be done using electronic forms and templates. When you're designing these forms and templates, the following issues must be taken into consideration:

- Which data can be collected using the same form?
- Validation. How easy is it to check that the data is complete and correct?

- Ensure traceability (date, project ID, configuration management data, etc.). Sometimes it is necessary to preserve data for a long time, making traceability even more important.
- The possibility of automatic processing.

As soon as the data is collected, analysis must start. At this point it is still possible to make changes and ask questions. Waiting too long decreases the chance of recovering the correct data and may negatively impact the motivation of testers to record accurately.

Step 5: Feedback Sessions

Feedback sessions are meetings involving members of the project team. This is an essential tool for analysis and interpretation of the measurement results. Proper feedback is also of importance for the motivation of those involved and the validation of the measurement data. At this step, it is also determined whether the goals have been achieved, which may even signal the start of a new GQM cycle. In this way, one is continuously improving the test process.

As a rule during feedback sessions, avoid complicated statistical techniques and models. Provide feedback to the testers and other stakeholders as quickly as possible. Show them what is being done with the information being gathered.

A more detailed description of a feedback session is provided later.

Step 6: Packaging of Measurement Results

To reuse measurement results and experiences, the results of the measurement program must be packaged. Packaging must be done in such a way that future project teams, or other parties from the organization, are able to use the measurement results.

GQM Definition

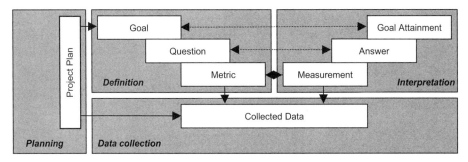

Figure 4–14   *The two main parts of the GQM method: definition and interpretation*

Application of GQM measurement by means of the process model divides the improvement cycle in two main parts (see figure 4–14). The first part consists of the definition process, during which goals, questions, metrics and additional procedures are defined (steps 1, 2, and 3). The second part (described in the next section) consists of the interpretation process, during which the collected data is analyzed, improvements are identified, and experiences are described (steps 4, 5, and 6).

The definition process for GQM measurement is well described in literature. Many books and papers are available on selecting the right metrics for a specific problem, such as, for example, *A Quantitative Approach to Software Management – The AMI Handbook* [Pulford, Kuntzmann-Combelles, Shirlaw 1995]. The GQM approach was initially introduced as a technique to define metrics, even though it already encouraged interpretation implicitly.

The definition process for GQM measurement consists of the following activities:

- Pre-study:
  Characterization of the organization and project, its problems and goals.
- Identify measurement goals:
  Refine informal improvement goals, rank and define them to correspond with GQM goals.
- Produce GQM plan:
  Use the GQM paradigm for the definition of questions and metrics. Interview project members to retrieve the necessary information.
- Produce measurement plan:
  Define environment in which the defined metrics are collected.
- Produce analysis plan, and start measuring:
  Define the analysis in charts and tables according to which the analysis is likely to be done, and start collecting data.

Tools are available for the first three of the activities. For the pre-study, questionnaires have been shown to be useful. For the definition of goals, templates are available and brainstorming sessions can be used. For the production of the GQM plan, interviews must be held that can be supported by abstraction sheets (see section 4.3.4).

GQM Interpretation

Once the goals, questions, and metrics have been defined and the matching plans are developed, data collection can start. Based on this data, an analysis will be performed aimed at answering questions and reaching goals. This is the *interpretation process*. Remember, it is often easy to get numbers; what is hard is to know that they are right and understand what they mean. Experience has shown that interpreting measurement data is a learning process within a team. Interpreting measurement data properly can be done according to the three principles of goal-oriented measurement:

- Measurement must reflect the interest of the data providers and must be based on the knowledge of the team.
- Only those that provide the data can determine its validity. They are the only ones who know all the details (including the data that was not measured) and are therefore the only people allowed to really interpret feedback material.
- Because of the limited amount of time available (e.g., caused by commitments to project planning), conflicts of interest may occur when the test team performs all the measurement tasks. Separate staffing may be needed to support the collection and analysis of the measurement data and perform those activities that do not necessarily have to be carried out by the test team.

To get the most out of measurement, the team must emphasize the interpretation to close the feedback loop. The main objective of measurement is to get interpretations from the team on the collected data. This data can be used to evaluate current processes and identify improvement opportunities. Depending on the results, immediate changes and adjustments to both the test process and the measurement process can be suggested. Through defining conclusions and action points during the interpretation process, test process improvement is started at the project and engineering level.

The motivation for testers to participate in measurement is mainly determined by the way the interpretation process is carried out. For this purpose, so-called *feedback sessions* can be introduced. These are structured meetings involving members of the project team and measurement team, during which measurement data is analyzed, conclusions are drawn, and corrective actions are identified. A set of guidelines should be developed to improve the organization of the feedback process. These guidelines can also help to identify why a specific feedback process goes wrong.

Quality measurement programs are unsuited to the evaluation of individual developers. Judgment of the performance of individuals based on measurement data violates almost every condition for a successful learning program and may even be illegal in some countries. If measurement is used in this way, the entire measurement program will fail, either quickly or within about a year.

4.3.4 Supporting Tools and Techniques

The following sections present some useful tools and techniques for measurement that are being used in day-to-day practice.

Goal Definition

Goal definition is important for measurement. It defines the scope of the measurement program for a period of time. Refining organizational or project goals into measurement goals is a difficult task that requires skills and knowledge. You must keep in mind that a goal must be reachable, must be measurable, and must be attainable by answering a set of (knowledge) questions. Two tools are available for goal definition: a measurement goal template, and a technique termed *the seven questions* (described later). Section 4.4 provides a number of standard goals and metrics. Of course, these are not anywhere near complete or exhaustive, but they can be a source for inspiration, especially to those who are not that experienced in applying software measurement by GQM.

Measurement Goal Template

Measurement goals can directly reflect business goals but also project goals or personal goals. To describe measurement goals in a uniform and reachable way, a template is available (see figure 4–15) [Basili and Rombach 1988].

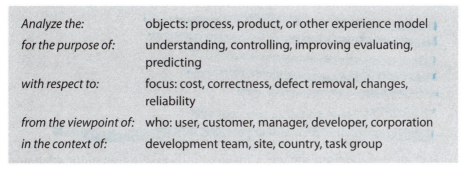

Analyze the:	objects: process, product, or other experience model
for the purpose of:	understanding, controlling, improving evaluating, predicting
with respect to:	focus: cost, correctness, defect removal, changes, reliability
from the viewpoint of:	who: user, customer, manager, developer, corporation
in the context of:	development team, site, country, task group

Figure 4–15 Template for a measurement goal

Figure 4–16 shows an example from a measurement project where the goal was to understand the usefulness of code metrics.

Analyze the:	the value of code metrics
for the purpose of:	understanding
with respect to:	their usefulness as reliability and maintainability indicators
from the viewpoint of:	the software engineers
in the context of:	the projects xxxx and yyyy

Figure 4–16   *Example of a defined measurement goal (using the template)*

The Seven Questions

Within a brainstorming session it is always possible to define many goals. However, these must be relevant to the business, represent strategic goals from management, and support high priority processes of the organization. Sometimes it will be clear for a (test) manager what the measurement goals must be (for example, a specific problem that needs attention), but often it is not obvious. In such cases, brainstorming and goal selection by a multi-criteria mechanism is a possibility.

It is also possible to define and select the measurement goals in a meeting. One mechanism to support goal definition and selection in a meeting is by asking the seven questions:

1. What are the strategic goals of your organization?
2. What forces have impact on your strategic goals?
3. How can you improve your performance?
4. What are your major concerns (problems)?
5. What are your improvement goals?
6. How can you reach your improvement goals?
7. What are possible measurement goals, and what are their priorities?

All members of the team should be involved in the definition of the goals and have an interest in achieving them. High motivation of team members can be expected when they set their own goals. However, management involvement is a critical success factor, and it should be clear to them how the measurement goals relate to the business goals and support business improvement.

Abstraction Sheets

The selected goals can be refined into questions and metrics based on interviews. The aim of the interviews is to capture the definitions, assumptions, and models of the team that are related to the goal. The main purpose of these interviews is to make the implicit knowledge of the engineers explicit. Furthermore, the interviews motivate the people for the measurement program because they realize that the data to be collected is related to their own issues.

The information acquired during the interviews must be combined because inconsistencies can exist between the different team members. Those differences become clear during the interviews and must be discussed and clarified.

The interview is supported by so-called *abstraction sheets*. The use of abstraction sheets during interviews provides a structured approach to focus on the relevant subjects regarding the goals and support the identification of issues that could be overlooked. An abstraction sheet summarizes the main issues and dependencies of a goal and represents this information on the following four quadrants of a sheet:

1. Quality Focus:
   What are the measured properties of the object in the goal?
2. Baseline Hypothesis:
   What are the expectations about the measurements? What is the current status of knowledge about the measured properties? The current knowledge is made explicit by drawing up baseline hypotheses.
3. Variation Factors:
   Which factors are expected to have an essential impact on the measured properties?
4. Impact on Baseline Hypothesis:
   How do the variation factors influence the measured properties? Which dependencies are assumed?

Object	Purpose	Quality focus	Viewpoint	Environment
Quality Focus Number of failures by severity (minor, major, critical)			*Variation Factors* Domain conformance Experience of engineers	
Baseline Hypothesis Distribution of failures by severity: minor: 60% major: 30% critical: 10%			*Impact on Baseline Hypothesis* More experienced engineers results in less fatal failures	

Figure 4–17   Example of an abstraction sheet

Hypotheses are grouped into two quadrants of the abstraction sheet and are matched to the questions of the other quadrants. The four quadrants can be checked because mutual relationships exist. For example, every metric in Quality Focus must have a hypothesis in the Baseline Hypothesis part, and for every metric in Variation Factors, its influence on the hypothesis must be defined in the Impact on Baseline Hypothesis quadrant. An example of an abstraction sheet is presented in figure 4–17. Abstraction sheets are a powerful tool for interviews during the definition process of a measurement program. Abstraction sheets can also be used to structure interpretation of measurement data.

Data Collection Tools

No GQM-specific data collection tools exist. However, some software is available that can be used for measurement. There are tools available that calculate some well-known metrics on test coverage. Database packages can be used to collect data. Testers can then enter specific data, such as effort spent on testing and retesting, into an electronic database. Current database tools provide functionality to easily create specific databases with user friendly interfaces. Finally, it is possible to build data collection forms with a word processor. Such forms must be filled in by the testers and subsequently included in some automated tool.

Feedback Sessions

Feedback sessions are meetings during which data are analyzed by the team based on the procedures defined in the GQM plan. These sessions are important to maintain interest and motivation for the measurement program. This is one of the reasons they should be held often.

There should be enough time between feedback sessions to ensure that there is enough new measurement data and the effort spent is being optimized. This is a kind of paradox: on one hand, feedback must be obtained often; on the other hand, this is not always feasible. In practice, a balance is achieved by running feedback sessions every six to eight weeks, depending on the project-specific goals.

Generally speaking, feedback sessions last between two and three hours. The attendees need to show a high degree of concentration for a feedback session. As a result, a maximum number of 10 slides presenting measurement results can be discussed. Decisions have to be made on which issues to discuss in a feedback session. In the first sessions of a measurement program, it might be necessary to discuss all available material.

Feedback sessions consist of the steps shown in table 4-3.

Table 4-3 *10 steps for feedback sessions*

	Feedback session steps
1	Freeze database with measurement data.
2	Create basic set of analysis slides.
3	Create additional set with new analysis.
4	Select feedback material.
5	Distribute feedback material.
6	Analyze feedback material in the session.
7	Draw conclusions, answer questions, and define action points.
8	Evaluate with project team.
9	Evaluate within GQM team.
10	Report.

The first step is to freeze the database in which the collected measurements are stored. With this data set it is possible to update the basic set of slides to discuss during the feedback session. Extra slides can also be created to study the specific issues raised by the team. Often the total set of slides is by then already too large. Therefore, step 4 must be carried out, during which a selection is made in cooperation with the test manager and team members on the subjects for the feedback session. The slides are always distributed to the attendees of a feedback session one or two days in advance to allow for preparation.

After the individual preparations, the feedback session can take place (step 6). The use of a moderator to guide the discussion during a feedback session is especially necessary for a project team larger than four people. The moderator explains which data is included in a presentation slide, explains the axes of a chart, and if a relationship is visible from a slide, the moderator points it out. After this explanation, the team is asked to interpret. Mostly, the first interpretation already results in a group discussion, which is finished with an overall interpretation and sometimes one or more action points. The conclusions are recorded, and the action points are assigned among the participants of the feedback session.

A feedback session is finalized by an evaluation with all participants involved, followed by an internal GQM team evaluation. The results, conclusions, and corrective actions are reported by the GQM team, including improvements for the measurement program. The specific feedback session then comes to an end, but since this is a continuous process, the next feedback session is already planned.

4.3.5 Bottom-Up Improvement

Most widely used test improvement methods provide a top-down approach. However, the application of bottom-up approaches is also recommended. Such methods, termed *software measurement*, are focused on collecting data on current practices within the organization. Although it is important to select the right metrics, the process by which the measurement data is analyzed is more important.

Measurement is the starting point for actually improving test processes and products at the project level. Interpreting measurement data is most important. The major benefit of measurement is to raise the level of understanding by the team—in short, learning. Organizations must include such learning activities in their regular planning.

The GQM approach is a powerful technique that supports the collection of data based on a specific problem or organization. The recommendation is to apply an approach such as GQM instead of just collecting some well-known metrics. Especially industrial organizations have positive experiences with GQM because both the method and the organization are goal driven.

Organizations need to improve continuously. This chapter does not claim that top-down improvement approaches such as the TMMi do not work. On the contrary, top-down approaches have proven to be valuable in establishing improvements. They provide a means to set up a solid test engineering working environment and to establish product quality targets. Experiences in practice have shown significant benefits.

This chapter does claim that organizations need to apply a bottom-up approach as well. When such a measurement-based approach is set up, testing will become better understood. Knowledge is the best basis for improvement, and knowledge has to be created within people. Since testing is still a human activity, we must begin to make use of bottom-up improvement approaches as soon as possible.

4.4 Analysis Using Measures, Metrics, and Indicators

Syllabus Learning Objectives

LO 4.4.1 (K2) Provide examples of the various categories of metrics and how they can be used in a test improvement context.

LO 4.4.2 (K5) Recommend appropriate metrics and indicators for tracking improvement trends in a particular improvement situation.

Measurements are important for the improvement of the test process to assess the consequences of any certain improvement actions by comparing data before and after the action has been implemented. Data analysis is essential for objective test process improvement and a valuable support to purely qualitative assessments, which might otherwise result in imprecise recommendations that are not supported by data.

In short, measurement should be a part of a test improvement program for the following reasons:

- To show the benefits of test improvement
- To understand the current situation (both for product quality and test process)
- For benchmarking

Often the terms *metric*, *measure*, and *indicator* are used interchangeably. While the semantic differences between the three are small in most circumstances, it is helpful to understand the different meanings.

Measure

Measures are quantifiable figures derived from a product, a process, or a resource. By definition, measures are quantitative, and in the software development industry they can be applied to products, projects, and processes. Measures should be documented and often are substantiated with estimated, planned, and actual values. Examples of measures include start and end dates, size, effort, and defects. Measures are also called *absolute measures* because they can be taken directly from data without requiring calculations.

> **Measure** The number or category assigned to an attribute of an entity by making a measurement [ISO 14598].

A measure is basically a value that is quantified against a standard at a point in time. For example, if we were to calculate store sales for January 2013, the standard would be the dollar and the total sales for January 2013 would be the measure. A single measure usually has little value without some context. How do we know if $25,000 in sales for that month is good or bad?

Metric

Metrics are used to evaluate products and/or processes, and they enable a quantitative comparison with other products and processes. They typically facilitate a common denominator type of comparison between two or more observed measures. Metrics are most often calculated from (basic) measures or their combinations and are typically compared with a baseline or an expected result. Metrics should deliver *orientation support*, that is, direction for planning and management of the key processes in an organization.

Suppose we track monthly sales over a 13-month period between January 2012 and January 2013. Now, we have some context to see if our January 2013 sales are trending up or down. A metric is the degree to which a particular subject possesses the quality that is being measured. It is based upon two or more measures. Total Monthly Sales is our metric.

> **Metric** A measurement scale and the method used for measurement [ISO 14598].

Indicator

Indicators compare a metric to a baseline or to an anticipated result. Indicators are collected over a time period to derive trends—often they can serve as early warning indicators. An indicator often consists of a measured variable, a goal (expected by historic experience, industrial average, or best practice), and an analysis technique, allowing a comparison between measurement and goal. It is the comparison between the measurement and the goal that permits one to recognize if some action has to be performed.

> **Indicator** A measure that can be used to estimate or predict another measure [ISO 14598].

In our example, the metric Total Monthly Sales gives us more context and understanding of the relationship between measures. However, the fact that the sales are trending up may not give us the complete perspective of how this store is performing. If we measure the store's sales against a baseline such as budgeted sales, then we get a truer indicator of performance. Total Monthly Sales to Budget can also be used as an indicator. This provides us with actionable information that we use to drive our business.

Standard Test Performance Indicators and Metrics

Measurement, in the context of test performance improvement, is the continuous process of defining, collecting, and analyzing data on clearly defined—quantifiable—attributes of test performance. These measurements indicate what the results are of the activities that are defined in previous steps to improve the test process. In other words, test performance indicators quantify the effects of the test performance improvement program.

A number of performance indicators can be used in almost every test improvement program. These commonly used performance indicators are based upon metrics on product quality, test effectiveness, lead-time, predictability, efficiency/cost, and test maturity. Note that for all metrics that are discussed hereafter it is important when measuring number of defects to make a distinction between the various priority levels of the defects found.

4.4.1 Test Effectiveness Metrics

Note that the metrics discussed under this heading provide information for the manufacturing view of quality as was discussed in Chapter 2.

Defect Detection Percentage (DDP)

The first indicator that can be used in almost any test improvement process, and is highly recommended by most test experts, is the Defect Detection Percentage (DDP). If you've found most (if not all) of the important Defects During Testing, and users/customers found few during real-life usage, your testing is good. Defect detection percentage is defined as the proportion of all the defects known that were actually found by testing. The DDP can be calculated per test stage (e.g., integration, alpha testing, beta testing) or for the all test stages together. DDP is a calculable metric used after a project is finished and users/customers have had some time to find the residual defects on a system.

Figure 4–18 shows the defects found during testing (the white area) and the defects found in a period after release (grey area). This period typically covers the first six months of real-life usage. Undetected defects (the black area in the graph) can of course not be taken into account, but they can be detected by the customer.

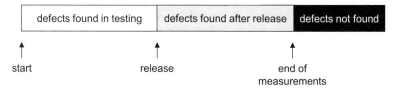

Figure 4–18 *DDP basics*

Three commonly used performance indicators are based on the defects found during alpha testing, during beta testing, and in the first three or six months after release. Finding defects six months after release will make the performance indicator (slightly) more reliable; three months will allow for more rapid feedback.

$$DDP\_alpha = \frac{\text{Defects found during alpha testing}}{\text{Defects found during \{alpha testing + beta testing + first 6 months after release\}}} * 100\%$$

$$DDP\_beta = \frac{\text{Defects found during beta testing}}{\text{Defects found during \{beta testing + first 6 months after release\}}} * 100\%$$

> **Defect Detection Percentage (DDP)**
> The number of defects found by a test phase divided by the number found by that test phase and any other means afterward.

Post-Release Defect Rate

This performance indicator is defined as the number of defects found by customers during a certain period after release of the product per kilo lines of code

(KLOC). If this rate decreases, then the customers' perceived quality will increase.

$$\text{Post-release defect rate} = \frac{\text{Number of defects reported post release}}{\text{Size (KLOC)}}$$

4.4.2 Test Efficiency / Cost Metrics

Cost of Quality Ratio

The cost of quality ratio is the ratio of "total effort spent on static testing (e.g., inspections and reviews)" and "total effort spent on dynamic testing (e.g., unit, integration, system test)." If this ratio increases, then the efficiency of the defect removal process will increase.

$$\text{Cost of quality ratio} = \frac{\text{Total effort spent on static testing}}{\text{Total effort spent on dynamic testing}}$$

Early Defect Detection

As stated, the efficiency of the defect removal process will increase if defects are found earlier in the process. Not only is this applicable for static versus dynamic testing, but also for unit and integration versus system and acceptance testing. The performance indicator "early defect detection" measures the total number of defects found during unit and integration testing (early dynamic testing) versus the total number of defects found during dynamic testing.

$$\text{Early defect detection} = \frac{\text{Total number of defects found during unit and integration testing}}{\text{Total number of defects found during dynamic testing}} \times 100\%$$

Relative Test Effort

A basic performance indicator is the ratio of the total test effort (or cost) versus the total project effort (or cost) prerelease. Post-release effort spent on activities such as maintenance and after-sales support is not taken into account.

$$\text{Relative test effort} = \frac{\text{Total effort spent on testing}}{\text{Total effort spent on project}} \times 100\%$$

Test Efficiency

This performance indicator is based on the number of defects found and the effort spent (per test phase). It provides support in determining if the test effort is focused on finding defects; in other words, is testing done efficiently? It is important to take only high-priority defects into account when calculating this performance indicator. Also, defects that are rejected because the tester incorrectly marked them as a defect must not be taken into account.

$$\text{Test efficiency} = \frac{\text{Number of defects found}}{\text{Test effort}}$$

Automation Level

The automation level is the ratio of the number of test cases that are executed automatically (e.g., using record and playback tools) to the total number of test cases executed (both manually and automatically).

$$\text{Automation level} = \frac{\text{Number of test cases executed automatically}}{\text{Total number of test cases executed}} \times 100\%$$

Test Productivity

This is the total number of test cases (or test design) for the product related to the total test effort required. Of course, this performance indicator can also be measured per test phase.

$$\text{Test productivity} = \frac{\text{Number of test cases}}{\text{Test effort}}$$

4.4.3 Lead-Time Metrics

Test Execution Lead Time

The lead time of testing is especially important during test execution because during test execution, testing is on the critical path of the project. Lead time is defined as the period (in days or weeks) between two milestones that identify the start and end of one or more test phases. The test execution lead-time performance indicator to test the product should of course be related to the size of the product. This performance indicator can be measured per test phase (e.g., alpha or beta).

$$\text{Test execution lead time} = \frac{\text{Lead-time test execution (in days)}}{\text{Product size (e.g., KLOC or number of requirements)}}$$

4.4.4 Predictability Metrics

Test Execution Lead-Time Slippage

This is the difference between the actual and estimated test execution lead time required for one or more test phases related to the estimated test execution lead time.

$$\text{Test execution lead time slip} = \frac{\text{Actual test execution lead time} - \text{Estimated test lead time}}{\text{Estimated test execution lead time}} \times 100\%$$

For project control and improvement purposes, it is often interesting to measure test lead time slippage against the estimation made at the beginning of the project and against the estimation made at the beginning of the test execution phase.

Effort Slip (or Cost)

This metric is the difference between the actual and estimated effort (or cost) required for one or more test phases related to the estimated effort (or cost).

$$\text{Effort slip} = \frac{\text{Actual effort} - \text{estimated effort}}{\text{Estimated effort}} \times 100\%$$

Test Case Slip

This is the difference between the actual and estimated number of test cases (or test designs) required for one or more test phases related to the estimated number of test cases (or test designs).

$$\text{Test case slip} = \frac{\text{Actual number of test cases} - \text{estimated number of test cases}}{\text{Estimated number of test cases}} \times 100\%$$

4.4.5 Product Quality Metrics

Metrics for Quality Attributes

A number of attributes are available with which product quality can be described (e.g., functionality, reliability, usability, efficiency, maintainability, portability). These are documented in the ISO 9126 standard [ISO 9126] and its successor, ISO 25000 [ISO 25000]. The attributes and the indicators associated with them are described in the ISTQB Advanced Level syllabus. For example, indicators associated with the software quality attribute reliability may take the form of mean time between failures (MTBF) and mean time to repair (MTTR).

The test process is one of the primary sources of information for measuring these software quality attributes. The capability of the test process to deliver meaningful and relevant product quality information may be considered an area for potential test process improvement.

Mean Time Between Failures (MTBF)

This is the number of post-release failures (defects) found during a defined period related to the duration of that period, e.g., six months.

$$\text{MTBF} = \frac{\text{Duration period (in weeks or days)}}{\text{Number of failures reported post-release during defined period}}$$

Table 4–4 shows a real-life example of metrics for quality attributes that were used during the testing of copier/printer software [van Veenendaal 2010].

Table 4–4 *Example of product quality metrics*

Quality characteristic	Sub-characteristic	Metric	Explanation
Functionality	Suitability	Functional implementation completeness: Number of missing functions detected during system testing / Number of functions described in requirement specifications.	How many functions have been implemented in relation to the number of functions specified in the requirement specifications?
		Functional implementation correctness: Number of correctly implemented functions confirmed during system testing / Number of functions described in requirement specifications.	What is the amount of functions that have been implemented according to the requirement specifications?
Reliability	Maturity	Mean copies between failures: Total number of copies during system testing / Number of defects, caused by controller software, detected during operation time.	How frequent are the defects of the controller software in operation?
		Defect detection: Absolute number of defects detected during all test phases / Number of estimated defects to be detected. Measured for each release.	What's the proportion of the defects found?

Quality characteristic	Sub-characteristic	Metric	Explanation
		Test completeness: Number of actually executed test cases / Number of test cases to be executed.	How reliable is the test process for product quality statements?
Maintainability	Analyzability	Availability of design documentation: Available design documentation (i.e., SW architecture, top-level design, analysis views, design views, and interface specifications) / Identified design documentation.	What's the proportion of design documentation available?
		Inspected design documentation: Inspected design documentation / Available design documentation.	How reliable and correct is the content of design documentation?
Functionality	Suitability	Functional implementation completeness: Number of missing functions detected during system testing / Number of functions described in requirement specifications.	How many functions have been implemented in relation to the number of functions specified in the requirement specifications?
		Functional implementation correctness: Number of correctly implemented functions confirmed during system testing / Number of functions described in requirement specifications.	What is the amount of functions that have been implemented according to the requirement specifications?

Coverage Indicators

The coverage of requirements and code achieved by testing may be used as indicators of product quality (assuming that higher product quality is related to higher coverage levels) during testing.

Requirements Coverage

Both requirements coverage and code coverage (see the next section) are indirect measures. This means that they do not directly relate to better or improved product quality but are indicators that higher product quality is very likely since more has been covered during testing. Requirements coverage is defined as the number of requirements tested compared to the total number of requirements that have been defined. Note that this performance indicator can be further refined, making a distinction between the number of requirements tested and the number of requirements tested and passed. Test management tools can be used to support the implementation of this performance indicator. If coverage levels increase, testing is becoming better and it is expected that product quality will also increase.

$$\text{Requirements coverage} = \frac{\text{Number of requirements tested}}{\text{Total number of requirements defined}} \times 100\%$$

Code Coverage

Code coverage is defined as the percentage of the total software code that is executed during testing. Various levels of code coverage exist, such as statement coverage, decision coverage, and condition coverage. Numerous tools are available to support code coverage measurements.

$$\text{Statement coverage} = \frac{\text{Software statements executed}}{\text{Total number of software statements}} \times 100\%$$

A statement is defined as an entity in a programming language that is typically the smallest indivisible unit of execution.

4.4.6 Test Maturity Metrics

Test Maturity

This is an organization's test maturity level in terms of the Test Maturity Model integration (TMMi) or the TPI NEXT model. It is assumed that when the maturity increases, the risk of not satisfying the project's test objectives regarding quality, lead time, and costs will decrease.

Please note that these metrics address the manufacturing, product, and value quality views described in chapter 2 but are not direct measures of the user's view of quality. Test managers may therefore want to measure user quality by taking specific measures of user/customer satisfaction, by measuring usability characteristics (especially relating to task efficiency and effectiveness), or by using qualitative measures of stakeholder views.

4.5 Exercises

The following multiple-choice questions will give you some feedback on your understanding of this chapter. Appendix F lists the answers.

4-1: Which of the following would you *not* select for causal analysis ?

　A: An incident reported by a user to the help desk

　B: A low level of planned test coverage

　C: Low levels of defect detection

　D: An issue raised by the project leader

4-2　What best describes the Pareto Principle?

　A: A large majority of problems are produced by a few key causes.

　B: The most significant problems arise from a few key causes.

　C: Analyzing a small sample of problems will lead to the principal causes.

　D: Most defects come from making a small number of errors.

4-3　Which of the following statements does *not* apply to Ishikawa diagrams?

　A: The backbone shows the main path to the defect.

　B: Standard categories can be used.

　C: Each possible cause is shown as a fishbone with an arrow symbol.

　D: The finer bones are less important than the major bones.

4-4　Which of the following statements applies to systems analysis?

　A: Systems with reinforcing feedback loops exhibit stable characteristics.

　B: A vicious circle is a positive reinforcing loop.

　C: A system that contains balancing feedback loops will reduce any difference between a current and a desired system state until a balanced state is achieved.

　D: A virtuous circle is a positive reinforcing loop.

4-5 Which of the following steps would not be performed when using formal reviews for causal analysis?

A: Defect selection

B: Analysis of specific defects

C: Alignment of analysis to business objectives

D: Analysis of generic defects

4-6 Which of the following statements regarding causal analysis would you agree with?

A: It is better to say, "I don't know" than guess.

B: For each problem, a cause can be shown, and that cause and problem are directly related to one another.

C: Spontaneous "gut feelings" based on experience are more likely to find root causes than ideas incubated over a period of time.

D: Members of the group with strong analytical skills are generally able to communicate ideas most effectively.

4-7 Which of the following statement is not true with respect to the GQM paradigm?

A: Implicit models give valuable input to the measurement program.

B: Measured data will be analyzed to identify whether the goals are attained.

C: In GQM, metrics are defined from a top-down perspective.

D: Knowledge acquisition techniques are used to capture the explicit models.

4-8 In a GQM measurement program, the following goal has been set: Evaluate the number of defects per component. What specific name does GQM use for such a goal?

A: Measurement goal

B: Knowledge goal

C: Improvement goal

D: Product quality goal

4-9 What is the purpose of the baseline hypothesis with GQM?

A: It defines the measured properties of the object in the goal.

B: It defines the expectations about the measurements.

C: It defines which factors are expected to have an essential impact on the measured properties.

D: It defines how the variation factors influence the measured properties.

4-10 To which ISO 9126 quality attribute does the product quality metric MTBF relate?

A: Portability

B: Reliability

C: Availability

D: Maintainability

5 Selecting Improvement Approaches

In the two previous chapters, a number of approaches, models, methods, and techniques were introduced for test process improvement. In fact, a very large number are available to choose from. Within these preceding chapters, some comparisons between the various approaches and models were made. This chapter discusses a set of guidelines for selecting the appropriate approach for test process improvement within a project or organization. References will be made to the comparisons and comments made regarding applicability of approaches and models in the previous chapters. Indeed, selecting the appropriate approach is not an easy and straightforward task for a test process improver. However, failure to select the correct approach may imply that the test process improvement project will fail before it has even begun. It is indeed a critical success factor with huge impact. In this chapter, we discuss each of the reasons for applying process models, content models, and analytical approaches and, finally, reasons for applying a mixed (or hybrid) approach. To conclude the chapter, we'll look at how analytical approaches are incorporated into the models we covered in chapter 3.

5.1 Selecting Test Process Improvement Approaches

Syllabus Learning Objectives

LO 5.1.1 (K2) Summarize reasons for best applying a test process improvement approach.

LO 5.1.2 (K5) Recommend a test process improvement approach in a specific scenario and for a given improvement scope.

As stated, this chapter is all about selecting the appropriate test process improvement approach for a project or organization. The guidelines described are provided to support this decision process. In addition to these guidelines, the critical success factors described in chapter 9 will influence the decision for a certain test process improvement approach. The decision about the approach is typically one that is made by a Test Process Group (TPG), steering committee, or other management group (see section 7.1). The test process improver often prepares a document describing recommendations on the approach to be applied as an input for the decision. If the result of the decision taken (i.e., the test process improvement approach) can be generally applied to the organization, it will typically be documented in a quality or test policy.

The guidelines presented in this chapter should by no means be taken as a set of mandatory requirements or unbreakable rules. They are only guidelines and should therefore be combined with knowledge about the specific project or organizational situation and, of course, with common sense.

5.2 Process Models

Reference models in general provide a body of information and best practices that form the core of the model. In the case of process (reference) models, a predefined scale of process maturity is mapped onto the core body of process information. In chapter 3, we discussed the software process improvement models CMMI and ISO/IEC 15504 and test process improvement models TMMi and TPI NEXT. In general, these (test) process models are best applied when the conditions in the following sections are met.

A Test Process Already Exists

With a test process already in place, a test process improvement model is often used to identify strengths and weaknesses. Based on an assessment, test process improvement models typically provide a list of recommendations where the current test process can or should be improved. The test process model is thus used as a process reference. Note that the test process models typically are not only useful for providing recommendations on where improvements can be made, they are often also useful for establishing test processes. To a certain level of detail, most process models also provide sample processes.

Comparisons or Benchmarking is Required Between Similar Projects

Since process models are basically reference process models, they can be used to assess a project. Process models typically provide an assessment framework with checklists and scoring rules. Using this assessment framework, you can assess projects and compare them to each another. This is typically not done to decide which project is more or less mature but much more to profit from mutual learning. If, for instance, one project has a higher level of maturity in test planning than another, the less mature project may benefit from the other project's test planning practices. When you work in this way, internal cross-project learning is stimulated, which is often a highly practical way to establish improvements. An additional benefit is that the level of resistance will typically be low because these practices have been shown to work in your projects.

Compatibility with Software Process Improvement Models is Required

Many development organizations use a software (or system) process improvement model such as CMMI. Launching a totally independent and different test improvement program in such environments is usually not the best option. Most often, especially when a software process improvement program is well established, it is best to not reinvent the wheel. Managers who finally understand what software process improvement is all about like to see how a test process improvement model compares to the model they are familiar with. There are many instances where TMMi was selected as the test improvement model because it is highly compatible with the popular CMMI. When trying to achieve CMMI level 3, many organizations discover that testing is only marginally addressed in the model and end up looking for ways to improve testing while still being compliant to the requirements stated by the process areas Verification and Validation. This is where TMMi is strong; achieving TMMi level 2 will automatically fulfill the requirements for the CMMI process areas Validation and Verification (with the exception of peer reviews).

Company Policy is to Attain a Specific Maturity Level (e.g., TMMi Level 3)

Especially in large multinational organizations, having a meaningful quality or test policy across all development sites and test organizations is difficult to achieve. The concept of a common maturity level to be achieved is very tangible and concrete. Driven by various business objectives, many large organizations have used this concept. An example is Philips Consumer Electronics (nowadays called Philips Lifestyle), where a number of years ago all development sites across the globe were required to be at least CMM or CMMI level 3. This was documented in a company-wide quality policy. If situations like this exist, then a specific project or organization has, of course, no other option than to follow this directive.

A Well-Defined Starting Point with a Predefined Path of Improvement is Desired

This is a very common reason for selecting and using process improvement models. In fact, we believe it is probably the most important reason. Most organizations like process improvement models because they make it easier to do process improvement when, based on an assessment, they can find out where they are and a road map is more or less provided for the next steps to take. The progression from one maturity level to another is an integral feature of process improvement models, which gives them their predefined "prescribed" character that many users like. As an example, the TMap approach [Pol, Teunnissen, and van Veenendaal 2002], being another example of a test content-based model, was initially developed and documented in a book of over 500 pages. Many testers liked it, classes were popular, and over 10,000 copies were sold. However, the main comment the authors received was, "I don't know where to start." TPI [Koomen and Pol 1999] (nowadays superseded by TPI NEXT) was established primarily for this reason, and it supported organizations in prioritizing all these best practices within TMap (now superceded by TMap NEXT). The organizations that were already using TMap were provided with an assessment tool to define a starting point and thereafter a predefined path of improvements (and therefore TMap best practices) to follow. Many organizations that do not use TMap have since adopted TPI NEXT as their process improvement model.

A Measure of Test Maturity is Needed (e.g., for Marketing Purposes)

Although there are other reasons for the need to have a measure of test maturity, the most common one is marketing. There are many organizations who want a maturity "label" for their organization to show to the external world how well they are doing things. Typically, companies that are offering services such as (test) outsourcing are interested in this. However, in practice this has often led to so-called *level scoring*. The content and improvements are not (that) important, but achieving the maturity level with minimum effort is. Therefore, if an organization is advocating a particular CMMI or TMMi maturity, it is always recommended to ask the question, Who has determined their maturity level? This question is especially relevant where a high level has been determined (e.g.,

4 or 5). In general, only when the assessment has been performed by an accredited lead assessor following a formal assessment process can the claim for a certain maturity level be substantiated. Unfortunately, there are many so-called level scoring organizations out there, some of which give process models a bad name. If you need a measure of test process maturity, look for professional and objective support, either from a reputable external source (e.g., a consultant) or an experienced testing services company. Avoid self-assessment for determining your maturity level; it is biased and unreliable.

Process Models are Respected and Accepted in the Organization

This factor can go both ways. We have been in organizations that had bad experiences using models such as CMMI and therefore were reluctant to use a formal test improvement model. A commonly heard comment was, "We do not want another CMMI!" On the contrary, in organizations that were already successfully applying a software process improvement model, introducing a model specifically for testing is often much easier (although the statement "yet another model" is occasionally also heard). Therefore, timing the introduction of a new model is critical. Generally speaking, in organizations where process models are respected and accepted, the introduction of test process improvement models is much easier and often successful.

Once a decision has been made to select a process model (among others, based on the conditions described in this section), the next question that comes to mind is, Which process model should be used? In such circumstances a list of characteristics that a thorough test process improvement model should adhere to is highly useful. Fundamentally, a test process improvement model should provide three essential benefits:

- Clearly show the current status of the test process in a thorough, structured, and understandable manner.
- Help to identify where improvements to that test process should take place.
- Provide guidance on how to progress from the current to the desired state.

Section 3.1.1 describes a number of specific characteristics that can help us understand the aspects of a test process improvement model that can generally be considered as "desirable." The areas are covered under the headings "Model Content," "Model Design," and "Formal Considerations."

Another decision that needs to made is whether to use a generic software process improvement model (that also addresses testing) or a specific test improvement model. Using SPI models can be advantageous if only a relatively high-level consideration of the testing process is desired. If details are important (and they often are), a test process improvement model is more appropriate. A strong mover behind the development of test process improvement models was the low level of testing detail provided by software development models (e.g., CMMI). This was often considered inadequate for thorough and practical test process improvement. However, there may still be reasons for an organization to limit itself to using a software process improvement model also for test process improvement (e.g., using a single model reduces effort for learning the model).

Section 3.2.3 provides a comparison between the leading software process improvement models CMMI and ISO/IEC 15504. Section 3.3.3 provides a comparison between the leading test process improvement models TMMi and TPI NEXT. Both sections may provide support when you're trying to make the decision regarding which improvement model should be used.

5.3 Content Models

In content (reference) models, no concept of different process maturity levels is provided, and they do not prescribe the path to be taken for improving test processes. The principal emphasis is placed on the judgment of the user to decide where the test process is and where it should be improved. In chapter 3, the content-based models CTP and STEP were discussed. In general, these (test) content model are best applied when the conditions in the following sections are met.

A Test Process Needs to be Established

When an organization is immature and does not yet have a test process, it doesn't much benefit from doing an assessment against a process model. The result of the assessment—e.g., "there is no test process"—is already known by the organization. The organization is much better off using a detailed content-based model that will help them to establish a test process. Content-based models will typically provide detailed processes and templates that can be used to define a standard process for the organization (or project).

An Assessment to Identify Costs and Risks Associated with the Current Test Process is Needed

Both CTP and STEP state that metrics are an essential part of their model. Having these metrics in place, and assuming they relate to the costs and benefits of testing, will make it possible to quantify costs and risks associated with the current test process. In practice, however, we have not seen many organizations applying CTP and STEP if they also have a full set of metrics. As a result, when metrics are not available, it may also be beneficial to use a test process model for assessing the current test process. Stating the costs and risks will be difficult in a quantitative way for both types of models if metrics are not available. Most likely the answer will be to state the costs and risks in a qualitative way.

Improvements Need to be Implemented in the Order Determined by Business Needs

Where improvements do not need to be implemented in the order specified by TMMi or TPI NEXT, but rather in the order determined by business needs, a content-based model may be the best choice. However, we believe that the test process models TMMi and TPI Next also have the possibility to be (or even should be) applied in a business-driven way. The criterion may be especially applicable when an analytical approach is used—for example, where GQM is applied, starting from business goals and identifying improvement areas in testing based on metrics. In such situations, a content-based model can be used to look for the solution to the identified test process issues.

Tailoring is Required to Ensure That the Test Process Fits the Company's Specific Context

When using a test process model, this is often perceived as being too strict, leaving the organization with less freedom when it wants to comply with the requirements. Organizations that want to have a higher sense of freedom may prefer to choose a content-based model where they can tailor whatever they want. This may be driven by the organization's culture (e.g., "mavericks who do not like standards"), but it can also be driven by the specific context of the organization. There may be circumstances where the standard test process models such as TPI NEXT and TMMi are very difficult to apply—for example, with process automation or crowd testing.

Discontinuous, Rapid Improvements and Changes to the Existing Test Process are Desired

When there is no long-term commitment or strategy for test process improvement, adopting a road map based on a process model doesn't make much sense. Typically, these types of organizations are looking for quick solutions based on day-to-day problems. For example, if defect management is problematic, the organization will benefit from looking at CTP and studying the best practices on defect management. On this basis, the organization can build a tailored defect management process. Some time later another issue may arise, and again the organization looks for a rapid improvement by considering what content-based models have to offer.

The set of desirable model attributes described section 3.1.1 can of course also be used to evaluate the content-based models. In section 3.4, a comparison is made between the test process improvement models (TMMi and TPI NEXT) and the content reference models (CTP and STEP). This comparison can also be of use during the selection process for a test improvement approach.

5.4 Analytical Approaches

Analytical approaches are used to identify problem areas in test processes and set project-specific improvement goals. Section 4.2 introduced Goal-Question-Metric (GQM) and analysis using measures, metrics, and indicators as analytical approaches. These analytical approaches are best applied when the conditions in the following sections are met.

Specific Problems Need to be Targeted

Causal analysis is a perfect mechanism to target specific problems that keep reoccurring or a major failure that occurred in production. For these types of problems, using a model (either process or content based) is typically not the way to go. Doing a detailed causal analysis, identifying root causes and possibly common causes where multiple problems are at stake, is usually what is needed. The specific problems are often context dependent and this is where analytical approaches are strong; they focus on the specifics of the project or organization.

Measures and Metrics are Available or can be Established and Taken

Sometimes a lot of data is already available—for example, from tools such as defect management, test management, or project management that have been in use for a while. With all this information lying around for free, setting up a measurement program and starting to analyze the available data is an easy way forward. The data can be transformed into measures and analyzed to enable recommendations for (test) process improvement to be established. The measurement program will quickly show results, and based on these initial results, it can grow.

Evidence for the Need of a Test Process is Required

In many organizations, testers are convinced the test process needs to be improved and a test process improvement program is required. Often, however, management doesn't see the need for this and is not ready to give their commitment. In such cases, a small-scale measurement program or causal analysis based on some major problems can be set up. The results from these analytical activities can then be used to gather evidence that a test process improvement program would be beneficial to the organization. Once management has been convinced and is committed, you may convert to a more model-based improvement approach.

Agreement is Needed About the Reasons for Change

This resembles the previous criterion but is different. In this case, management is already convinced that something needs to be done about testing. However, there is discussion about the main business objectives and the problems that are related to them. Where can a test improvement program make a significant contribution, and where is this contribution needed most? To be able to answer these and other questions, an analytical measurement or causal analysis approach can be used. By performing an analysis, the most important reasons for change can be substantiated and agreement between stakeholders can be established. Based on this agreement, test improvement goals can be defined.

The Root Cause of the Problem is not Necessarily Within the Control of the Test Process Owner

There are many problems that we as testers suffer from that we cannot solve ourselves. Examples can be found in the areas of configuration management, requirements management, and project management. Using a test (improvement) model doesn't help to solve these types of problem. Doing causal analysis that shows that the root cause is somewhere other than the test process can help to raise awareness and make the problem area more visible (e.g., that test design rework is often the result of poor requirements management, or many regression tests are needed because of poor configuration management). Of course, such analysis can also be done by means of a measurement program.

A Small-Scale Evaluation or Improvement Pilot is Required/Budgeted For

If there are few resources available for improvements, then using full-blown reference models is often not really helpful. You can focus on only one or two critical issues. That's all there is time for. Using analytical approaches can reveal these one or two critical issues (in terms of both impact and/or frequency of occurrence), and test improvement recommendations can be identified based on the analysis. The highly focused effort with limited resources can subsequently address the identified recommendation, after which the test improvement program stops (at least for a while).

A Pilot is Required to See Whether a Larger-Scale Investigation is Needed

This resembles strongly the criterion "Evidence for the need of a test process is required" mentioned earlier. Clearly, there is a need to convince management and get their commitment on a test improvement program. A causal analysis could be used to quickly identify a suitable improvement area (one that matters). By doing a pilot on a project and then measuring the results (costs/benefits) of the pilot, you can make a decision with stakeholders on whether a larger-scale investigation or improvement program is needed and can be budgeted for.

There is a Need to Test Hypotheses about the Causes, Symptoms, and Effects of Problems

After having studied the Goal-Question-Metric (GQM) approach in the previous chapter (see section 4.3), it should be clear to you that analysis is one of the essential steps with the GQM approach. Abstraction sheets can be used to define a baseline hypothesis and identify variation factors and their impact on the baseline hypothesis. So, when there is a need to test hypotheses and gather evidence about the causes, symptoms, and effects of problems and of proposed improvements, clearly an analytical approach (e.g., GQM) is the way to go.

The Organizational Culture Values/Trusts Internally Developed Analysis Based on Local Evidence

This is a selection criterion that is hard to argue with. Sometimes it all depends on the organizational culture as to what is "possible" and what can be used. If there is a large "not invented here" syndrome, then one may face huge difficulties in introducing an external model. Despite taking change management into account, it sometimes just doesn't work due to the organizational culture. The organizational culture values and trusts internally developed analysis based on local evidence more than externally built models (reference or content). Section 9.2 discusses issues concerning improvement culture in more detail.

Stakeholders from Many Areas are to be Involved Personally in the Analysis

When the context of testing involves many different stakeholders, which is often the case in situations such as testing a system-of-systems, testing multidisciplinary systems, having multiple (possibly remote) development groups, and testing safety-critical systems, then the analysis of testing issues often needs the involvement of many stakeholders (at least initially). In such complex situations, models are often an abstraction of reality that is too simple. Therefore, in addition to these models, brainstorming sessions and other techniques need to be used in a test improvement program. Different stakeholders representing many areas within (or even outside) the organization need to be involved in the analysis, making it appropriate to (also) use analytical approaches.

The Team has Control of the Analysis

Having control but also having the resources, knowledge, and skills to perform an analysis is another reason to choose an analytical approach. Clearly, this is almost like a precondition for being able to select and use analytical approaches. Having control means testing has the authority to organize causal analysis sessions (assuming this is accepted by stakeholders) and has access to the measurement database needed to perform data analysis. From chapter 4 you can see that performing causal analysis and executing a measurement program are not straightforward tasks. Both require specific knowledge and skills, and the possession of these skills is needed by testing to be able to use analytical approaches effectively and efficiently.

5.5 Mixed Approaches

Most widely used test improvement models are used with a top-down approach. However, it is also recommended to apply bottom-up, analytical-based approaches. Top-down approaches have proven to be valuable in establishing improvements. They provide the means to set up a solid test engineering working environment and to establish product quality targets. Experiences in practice have shown significant benefits of this approach. However, organizations also need to apply a bottom-up approach, such as causal analysis of day-to-day problems and the gathering and analysis of process and product metrics. By setting up a measurement-based approach in their organizations, testing will become better understood. Remember, knowledge is an important basis for improvement. The models can be used to define the strategic vision for the next year(s) and provide long-term improvement goals. Bottom-up analytical approaches may well be used to identify some critical issues that need to be solved today rather than tomorrow and thus provide short-term improvement goals.

In practice, we almost never find just a model-based, content-based, or analytical approach being applied in isolation. It may be the case that one of these approaches is leading, but it will most likely be blended with another one. Therefore, in practice, we often have a mixed approach, even if a process model approach is chosen. Here are a couple of examples of mixed approaches, such as the use of analytical approaches within a process model or content model:

- Usage of causal analysis during a TMMi test improvement program
- Usage of metrics during a STEP test improvement program

More and detailed examples of this are provided in the next section.

5.6 Analytical Approaches and Improvement Models

Applying analytical approaches to achieve test process improvement is considered a valuable practice by all of the models we covered in chapter 3. If you choose to use one of these models, you may be guided to implement analytical measures to achieve improvement, or you may choose to use the model to verify the results of your analysis. In the following sections, we provide some examples of how the models described in chapter 3 are blended with analytical approaches.

5.6.1 Analytical-Based Improvement with CMMI

Software process improvement models, such as CMMI, place considerable emphasis on the ability to perform causal analysis for improving the maturity of the software process. In fact, Causal Analysis and Resolution (CAR) is described in CMMI as a separate process area consisting of the following Specific Goals (SG) and Specific Practices (SP):

Specific Goal SG1: Determine causes of defects
    SP 1.1 Select data for analysis
    SP 1.2 Analyze causes

Specific Goal SG2: Address causes of defects
    SP 2.1 Implement the action proposals
    SP 2.2 Evaluate the effect of changes
    SP 2.3 Record data

Also, measurement is an important aspect in all software process improvement models. CMMI has a dedicated process area on measurement within the Support category. This process area, called Measurement and Analysis, consists of the following Specific Goals (SG) and Specific Practices (SP):

Specific Goal SG1: Align measurement and analysis activities
    SP 1.1 Establish measurement objectives
    SP 1.2 Specify measures
    SP 1.3 Specify data collection and storage procedure
    SP 1.4 Specify analysis procedures

Specific Goal SG2: Provide measurement results
    SP 2.1 Collect measurement data
    SP 2.2 Analyze measurement data
    SP 2.3 Store data and results
    SP 2.4 Communicate results

In addition to the process area Measurement and Analysis, CMMI defines the Generic Practice "Collect Improvement Information" (GP3.2). Being a generic practice, this must be applied by each process area and deals with collecting measures, measurement results, and improvement information derived from planning and performing the specific process to support future use and improvement of the organization's process and process assets.

5.6.2 Analytical-Based Improvement with TPI NEXT

The TPI NEXT model considers some aspects of causal analysis at both the "efficient" and "optimizing" levels of test process maturity. Table 5–1 shows the three checkpoints to be achieved that relate to causal analysis.

Table 5–1 *Causal analysis checkpoints TPI NEXT*

Maturity level	Key area	Checkpoint number	Checkpoint description
Efficient	Degree of Involvement	02.e.2	Testers contribute to the impact analysis of defects.
Efficient	Defect management	10.e.4	Trends are identified. For this, more information is recorded about a defect, the subsystem, priority, program and version, test basis and version, root cause, all status transitions, and problem solver.
Optimizing	Defect management	10.o.3	Defects are analyzed for common properties and recommendations are made to avoid future defects.

TPI NEXT has a dedicated key area for metrics; especially at the efficient and optimizing levels, the metrics are used for the purpose of improving the (testing) process. TPI NEXT also provides some examples of metrics typically used at the "efficient" and "optimizing" levels. Table 5–2 shows some of the metrics proposed by the TPI NEXT process model.

Table 5–2 *Example Metrics TPI NEXT*

Maturity level	Measure	Metric	Checkpoint description
Efficient	Test basis stability	Number of added, updated, and removed test cases	The test process efficiency benefits if test case design can be done "first time right" due to stable test basis in sufficient quality.
Efficient	(Re)test	Number of tests and retests	Indicates how many (re)tests are necessary in order to test an object.
Optimizing	Test design effort	Average time spent on designing a test case	This metric over the course of several test projects helps to optimize resource estimation.
Optimizing	Waiting time per cause	Idle time / working hours in "standstill" as a percentage of the total test hours	Shows where measures should be taken to eliminate future obstruction of the test process.

5.6.3 Analytical-Based Improvement with TMMi

TMMi considers causal analysis as part of process maturity level 5, "optimizing." At this highest level of test process maturity, TMMi defines the process area Defect Prevention (PA 5.1) and two Specific Goals, one of which (SG1) fully covers the determination of root and common causes of defects. The specific goal is achieved by performing the following three specific practices:

SP1.1   Define defect selection parameters and defect classification scheme
SP1.2   Select defects for analysis
SP1.3   Analyze causes of selected defects

TMMi has many instances where it addresses measurement practices. It has a dedicated process area called Test Measurement that has the same specific goals and specific practices as the CMMI process area Measurement and Analysis. However, note that its subpractices are most often different. Within this process area TMMi provides many examples of commonly used test metrics. In addition, TMMi also has the same Generic Practice Collect Improvement Information (GP3.2) as the CMMI.

However, TMMi also has a process area called Advanced Reviews where peer review measurement results are used to adjust the test approach. Finally, already at TMMi level 2, within the process area Test Policy and Strategy, the specific goal "Establish test performance indicators" (SG3) is introduced to establish a set of goal-oriented test process performance indicators to measure the quality of the test process. The specific goal is achieved by performing the following two specific practices:

SP3.1   Define test performance indicators
SP3.2   Deploy test performance indicators

If you look back at the discussion in section 3.1.3 about the differences between continuous and staged representations in test process reference models, you will recall that models using the staged representation can suffer from the "all or nothing" syndrome. If, for example, all but one of the maturity level 2 goals are satisfied, the model still places the test process at maturity level 1. This can result in an unrealistically negative impression of the achieved test process maturity and could demotivate those striving to make improvements. Having a set of test performance indicators in TMMi helps considerably against this "all or nothing" syndrome. Statements like "We worked all year and achieved a lot, but (according to the model) we're still where we started!" may result in frustration in the test improvement team and could lead to incorrect management perceptions ("What? Still at maturity level 1 after all that investment? You promised me improvements!"). Hence, we find here another reason to combine model-based approaches with analytical-based appproaches. The defined and established test performance indicators should provide measurable and tangible results, although possibly still being at the same maturity level. TMMi provides us with the following examples of test performance indicators:

- Test effort and cost
- Test lead time
- Number of defects found
- Defect detection percentage
- Test coverage
- Test maturity level

Refer to section 4.4 for an explanation and definition of these and other test performance indicators.

5.6.4 Analytical-Based Improvement with CTP and STEP

Both CTP and STEP are limited when it comes to causal analysis, as described in chapter 4. There are some elements of causal analysis present in both models, but the core functionality of causal analysis is not really addressed. When one looks at both CTP and STEP (and, in fact, most content-based models), their focus is very much on providing thorough test content for their users and not so much on the improvement process itself. The latter is addressed, but only marginally.

However, both models do emphasize the importance of metrics. The STEP model explicitly identifies measurement as one of the activities within its "measure behavior" phase. However, no specific details are provided on this. CTP describes a number of metrics relevant to the critical testing processes (see table 3–27). These may be applied to improving the test process. In its high-level approach to test process improvement, CTP proposes to do the following:

- Gather detailed metrics on these critical testing processes.
- Recommend improvements based on these metrics and develop an improvement plan.

In summary, one can conclude that content-based models are less blended with analytical improvement approaches than process improvement models such as CMMI, TMMi, and TPI NEXT, partly due to the limited focus of content-based models on the improvement process. The three process improvement models mentioned earlier encompass many of the analytical approaches described in chapter 4.

5.7 Exercises

The following multiple-choice questions will give you some feedback on your understanding of this chapter. Appendix F lists the answers.

5-1 What is considered a valid reason for using a process model to improve testing?

  A: A test process already exists.

  B: A test process needs to be established.

  C: Specific problems need to be targeted.

  D: Evidence for the need of a test process is required.

5-2 What is considered a valid reason for using a content model to improve testing?

  A: Comparisons or benchmarking is required between similar projects.

  B: Compatibility with software process improvement models is required.

  C: Improvements need to be implemented in the order determined by business needs.

  D: Agreement is needed about the reasons for change.

5-3 What is considered a valid reason for using an analytical approach to improve testing?

  A: A measure of test maturity is needed (e.g., for marketing purposes).

  B: Process models are respected and accepted in the organization.

  C: Tailoring is required to ensure that the test process fits the company's specific context.

  D: The root cause of the problem is not necessarily within the control of the test process owner.

5-4 The usage of causal analysis during a TMMi test improvement program is an example of which of the following?

A: Model-based approach

B: Content-based approach

C: Analytical approach

D: Mixed approach

5-5 Which of the following TMMi process areas is *not* also related to an analytical approach ?

A: Test Measurement

B: Advanced Reviews

C: Test Policy and Strategy

D: Defect Prevention

E: None of the above

6 Process for Improvement

The implementation of test process improvements is likely to be more effective if the improvement process itself is supported by a standard description. One such description, the IDEAL process improvement framework, is described in this chapter. We describe the individual IDEAL phases, explain the activities to be performed, and provide an overview of the principal output documents: the assessment plan and the test improvement plan.

6.1 Introduction

Syllabus Learning Objectives

LO 6.1.1 (K2) Summarize the key elements of a test policy.
LO 6.1.2 (K6) Create a test (improvement) policy.

6.1.1 IDEAL Process Improvement Framework

Primarily, the models described in chapter 3 provide a list of best practices and/or a description of a mature test process. They typically do not offer a standard approach to a deployment and improvement program in an organization. To support the implementation of these types of improvement models, the Software Engineering Institute (SEI) has developed a framework model for process improvement: IDEAL [McFeeley 1996].

The IDEAL model has proven to be very useful when implementing both model-based and analytical-based test improvements. IDEAL offers an extensive and practical reference standard for improvement processes and also shows what needs to be done when implementing test process improvements in an organization. The model contains a five-phase improvement cycle as shown in table 6–1.

> **IDEAL** An organizational improvement model that serves as a road map for initiating, planning, and implementing improvement actions. The IDEAL model is named for the five phases it describes: initiating, diagnosing, establishing, acting, and learning.

Table 6-1 The IDEAL five-phase improvement cycle

Acronym	Phase	Goal
I	Initiating	Establishing the initial improvement infrastructure for a successful improvement process
D	Diagnosing	Determining the organization's current state as opposed to what it wants to achieve
E	Establishing	Planning and specifying how the chosen situation will be established
A	Acting	Executing the plan
L	Learning	Learning by experience and improving the abilities to implement changes

In addition to IDEAL, there are several other models for the implementation of process improvement. In general, all of these models are based on Edward Deming's Plan, Do, Check, Act (PDCA) cycle (see section 2.4.1). The Deming cycle starts with making a plan that determines the improvement goals and how they will be achieved (plan). Then the improvements are implemented (do), and it is determined whether the planned advantages have been achieved (check). Based on the results of this assessment, further actions are taken as needed (act).

This chapter is about the phases and activities of IDEAL. The phases of an improvement program in accordance with IDEAL are shown in figure 6-1.

Before we get to each phase of the IDEAL model, the next section describes the need to first establish an overall test policy that also addresses test process improvement. The test policy is basically the driver and starting point for all test improvement activities. The test policy is also a means to create management commitment. Before starting with the test process improvement, you should know why you are doing this, what (business) problems will be addressed, and what the main principles for testing are in your organization.

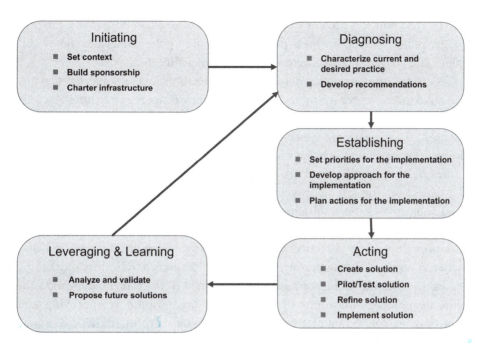

Figure 6–1 *Phases of an improvement program according to IDEAL*

6.1.2 Test Policy

When an organization wants to improve its test process, it should first clearly define a test policy [van Veenendaal and Wells 2012]. There are several questions that should be answered up front by means of a test policy that are relevant to test process improvement:

- What is the problem?
- What are we trying to achieve?
- Why are we doing test process improvement?

The test policy describes the organization's philosophy toward testing (and possibly quality assurance). It is set down either in writing or by management direction and lays out the overall objectives regarding testing that the organization wants to achieve. This policy should be developed in cooperation with stakeholders, such as information technology, research and development, and product development departments. It should reflect the organizational values and goals as they relate to testing.

The test policy is preferably complementary to or a component of a broader quality policy or even business policy. This quality policy describes the overall values and goals of management with regard to quality.

As stated, the test policy defines the organization's overall objectives, goals, and strategic views regarding testing. A test policy is necessary to attain a common view of testing and its objectives between all stakeholders within an organization. This common view is required to align test activities (including process improvement) throughout the organization. The test policy should address testing activities for both new development and maintenance projects.

Objectives for test improvement should be stated within the test policy. These objectives should subsequently be translated into a set of key test performance indicators. The test policy and the accompanying performance indicators provide a clear direction and a means to communicate expected and achieved levels of testing performance. The performance indicators must show the value of testing and test process improvement to the stakeholders and provide quantitative indications of whether the organization is improving and achieving the defined set of test (improvement) goals. Within the TMMi model, the definition of a test policy is even part of the model itself, within the level 2 process area Test Policy and Strategy. By comparison, the TPI NEXT model includes a single checkpoint for whether the test policy is followed.

Modification of the test policy and test strategy is usually required as an organization's test process evolves and moves to a higher maturity level. The test policy may also reference a standard for testing terminology to be used throughout the organization.

Where a written test policy exists, it may be a short, high-level document that accomplishes the following objectives:

- Provides a definition of testing, such as building confidence that the system works as intended and detecting defects
- Lays out a fundamental test process, such as, for example, test planning and control, test analysis and design, test implementation and execution, evaluation of test exit criteria and test reporting, and test closure activities
- Describes how to evaluate the effectiveness and efficiency of testing—for example, by the percentage of defects to be detected (Defect Detection Percentage or DDP) and the relative cost of defects detected in testing as opposed to after release
- Defines desired quality targets, such as reliability (e.g., measured in terms of failure rate) or usability

- Specifies activities for test process improvement, such as, for example, application of the TMMi or TPI NEXT model or implementation of recommendations from project retrospectives

A test policy might typcially include the following elements [van Veenendaal and Wells 2012]:

- A definition of testing
- A definition of debugging (fault localization and repair)
- Basic views regarding testing and the testing profession
- The objectives and added value of testing
- The quality levels to be achieved
- The level of independence of the test organization
- A high-level test process definition
- The key responsibilities of testing
- The organizational approach to and objectives of test process improvement

> **Test policy** A high-level document describing the principles, approach, and major objectives of the organization regarding testing.

An anonymized real-life example of a short one-page test policy is provided in figure 6–2.

228 6 Process for Improvement

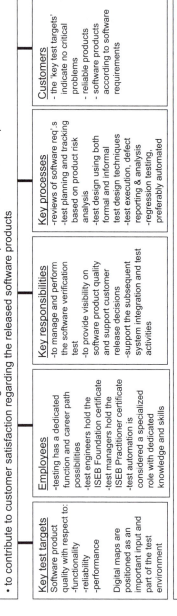

Figure 6-2 Example of a test policy

6.2 Initiating the Improvement Process

Syllabus Learning Objectives

LO 6.2.1 (K2) Summarize the activities of the Initiating phase of the IDEAL improvement framework.

LO 6.2.2 (K4) Analyze business goals (e.g., using corporate dashboards or balanced scorecards) in order to derive appropriate testing goals.

LO 6.2.3 (K6) Create an improvement strategy (including the scope of the test process improvement) for a given scenario.

The IDEAL model starts with the phase called *Initiating*. In the initiating phase, the infrastructure for a successful change program is established. Actions taken at this initial stage directly influence the final results of the improvement process. Poorly initialized improvement processes may deliver unsatisfactory results and significantly reduce the chances of being able to take any future improvement initiatives.

The goals and expected results with respect to the change program and what needs to be contributed by the different parties concerned are defined. The goals of a test improvement implementation need to be in line with the quality goals and the organizational goals. In this phase, the goals cannot always be formulated according to the SMART model (specific, measurable, achievable, realistic, and time-bound), which is why the goals are specified in more detail in the establishing phase.

In this phase, management commitment requires explicit attention; management commitment is needed from test management, IT management, and business management.

At the initiating phase, a number of people-related critical success factors must be considered; these can have an influence on achieving improvement objectives:

- Level of knowledge—for example, people who have a lack of knowledge, for instance of testing issues, may as a consequence be adverse to changes.
- Organizational culture—for example, the organization may not be process-oriented and yet you are trying to define mature test processes.

> **Initiating (IDEAL)** The phase within the IDEAL model where the groundwork is laid for a successful improvement effort. The initiating phase consists of the following activities: set context, build sponsorship, and charter infrastructure.

- People culture—for example, there is culture where people get blamed if a failures occurs, and as a consequence, there may be strong resistance to defining a test measurement program.
- Level of acceptance—for example, an initiative for software process improvement was started a few years ago and failed. As a consequence, people look at this new initiative very skeptically.

Recommendations for test improvement should be sensitive to these people issues and be able to suggest alternative improvement strategies depending on the styles, culture, and needs of the people in the organization.

The initiating phase has the following main activities:

- Identify stimulus for change
- Set objectives for test improvement
- Set context
- Build sponsorship
- Charter infrastructure

Each of these activities is discussed in the following sections.

6.2.1 Identify Stimulus for Change

As a first step in establishing the need for improvement, IDEAL refers to the identification of a "stimulus for change" that generates awareness about the need for process improvement. The stimulus can come from a number of sources:

- Dissatisfaction with the results of current testing (e.g., poor testing efficiency)
- Unexpected incidents (e.g., major failures in production)
- Changing circumstances (e.g., organizational change or changes to quality or test policy)
- Customer demand (e.g., to achieve a formal certification for test maturity)
- Market trends or information taken from an internal measurement repository (e.g., a benchmark result that indicates that achieved levels of quality are too low)

Areas for improvement may be captured and defined based on preliminary analysis and interviews with stakeholders. As part of the analysis it may be necessary to determine current indicators such as the total cost of quality, based on the total cost of failures in production and the total cost of testing.

The proposed change needs to contribute to the success of the organization and needs to complement any existing quality and organizational goals. The extent to which the process change is in accordance with the organization's goals largely determines the success of the change.

6.2.2 Set Objectives for Test Improvement

Clear objectives for test improvement are needed to provide a clear focus and to enable the activities to be reviewed against the objectives. These are a key to success. The objectives of test process improvement must always be established in relation to business values and goals. There are typically three steps for setting objectives for test improvement:

- Establish a general vision for the (improved) future
- Set specific objectives
- Align testing improvement to business goals

The general vision and the objectives for test improvement are typically documented in the organization's test policy (see section 6.1.2).

Establishing a General Vision for the Future

Test process improvement must focus on the (business) benefits required by a sponsoring stakeholder and a vision of the overall objectives to be achieved. Improvement initiatives need such a vision of the future for the following reasons (for example):

- Sponsors need to be convinced of the return on investment before committing resources.
- The management of any necessary changes must relate to agreed-upon objectives. Any improvement action should contribute directly or indirectly to achieving the agreed-upon objectives.

Inability to define a common vision may result in failure of the proposed test improvements (see chapter 9):

- Poorly defined objectives may hide unresolved conflicts of interest.
- We may focus on inappropriate or unachievable objectives that may be a waste of resources and/or fail to deliver improvements.

Although all of this may sound very obvious to the reader, we have come across many organizations that have been attempting to improve the testing process for some time unsuccessfully. Asking the questions "Why?" and "What are the business objectives behind the improvement process?" resulted in total silence. No common objectives were established and agreed upon up front. Only with real management commitment and clear (business) objectives can test process improvement be successful.

Setting Specific Objectives

As stated, specific, well-defined objectives are needed for any test process improvement for the following reasons:

- They enable appropriate actions to be taken.
- The success (or failure) of the improvement efforts can be defined and reported back to management and other stakeholders.
- Commitment can be obtained from management and other stakeholders.

A number of possibilities are available to enable objectives to be represented:

- Quantitative objectives with metrics. For example, the Goal-Question-Metric (GQM) method (see section 4.3) enables metrics to be defined and can be used to link objectives (goals) with measurable results.
- Objectives expressed as maturity levels. If test process improvement is to be conducted using a process model, objectives may also be represented in a form appropriate for the model in question. This typically involves defining specific levels of maturity to be achieved either for the test process as a whole (e.g., managed) or for individual aspects of the test process (e.g., test design). This type of objective is often applied as a marketing vehicle by (test) organizations providing testing services to the market (for example, organizations that perform outsourced testing).
- It is also possible to have qualitative objectives, perhaps supported by appropriate scales (e.g., from "very bad" to "very good" or "getting better" to "getting worse"). However, it is strongly recommended to combine qualitative objectives with quantitative objectives.

Aligning Testing Improvements to the Organization

Test process improvements must never be done in isolation. They must be aligned to the business goals and objectives of any software process improvements being performed and any organizational improvements taking place (see chapter 2).

Corporate dashboards and balanced scorecards can be used by the organization to allow test improvements to be aligned to organizational improvement targets.

Corporate Dashboard

A corporate dashboard is an easy-to-read, often single-page source of information showing graphical presentations of the current status (snapshot) and historical trends of an organization's key performance indicators. They allow managers to monitor the contribution of the various processes and departments in their organization and enable instantaneous and informed decisions to be made at a glance.

Using corporate dashboards provides the following benefits:

- Visual presentation of performance indicators
- Ability to identify and correct negative trends
- Ability to make more informed decisions based on collected data
- Alignment of strategies and organizational goals
- Ability to save time compared to studying multiple reports
- Ability to gain total overall visibility instantly

Figure 6–3 shows an example of a corporate dashboard. Note that it is not intended for the reader to be able to read every detail of this figure but to get a feeling of what a corporate dashboard can look like. Dashboards are rapidly becoming more popular within testing and are used by some test managers to show the status of testing; for example, a one-page dashboard might show status regarding requirements coverage, test progress, defect status, and product quality.

> **Corporate dashboard** A dashboard-style representation of the status of corporate performance data.

234 6 Process for Improvement

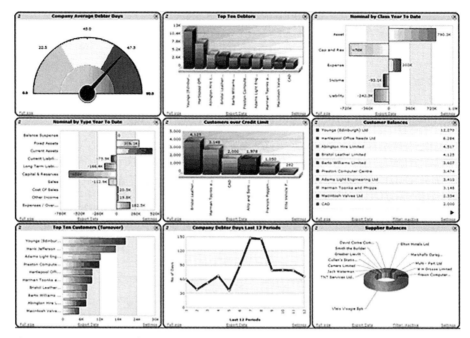

Figure 6-3 Example of a corporate dashboard

Balanced Scorecard

The balanced scorecard is a strategic planning and management instrument that is used extensively to align business activities to the vision and strategy of the organization, improve internal and external communications, and monitor organization performance against strategic goals. It was originated by Drs. Robert Kaplan and David Norton [Kaplan and Norton 1996] as a performance measurement framework that added strategic nonfinancial performance measures to traditional financial metrics to give managers and executives a more "balanced" view of organizational performance. The balanced scorecard has evolved from its early use as a simple performance measurement framework to a full strategic planning and management system.

Recognizing some of the weaknesses and vagueness of most management approaches, the balanced scorecard approach provides a clear indication as to what companies should measure in order to "balance" the financial perspective. The balanced scorecard is a management system (not only a measurement system) that enables organizations to clarify their vision and strategy and translate them into actions. It provides feedback regarding both the internal business

> **Balanced scorecard** A strategic tool for measuring whether the operational activities of a company are aligned with its objectives in terms of business vision and strategy.

processes and external outcomes to continuously improve strategic performance and results.

The balanced scorecard suggests that we view an organization from four perspectives and that we develop metrics, collect data, and analyze it relative to each of these perspectives (see figure 6–4).

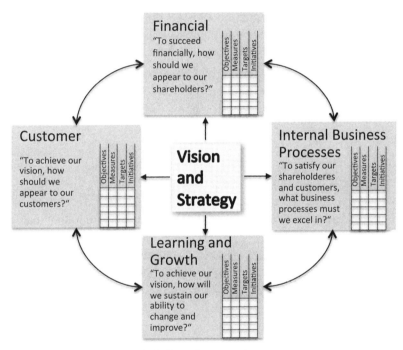

Figure 6–4   *Four perspectives of a balanced scorecard*

- The learning and growth perspective includes employee training and corporate cultural attitudes related to both individual and corporate self-improvement.
- The business process perspective refers to internal business processes. Metrics based on this perspective allow the managers to know how well their business is running and whether its products and services conform to customer requirements (the mission).

- The customer perspective relates to the importance of customer focus and customer satisfaction in any business.
- The financial perspective reflects the traditional need for financial data.

Some examples of aligning business value to test improvements are shown in the following sections. This list provides test and quality topics that can be used as a source of inspiration to integrate testing into a corporate dashboard or balanced scorecard. Note how some of the targets almost explicitly relate to the views of quality introduced in chapter 2.

Learning and Growth

- People targets—for example, job satisfaction, staff turnover, and sickness, which may align to any of the quality views but will also affect the transcendent view of quality (trust, reputation)
- Innovation and improvement targets—increased number of new products to market, speed to market, and process/framework/standards accreditation (e.g., TMMi or industry standard) aligned to the "value" view of quality

Customer

- Customer targets—for example, improved market share, improved customer satisfaction, improved risk management process; also aligned to the user view of quality
- Improved product quality—aligned to the product, manufacturing, and user views of quality
- Social involvement/political targets—for example, environmental impact of the organization, reputation, and publicity, which may align to any of the quality views but will also affect the transcendent view of quality (trust, reputation)

Internal Business Processes

- Internal targets—for example, greater predictability of project outcomes, reduced faults/failures during the software development, reduced project elapsed time, and reduced effort/costs aligned to the manufacturing view of quality

Financial

- Financial targets—for example, productivity improvements, improved revenue, improved profit, improved financial turnover; also aligned to the value view of quality, test productivity, and/or costs of quality

Note how the preceding list is explicitly linked to the four perspectives of the balanced scorecard.

6.2.3 Set Context

The management needs to determine how the change effort fits the quality and business strategy. Which specific organizational goals will be realized or supported by the test improvements? How are current projects influenced by the improvement? Which proceeds need to be yielded—for example, in terms of fewer issues and incidents or the shortening of the lead time for test execution? During the project, the context and effects will become more concrete, but it is important to be as clear as possible early in the project.

Part of setting the context is related to defining the scope of the test process improvement project. This includes obtaining answers to the following questions:

- General process scope: Which processes other than the test process are in scope?
- Test process scope: Which parts of the test process need to be addressed?
- Test levels: Which test levels are within the scope of the improvement program?
- Project scope: Are project(s) or the organization in scope?

6.2.4 Build Sponsorship

Gaining support from the responsible managers, or building sponsorship, is extremely important in improvement projects. This involves test management, IT management, and business management sponsorship because all these stakeholders will be influenced by the change.

Sponsorship is important during the entire project, but because of the insecurity caused by changes, active support at the beginning of the project is especially important. Providing support for the improvement program is a major part of sponsorship, but sponsorship also includes, for example, providing active participation or promoting the project when there is resistance. During this activity, stakeholders are presented with the results from the previous step of the improvement process; for example, the objectives for test improvement and test policy and their commitment to these results needs to be obtained. Without their commitment, the improvement project will fail in the short or medium term.

6.2.5 Charter Infrastructure

As a final activity in the initiating phase, the way in which an improvement project is executed is determined. An organizational infrastructure such as a Test Process Group is put in place, and it must be described explicitly, including responsibilities and qualifications.

Usually the infrastructure consists of a project board guiding several improvement teams. In the project board are the sponsor, possibly the other sponsors of other improvement projects, the manager of the improvement program, and possibly an external consultant. In addition, there is often an (external) test expert. The project board is ultimately responsible for the improvement program and agrees on plans, milestones, and final results. It has the ultimate power to decide and is the highest level of escalation.

Organizational issues are described in further detail in section 7.2.

6.3 Diagnosing the Current Situation

Syllabus Learning Objectives

LO 6.3.1 (K2) Summarize the activities of the Diagnosing phase of the IDEAL improvement framework.

LO 6.3.2 (K6) Plan and perform assessment interviews using a particular process or content model in which an awareness of interview style and interpersonal skills are demonstrated.

LO 6.3.3 (K6) Create and present a summary of the conclusions (based on an analysis of the findings) and findings from an assessment.

LO 6.3.4 (K2) Summarize the approach to solution analysis.

LO 6.3.5 (K5) Recommend test process improvement actions on the basis of assessment results and the analysis performed.

6.3 Diagnosing the Current Situation

> **Diagnosing (IDEAL):** The phase within the IDEAL model where it is determined where one is, relative to where one wants to be. The diagnosing phase consists of the following activities: characterize current and desired states and develop recommendations.

High Level Overview

In the *Diagnosing* phase it is determined where the organization stands as opposed to what it wants to achieve. The current state of the organization is determined and its desired future state is clearly formulated.

The diagnosing phase consists of the following main activities:

- Characterize the current and desired states
- Develop recommendations

At the end of the diagnosing phase, a test assessment report is available.

Characterize Current and Desired States

The activities performed depend largely on whether the approach to be taken to test process improvement is model-based (chapter 3) or analytical (chapter 4).

If a model-based approach is to be used, then an assessment will be planned and performed in which measurements are compared to a reference standard such as, for example, TMMi level 2. A test process improvement model can be used to define the desired state.

An assessment, either formal or informal, is conducted to determine the current state. The proposed practices of a test improvement model may be used as a checklist to determine the maturity of the test processes. The desired state must align with the stimulus for change as determined in the initiating phase and it must be within the realm of possibility for the organization.

If an analytical-based approach is to be adopted, the various causal analysis techniques described in chapter 4 may be applied and metrics, measures, and indicators analyzed. Refer to section 6.3.5 for more information about analyzing results.

> **Process assessment** A disciplined evaluation of an organization's software processes against a reference model [After ISO/IEC 15504].

Develop Recommendations

The recommendations suggest a way of proceeding in subsequent activities. Which test processes are addressed first? Which part of a test process is to be addressed and in what way? The recommendations may be formulated under the guidance of (internal or external) test experts in the specific process area, and they are typically formulated in a test assessment report.

Detailed Tasks

The Expert Level syllabus breaks down the principal activities defined in IDEAL into the following tasks:

- Planning the assessment
- Preparing for the assessment
- Performing interviews
- Giving feedback
- Analyzing results
- Performing solution analysis
- Recommending improvement actions

A detailed description of these individual tasks is given in the following sections.

6.3.1 Planning the Assessment

The purpose of the planning phase is to come to an agreement with the sponsor about scope, costs, activities to be carried out, timeline, planned feedback sessions, and reports. The planning is executed using the assessment request (the documented or undocumented request to conduct an assessment) and discussions between the client and the (intended) assessor.

Prior to its initiation, a plan for the assessment is formulated. This plan is distributed to all key stakeholders, among which are the assessment sponsor and the assessment team.

There are three main inputs to the assessment plan, as follows:

1. The purpose of the assessment—for example, determining if a particular TMMi level has been attained, determining the defects in certain process areas, or identifying recommendations for optimizing the test process
2. The scope of the assessment—defines how wide-ranging the assessment is, including organizational elements, process areas, and projects that will be covered

3. The constraints—for example, availability of key resources, the maximum duration of the assessment, specific organizational areas to be excluded from the assessment, and any confidentiality agreements that need to be taken into account

The assessment plan identifies the activities, resources, schedules, and responsibilities and includes a description of the intended assessment outputs. If the assessment is not intended to include all aspects of the test process, the planning identifies which aspects are to be covered and in which sequence. It should also explicitly state which aspects are not covered.

If the TMMi model is used, a decision needs to be made about whether a formal or an informal assessment is required. A formal assessment has enough depth to officially determine to what extent an organization meets the requirements as defined in the model.

An informal assessment does not lead to an official result about the process maturity; it provides only an indication. An informal assessment is often used to identify the major improvements that need to be made, and it can also be used to determine the progress of an improvement implementation. This form of assessment is often adequate as an initial survey.

The roles and responsibilities for performing assessments are described in section 7.2.

6.3.2 Assessment Preparation

The purpose of the preparation phase is to prepare everything needed to conduct the assessment and to make a detailed schedule for the (optional) kick-off meeting, interviews, progress reports, feedback sessions, presentation, and report. Depending on the scope and size of the assessment, the detailed schedule may already have been defined in the planning phase.

During this phase a document study is conducted, the purpose of which is as follows:

- To gain insights into the current testing process prior to interviewing those involved.
- To prepare particular questions for the interview.
- To perform formal elements of the assessment that do not require discussion. For example, the documents may be checked to ensure completeness and conformity to standards.

The document study starts with providing the organization with a checklist, in which the required test documentation can be found. Typical documents for an assessment of the organization include test policy and test strategy. For project assessments, the test plans, test specifications, defect reports, and test reports are in focus.

When the assessor has been provided with this documentation, the document study can be started to gain initial information about the current situation within the organization. The findings are documented in the initial version of the assessment report. It is important that when the findings are documented, their source is also recorded, so the results of the assessment can be verified.

Part of the assessment preparation includes ensuring that a suitable environment exists for conducting the planned interviews. Interview participants will not be able to freely give information if they are not comfortable, if there are constant disturbances, or if confidentiality cannot be guaranteed. A self-contained, quiet room away from the interviewee's own working area is generally acceptable.

6.3.3 Performing Interviews

The purpose of the interview phase is to collect information about the current test practices. The following activities need to be executed:

- Conducting interviews as a means to gather and verify information
- Performing a preliminary result analysis, which can lead to additional questions in successive interviews or even to the planning of additional interviews

Interviews are performed according to the assessment plan, and the content is generally guided by the model being used.

Interviews are mostly conducted on an individual basis to allow the interviewee freedom to express views and to ensure that a "secure" environment exists. The interviewer should always discuss the importance of confidentiality for interviewees and information providers prior to an assessment taking place, particularly if sensitive issues are likely to arise.

It may be tempting to conduct group discussions instead of individual interviews. Even though this might save time, the quality of the information received may suffer from group dynamics. Individuals react differently to group discussions depending on their personality types; some may dominate discussions with their own opinions and others may feel reluctant to contribute. These effects should not be allowed to influence information gathered in the assessment.

A wide range of skills are required for a successful interview. These are described in more detail in section 7.3.1.

6.3.4 Giving Feedback

At the end of the interviews an initial feedback may be given. This is particularly helpful in confirming initial assessment findings with the interviewee and for clarifying any misunderstandings.

The initial feedback may also take place based on several interviews and to a larger audience. It will then typically provide an overview of main points to stakeholders and may be an important opportunity to manage their expectations regarding final results and recommendations. Care should be taken to maintain the rules of confidentiality at all times and to avoid assigning blame for any problems identified.

6.3.5 Analyzing Results

The analysis of results is conducted according to the overall approach adopted to test process improvement.

If a model-based approach is adopted, the assessment results are compared to the model. When a process model such as TMMi or TPI NEXT is used, the assessment results are evaluated against the conditions (e.g., specific practices or checkpoints) for achieving a given process maturity level described in the model. When a content model such as CTP is used, results are compared against the practices recommended by the model. The latter will be expert-based because no clear set of conditions is defined by the content-based models.

If an analytical-based approach to test process improvement is adopted, the analysis of results is one of the principal activities performed and the techniques described in chapter 4 are applied:

- Analysis of metrics.
  For example, if Defect Detection Percentage (DDP) is being applied as an indicator and has fallen below the required level, a causal analysis of failures found in production should be performed.
- Analysis of interactions between different process components using systems thinking [Weinberg 1992].
  For example, the results of interviews with a test manager may show that there is frustration about stakeholders not reading the test status reports they create. The reports have therefore become increasingly poor quality

with many items missing. Interviews with the stakeholders indicate that the reports started off much too lengthy and are not directed at their actual information needs. At meetings with the test manager, stakeholders showed little interest for issues raised in the reports by the test manager. Using systems thinking, the interactions between the stakeholders and test manager show a negative reinforcing loop (vicious circle), which results in a steady decline in the quality of the test status reports. The worse the reports are, the less they are read by the stakeholders and the less motivated the test manager becomes to write good reports.

- Analysis of tipping points
  Certain aspects of the Tipping Point theory [Gladwell 2000] can help identify specific points in a system where apparently insignificant events may result in the rapid worsening of a situation. In the context of test processes, the failure to maintain a master test plan, for example, may be considered a tipping point that signals to the entire test team that test documents in general are not usable and a waste of time. The neglect of test documents may spread rapidly throughout the team by word of mouth until no test documentation is created at all. This may be the result observed in assessment interviews. Performing analysis of these results using Tipping Point theory may help expose the cause.
- Analysis of benchmarks
  Some results may need to be compared with "normal" or "standard" benchmarks created by a project, an organization, or a branch of industry. Process models also include a form of benchmark. The analysis provides information about whether the benchmarks (perhaps defined as service-level agreements) are achieved and how far below or above the benchmark the results are.

6.3.6 Performing Solution Analysis

Solution analysis is used to identify potential solutions to problems and then to choose between those solutions. It helps to define concrete and feasible recommendations. The task of solution analysis typically involves a variety of individual activities, and different approaches can be adopted. The following activities are among those that may be included:

- Performing cost-benefit analysis
- Identifying the risks of implementing solutions
- Identifying any constraints or requirements on proposing solutions

6.3 Diagnosing the Current Situation

- Identifying conflicts and dependencies between possible solutions
- Prioritizing the possible solutions according to one or more of the preceding points

A number of approaches may be adopted to performing solution analysis:

- If a model-based approach has been used, solutions may be obtained from the model. If the TPI NEXT model is used, the TPI matrix shows the earliest cluster not achieved, and the checkpoints not achieved in that cluster provide the "solution." Care must be taken when following models in this manner; the "next practice to adopt" proposed by the model may not provide the necessary solution and could even make it worse. Adopting the recommendations suggested by models should not be a substitute for judgment exercised by experienced testing professionals. In general, any recommended solution should be evaluated against the test policy and the stated test improvement objectives. Does this recommendation contribute to achieving these objectives?
- If systems thinking [Weinberg 1992] has been used for the analysis of results, the theory may now also be of assistance in helping to identify solutions. Taking the "vicious circle" example mentioned in section 6.3.5, an analysis of the system may reveal ways to break the negative reinforcing loop. In this case a relatively simple solution may be may proposed by, for example, agreeing with stakeholders about what kind of information they need in test status reports, how often they need the information, and how they would prefer the information to be presented (raw data, graphics, etc.). Using systems thinking is particularly useful if the interrelationships between different parts of a system (e.g., a test process) are complex. There may be different loops within a system, some of them balancing (i.e., stabilizing), some reinforcing (i.e., destabilizing). Either type may be identified as having a good (virtuous) or bad (vicious) impact on the system behavior. Systems thinking helps us to untangle the complexity and understand interactions more clearly. Once this is achieved, solutions can be analyzed more thoroughly and systematically. Performing solution analysis in this manner may result in well-targeted recommendations, but the analysis process also consumes more resources compared to, for example, adopting the solution(s) proposed by a model. This is also one of the benefits of using a model-based approach.
- Tipping Point theory may be particularly useful if solutions are needed that will need to be adopted by a large number of people (e.g., a department or

organization). Considering the "bad documentation" example mentioned in section 6.3.5, we try to identify a solution that may be relatively simple but can trigger wide-ranging improvements. For example, the solution may be to start regularly updating test plans and making this well known. With Tipping Point theory, part of the solution is not just the actual change but the way the message ("from now on, documents are updated and useful") is delivered to the people and becomes rapidly adopted by them. This kind of "viral" adoption doesn't just happen by itself; we need to identify key people who will spread the message to the team and motivate them to adopt the new measures. These are well respected, knowledgeable people who have good connections and like to share information and knowledge. The end result (solution) in this example may be that a whole department sees the benefits of keeping test documents up to date and adopts this not just for test plans but for all required documents. Time is needed to construct solutions developed using Tipping Point theory. Most of this time is devoted to strategic issues rather than the actual "impulse" change.

Sometimes finding a solution does not actually involve analysis as such. Consider the following two "approaches":

- Adoption of preconceived ideas is, unfortunately, commonly practiced. The underlying philosophy behind this approach is "Don't bother me with the details; I've already made my mind up." A typical preconceived solution might be the reorganization of a testing department in order to improve testing. The decision to reorganize is already made (perhaps motivated by factors other than to improve testing), and the results of the test process improvement activities are expected to confirm the preconceived solution. Since a solution analysis stage is not actually carried out, this can initially be a relatively cheap approach. Clearly, the disadvantage is that the preconceived solution may not improve testing and may even make it worse. Depending on the motivation for the preconceived solution, the success of future test process improvement initiatives may be endangered if they are perceived as biased or manipulative.
- Scope for selection of a solution may be limited if specific requirements or constraints have been stated by a customer or stakeholder. If, for example, a tool is proposed as part of a solution, the actual tool selected may be constrained by commercial issues such as licenses or preferences for a particular vendor. Required standards may also impose constraints on the proposed solution. If company standards stipulate, for example, that a par-

ticular test environment may only be located onshore, then test process improvements involving testing infrastructure are constrained by these requirements. The advantage for the solution analysis task is that the scope for proposed solutions is very clearly defined. The disadvantage is that the required improvement could be suboptimal.

Clearly, when solution analysis is performed, a mix of different approaches may be applied to provide a tailored result for the specific project or organization context. The methods described in this section are often applied in the context of a workshop and/or brainstorming session.

6.3.7 Recommending Improvement Actions

At the end of the diagnosing phase, the final activity performed is to give the organization feedback about the assessment findings and recommendations. This is typically performed in two stages.

Preliminary Stage

- The preliminary assessment report and/or presentation are created. The use of a standard template is recommended. (Typical contents are described in the section "The Assessment Report.")
- The assessment results and recommendations are presented to the stakeholders. Depending on the scope of the test improvement, this may be a series of presentations to individual stakeholder groups or a single presentation to all stakeholders.
- Findings and recommendations are validated by the stakeholders. The presenter will require a wide range of skills (see chapter 7) to enable this validation to take place successfully. This is the stage where stakeholders (especially those that were not involved in interviews) are probably hearing findings and recommendations for the first time; these may not always be to their liking! The validation of results and recommendations is not a negotiation; the presenter must keep the focus on ensuring that there are no mistakes or misunderstandings in the preliminary report and on gaining overall recognition that the findings are valid.

Final Stage

- Any agreed-upon corrections from the preliminary stage are implemented.
- The final assessment report is created and issued.

> **Assessment report** A document summarizing the assessment results; e.g., conclusions, recommendations, and findings.

The Assessment Report

An assessment report typically contains the following items:

- A management summary, including scope and objectives
- Planning details
- The time period in which the assessment was conducted
- Names and roles of people interviewed
- Subjects covered in the interviews
- Name of interviewers
- Location of interviews
- An overview of the method that was used to conduct the assessment.
- A list of inputs (documents, interview reports) that were used for the assessment
- The findings ("the evidence") that were collected during the document study and the interviews
- Results of the analysis (the assessment conclusions), which should address both positive aspects and aspects that need improving. The results should be related to the specified test improvement objectives.
- A list of concrete recommendations, including, for each recommendation, an identifier, possible impact, objective it relates to, estimated costs, time scales, and risks of implementation

Tips

The following tips will help you write good assessment reports:

- High-level, coarse-grained recommendations should be decomposed into smaller recommendations with specific goals where possible. This will make the task of planning and controlling the test improvements easier.
- A frequent mistake is to pack the assessment report with large amounts of information by incorrectly assuming that lengthy reports are good reports. Avoid reporting relatively insignificant low-priority findings; stakeholders will probably not have time to read them all and they may even distract from the most important points.

- It is always good to have an independent review on the report and presentation. The reviewer should preferably first study the findings and the assessment conclusions and ask the question, "Do the conclusions reflect the findings?" Finally, the reviewer should study the management summary and ask the question, "Does the management summary reflect the findings, conclusions, and recommendations stated in the report?" All of this may seem obvious to the reader, but we have learned throughout our experiences that these question reveal many mistakes in the report. Thus, reading an assessment report from the start to the end during the review is preferred to reading from back to front.

6.4 Establishing a Test Improvement Plan

Syllabus Learning Objectives

LO 6.4.1 (K2) Summarize the activities of the Establishing phase of the IDEAL improvement framework.
LO 6.4.2 (K4) Select and prioritize recommendations using a given criteria list.
LO 6.4.3 (K2) Compare top-down and bottom-up improvement approach.
LO 6.4.4 (K2) Summarize the typical contents of a test improvement plan.
LO 6.4.5 (K6) Create a test improvement plan.

During the *Establishing* phase of the IDEAL improvement framework, a detailed plan is developed to implement the developed recommendations. The general goals as laid down in the initiating phase are further specified in SMART goals, and the recommendations made in the assessment report are prioritized. The following main activities are performed in the establishing phase:

- Set priorities
- Develop an approach
- Plan the improvements

The end result of this phase is typically a test improvement plan.

> **Establishing (IDEAL)** The phase within the IDEAL model where the specifics of how an organization will reach its destination are planned. The establishing phase consists of the following activities: set priorities, develop an approach, and plan actions.

6.4.1 Set Priorities

The recommendations from the assessment report are prioritized according to a list of criteria, each of which may be weighted according to the need for the improvement and the stakeholders involved. For example, it is futile to implement all five process areas of TMMi level 2 at once. When priorities are set, it is determined which process area(s), and which recommendations are implemented first. Several factors, such as available resources, visibility of the results, likely resistance, and contribution to organizational goals should be taken into account. At a minimum, the following factors should be considered:

- Duration of improvement—A balance needs to be achieved between short-term and long-term improvements. Short-term improvements ("quick wins") have the advantage of quickly showing return on investment and may have a strong motivational impact on the implementing team. Long-term improvements may address some of the fundamental improvements in the testing process, including cultural and organizational issues.
- Implementation risk—Many improvements require a change to existing testing practices. There is a risk of failure associated with each of those improvements (see chapter 8 for more on managing change).
- Link to objectives—A clear association must be made between the proposed improvement and the stated objectives of the business.
- Leverage—How much impact will this improvement have on specific objectives (e.g., high, medium, low)?

6.4.2 Develop an Implementation Approach

Using the recommendations and priorities, a strategy is developed for achieving the desired situation and the desired process maturity level. The resources needed to achieve them are identified.

Technical factors to be considered include new methods, techniques, and resources. Attention must be paid to training, developing process descriptions, and possible tool selection.

Nontechnical factors to be considered include knowledge and experience, implementation approach, resistance, support, sense of urgency, and the organization's culture, among other things.

The two principal strategies/approaches for the implementation can be distinguished as follows (see table 6–2).

- Top-down
- Bottom-up

Note that the results of the bottom-up strategy may be used for a subsequent top-down rollout of proven improvement measures.

Table 6–2 *Implementation approaches*

	Top-down	Bottom-up
Scope	Typically covers several projects or an entire organization.	Typically covers no more than one or two projects.
Ownership	Dedicated improvement team.	Project team.
Approach	Typically formal based on a test improvement plan. Detailed analysis of results is required in order to find commonalities (good and bad practices) between the different projects.	Less formal, often a more analytical approach and/or prototyping in order to gain experience and build support.

For the top-down approach, presentation and negotiation skills are particularly relevant in achieving consensus on objectives and recommendations (see section 7.3). Critical success factors with this approach are managing people effectively, obtaining sponsorship, and managing expectations. The bottom-up approach may be adopted where funding for a test improvement program is limited and costs/benefits first need to be demonstrated.

6.4.3 Planning the Improvements

With the approach defined, detailed actions can be determined. Together with information taken from prior activities, these are combined into a test improvement plan including, among other things, actions, schedule, milestones, decision points, resources, responsibilities, measurements to be taken (including performance indicators), tracking mechanisms, risks, and implementation strategy.

> **Test improvement plan** A plan for achieving organizational test process improvement objectives based on a thorough understanding of the current strengths and weaknesses of the organization's test processes and test process assets [After Chrissis, Konrad, and Shrum 2004].

The primary planning activities are listed here:

- Prioritizing and combining groups of related improvements into packages (step-by-step improvement)
- Linking the improvement issues to the recommendations and required performance indicators for achievement
- Deciding on an approach for process improvement
- Scheduling the changes
- Establishing groups or teams to implement the improvements
- Assigning tasks
- Documenting the above-mentioned points in a test improvement plan

The test improvement plan is typically an action plan with a timeframe of one year or less focused on detailed planning of test improvement activities.

If test process improvements are taking place across the entire organization, perhaps in parallel with other process improvement initiatives, a longer-term strategic action plan may be created. This brings together the organization's process improvement strategy into a cohesive plan covering the next three to five years.

6.5 Acting to Implement Improvement

> **Syllabus Learning Objectives**
>
> LO 6.5.1 (K2) Summarize the activities of the Acting phase of the IDEAL improvement framework.
>
> LO 6.5.2 (K4) Select an appropriate pilot from a list of possibilities.

This phase is about concrete activities. This is where the action is! The recommendations must be specified in detail and must be implemented according to the test improvement plan. Obviously this phase consumes the most effort, because while developing the solution takes up about 30 percent effort, implementing the solution takes up about 70 percent [Cannegieter 2003].

> **Acting (IDEAL)** The phase within the IDEAL model where the improvements are developed, put into practice, and deployed across the organization. The acting phase consists of the following activities: create solutions, pilot/test solution, refine solution, and implement solution.

The following main activities are performed in the *Acting* phase:

- Create solutions
- Pilot/test solutions
- Refine solutions
- Implement solutions

Create Solution

The acting phase begins with developing solutions to address the broadly outlined problems. These solutions should contribute to achieving the desired situation. The solutions can include processes, templates, tools, knowledge, skills (training), information, and support. The solutions, which can be quite complex, are often developed by improvement teams (see section 7.1.1). An approach using improvement teams that has proven to be successful is the improvement team relay [Zandhuis 2009]. In an improvement team relay, a number of succeeding improvement teams develop and implement (parts of) the solution in a short time. Some advantages of the improvement team relay include reducing the lead time that would be required if only one overall improvement team was used, achieving results quickly, and allowing for more exact guidance. Every improvement team needs to have a clear goal and be given a clear assignment by the management. As many employees as possible need to be involved in actually working out the solutions; an external consultant can provide guidance and content input.

Tip: Process Documentation Structure

In an early phase of the improvement project a document overview should be established. In one test improvement project one of the authors was involved in, the process documents were initially delivered separately by different teams for their particular improvement action. When all individual documents came together, it was obvious that an overall architecture, tying all parts together into one bigger picture from the start to the end of the test process, was missing. Once this overall architecture had been developed, it became the starting point of a structure or hierarchy for all the other test process documents in the quality system. By thinking about a thorough structure for your process documents at the beginning of your project, you can save a lot of time on reworking and restructuring later.

6.5.1 Selecting and Executing a Pilot

Pilot/Test Solution

Following Tom Gilb's advice, "If you don't know what you are doing, don't do it on a large scale," the created solution first needs to be tested in one or more pilot projects. Sometimes only practical experience can show the exact impact of a solution. In pilots such as this, usually one or more projects are appointed in which the improvements are implemented and evaluated before they are adopted by additional projects.

Piloting a proposed improvement is an effective way of reducing the risk of implementation failure, gaining experience and building support. This is especially important where those improvements involve major changes to working practices or place a heavy demand on resources. Selection of a pilot should balance the following factors:

- Realism. For example, is the pilot representative of the "real world"?
- Scalability of solution. For example, can the results from the pilot be used in all contexts?
- Impact on current projects. Particular care is required if existing practices are to be replaced by the improved practices during the pilot.
- Risk of failure, that is, the risk that the pilot itself may be a failure.

Refine Solution

With the use of the results of the test or pilot, the solution can be optimized. Several iterations of the test-optimizing process may be necessary to reach a satisfactory solution that will work for all projects. A solution should be workable; waiting for a "perfect" solution may unnecessarily delay the implementation.

If the analysis of lessons learned from performing the pilot yields positive results, the decision may be made to roll out the improvements to other parts of the organization and/or other projects.

6.5.2 Manage and Control the Implementation

Once the solutions are deemed workable, they can be implemented throughout the (test) organization. This is usually the most radical activity, and it can provoke much resistance. Several implementation approaches can be used:

- Big bang: All the organizational changes are implemented at the same time.
- One project at a time. In every project, the change is implemented at a set moment in time.
- Just in time: The change is implemented when the process is executed.

Basically the implementation of the test improvement plan is performed and monitored and progress toward achieving improvement goals is reported. The measures, metrics, and indicators specified in the test improvement plan are collected and compared to the established objectives.

No one implementation approach is better than the other; the approach should be chosen based on the nature of the improvement and organizational circumstances. For a major change, implementation may require substantial time, resources, effort, and attention from the management.

The rollout of improvements follows a defined process, especially where an entire organization is affected by the change. Chapter 8 is devoted entirely to this critical aspect of test process improvement.

6.6 Learning from the Improvement Program

Syllabus Learning Objectives

LO 6.6.1 (K2) Summarize the activities of the Learning phase of the IDEAL improvement framework.

The *Learning* phase completes the improvement cycle. One of the goals of the IDEAL model is to continuously improve the ability to implement change. In the learning phase, the entire IDEAL experience is reviewed to determine what was accomplished, whether the intended goals were achieved, and how the organization can implement change more effectively and efficiently.

During and after implementation of the test improvement plan, project retrospectives are performed with the stakeholders. The organization or person that has implemented the improvement usually manages the retrospectives, which are typically performed as workshops.

The following activities are performed in the learning phase:

- Analyze and validate
- Propose future actions

> **Learning (IDEAL)** The phase within the IDEAL model where one learns from experiences and improves one's ability to adopt new processes and technologies in the future. The learning phase consists of the following activities: analyze and validate, and propose future actions.

Analyze and Validate

This activity answers several questions:

- How did the improvement program go?
- What has been accomplished; have the initial goals been achieved?
- What worked well?
- What could be done more efficiently or effectively?

Using these questions for guidance, lessons learned are collected, analyzed, summarized, and documented.

Propose Future Actions

Based upon the previous activity, recommendations are formulated that are intended to improve future improvement programs. These recommendations are provided to upper management for consideration, which may include performing a new improvement cycle.

6.7 Exercises

The following multiple-choice questions will give you some feedback on your understanding of this chapter. Appendix F lists the answers.

6-1 Which phase of the IDEAL framework relates to the following goal: "Determining the organization's current state as opposed to what it wants to achieve"?

    A: Initiating

    B: Establishing

    C: Acting

    D: Diagnosing

6-2 Which is the correct order for the phases of a test improvement cycle?

   A: Initiating, establishing, diagnosing, acting, learning

   B: Initiating, diagnosing, establishing, acting, learning

   C: Initiating, acting, establishing, diagnosing, learning

   D: Initiating, diagnosing, acting, establishing, learning

6-3 Which is of the following is not a main purpose of the document study to be carried out during the assessment preparation phase?

   A: Gain insights into the current testing process prior to interviewing those involved.

   B: Gather and verify information.

   C: Prepare particular questions for the interview.

   D: Perform formal elements of the assessment that do not require discussion. For example, the documents may be checked to ensure completeness and conformity to standards.

6-4 During an assessment, when will the initial feedback be provided?

   A: After analyzing the assessment results

   B: When presenting the assessment report

   C: At the end of the diagnosing phase

   D: At the end of the interviews

6-5 When assigning priorities to the recommendation from an assessment, which of the following factors needs to be taken into account?

   A: Implementation risk

   B: Added value for objectives

   C: Duration of the improvement action

   D: All of the above

6-6 Which of the following is an activity that will typically be performed as part of the learning phase of a test improvement cycle?

   A: Analyze and validate

   B: Plan actions

   C: Develop recommendations

   D: Refine solutions

6-7 Which of the following strategies/approaches for an implementation best matches the following characteristics?
- Less formal; often an analytical approach and/or prototyping in order to gain experience and build support can be distinguished
- Typically covers no more than one or two projects

A: Big bang

B: Just in time

C: Bottom-up

D: Top-down

6-8 Which of the following activities will typically be performed as part of the acting phase of a test improvement cycle?

A: Selecting and executing a pilot

B: Developing an implementation approach

C: Planning the Improvement

D: Analyzing and validating the solution

6-9 Which of the following would typically be part of a test policy?

A: Acceptance criteria

B: Main tasks for each test level

C: Generic risks for the products to be developed

D: The objectives and added value of testing

6-10 Which factor should be taken into account when selecting a pilot?

A: Is the pilot project lightweight, therefore making the chances of a successful pilot better?

B: Can the results from the pilot be used in all contexts; that is, is the solution scalable?

C: If the project is already late, would it be OK to delay it further due to a pilot?

D: Is the project a high-profile project, thus already having the required level of management attention?

7 Organization, Roles, and Skills

Getting organized will help manage your improvement plans effectively and ensure that test process improvements have a lasting positive impact. This chapter starts by considering different forms of organization that can be set up to manage test improvement programs and then describes the roles of the test process improver and the test process assessor.

As with any organization, success depends on having the right people with the right knowledge and skills. This chapter takes a practical look at the wide range of technical and social skills needed.

7.1 Organization

Image you're a test manager and you've just presented your project's test improvement plan to the organization's line management. You've proposed some quick wins for your project, but there are also a number of longer-term improvements required. Great! They like your proposals; now you can go ahead and implement the changes. Now the nagging doubts start. You know you have time to implement some of the quick wins in your project, but who is going to take on the longer-term improvements needed? Without someone to take on responsibility for the overall improvement plan, this could be simply too much for you as a test manager.

You may also be concerned that your ideas are confined to your project. Wouldn't your colleagues be interested in what you are doing here? If you had some kind of organized group of skilled people who could pick up your test improvement plan and also look beyond the project for benefits elsewhere, that could help everyone. This is where a test improvement organization comes in (and it may be embedded within the regular test organization). It gives you the ability to focus on one specific area, test improvement. It's where the test process improver plays a leading role.

The sections that follow look at the process improvement organization and how it is made up, both structurally and from a human resources point of view. Test improvement organizations are principally found at the departmental or organizational level. The principal focus will be placed on the structure of a typical test improvement organization (the Test Process Group) and its main function. The impacts of outsourcing or offshoring development on this organization are then outlined.

Syllabus Learning Objectives

LO 7.1.1 (K2) Understand the roles, tasks and responsibilities of a Test Process Group (TPG) within a test improvement program.

LO 7.1.2 (K4) Evaluate the different organizational structures to organize a test improvement program.

LO 7.1.3 (K2) Understand the impact of outsourcing or offshoring of development activities on the organization of a test process improvement program.

LO 7.1.4 (K6) Design an organizational structure for a given scope of a test process improvement program.

7.1.1 The Test Process Group (TPG)

The organization that takes responsibility for test process improvement can be given a variety of different names:

- Process Improvement Group (PIG, although people may not like being a member of the PIG group)
- Test Engineering Process Group (TEPG)
- Test Process Improvement Group (possible, but the abbreviation "TPI group" may give the impression that the group is focused only on the TPI model)
- Test Process Group (TPG), the term used in this chapter (see Practical Software Testing [Burnstein 2003])

> **Test Process Group (TPG)** A collection of (test) specialists who facilitate the definition, maintenance, and improvement of the test processes used by an organization [After Chrissis, Konrad, and Shrum 2004].

Irrespective of what you call it, the main point is that you understand the following different aspects of a TPG:

- Its scope
- Its structural organization
- The services it provides to stakeholders
- Its members and their roles and skills

TPG Scope

The scope of a TPG is influenced by two basic aspects: level of independence and degree of permanency.

An independent TPG can become the "owner" of the test process and function effectively as a trusted single point of contact for stakeholders. The message is "The test process is in good hands. If you need help, this is who you come to." In general, you should aim to make the TPG responsible for the test process at a high organizational level, where decisions can be taken that influence all, or at least many, projects and where standardized procedures and best practices (e.g., for writing test design or the test plan) can be introduced for achieving maximum effectiveness and efficiency. At project level, a test manager has more say in how to manage and improve the test process on a day-to-day basis. A TPG that is set up with only project scope could end up in conflict with the test manager and will often be unable to cross-feed improvements to or from other similar projects. This is just a general rule, of course, that may not hold true in big projects (we know of a project with over 100 testers that lasted more than five years and had a dedicated TPG organization).

Of course "independent" does not mean that they are not accountable to some other person or department. As you will see later, the structure of a TPG ideally includes elements that directly involve higher levels of management.

The aspect of permanency gives the TPG sufficient scope to enable medium- and long-term improvements to be considered. Improvement plans can be more effectively implemented and controlled. TPGs that are "here today and gone tomorrow" often lack consistency in their approach to test process improvement and tend to focus only on short-term issues. At the project level, improvement plans may be at the mercy of key players whose tasks could get re-prioritized, leaving test process improvement initiatives "high and dry." You should try to avoid these ad hoc TPGs; they are limited in scope and often limited in value.

You may well see changes to the scope and permanency of the test process improvement organization as improvements in their own right. Typically, independent and permanent TPGs are found in more mature organizations where test process improvements are frequently driven by gathered metrics. Organizations striving for this level of "optimizing" test process maturity will consider the setting up of a TPG as part of their test process improvement strategy. If we look at the TMMi model, for example, we see that maturity level 2 organizations have a type of TPG within projects. As the organization matures to TMMi level 3, the TPG typically becomes a more permanent organization.

TPG Organization

The IDEAL model [McFeeley 1996] proposes the structure of a Test Process Group consisting of three distinct components. Even though this would be relevant mostly for larger organizations, smaller organizations can still benefit from considering this structure, which includes sample charters for each of the elements outlined in the following section.

The structure of a TPG for a large organization is shown in figure 7–1.

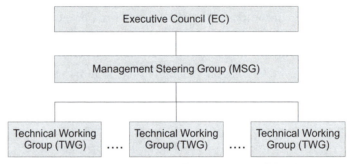

* Based on: Bob McFeeley/Software Engineering Institute (SEI), "IDEAL: A User's Guide for Software Process Improvement"

Figure 7–1   *TPG for a large organization*

The Executive Council (EC) deals with strategy and policy issues. It establishes the approaches to be used for test process improvement (e.g., analytical, model-based), specifies what the scope of the TPG should be, and defines test process ownership. Typically, the EC would be the same high-level body that sets up the overall testing policy for the organization. Indeed, aspects relating to test process improvement would often be included as part of the test policy. Given that the TPG cannot function as an "island" within an organization, the EC defines the interfaces to other groups that deal with IT processes, such as a Software

Engineering Process Group (SEPG), and resolves any scoping and responsibility issues between these groups. It would be unlikely for the EC to meet often, unless major changes are being proposed with wide-ranging impact.

The operational management of the TPG is performed by the Management Steering Group (MSG). This is a group of mostly high-level line managers (e.g., the manager of the test organization), program managers, and perhaps senior test managers who regularly meet to set objectives, goals, and success criteria for the planned improvement. They steer the implementation of test process improvements in the organization by setting priorities, monitoring the high-level status of test process improvement plans, and providing the necessary resources to get the job done. Of course, some of these resources may come from their own budgets, so the test process improver will need to convince the MSG members that improvement propopsals are worthwhile (e.g., by means of a measureable business case). The soft skills mentioned later in this chapter will be of particular value in such situations. The MSG is not involved in implementing changes; it sets up other groups to do that (see the next paragraph below). Depending on the amount and significance of test process improvements being undertaken, the MSG typically meets on a quarterly or even monthly basis.

Technical Working Groups (TWGs) are where the individual measures in improvement plans are implemented. Members of these teams may be drawn from any number of different departmements, such as development, business analysts, and of course, testing. The individual tasks performed may range from long-term projects (as might be the case for a test automation initiative) to short-term measures, such as developing new checklists to be used in experience-based testing or testability reviews. The MSG may set up temporary TWGs to perform research tasks, investigate proposed solutions to problems, or conduct the early proof-of-concept tasks needed to build a business case for larger-scale improvement proposals. As a result of these activities, it would be expected from a TWG that they adjust their original plans to incorporate lessons learned and take into account any changes proposed by the MSG (the IDEAL model calls these short-term plans *tactical action plans*). Note, however, that the TWG reports to the MSG, so any changes made from within the TWG itself must be justified to the MSG.

Now, you may be asking yourself, "Is a TWG a permanent part of the overall TPG or not?" The TWG proposed in the IDEAL model suggests that they are nonpermanent and disband after their tasks and objectives have been completed. This may be true for some TWGs, but we would suggest that permanent

TWGs are also required to achieve the consistency and permanency mentioned earlier in the section on TPG scope.

If your organization is relatively small (say, less than 30 testers), the structures proposed by the IDEAL model may appear rather heavy weight. In this case, you can scale the whole idea down to suit your organization's size. You can start, for example, with just a single person who is allocated test improvement responsibility and who meets regularly with senior management to talk about these issues. It's not necessary to call this a Management Steering Group, but the person would basically be performing the same kind of function.

Establishing an organizational structure for test process improvement may not be trivial; it may be necessary to initiate decision-making at the highest levels of management (e.g., when setting up an Executive Council or Management Steering Group). The practice of outsourcing and offshoring generally increases the complexity of organizations. These are discussed in section 7.1.2.

Services Provided

We like to think of a Test Process Group containing individual permanent TWGs as service providers to the overall IT organization. By adopting a standardized "industrialized" approach to test process improvement, they are able to offer standard packages for projects and the Management Steering Group. The group might typically provide the following services:

- Performing test process assessments
- Providing coaching and training in testing
- Providing individual consultancy to projects to enable improvements to be rolled out successfully

Note that in this book we are considering the Test Process Group principally from the aspect of test process improvement. It is not uncommon for a TPG to provide other general testing services, such as creation of master test plans, implementation of testing tools, and even some test management tasks.

TPG Skills

A thorough description of the skills needed by the test process improver is provided in section 7.3. The social skills and expertise that need to be represented in a Test Process Group are summarized here.

Social skills:

- Consultancy
- Conflict handling
- Negotiation
- Enthusiasm and persuasiveness
- Honest and open attitude
- Able to handle criticism
- Patience

Expertise

- Structured testing
- Software process improvement
- Test process improvement models
- Analytical approaches (e.g., test metrics)
- Test processes
- Test tools
- Test organization

What Can Go Wrong?

Creation of a TPG doesn't, of course, guarantee success. Here are just a few of the risks that need to be considered:

- The TPG is perceived by stakeholders as "just overhead." Remember, if the TPG is established as an overall entity within an organization, there may be people who critically view the resources it consumes.
- The TPG is unable to implement improvements at the organizational level. This may, for example, be due to insufficient backing from management because responsibilities are not clearly defined (e.g., who "owns" the test process), a lack of coordination, or simply not having the right people involved.
- Some TWGs are disbanded, resulting in loss of continuity and know-how.
- The products of the TPG are not pragmatic or flexible enough. This applies in particular to standardized templates and procedures.
- The people making up the TPG don't have the necessary skills.

It's the task of the test process improver to manage and mitigate these risks. Many of them can be managed by showing the value a TPG adds whenever possible.

7.1.2 Test Improvement with Remote, Offshore, and Outsourced Teams

When two people exchange information, there is always a "filter" between what the sender of the information wishes to convey and what the receiver actually understands. The skills needed to handle these kinds of communications problem are discussed in section 7.3. However, the organizations to which the communicating people belong can also influence the ability of people to communicate effectively. This is particularly the case when people are geographically remote from each other (perhaps even offshore) and where development and/or test processes have been outsourced.

For providing an effective and professional message, research has taught us that only 20 percent is determined by the "what" part (e.g., words, conversation, email), 30 percent is determined by the "how" part (e.g., tone of voice), and no less than 50 percent by the "expression" part (e.g., face, gestures, posture). In outsourced and distributed environments thus, at least 80 percent of the communication becomes challenging.

The test process improver needs to communicate clearly to stakeholders on a large number of issues, such as resources, root causes, improvement plans, and results. It is therefore critical to appreciate the impact of outsourcing or offshoring on a test process improvement program. Probably the following questions are the two most significant questions to consider:

- Are there any barriers betweeen us?
- Are communication channels open?

Contractually, it is common to find that the outsourced test process cannot be changed by anyone other than the "new" owner, making improvement initiatives difficult or even impossible. Even if there is some scope for getting involved, the test process improver faces a wide range of different factors that might disrupt their ability to implement improvement plans. These may be of a political, cultural, or contractual nature. On the political front, it could be, for example, that the manager of an onshore part of the organization resists attempts to transfer parts of the test process to an offshore location. There may be subtle attempts to show that suggested improvements "won't work there," or there may be outright refusal to enact parts of the plan, perhaps driven by fear ("If I cooperate, I may lose my job"). Cultural difficulties can also be a barrier to test process improvement. Language and customs are the two most significant issues that can prevent proper exchange of views regarding a specific point. Perhaps people are using different words for the same things (e.g., test strategy and test approach), or it could be that long telephone conferences in a foreign language, not to mention different time zones, create barriers to mutual understanding.

For the test process improver, keeping communications open means keeping all involved parties fully informed about status and involved in decision-making. Status information needs to be made available regarding the improvement project itself (don't forget those time zones), and decisions on improvements need to be made in consultation with offshore partners. This might mean, for example, involving all parties in critical choices and decisions (e.g., choice of pilot project or deciding on the success/failure of improvements) and in the planning of improvements and their rollout into the whole organization.

Good alignment is a key success factor when dealing with teams who are geographically remote or offshore. This applies not just to the communications issues just mentioned but also to process alignment, process maturity, and other "human" factors such as motivation, expectations, and quality culture. Clearly, the success of test process improvements will be placed at higher risk if the affected elements of an organization apply different IT processes (e.g., for software development) or where similar processes are practiced but at different levels of maturity (e.g., managed or optimizing). Where expectations and motivation are not aligned, you might find increased resistance to any proposed improvements. People generally resist change, so if their expectations and motivation are not aligned, you can expect conflict.

Mitigating the Risks

The likelihood of all of the risks just described is generally higher with remote and offshore organizations or where outsourcing is practiced. The test process improver should appreciate these issues and propose mitigating measures should any of the risks apply. What can be done? It may be as simple as conducting joint workshops or web-based conference calls to align expectations. You may introduce a standardized training scheme such as ISTQB to ensure that both parties have a common understanding of testing issues. On the other hand, you may propose far-reaching measures like setting non-testing process maturity entry criteria before embarking on test process improvements. This could mean a major program in its own right (e.g., to raise maturity levels of particular IT processes to acceptable levels). Implementing such changes are outside of the test process improver's scope, but they should still be proposed if considered necessary. In general, practicing good governance and setting up appropriate organizational structures is a key success factor to any outsourcing program involving onshore and offshore elements.

For test process improvements to take effect, you need to appreciate which organizational structures and roles are defined for dealing with these distributed teams (e.g., offshore coordinators) and then ensure that test process improvement can be "channeled" correctly via those people. Once again, we are looking at good soft skills from the test process improver to forge strong links with those responsible for managing remote, offshore, and outsourced teams; it can make the difference between success and failure for getting test process improvements implemented.

7.2 Individual Roles and Staffing

Syllabus Learning Objectives

LO 7.2.1 (K2) Understand the individual roles in a test process improvement program.

In the preceding chapters of this book, and in particular in the discussions earlier in this chapter, the role *test process improver* has figured strongly. That's hardly surprising given the nature of the book, but we now bring the various aspects we've discussed so far together into a definition of the role itself. In addition, we'll describe the specific roles for supporting test process assessments. Individual organizations may, of course, tailor these role definitions to suit their specific needs.

Note that having an independent and permanent Test Process Group will generally make it easier to establish these specific roles and provide a solid organizational structure for skills development. In general, it is highly recommended to make these roles formal and therefore part of the human resource process and structure.

7.2.1 The Test Process Improver

The description of the test process improver's role could be summarized quite simply as "Be able to do all the things contained in this book." That would be a bit too simple, and after all, it's useful to have a point of reference from which to get a summary. The expectations discussed in this section are based on the business outcomes for the test process improver, as described in the ISTQB document "Certified Tester Expert Level, Modules Overview" [ISTQB-EL-OVIEW]. Note that the skills and experience are shown as "desired"; each organization would need to decide for itself what is actually "required."

In general, the test process improver should be perceived by fellow testers and stakeholders as the local testing expert. This is especially true in smaller organizations. In larger organizations, the test process improver could have more of a managment background and be supported by a team of testing experts.

Tasks and expectations

- Lead programs for improving the test process within an organization or project.
- Make appropriate decisions on how to approach improvement to the test process.
- Assess a test process, propose step-by-step improvements, and show how these are linked to achieving business goals.
- Set up a strategic policy for improving the test process and implement that policy.
- Analyze specific problems with the test process and propose effective solutions.
- Create a test improvement plan that meets business objectives.
- Develop organizational concepts for improvement of the test process that include required roles, skills, and organizational structure.
- Establish a standard process for implementing improvement to the test process within an organization.
- Manage the introduction of changes to the test process, including cooperation with the sponsors of improvements. Identify and manage the critical success factors.
- Coordinate the activities of groups implementing test process improvements (e.g., Technical Working Groups).
- Understand and effectively manage the human issues associated with assessing the test process and implementing necessary changes.
- Function as a single point of contact for all stakeholders regarding test process issues.
- Perform the duties of a lead assessor or co-assessor, as shown in section 7.2.2 and section 7.2.3, respectively.

> **Test process improver** A person implementing improvements in the test process based on a test improvement plan.

Desired skills and qualifications

- Skills in defining and deploying test processes
- Management skills
- Consultancy and training/presentation skills
- Change management skills
- Soft skills (e.g., communications)
- Asessment skills
- Knowledge and skills regarding test improvement models (e.g., TPI NEXT and TMMi)
- Knowledge and skills regarding analytical-based improvements
- (Optional) ISTQB Expert Level certification in Improving the Test Process and preferably ISTQB Full Advanced certification providing the person with a wide range of testing knowledge. (Note that for TMMi, a specific qualification is available: TMMi Professional.)

Desired experience

- Experience as a test designer or test analyst in several projects
- At least five years of experience as a test manager
- Experience in the software development life cycle(s) being applied in the organization
- Also helpful is some experience in test automation

7.2.2 The Lead Assessor

Tasks and expectations

- Plan the assessment of a test process.
- Perform interviews and analysis according to a specific assessment approach (e.g., model).
- Write the assessment report.
- Propose step-by-step improvements and show how these are linked to achieving business goals.
- Present the assessment conclusion, findings, and recommendations to stakeholders.
- Perform the duties of a co-assessor (see section 7.2.3).

> **Assessor** A person who conducts an assessment; any member of an assessment team.
>
> **Lead assessor** The person who leads an assessment. In some cases (for instance, CMMI and TMMi) when formal assessments are conducted, the lead assessor must be accredited and formally trained.

Required skills and qualifications

- Soft skills, in particular relating to interviewing and listening
- Writing and presentation skills
- Planning and managerial skills (especially relevant at larger assessments)
- Detailed knowledge and skills regarding the chosen assessment approach
- (Desirable) At least ISTQB Advanced Level Test Manager certification (Full Advanced qualification recommended so that other areas of testing are also covered)
- For formal TMMi assessments, accredited as a TMMi lead assessor [van Veenendaal and Wells 2012]
- For informal TMMi assessments, TMMi experienced or accredited assessor [van Veenendaal and Wells 2012]

Required experience

- At least two assessments performed as co-assessor in the chosen assessment approach
- Experience as a tester or test analyst in several projects
- At least five years of experience as a test manager
- Experience in the software development life cycle(s) being applied in the organization

7.2.3 The Co-Assessor

When performing interviews, the lead assessor is required to perform several tasks in parallel (e.g., listen, take notes, ask questions, and guide the discussion). To assist the lead assessor, it may be helpful to define a specific role; the co-assessor.

Tasks and expectations

- Take structured notes during assessment interviews.
- Provide the lead assessor with a second opinion where a specific point is unclear.

- Monitor the coverage of specific subjects, and where necessary, remind the lead assessor of any aspects not covered (e.g., a specifc checkpoint when using the TPI NEXT model).

Required skills and qualifications
- Soft skills, in particular relating to note-taking
- Good knowledge of the chosen assessment approach
- (Desirable) ISTQB Foundation Level certification

Required experience
- Experience as a tester or test analyst in several projects

7.3 Skills of the Test Process Improver/Assessor

In the previous sections we looked at the roles and organization of test process improvement. We briefly listed some of the skills we would expect to find in these organizations and the people performing those roles. This section goes into more detail about those skills and provides insights into why they are of importance when performing the various tasks of a test process improver.

Syllabus Learning Objectives

LO 7.3.1 (K2) Understand the skills necessary to perform an assessment.

LO 7.3.2 (K5) Assess test professionals (e.g., potential members of a Test Process Group / Technical Working Group) with regard to their deficits of the principal soft skills needed to perform an assessment.

LO 7.3.3 (K3) Apply interviewing skills, listening skills and note-taking skills during an assessment, e.g., when performing interviews during "Diagnosing the current situation."

LO 7.3.4 (K3) Apply analytical skills during an assessment, e.g., when analyzing the results during "Diagnosing the current situation."

LO 7.3.5 (K2) Understand presentational and reporting skills during a test process improvement program.

LO 7.3.5 (K2) Understand persuasion skills during a test process improvement program.

The key skills we will be discussing are shown in figure 7-1.

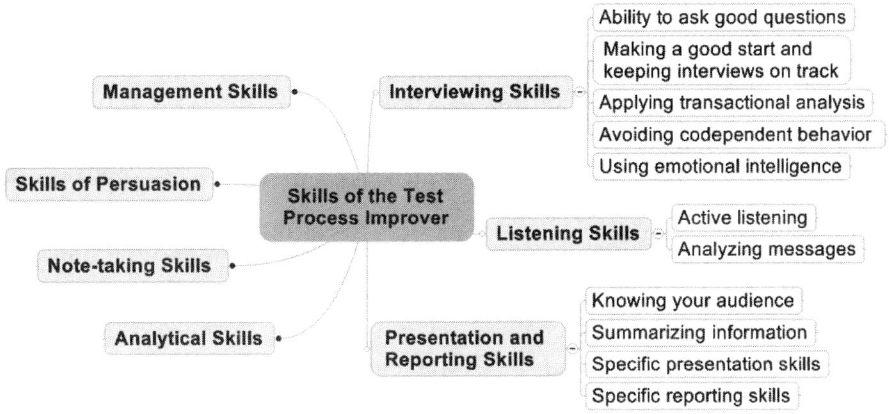

Figure 7-2 *Skills of the test process improver*

Note that an independent and permanent TPG (discussed earlier in section 7.1.1) should be responsible for development of specific skills needed for test process improvement. These can also be beneficial for test management and may be acquired together with test management skills.

Before we discuss some of the skills in more details, a word of advice: We, as humble test process improvers, are generally not trained psychologists. Certainly an appreciation of this fascinating subject can help you in performing good interviews, but you should focus on the practical uses rather than the theory. This is where some of the literature on "soft skills for testers or test managers," in our opinion, is not entirely helpful—too much theory; not enough practical hints on how to apply it.

7.3.1 Interviewing Skills

Interviewing is a key activity in performing assessments. You need information to find out where you are in the test process, and much of that information comes from talking to people. In the context of test process assessment, the talking is generally done in the form of interviews. If you have poor interview skills, you are unlikely to get the most out of the precious time you have with the people that are of most interest to you, like test managers, testers, project leaders, and other stakeholders.

If you conduct interviews without having sufficient practice, you could experience some of the following (unfortunately typical) symptoms:

- In a bad interview, the interviewee feels like they are partaking in an interrogation rather than an open interview. This is a common mistake, particularly if you are using a test process improvement model. For the beginner, it's tempting to think of the checkpoints in the model as being "ready-made" questions; they are not. For the interviewee, there is nothing more tedious than checkpoints being read out like this: "Do you write test plans? Answer yes or no." After the 10th question like that, they will be heading for the door.
- In a bad interview, the interviewer doesn't respond to answers correctly. People give more than factual information when they answer your questions. Ignoring the "hidden messages" may result in the interviewer missing vital information. Look at the expression on their face when they answer your question and be prepared to dig deeper when answers like "In principle we do this" are given. In this case, you should follow up by asking, "Do you actually do this or not? Give me an example, please." In section 7.3.2, we will discuss the ability to listen well as a separate skill in its own right.
- In a bad interview, the interviewer might get manipulated by the interviewee, by evasive responses, exaggerated claims, or (yes it can happen) half-truths.

So that's what can make bad interviews. Now, what are the principal skills that can help to conduct good interviews? These are the ones we'll be focusing on:

- Ability to ask good questions (the meaning of *good* will be discussed soon)
- Applying transactional analysis
- Making a good start, keeping the interview on track, and closing the interview
- Avoiding codependent behavior
- Using emotional intelligence

Some of these skills may also be applied in the context of other skill areas covered in later sections, such as listening and presenting.

Asking Good Questions

What is a "good" question? It's one that extracts the information you want from the interviewee and, at the same time, establishes a bond with that person. People are more likely to be open and forthcoming with information if they trust the interviewer and feel relaxed and unthreatened.

The best kind of questions for getting a conversation going are so-called *open* questions, ones that demand more than a yes or no answer. Here are some typical examples:

- How do you specify the test cases for this function?
- What's your opinion about the current software quality?
- Explain for me the risks you see for this requirement.

Now, asking only open questions is not always a good strategy. Think about what it's like when a young child keeps asking "why." In the end you are exhausted with the constant demand for information. That's how an interviewee feels if you keep asking one open question after another. They feel drained, tired, and maybe a bit edgy. You can get around this by interspersing open questions with so-called *closed* questions. They are quick yes/no questions that help to confirm a fact or simply establish a true or false situation. Here are some examples of closed questions:

- Have these test cases been reviewed?
- How many major defects did you find last week?
- Did you report this problem?
- Did you use a tool for automating tests in this project?

Closed questions work like the punctuation in a sentence. They help give structure and can be useful to change the tempo of an interview. A long exchange involving open questions can be concluded, for example, with a short burst of closed questions. This gives light and shade to an interview; it gives the interviewee the chance to recover because the interviewer is the one doing most of the talking. Sometimes a few "easy" closed questions at the start of an interview can also help to get the ball rolling. Remember, though, too many closed questions in one continuous block will lead to the "interrogation" style mentioned earlier and will not deliver the information you need.

Test process assessments generally involve the conduct of more than one interview. This presents the opportunity to practice what is sometimes called the "Columbo" interviewing technique (named after the famous American detective series on television). This technique involves the following principle aspects:

- Asking different people the same question
- Asking the same person very nearly the same question
- Pretending to be finished with a subject and then returning with the famous "Oh, just one more point" tactic

Even though it was entertaining to watch Columbo do this, there's a lesson to be learned. If people are in any way exaggerating or concealing the truth, this kind of questioning technique, used with care, might just give you a hint of what you are looking for: reality.

When an interview is nearly over, one of the most obvious questions that can be asked ask is a simple, "Did I miss anything?" It's not uncommon for people to come to interviews prepared to talk about some testing-related issues that they really want to discuss. Maybe your interview didn't touch directly on these issues. Asking this simple question gives people the chance to say what they want to say and rounds off a discussion. Even if this isn't of direct relevance to test process improvement, it can still provide valuable background information about, for example, relationships with stakeholders or between the test manager and the testers. These are the areas that you might miss if, for example, you are following a model-based approach and focus too much on coverage of the model's checkpoints.

Applying Transactional Analysis

Transactional analysis focuses on the way people interact with each other and provides a framework with which verbal exchanges (transactions) can be understood.

The framework described by Abe Wagner [Wagner 1996] identifies six "inner people" that all of us have. Three of them (Wagner also calls them "ego states") are effective when it comes to communicating with others and three are ineffective. Let's consider the effective inner people first (see table 7–1).

Table 7–1   Effective inner people

Inner person	Description
Natural child	• Responds spontaneously to situations • Expresses subjective feelings rather than objective facts • Demands recognition from others for their ideas and inputs • Needs a framework within which they feel comfortable • Needs stimulation to trigger their creativity
Adult	• Thinks and behaves logically • Is rational and reasonable • Deals in objective facts rather than subjective feelings
Nurturing parent	• Is firm with others • Listens and is understanding • Has a sensitive and caring style

> **Transactional analysis** The analysis of transactions between people and within people's minds; a transaction is defined as a stimulus plus a response. Transactions take place between people and between the ego states (personality segments) within one person's mind.

Now let's consider the ineffective inner people (see table 7–2). These are the "ego states" that we need to avoid in an interview situation, as either interviewer or interviewee or, worst of all, as both.

Table 7–2   Ineffective inner people

Inner person	Description
Critical parent	• Thinks they know best and likes to "tell others off" • Uses a range of mechanisms to admonish people, such as gestures (e.g., finger pointing), tone (e.g., shouting), style (e.g., sarcasm)
Rebellious child	• Gets angry easily and remains so • Is generally negative about people and projects • Does not want to listen to reasoned argument • Is manipulative (e.g., tells half-truths or omits certain facts) • May deliberately undermine or delay a conversation
Compliant child	• Feels inadequate and blames self • Talks in a soft, submissive voice • Whines and complains • Is very careful about what they say • Adopts a self-protective style

The ability to perform transactional analysis is a skill that can be applied by anyone needing a good understanding of how people communicate with each other. This is typically the case for managers but also, in the context of performing interviews, for test process improvers.

So how can transactional analysis be useful to the test process improver as an interviewing skill? Taking your own role as interviewer first, it means that you must strive to establish an "adult-to-adult" interaction with the interviewee. As an interviewer, you must ensure that your "adult" inner person is in the forefront. You are reasonable, understanding, and focused on information gathering. You must not be judgmental ("Oh, that's bad practice you have there"), blaming ("You can't be serious!"), or sarcastic ("These reports remind me of a long book I'm reading"). This "critical parent" style is not going to be at all helpful; it could bring out the argumentative "rebellious child" or the whining, self-protective "compliant child" in the interviewee. You could end up in an argument or cause the interviewee to close up.

Recognizing the inner person shown by the interviewee is an essential skill needed by the interviewer. If you, the interviewer, have an "adult" interviewee before you, you can expect a good, factual exchange of information and you can press on with your questions at a reasonbly fast pace.

Interviewing someone showing their "natural child" will mean that you will occasionally need to refocus the discussion back to an objective one. You will need to practice your listening skills here and give objective summaries of what you have understood back to the interviewee (see the discussion of active listening in section 7.3.2).

With interviewees who emphasize their ineffective inner persons, the interviewer may have a much more difficult task in getting the information they need. The "rebellious child" might resent the fact that they are being interviewed, they may exaggerate the negative aspects of the project, they might be devisive and withhold information, and they may challenge the questions you ask rather than answer them.

The "rebellious child" and the "compliant child" often show themselves at the start of interviews. This critical stage of the interview is where we, the interviewer, need to be patient, reassuring, and yet firm (see the discussion of getting started in a bit). Explain what the interview is about and why it is being conducted in terms of benefits. Emphasize your neutrality and objectivity. Your aim is to bring the discussion around so that the interviewee is communicating as one of their three effective inner persons (preferably the "adult"). If this approach does not succeed and the interviewee persistently shows an ineffective inner peson, you may be justified in breaking off the interview to seek a solution (e.g., resolve problems in a project, nominate an alternative interviewee). Making the decision to terminate an interview may be a last resort, but it is preferable to conducting an ineffective interview.

Having skills in transactional analysis can help interviewers to be more discerning about the answers and information they are receiving from an interviewee. In this book, we have only touched on the basics of transactional analysis. If you want to develop your skills further in this area, we suggest you start with Isabel Evan's book *Achieving Software Quality through Teamwork* [Evans 2004], which provides a useful summary and some examples. The works of Abe Wagner, specifically *The Transactional Manager* [Wagner 1996], give further understanding on how transactional analysis can be applied in a management context.

Getting Started, Keeping the Interview on Track, and Closing the Interview

Test process assessments generally involve conducting interviews that should last no more than two hours. This may sound like a long time, but typically there will be several individual subjects to be covered. If practically possible, it can be effective to schedule shorter, more frequent interviews (e.g., each lasting one hour) so that the interviewee's concentration and motivation can be maintained.

Without a controlled start, you might fail to create the right atmosphere for the interview. Without the skills to keep an interview under control, you may find that some subjects get covered in too much detail while others are missed completely. Here are some tips that will help you in these areas; they provide an insight into the skills needed to conduct an interview (see section 6.3.3):

- Don't dive straight into the factual aspects of an interview. Remember, the ability to make "small talk" at the start of an interview is a perfect chance to build initial bonds with the interviewee and establish a good level of openness (e.g., talk about the weather, the view from the office, the journey to work).
- Tell the interviewee about the purpose of the interview, what is in scope and out of scope, and the way it will be conducted. Doing so before the first question is asked will reassure the interviewee and enable the discussion to be more open. This "smoothing the way" requires both interviewing skills and the ability to understand the nonfactual aspects of what is said (see the discussion of transactional analysis earlier). Remember, the interviewee may be stressed by their project workload, concerned that having a "good" interview must reflect well on their work or project, or simply withdrawn and defensive because they have not been informed adequately. Running through a quick checklist like the following can help an interview start out well:
    - Thanks: Thank them for taking time from their work (they are probably busy).
    - Discussion, not interrogation: We are going to have a discussion about the test process.
    - Confidentiality: All information will be treated confidentially.
    - Focus: The assessment is focused on the test process, not you personally.
    - Purpose: The interview will help to identify test process improvements.
- Interviews should be conducted according to the plans and preparations made (see section 6.3.2). However, interviews rarely run exactly as planned,

so flexibility must be practiced by the interviewer. Some issues may arise during the interview that justify further discussion, and some planned items may turn out to be redundant (e.g., if the interviewee simply states, "We have no tools here" it's pointless to discuss issues of test automation any further). The interviewer should adjust the plan as required to keep the flow of the discussion going. If topics arise that you prefer to discuss later (e.g., because they are not in the agreed-upon scope), then explicitly communicate this to the interviewee, but try not to defer too often; it can give the impression that you are not interested in what the interviewee is saying.

- The end of the interview is determined by the assessor and is normally based on achievement of agreed-upon scope or time constraints. Even with the most well-planned and -conducted interviews, time can run out. If this happens, make sure the interviewee is made aware of the areas in scope that could not be covered and make arrangements (where possible, immediately) for a follow-up interview. Get used to mentally running through the following checklist when closing the interview:
  - Thank the interviewee for their time.
  - Ask the interviewee if the interview met their expectations and if any improvements could be made.
  - Tell the interviewee what will happen to the information provided.
  - Briefly explain what the remainder of the assessment process looks like.
- In exceptional situations, the assessor may decide to break off the interview. Perhaps the interview room doesn't provide enough privacy, maybe the interviewee is simply unable or unwilling to answer questions, or maybe there are communication difficulties that cannot be overcome (e.g., language or technical problems).

Avoiding Codependent Behavior

Codependence can occur in a number of situations, especially where we need to reach agreement on something. For the test process improver, these situations typically occur when proposing, agreeing upon, and prioritizing improvements to the test process (see section 6.4) and when they perform interviews. An awareness of codependence can help the interviewer in two principal ways: to identify situations where a test process contains codependencies and to prevent codependencies from developing during an interview between interviewer and interviewee.

A typical codependency in a test process might be, for example, when the test manager takes on the task of entering defect reports into a defect manage-

> **Codependent behavior** Excessive emotional or psychological dependence on another person, specifically in trying to change that person's current (undesirable) behavior while supporting them in continuing that behavior.

ment tool to compensate for the inability of testers to do this themselves (e.g., through lack of skills, time, or motivation). The testers are content to live with this situation and come to rely on the test manager to take on this task for them. The test manager gets more and more frustrated but can't find a way out without causing difficulties in the team. They don't want to let the team down, so they carry on with the codependent situation until it becomes a "standard" part of their test process. When performing interviews, the test process improver needs to recognize such codependencies and get to the bottom of why this practice has become standard. Improvement suggestions then focus on the reason for the codependency; suggestions in this case may be to give testers adequate training and resources in using the defect management tool. The independence of the test process improver is important in resolving such codependent situations; both sides in the codependency can more easily accept a proposed solution from someone outside of the particular situation.

Codependencies can develop during an interview when the interviewer compensates for the test process difficiencies revealed in the conversation by the interviewee. Perhaps the interviewee is known and liked by the interviewer and the interviewer doesn't want to make trouble for the interviewee by identifying weaknesses in their part of the test process. If the interviewer makes this known by saying things like, "Don't worry, I'll ignore that," "Never mind," or, with a grin, "I didn't hear that," the interviewee comes to expect that their parts of the test process that need correcting will remain untouched. There are several reasons codependency can develop in an interview, but the end result is always the same. In the words of Lee Copeland, we end up "doing all the wrong things for all the right reasons." Once again, using an independent (external) interviewer can help avoid such codependencies. Even then, however, interviewers still need the necessary skills and experienec to recognize and prevent codependent situations from developing in interviews. We must never deny the presence of risk because you or someone you like might be criticized if you mention it.

Ability to Apply Emotional Intelligence

An understanding of emotional intelligence (EI) is important for test process improvers when performing interviews. Generally speaking, the concept of IE (see *Emotional Intelligence: Key Readings on the Mayer and Salovey Model* [Mayer 2004]) recognizes that factual information is often just one aspect of the information being communicated, (we will discuss this further in section 7.3.2) and that it's critical to process the nonfactual "emotional" content of messages correctly. A model developed by Mayer and Salovey [Mayer 2004] notes that people vary in their ability to communicate and understand at the emotional level and describes four types of skills that are important in dealing with emotions (see table 7–3).

Table 7–3 Types of emotional ability

Emotional ability	Description
Perceiving emotions	The ability to detect and interpret emotions in others and in ourselves
Using emotions	The ability to harness emotions to enable thinking and analysis of problems
Understanding emotions	The ability to appreciate complicated relationships among emotions and how they might develop over time
Managing emotions	The ability to regulate emotions in both ourselves and others.

The emotionally intelligent test process improver can do the following:

- Perceive changes of mood during an interview by recognizing them in an interviewee's face and voice. Perhaps a question that pinpoints a weakness in the test process causes the interviewee to frown or to become hesitant.
- Use perceived emotional information to obtain specific information or views from the interviewee. Perhaps an open follow-up question is asked to obtain more information (e.g., What is your feeling about that?)
- Can manage emotions to achieve the objectives of the interview. Perhaps the interviewer uses small talk to create a relaxed mood and encourage the interviewee to talk openly.

The ability-based model proposed by Mayer and Salovey also enables IE to be measured, but it is not expected that test process improvers can conduct these measurements themselves.

> **Emotional intelligence** The ability, capacity, and skill to identify, assess, and manage the emotions of one's self, of others, and of groups.

Test process improvers should use their emotional skills with care during an interview. In particular, the management of emotions, if incorrectly used, may lead to a loss of the "adult-adult" situation you are aiming for in an interview (see the discussion on transactional analysis earlier in this chapter).

7.3.2 Listening Skills

Have you ever played the game where five or more people stand in a line and each passes on a message to the next person in line? When the message reaches the end of the line, the first and the last person write down their messages and they are compared. Everyone laughs at how the original message has changed. For example, a message that started as "Catch the 9 o'clock bus from George Street and change onto the Red Line in the direction of Shady Grove" transforms into "Catch the red bus from Michael Street and change there for Shady Lane." This bit of fun demonstrates the human tendency to filter information, to leave out or add certain details, to transform our understanding, and to simply get the details mixed up. This transformation effect makes life difficult for developers and testers when they try to interpret incorrect, incomplete, or inconsistent requirements.

When conducting interviews, this is not going to happen to the same degree as illustrated in the example, but there is always a certain degree of transformation that takes place. Maybe you miss an important detail, maybe you interpreted "test data" to be the primary data associated with a test case instead of the secondary, background data needed to make the test case run, or maybe you mixed up the names of departments responsible for particular testing activities.

What can you do about this? Where requirements engineers have techniques available to overcome the problem, such as documenting requirements in a normalized format or applying requirements templates and rules, interviewers need other approaches that can be applied in real-time interview situations. In these situations, the following two approaches can be of particular use:

- Practice active listening
- Analyze messages

Active Listening

When you practice this technique in an interview, you are continuously applying following steps:

- Ask a question.
- Listen carefully (apply the transactional analysis discussed earlier).
- Maintain eye contact (but don't stare!).
- Make the interviewee aware that you are listening and interested in what they are saying, perhaps with an occasional nod or a quietly spoken "Okay, aha." Don't look out of the window or busy yourself with other tasks, other than taking occasional notes.
- Wait until the interviewee is finished speaking and avoid interrupting them unless it is absolutely necessary (for example, if they misunderstood the question or are moving way off the subject).
- Once the interviewee has finished with their answer, give them feedback by repeating what you have understood. This isn't a playback of every word; it's a summary of the message you understood, perhaps broken down into the constituent parts discussed earlier when we covered transactional analysis.
- Listen for confirmation or correction.
- Continue with the next question.

This continuous cycle of asking, listening, and giving feedback eliminates many of the misunderstandings and transformational errors that might otherwise result in incorrect findings and ultimately even incorrect proposals being made for test process improvement.

Analyze Messages

When someone communicates with us, they don't just give us facts. You may have heard the expression "reading between the lines." This comes from the general observation that messages (spoken words or written text) often convey more than their factual content, whether this be deliberate or accidental.

Analyzing the messages you receive helps you understand the hidden, nonfactual elements being communicated. With careful listening and an appreciation for the different components in spoken messages, you can improve your ability to understand effectively and make the most of available interview time. The four components of a message (transaction) identified by Schulz von Thun [von Thun 2008] are described in abbreviated form in table 7–4.

Table 7-4 Message components

Message component	Sender communicates …	… receiver understands
Factual component	• Data • Facts • Statements	• Correctness • Completeness • Relevance
Relationship component	• This is what I think about you (not always spoken; e.g., body language, tone of voice). • This is how I see our "chemistry." • Respect, friendliness • Disinterest, contempt	• Acceptance • Level of respect • Rejection • Do we appreciate each other?
Appeal component	• What I would like you to do • Advice • Political messages	• This is what the sender wants me to do • An opinion I should take
Self component	• This is how I am and how I think (my personality). • Intentional, unintentional	• What makes the sender "tick"

Let's see how these four components may be identified in a typical message. Imagine you are at the weekly project status meeting. One of the team leads looks at the test manager and says, "I've entered all the defects into the tool!" The tone is one of exhaustion and exasperation. The team lead raises both arms over his head as he makes the statement. Now, suppose you want to find out if the defect management is working effectively. How might you analyze this statement according to the four components mentioned in table 7–4 (from the sender's point of view)? This is shown in table 7–5.

Table 7-5 Example of message components

Message component	Statement: "I've entered all the defects into the tool!"
Factual component	• The defects have been entered into the tool.
Relationship component	• "I always have to enter these defects." • "I never get any help!"
Appeal component	• "I would really appreciate it if you could find someone to do this tedious job."
Self component	• "I always get the tedious jobs!" • "In this project I'm not really appreciated!"

If you focused on just the facts in this example, you are unlikely to identify ways to improve the defect management. Breaking the message down into its components and then looking at, you might find that the "appeal" component, for example, reveals possibilities for making suggestions. You might see the potential in using additional tool support to make defect entry easier or in training testers to use the defect management tool more efficiently. You would need to find out more before you can actually make these specific suggestions, but with transaction analysis skills, you can more easily identify promising areas for improvement.

In interview situations the ability to analyze messages can also be useful when deciding on the next questions to ask. In that sense, you can also consider this to be an interviewing skill (see section 7.3.1). In this example, your next question might be one of these:

- How do testers record defects in your project?
- Does everyone have access to the defect management tool?
- Are all testers able to use the defect management tool correctly?

Analyzing the message is not an easy skill to develop, but it helps you to "listen" well, it can give you better interview techniques, and it can be a useful method to identify potential improvements.

7.3.3 Presentation and Reporting Skills

As experts in the field of test process improvement, one of the most important things we need to do is to get our message across effectively and to the right people. Without these skills, we will fail to get the necessary commitment from decision makers for the specific improvements we propose and the people affected by those improvements will not fully "buy in" (refer to chapter 8, "Managing Change").

At the Expert Level, it is expected that you already have the basic skills of presenting information (e.g., using slides or flip charts) and writing reports such as test status reports [ISTQB-CTAL-TM]. This section builds on your existing knowledge by considering the following key elements:

- Knowing your audience
- Summarizing information
- Developing your presentation skills
- Developing your reporting skills (including emails)

Knowing Your Audience

If you are unaware of a person's role and responsibilities and their relevance to the test process as a stakeholder, there is a good chance that your message will not come across as well as it should. Testers or developers who need details will find it difficult to relate high-level presentations and reports to their specific tasks. Line managers need sufficient information to make the right tactical (i.e., project-relevant) and/or strategic (i.e., company-wide) decisions. Give them too much detail and they will likely come back to you with questions like, "What does all this mean?" or statements like, "I can't make sense of all this detail." At worst they might simply ignore your message entirely and potentially endanger the chances of implementing your proposed test process improvements.

So how can you sharpen your awareness of stakeholder issues and recognize specific attributes in the people you interact with? One way is to consider the different categories of stakeholders as discussed by Isabel Evans [Evans 2004] and in chapter 2. Each of the stakeholder categories (e.g., developers, managers) has a distinct view of what they consider quality. Recognizing these categories of stakeholders is an essential skill when reporting and presenting because it enables you to adjust the type and depth of information you provide on the test process and any proposed improvements. Developers want detailed information about any proposed changes to, for example, component testing procedures or specifications; they take a "manufacturing-oriented" view of quality. Managers will want consolidated data on how proposals will impact their available resources and overall test process efficiency; they have a "value-oriented" view of quality.

You can extend this concept to include personality types and by considering how specific individuals in a project or organization relate to each other. There are a number of such categorizations that can be used here. Dr. Meredith Belbin provides a scheme that enables us to recognize the principal strengths and weaknesses of a particular person [Belbin 2010]. Work carried out in the field of test team dynamics has shown that natural personality traits can be used to group types of people together based on their behavior. Dr. Belbin carried out research in this field and found nine distinct role types (Team Worker, Plant, Coordinator, Monitor Evaluator, Completer, Finisher, Shaper, Specialist, Implementer, Resource Investigator). Compare, for example, the two Belbin roles Shaper and Monitor Evaluator, which are shown in table 7–6 in highly condensed form:

Table 7–6 Example of Belbin roles

	The Shaper	**The Monitor Evaluator**
Strengths	• Challenges the ideas of others • Is dynamic • Has energy to get things done	• Works quietly and studiously • Thinks objectively • Shows good judgement
Weaknesses	• Is easily provoked • Easily hurts people's feelings	• Not much "power" • Relatively uninspiring

Test managers need to know about these roles to support team building and to understand group dynamics. Test process improvers can also use them to help direct their message in the most appropriate way. Let's say, for example, that you are presenting a test improvement plan to some people and you know from previous experience they include Monitor Evaluators and Shapers. If some of your proposed changes could meet resistance, who would you pick to introduce and pilot them? Would you address the Monitor Evaluators or the Shapers? Our choice would be the Shapers, the people with the power to get things done in the face of possible resistance. This doesn't mean we would ignore the others in the group, but it does mean we would pay extra attention to the views of the Shapers, getting their feedback and assessing their commitment to introduce the proposed changes.

If you prefer to use something other than the Belbin roles, the Myers-Briggs Type Indicator (MBTI) is an alternative (see also section 8.6.1). A further option might be to consider the work of Abe Wagner on transaction analysis [Wagner 1996] mentioned earlier. The Myers-Briggs Type Indicator (MBTI) is an instrument that describes individual preferences for using energy, processing information, making decisions, and relating to the external world [Briggs Myers and Myers 1995]. These preferences result in a four-letter "type" that can be helpful in understanding different personalities. The personality types exhibit different ways in which people communicate and how you might best communicate with them. You may have taken an MBTI test in the past. For those who haven't, here is a basic outline of the MBTI's four preferences. Each preference has two endpoints:

- The first preference describes the source of your energy—introvert or extrovert.
- How one processes information is the next preference—sensing or intuitive.
- Decision-making is the third preference—thinking or feeling.

- The fourth preference—judging or perceiving—deals with how an individual relates to the external world.

Summarizing Information

Test process assessments often result in a large amount of information being collected, regardless of whether a model-based or analytical approach is followed. Consolidating and summarizing this information to make it "digestible" for the intended stakeholders is a key skill. Without the ability to strip out non-essential details and focus on key points at the right level of abstraction, there is a good chance you will swamp your intended audiences with information. In addition, you will find it more difficult to identify the improvements that will really make a difference to the test process. Here are a few tips that will help you to summarize and consolidate information:

- Deliberately limit the time or physical space you have in which to make your points. This could be, for example, a maximum number of slides in a presentation or maximum number of pages in a report. This approach applies in particular to management summaries, which rarely exceed one or two slides/pages. The motto here is "Reduce to the maximum" (i.e., maximum information for the minimum outlay of time or physical space).
- Don't try to cover everything. Use the Pareto Principle to find the 20 percent of information that accounts for 80 percent of what really matters. You will not be thanked for including all the minor points in your report or presentation just for the sake of being thorough and complete.
- Always relate your summary points to the appropriate stakeholder. Describe what a proposed improvement would mean for them, and where possible, try to use their own "language," whether it's the language of a manager (fact and figures, costs and benefits) or the language of the test manager (specific test documents, steps in the test process).
- When summarizing, it can be easy to "oversell" the benefits of a proposed improvement by using sweeping statements and generalizations. Your summary must not be vague or exaggerated. Keep time frames and estimates of effort realistic. Be honest about the risks of implementing changes.
- Use diagrams and illustrations rather than tables of data and complex sentences. In general, remember that "a picture is worth a thousand words."

Developing Your Presentation Skills

Complete coverage of presentation skills is outside the scope of this book. As noted at the start of this section, it is assumed that the Expert Level test process improver starts with the level of knowledge needed for the Advanced Level test manager. Here, we'll provide some tips on how to create good test process improvement presentations and how to deliver them.

The following tips will help you get the content right in your presentations:

- Use the right mix of text and graphics. Reports and presentations that are full of text will not invite the listener or reader to follow your message. How much is "too much" is often a matter of experience and personal preference.
- Proposals must be based on evidence. Always state where your evidence comes from (direct measurements during analysis, statements made during assessment interviews, industry benchmarks, best practices, personal experience in comparable situations). In particular for test process improvement, evidence must clearly show where the test process is now and where improvements will bring benefits.
- Ensure that the evidence used does not represent a special case. Focus on systematic issues that have been noted in several situations (e.g., "We always forget to report on risks") rather than individual problems (e.g., "We delivered the report late three weeks ago").
- Have your presentation reviewed by a collegue (and perhaps a co-assessor) who will look it with a critical mindset.

The following tips relate to improving the delivery of your presentations:

- Create a broad time plan for the presentation. Allow 10 percent of the available time for start-up points such as introductions, scope, and agenda. The main part of the presentation should take up approximately 75 percent of the available time, and the remaining 15 percent should be reserved for summarizing, obtaining feedback, and answering questions. If you are using slides in a presentation, allow for a minimum of three minutes per slide on average. A presentation scheduled for one hour will enable you to present around 15 slides for the key messages in the main part.
- Remember, the end of the presentation is important. Don't stop suddenly by saying, "Well I suppose that's it because we're out of time now" or "You can read the rest in my report." Know when you have presented the last item.

- When you're presenting test process improvement suggestions, there must be a summary of what the results of the assessment are, what needs improving, and what decisions have to be made.
- Anticipate questions by having answers prepared and backup information available. If questions come during the presentation that can be answered right away, then do so; otherwise note them down (e.g., on a flip chart) and answer them at the end of the presentation.
- Always relate to your audience. Make visual contact during the presentation, encourage feedback, and give concise answers to any questions received.
- Use body language effectively. Do not raise or point your finger, and be aware of certain signs of nervousness (e.g., repeated actions, folded arms) and of insincerity (e.g., no eye contact, hesitancy, turning away) in both yourself and your audience.
- Learn from others. Listen to the people who are present (e.g., at conferences, at meetings). If you think they are good presenters, ask yourself why and maybe model your own style on theirs.
- Practice your presentations with colleagues.
- Be open-minded and not defensive.

Developing Your Reporting Skills

The following tips relate to getting the content right for your reports:

- Understand the proper use of diagrams, charts, and graphics. Earlier, we mentioned the common expression "A picture is worth a thousand words," but if the picture tells you nothing or conveys the wrong message, then it's worthless. Always give the reader some help in getting the right message. Uncommented diagrams can easily be misinterpreted.
- As with presentations, be sure you state the source of any data and evidence you provide, unless this breaks any confidentiality agreements you may have made (e.g., with an interviewee).
- Avoid unneccesary content. Before you write anything, ask yourself, "Who will be interested in reading this?" and "Why am I writing this?" Apply the motto "Reduce to the maximum" by writing as much as necessary and as little as possible.
- Maintain the trust of your intended audience at all times. If people don't trust what you say, they will not read what you have written. Always tell the truth. Never hide relevant information. Don't spread rumors. Maintain an objective, professional style.

- Practice your reporting skills. Books can also be of help in giving ideas and tips (see *Information Dashboard Design: The Effective Visual Communication of Data* [Few 2006] and *Envisioning Information* [Tufte 1997])

Developing Your Email Skills

Test process improvers, like many of us, frequently using email to communicate. This is an area where written communication can often break down. (How often do you hear people saying, "I didn't mean it that way" when others respond unfavorably to a badly written email?) You can improve your email-writing skills by considering the following points:

- Avoid text in red, capital letters and in large font sizes. Equally bad, the ! character should be used with care. In an email, all of these attempts to provide emphasis can easily be interpreted as "shouting."
- Don't make jokes or use slang in your email messages. Both can easily be misinterpreted, especially where different cultures are involved.
- Never make threats or hurtful comments. Even if you are irritated by an email, think before you write a response. Ask yourself, "Would I use the same words tomorrow?" and "Would I be comfortable with anyone else reading this?" Sometimes it helps to not respond instantly but instead to wait a few hours and rethink your answer.
- In general, in the context of test process improvement, write emails as you would professional documents.

7.3.4 Analytical Skills

An analytical approach to test improvement is based on a number of specific skills that help test process improvers summarize information, identify trends, and differentiate between causes and effects. Several of these skills are described in chapter 4. In addition, the test process improver needs many other skills that are briefly described in this section.

Knowledge of statistical techniques will enable the correct interpretations to be drawn from data, particularly regarding the statistical significance of data. For example, if data relating to test environment availability is collected, statistical techniques can be used to analyze the data and show whether the availability has been below a required level on a statistically significant number of days (the meaning of *significant* would, of course, need to be defined as well).

A basic knowledge of statistics will enable correlations between different parameters to be detected. Is the fall in the number of high-severity defects found in production strongly correlated to the number of test cases that are automated or is this coincidental? Could there be other parameters that are more strongly correlated to this trend, such as improvements in the risk-based testing strategy?

Test process improvers must be aware that a more subjective type of analysis can be more appropriate. Take, for example, improvements made to the testing of software usability. It may be more appropriate to use a more subjective questionaire-based approach to demonstrate improvements than attempt to perform purely statistical analysis. An example of this is the standardized and publicly available survey "Software Usability Measurement Inventory" [URL: SUMI].

Don't forget that the transaction analysis skills we described in section 7.3.1 can also be used for the analysis of inteview results (Were they trying to tell us something there? What was the hidden meaning behind that statement?).

Finally, the ability to analyze systems and their interactions is a key skill, especially where many data flows and dependencies exist between the different parts of a system (which may contain both hardware and software components). What feedback loops can be defined in the system? Are they positive and reinforcing (i.e., they help to stabilize the system) or are they negative and destabilizing? Refer to *Quality Software Management, Volume 1* [Weinberg 1992] for more on systems analysis. Skills in modeling system architectures using the standard notations used in software development are recommended.

7.3.5 Note-Taking Skills

Interviews combine many of the skills needed by the test process improver. Taking good notes may sound like any easy task, but remember, if an interviewer is conducting an interview by themselves (i.e., without the support of a co-assessor), they will be simultaneously occupied in asking good questions, listening carefully, understanding and analyzing the answers they receive, and keeping the overall interview on track. Add to this the task of note taking and it becomes apparent that anything that can reduce the workload on the interviewer is going to benefit the interview as a whole. Of course, one solution is to conduct interviews together with a co-assessor and thereby relieve the overall workload on the lead assessor. Unfortunately, this is not always an option, so good note-taking skills are required by both lead assessors and co-assessors.

An effective way to take notes is to summarize and group related information on a mind map [Buzan and Buzan 1995]. These diagrams enable us to connect related items of information easily and join them to form a tree-like

> **Mind map**   A diagram used to represent words, ideas, tasks, or other items linked to and arranged around a central key word or idea. Mind maps are used to generate, visualize, structure, and classify ideas and as an aid in study, organization, problem-solving, decision-making, and writing.

structure. The resulting "big picture" can cover a wide range of individual topics and may contain a combination of text, sketches, or symbols.

Section 4.2.2 discusses the use of mind maps as a way to support gathering and organizing the information for analytical approaches to test process improvement (and also shows an example). Considered from the note-taking aspect, the main benefits of using mind maps are as follows:

- Note-taking is quicker compared to writing down text in natural, long-hand format.
- The main areas of interest are better organized, especially if a template mind map has been prepared in advance that contains the broad areas to be covered.
- There is more time to focus on conducting an interview. Sometimes pre-prepared mind maps can be extended by having some key "open" questions written down and ready for asking. This generally gives interviewers more control over the interview.
- Post-inteview analysis is more effective. The associations drawn on the mind maps help us to recall significant points and to develop any key ideas where improvements might be required.
- Where a brief summary of the interview is required shortly after its conclusion, the "big picture" nature of mind maps helps to summarize the main points. You don't have to leaf through pages of notes written in prose. Note that some good freeware tools for mind mapping are available and are very easy to learn.

Despite the benefits of note-taking with mind maps, the test process improver may prefer other approaches. During interviews, these may include the use of keywords, shorthand notations, or even natural text (especially useful for capturing significant statements as direct quotes). Certain types of information, such as organizational structures or team communication charts, can also be captured with a variety of diagrams.

Here are some further tips on note taking:

- Avoid using a laptop when taking notes during an interview. This might be seen by the interviewee as a barrier and could prevent free discussion from developing.
- Try not to use a red pen for taking notes. This can be a distraction for the interviewee due to the association in many countries of red with danger or "wrong."
- Always ask for permission from the interviewee if you wish to make audio or video recordings of the interview. In particular, there should be a clear agreement made regarding use and disposal of the recordings. In general this is not a recommended practice because it usually makes the interviewee respond less freely.
- If workshops are organized to discuss or develop improvement proposals, the notes taken should be made accessible to all contributors. This encourages interaction and improves the group buy-in to any notes taken.

7.3.6 Skills of Persuasion

You cannot expect stakeholders to simply say yes to improvement proposals, especially if significant changes to work practices are needed or where major funding is required. In some situations, you may not be the first to propose particular improvement measures; perhaps previous attempts failed, leaving stakeholders cautious and even skeptical about similar proposals. Obtaining management backing and buy-in is highlighted in chapter 8 as being one of the key activities at the start of the improvement cycle. Several of the skills described previously are needed at this important stage to give proposals the best chance of being adopted. These include good presentation and reporting skills, ability to summarize information, and skills of persuasion.

The 30-Second Message

The technique was developed by Milo Frank [Frank 1990] and is particularly useful when only very limited time is available to get your message across to busy people, such as line managers or senior company executives. The technique is really quite simple and consists of the following steps:

- Set objectives
- Select audience
- Choose an approach

- Use a "hook" to get attention
- Know the subject
- Ask for what you want, or at least for a next step toward achieving the objective

A 30-second message is something a test process improver plans and prepares in advance. When the right situation arises (e.g., you meet the CIO in the coffee room or after a meeting), you are ready to implement the plan. Table 7-7 shows the planned outline for a 30-second message.

Table 7-7 Example plan for a 30-second message

Element of 30-second message	Content
Objective	Get the chief information officer (CIO) to buy in to using reviews.
Audience	CIO
Approach	Appeal to possible savings. Time and money invested now result in finding bugs early and bringing savings later.
Hook	You must be fed up with projects being late due to showstoppers found in acceptance testing; review techniques can help prevent this by finding problems in the requirements.
Subject	Reviews are a proven technique that can find up to 70 percent of defects in requirements. Rules and checklists are used to find the most common errors. Defects are not propagated to the later stages of development.
Ask for it	Why not give reviews a try on the next software release of our project?

The 30-second message is a good way to approach persuading individuals. You should also consider which basic approach to adopt in persuading a group. The two approaches ("push" and "pull") are briefly outlined next.

The "Push" Approach

This is a low-cost approach that for many is a "natural" style of persuading people regarding an idea or proposal. The success of the push approach is highly dependent on the level of trust and standing enjoyed by the person doing the persuading. Effectively, they are saying, "Follow me, I know best." If everyone has trust in that person, they are more likely to be persuaded that the idea, which is presented as the only possibility available, is worth following. This is one of the reasons organizations sometimes hire external experts to do an assessment and report to management. They are respected and have the required authority.

If a test process improver enjoys this high standing with their stakeholders, and if they support their proposal with facts and information, then people will be persuaded to follow their proposals.

The problems with adopting this approach may only reveal themselves at a later stage. Maybe people were unconvinced of the proposal but were happy that someone was taking a lead. Maybe people had their own ideas but were afraid to bring them forward as alternatives. Now they start to "chip away" at to ideas as they are introduced and begin to undermine the proposals they initially signed up for. Clearly, if people have been persuaded to follow a particular course by a strong-minded, persuasive person, the implementation of that proposal is also likely to run into trouble if that person should becomes unavailable (e.g., an external consultant whose contract runs out).

The "Pull" Approach

This approach is based on reaching consensus among the stakeholders affected by a proposal. It takes more time and effort because of the discussions and workshops needed, but the adoption of a proposal reached this way is likely to have more chance of achieving lasting benefit. The group identifies more strongly with the proposal as being "theirs" and is more likely to find solutions to any problems should they occur. The test process improver often facilitates the discussions and helps the group reach a mutually acceptable solution.

7.3.7 Management Skills

The tasks of the test process improver require both specialization and a wide range of general management skills. This is the reason those taking the ISTQB certification examnation are required to also have at least the Advanced Level certificate in Test Management. A few examples illustrate the relevance of management skills for the test process improver:

- Prioritizing and scheduling test process improvements
- Estimating the effort required to implememt test process improvements
- Monitoring the implementation of a test process improvement plan
- Identifying and interacting with stakeholders
- Making decisions about the need for test process improvements
- Leading a Test Process Group

Describing the management skills required by the test process improver is outside the scope of this book. It is recommended that the reader consult the wide range of books available on the subject and, in particular, those relating to test management. A good start would be, for example, Rex Black's book on managing the testing process [Black 2009].

7.3.8 Summary

All of the soft skills described in this section need practice. Reading about it is a good start, but you have to get out there and apply them. This will ask a lot of you at times, but with a bit of bravery and practice, your skills will improve. Our tip: Be conscious of when somebody is exhibiting good soft skills. What makes them good? Note it and try to emulate these skills yourself. We frequently learn from people by doing this.

7.4 Exercises

The following multiple-choice questions will give you some feedback on your understanding of this chapter. Appendix F lists the answers.

7-1 What would you expect to find in the organization of a Test Process Group?

A: Executive Council

B: Lead Assessor Group

C: Offshore Steering Group

D: Test Engineering Process Group

7-2 What would you consider to be *not* within the test process improver's scope in implementing test improvement with offshore teams?

A: Achieving non-testing process maturity "entry criteria" before embarking on test process improvements

B: Checking that governance and organizational structures are in place and requesting necessary improvements

C: Checking that effective communication between teams can take place and requesting necessary improvements

D: Ensuring that motivation, expectations, and quality culture are aligned

7-3 Which task would you *not* expect a test process improver to perform?

A: Manage the introduction of changes to the test process.

B: Manage the human issues associated with assessing the test process.

C: Raise the maturity level of IT processes.

D: Perform the duties of a lead assessor.

7-4 Which of the following is a task typically performed by a lead assessor?

A: Set the business goals.

B: Check the assessment report written by the co-assessor.

C: Accept the test improvement plan.

D: Perform interviews and analysis.

7-5 Which of the following actions indicates *bad* interviewing skills?

A: Asking open questions at the start of an interview

B: Asking "effective inner people" factual questions

C: Ensuring that a codependent bond is established between interviewer and interviewee

D: Making notes

7-6 What activity would you perform after completion of an assessment interview?

A: Briefly discuss the conclusions with the interviewee.

B: Explain what the nexts steps are.

C: Give the interviewee feedback on their personality type.

D: Discuss common issues arising from other interviews.

7-7 What is important for the assessor to do when practicing active listening during an interview?

A: Give regular feedback to the interviewee on how well they are performing.

B: Manage time to ensure that the discussion fits into the allocated time period.

C: Repeat your understanding of what the interviewee said.

D: Ask open questions.

7-8 What can help deliver good presentations?

A: Discouraging people from asking questions.

B: Remaining seated with arms crossed.

C: Making sure you always look at the slide that is currently shown.

D: Keeping to a broad time plan.

7-9 Why do you need a "hook" in a 30-second message?

A: To help establish objectives with the person you want to talk to

B: To "catch" the right person to give the message to

C: To get attention for the message

D: To agree to the next step

7-10 How can you improve your written skills with regard to emails?

A: Keep to one main subject.

B: Ensure that you get people's attention by using different colors for main points.

C: Make sure that if you say something bad about someone, the email does not get forwarded.

D: Use an occasional light-hearted joke to make the email more fun to read.

8 Managing Change

The best plans, the most exciting ideas, the most promising objectives—they are practically worthless if they can't be put into practical use. This can be one of the most challenging and rewarding stages of improving test processes. If the actual changes become adopted and if the expected benefits are achieved, you have achieved your ultimate objective: to improve the test process to the benefit of the organization, its stakeholders, and its staff. Conversely, this can be the stage where you end up with that sinking feeling of failure. Why aren't they doing what was planned? Don't they know this is going to benefit them too? Why are they resisting so much? The answer? "They" are humans and "they" don't always behave as you would expect. Remember, most people don't like change. Therefore, change doesn't just happen; it needs careful consideration and management.

This chapter considers the critically important task of actually implementing the planned changes within the project or organization. We will look at the basic steps to follow and place a strong focus on the human aspects of implementing changes successfully.

Changes are not exclusive to the test process. Especially in the IT industry, you might hear people say, "The only thing that is constant here is change." Anyone who wants to introduce change will benefit from reading this chapter: line managers, team leads, human resources managers, and, yes, process improvers. If you are on the receiving end of changes (and who isn't), you will also benefit by reflecting on the human issues involved in changing the way you do things. If you understand what is going on, why you feel the way you do and what you can do about it, you will be better prepared the next time "change" affects you.

8.1 Introduction

Syllabus Learning Objectives

LO 8.2.1 (K2) Summarize the fundamental change management process.

LO 8.2.2 (K6) Create a test improvement plan considering change management issues, with appropriate steps and actions.

LO 8.3.1 (K2) Summarize the role of human factors in the change management process.

LO 8.3.2 (K4) Analyze people's attitudes to change and relate them to the Satir model.

LO 8.3.3 (K5) Recommend measures to create acceptance of the changes by the people involved.

To introduce the subject of change, let's consider what typically happens when change is badly managed. This could happen, for example, if a manager makes a surprise announcement at a meeting; for example, "Tomorrow everything will be done like this" (pointing, perhaps to a poster on the wall) or "From now on we will be better." Maybe a trolley-load of documents is wheeled into the room and the manager proudly announces, "The new test process is here; use it" or, more subtly, "We will all be receiving a new tool tomorrow; this will improve our productivity."

We expect that many of you have experienced similar situations; imposing change like this simply doesn't work. Why? Well, because the two principal ingredients for sucessful change are missing:

- A framework or process within which change can take place
- A proper consideration for the human aspects of change

We need to consider both people and processes to create the right conditions for change. This means thinking about both of these aspects in advance of implementing changes and then managing the change right through to completion.

In the sections that follow, we will look at the fundamental change process. This will give you practical information about what to do and when. At each stage in the process we will ask the questions, "Where do people fit into this?" and "What can we do to help ourselves and others to change (their testing process)?" To help answer these questions, we will draw on some of the excellent guidance and ideas provided by Naomi Karten [Karten 2009], Virginia Satir [Satir, et al. 1991], and Malcom Gladwell [Gladwell 2000], (among others).

An appreciation of these various issues will help to establish a culture of improvement in which change is regarded as something that is "normal" and can be properly managed.

8.2 Overview

The principal ideas mentioned in this chapter are interwoven within the framework of change management and a fundamental change management process.

Before going into the details of this process, we'll describe the basic steps in the fundamental change process and provide an overview of the two main pieces of work referred to: the Satir model and the theory of tipping points.

> **Change management**
> (1) A structured approach to transitioning individuals and organizations from a current state to a desired future state.
>
> (2) A controlled way to effect a change, or a proposed change, to a product or service.

8.2.1 The Fundamental Change Process

A number of models of the change process have been proposed, but they all share broadly the same principles as the model used in this chapter. The fundamental change model includes the following steps, or phases:

- **Preparing for change**

In this first step, the stage is set for the changes to be made, starting with the initial "spark" that establishes the need for improvement. Convincing sponsors and stakeholders that change is needed builds the momentum needed to get moving toward changes to the test process. With the backing of those people, you can set up the team needed to implement the changes and move forward.

- **Deciding what to do**

The next step is to draw up a vision of where you want to go. How will the improved test process look when you are done? Objectives need to be set and aligned to the goals of the organization. In your approach, you will also need to balance out long-term improvements with the need to show short-term "quick wins."

- **Implementing the changes**

As the Expert Level syllabus points out, this is where you "make it happen." More correctly, it's where you enable the people whose work practices and responsibilities are the focus of change to actually adopt them. This is where effective communication, motivation, and an understanding of people's responses to change are critically important for successful improvement.

- **Making the changes stick**

Creating a new culture of improvement is at the heart of this step. This is where you need the patience and stamina to keep the ball rolling and provide all those involved with encouragement and support.

These steps may give the impression that the fundamental change process is purely sequential in its approach, but this is not so. There is likely to be a strong degree of overlap between the different steps, and the process itself may be iterative, with small increments of change being implemented in parallel to one another. For the test process improver, it's important to know the stage at which a particular improvement has been achieved. Failure to manage this properly could result in confusion and might even endanger the success of the overall improvement program.

The IDEAL model of test process improvement also covers some of the issues mentioned in the fundamental change process just summarized. This comes as no real surprise because both models are involved in the overall objectives of test process improvement. An important distinction in this chapter, however, is that the focus is placed on the process of change itself and how to do this successfully. This places a strong emphasis on the two steps involved with implementing the changes and making them stick. Where relevant material is also covered the IDEAL model (chapter 6), appropriate references will be made.

8.2.2 The Satir Model

The way people respond to change is well captured in a model developed by Virginia Satir and eloquently described by Naomi Karten [Karten 2009]. Anyone who has been through a change (and who hasn't) will find themselves agreeing with the intuitive and logical structure of the model, which fits well into the framework of the fundamental change process described earlier. The Satir model describes how people change from a defined starting point ("the initial status quo") to a new and better end state ("the end status quo") by passing through specific phases:

- **Impact of a *foreign element* (also known as *jolt* or *trigger*)**

A jolt can come from a number of sources, such as the announcement of a new organizational structure. The key point is that the jolt causes a reaction that pushes a person away from their current status quo and, initially, into a state of chaos.

- **Period of chaos**

Following the jolt, a person enters a state where uncertainty, insecurity, confusion, or even anger dominates. In this state, you can expect people to react emotionally and not logically. It's a period of reduced productivity that can vary in its depth and duration, depending on the nature of the initial jolt and the measures taken (partly by test process improvers) to alleviate the negative aspects of chaos.

- **Development of *transforming ideas***

During this phase, people start to look for ways out of their chaos. A more positive approach is adopted as ideas begin to form at the team level. Of course, test process improvements will include such transforming ideas in the form of specific proposals documented in the test improvement plan. These proposals guide the process of finding transforming ideas.

- **Practice and integration**

The climb out of chaos involves implementing the transforming ideas so that those affected can achieve the intended improvements. There will be setbacks and successes during this phase, and some people will adopt changes more readily than others. Ultimately, people get used to the changes by practicing them and integrating them into their regular working procedures. As people begin to "see the light," they become steadily more enthusiastic about the changes and pull up the slower adopters. A new status quo is reached when these practices have been generally accepted as being the "normal" way of doing things.

As you will see in the rest of this chapter, test process improvers can do a lot to manage the introduction of improvements by appreciating the human aspects of the change process and by taking specific measures to manage those changes.

Note that the Satir model is generally applicable to virtually any situation where people change a particular aspect of their lives from an initial state to a new state. The identified phases may overlap and iterations may occur, especially where the introduction of new transforming ideas acts as new jolts. Test process improvers must take care not to introduce fresh jolts to people who are already in chaos. This can have the effect of deepening and lengthening the period of chaos, with potentially harmful impact on the organization and its employees.

The diagram in figure 8–1 combines the fundamental change process with the Satir model (symbols used taken from *Changing How You Manage and Communicate Change: Focusing on the Human Side of Change* [Karten 2009])

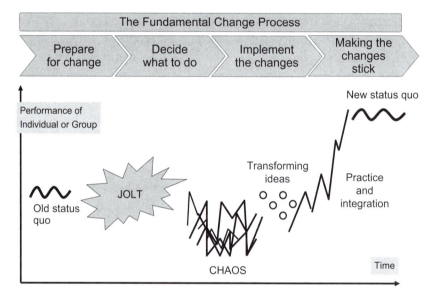

Figure 8–1   The fundamental change process and the Satir model

8.2.3 Tipping Points and Change

An appreciation of tipping point concepts [Gladwell 2000] will give us ideas about how to implement improvements effectively, especially where those changes affect a large number of people, such as in a large department or organization. In common with the Satir model, Tipping Point theory focuses on the people aspects of change. As noted in section 4.2.3, certain aspects of Tipping Point theory (such as the concept of "broken windows") can help you to analyze test processes and identify the root causes of problems.

Some of the key aspects of tipping points are summarized next.

The Basic Concepts

Tipping Point theory focuses on the point at which small changes can have big effects, where change becomes "viral," rather like an epidemic of influenza. Some of the basic concepts are as follows:

- Stickiness: There are specific ways to make a message memorable (*sticky* is the word used by Gladwell). Small changes to the way information is structured and presented can make a huge difference. Good soft skills and care are needed to get the message across as intended; there is unfortunately a thin line between success and failure here.
- Context: You need to be sensitive to the context in which rapid adoption of changes occurs. A good example is making improvements to the working environment (some colorful posters, new plants, more ergonomic workplaces). These changes may be small and yet create a constructive atmosphere that makes people more receptive to change.
- Group influence: Groups can play a major role in spreading information and ideas quickly, mainly because peer pressure exists between their members and because a kind of group knowledge and memory develops. It's important that groups are small enough to enable members to know each other. Having more than 150 people in a group is inadvisable because structural impediments start to occur that inhibit the ability of the group to agree and act with one voice. Groups are good units to take on responsibility for implementing particular improvements.
- Small steps lead to bigger steps: To create one "wave" of movement, you often have to create many small movements first. This is what Gladwell refers to as the "paradox of epidemic" and is a significant concept for test process improvers to realize, particularly when proposing improvements.

The Champions of Change

One critical factor in achieving rapid, epidemic-like change is the nature of the messengers who spread the word. The following "champions of change" are identified:

- **Connectors**: These people bring others together; they seem to know everyone and they make contacts very easily. They are friendly but casual, self-confident, sociable, and energetic. Generally speaking, the closer an improvement proposal comes to a connector, the more "energy" it has and the greater its chances of a successful implementation.

- **Oracles:** (Gladwell calls them *mavens*): These people are like walking "data banks" of knowledge. They are socially motivated and want to help people by sharing their knowledge. People tend to actively seek out oracles, especially when there is uncertainty about what is fact and what is fiction.
- **Salespeople:** These people are especially useful when others are unconvinced about improvements. They are expressive and fun and work with others at the emotional level. A good salesperson is hard to resist (don't we know it!).

So the idea is that test process improvers use their knowledge of these types of people and the powerful ideas expressed in the Tipping Point theory to help get change implemented, in particular where large numbers of people are involved.

We have now looked briefly at three main areas in change management: the fundamental change process, the Satir model, and Tipping Point theory. The rest of this chapter takes a more detailed look at the activities within the fundamental change process and weaves together the process and people aspects.

8.3 Prepare for Change

This phase includes the following principal activities:

- Establish the need for improvement
- Create a sense of urgency
- Establish the improvement team

These activities are similar to the activities for the initiating stage of the IDEAL model described in chapter 6. We describe the change management aspects of these activities in the following sections.

8.3.1 Establish the Need for Improvement

Getting started with test process improvement comes about from receiving an impulse. Without this it's questionable whether the effort is justifiable, and sooner or later you are going to find it hard to answer questions like, Why are we doing this? Typically, the need for improvement comes from one or more of the following situations:

- Disaster strikes
- You receive stakeholder feedback
- You see the need yourself
- It's your policy

Disaster Strikes

You have probably been in this situation before. Something horrible has happened (e.g., a severe system crash) and testing is considered to be partly or wholly to blame. Depending on the severity of the disaster, there are likely to be investigations that lead to specific decisions being taken, such as "improve the testing process!"

Now, there is a lot of negativity surrounding this kind of situation. After all, organizations can lose substantial amounts of money, companies can suffer a blow to their image, and people can be hurt. However, one small crumb of comfort comes from the high-priority and management attention given to test process improvements. Being in the spotlight may not always be desirable, but test process improvers certainly will benefit from strong management backing and convincing arguments for improvement suggestions. However, the human aspects of changes resulting from software disasters will need very careful management.

You Receive Stakeholder Feedback

When you talk to stakeholders about testing, they rarely say straight out, "We need test process improvement." The feedback you receive often gives you hints; you may hear statements like, "We find the faults too late" or "Testing is too expensive," and sometimes you might just hear general statements like, "There's something wrong with our testing." Often these statements will be mixed in with more general discussions on IT, and you might not even be present when these things are mentioned. To ensure that you receive feedback about testing, you need to be sure that your line managers, salespeople, and consultants are sensitive to statements like these and pass on the feedback to you.

Depending on the importance and relevance of the stakeholder, a test process improver should consider all forms of feedback (both positive and negative) as an initial stimulus for establishing the specific need for test process improvement. Certainly, if you receive feedback from a CIO or senior VP, it's time to get active! However, it would be advisable to check back first with the stakeholder and address any specific issues, especially those relating to the human aspects. It's quite possible that the originator will modify their feedback once they realize the potential consequences of making the required test process improvements.

You See the Need Yourself

In our daily working lives in projects, working groups, and organizations, we frequently get the opportunity to exchange views about testing with colleagues. This could take place in a formal situation, like a project meeting, or it could be a casual conversation in the coffee room or over lunch. These exchanges of views provide valuable input and stimuli that can lead you to recognize the need for test process improvement. You need to be aware of these stimuli. Maybe some programmers mention over lunch that their component test process could be improved, maybe a tester has a good idea that they would rather discuss informally with their team, and maybe you hear lots of complaints about a specific aspect of testing (e.g., "The test environment is always down").

Of course, project leaders should be alert to these kinds of issues, but test process improvers also need to be sensitive to any ideas or issues relating to testing. They need to recognize trends and issues in what they are hearing and present them in a coherent form for discussion and further analysis. They are also alert, for example, to any "broken windows" in the test process that might be negatively influencing it. They might hear people saying things like, "Nobody ever seems to maintain their test cases properly after a change; why should I bother?" These are clear signs of a test process in need of improvement.

Where necessary, potential improvement issues should be discussed with the project leader and with the group of people from which the ideas and comments originate. Project retrospective meetings are excellent opportunities for this kind of exchange of views (see section 6.6). This is where soft skills can be particularly useful (see section 7.3) so that a discussion can be started that enables the group to arrive at collective conclusions. The significant thing here is that establishing the need for improvement comes from within, that is, from the people who are feeling the pain or seeing the opportunities. This group "buy-in" can be a major plus if the ideas subsequently result in the introduction of specific improvements.

It's Your Policy

A test process that has achieved a high level of maturity includes an element of self-improvement. This means the test process improver can consider improvements to be a standard, even regular occurrence that is anchored within the process. They might even be integrated into a quality management policy or a company test improvement policy. Establishing the need for improvement doesn't depend on disaster striking, you don't need to wait for stakeholders to give you feedback on where testing might be failing them, and you don't need to rely entirely on the test process improver channeling issues into a collective view of where to improve; improvement is a continuous activity that is simply defined as an integral part of a mature test process. Some organizations, for example, might install a policy that calls for test process assessments to be performed annually on all projects above a certain level of criticality. If the assessment identifies areas for improvement, then measures are defined as a matter of standard procedure. Often the improvement measures are oriented toward tuning the test process or recovering from occasional slippages regarding specific practices (e.g., using the latest metrics in test effort estimations). Given this level of predictability and proactiveness, the human impact of change is much reduced; people may not always welcome the "standard" assessments, but they are rarely plunged into a state of deep chaos afterward.

8.3.2 Create a Sense of Urgency

Once the need for improvement has been established, it's time to gather the information needed to make a case to important decision-makers (i.e., the ones likely to be funding any improvements). The information you gather should be as objective and relevant as possible. Try not to use words like *too many* or *too expensive* because they are open to interpretation. If only subjective arguments can be used, care should be taken that they are reasonable and realistic; decision-makers are used to hearing exaggerated stories from people requesting funding, so "overselling" in an effort to create a sense of urgency could easily end up in failure. You should typically ask the following kinds of questions:

- How many high severity defects were found in production and how much did it cost to fix them?
- How many user complaints have been received about particular parts of an application?
- What are some actual problems experienced in the test process and what was their impact on efficiency or testing effectiveness?
- What risks (likelihood and potential impact) are associated with not improving the test process?

Creating a sense of urgency and gaining stakeholder backing will require many of the soft skills mentioned in chapter 7. High on the list are skills of persuasion and presentation. In addition, test process improvers should recognize that stakeholders may not react rationally to the news that the test process needs improvement; this must be handled with tact and care. Sponsors of improvement will want to be reassured about the change process and how it will be managed, so proposals for keeping them informed about status, problems, and risks should not be forgotten.

Assuming that stakeholder backing has been obtained, this should be made known to those affected by changes. They will need to know that there is support for the changes, especially if they are far reaching.

8.3.3 Establish the Improvement Team

Chapter 7 deals in length with the organization and roles found in an improvement team. When it comes to implementing change, the Test Process Group mentioned in section 7.1.1 will typically be assisted by individuals who can play a significant supporting role in getting the changes implemented and making them stick. When preparing for change, test process improvers need to identify these individuals (the "champions of change" and the "early adopters") and get them on board.

Identify Champions of Change

To identify the individuals who will support the improvement activities, test process improvers should consider people in the organization who can be the "champions of change," as mentioned in section 8.2.3. This applies in particular to improvements that need to be rolled out to many people across an organization. Depending on the number of people affected by the planned improvements and the specific nature of the changes themselves, it may be necessary to identify a particular mix of these special people, which include connectors, oracles, and salespeople. If there is likely to be a lot of convincing to be done, you would look for salespeople, if changes are more technical in nature (e.g., introduction of a new tool), it would be wise to identify suitable oracles with specific knowledge, and if you need to spread the word across a wide range of organizational units, connectors will be needed. If you are really fortunate, one person may be able to perform more than one of these roles, but that would be exceptional.

Identify Adopters of Change

The champions of change will tend to be more effective if the people affected by the changes are willing and enthusiastic. These are the so-called *early adopters* of change; they are generally open to change, they are unlikely to give up easily in the face of difficulty, and they will tend to withstand any setbacks during the implementation of improvements. Often these early adopters can be easily identified in an organization; maybe you know them yourself, sometimes you may need to ask around, and in some cases they come forward as willing volunteers.

If early adopters are not so easy to identify early, the test process improver may prefer to conduct an evaluation, as proposed by Kirton [URL: Kirton] (please read section 8.7, "Data Privacy," before you do that). According to Kirton, we all have an element of adaptor or innovator in us. *Adaptors* tend to be disciplined and efficient; they are team-oriented problem solvers. *Innovators* are challengers of accepted theory and have ideas that can sometimes be quite radical. Kirton assumes that all people have a creative side to them and gives us an evaluation method to answer the question, Will someone prefer to be creative within the rules or by breaking the rules?

Determining whether a person is an adaptor or innovator is generally useful to show their preferred approach to adopting change. If test process improvers see a need for gradual change that involves, for example, the extension of existing testing practices, it would be better to focus initial attention on people with a strong adaptor side. If you are looking to break open current practices and introduce something completely new (e.g., introduction of agile testing), you would favor people with a stronger innovator side.

Early adopters who are also in a decision making position (e.g., a project leader or test manager) are the prime candidates for early involvement, especially if improvements are first to be introduced in pilot projects. Early adopters in these positions will significantly influence the choice of pilot project (see section 6.5.1).

8.4 Decide What to Change

This phase includes the following principal activities:

- Establish a vision for the future.
- Set specific objectives and align to business goals.
- Decide on the implementation strategy.
- Balance long-term and short-term benefits.

These activities are similar to the activities for the initiating stage of the IDEAL model described in chapter 6. We'll describe the change management aspects of these activities in the following sections.

8.4.1 Establish a Vision of the Future

A vision for the future is not just something required to convince stakeholders and line managers of the need for and the reasoning behind test process improvements (refer to section 6.2.2); it's an essential element of the change process. Certainly, people affected by improvement will be generally interested in aspects like return on investment, broad objectives, and the scheduling of specific changes, but for people to get behind the required changes, they must be able to see a vision of their future working practices. Using the term introduced by Satir (see section 8.2.2), what will the *new status quo* feel like? How will the new, improved test process affect people?

This vision for the future needs to be firmly established and agreed upon with stakeholders before any improvements are rolled out. Once this is achieved, the test process improver should consider how best to communicate the new vision to affected people and might prepare presentations and other materials showing the "big picture." These will be needed when communicating for buy-in and understanding at the start of the "make it happen" phase of the change process (see section 8.5.1).

8.4.2 Set Specific Objectives and Align to Business Goals

Measurable objectives that are aligned to business goals are essential so that the benefit of test process improvements can be shown and their introduction can be performed in a controlled way. When communicating for buy-in and understanding, test process improvers will typically refer back to these aspects. (Further details are described in section 6.2.2).

8.4.3 Decide on an Implementation Strategy

The implementation strategy is part of the test improvement plan (see section 6.4.2). The strategy typically includes a consideration of which improvements are to be performed using a top-down approach and which shall use a bottom-up approach.

Top-down strategies implement improvements first at the higher organizational levels. The focus lies on the common ground between projects so that the improvements have a positive effect on as many individual projects as possible.

A top-down strategy will affect a relatively large number of people and the need for good communication will be high. When deciding on the implementation strategy, the availability of connectors to spread the word throughout the affected projects and departments will be a significant consideration in managing the change.

Bottom-up strategies implement improvements first in selected projects and spread successful improvements into other projects as required. The initial focus lies on demonstrating the value of specific improvements. If early adopters can be identified and any support required can be provided from oracles, this strategy will have a good chance of success.

8.4.4 Balance Short-Term and Longer-Term Benefits

Part of the test improvement strategy is to create a balance between the short-term improvements (often referred to as *quick wins*) and those that require more time to take effect.

Quick wins can have a significant effect on both the test process itself and the change process. Clearly, if specific problems can be fixed quickly, there will be a reconizable improvement to the test process (e.g., delays in executing tests due to low availability of the test environment may be quickly fixed by purchasing and installing a new environment). The impact of quick wins on the overall change process are also significant. Here are two of the most important aspects:

- Motivation rises: When quick improvements are made, the message is clear: things are happening for the better. Early adopters are empowered, and some sceptics may begin to change their views. As the level of motivation rises, extra momentum is added to the overall change process.
- References are achieved: Successful improvements serve as excellent references for achieving buy-in for other improvements. Salespeople have some material to work with in convincing others of the need for particular improvements.

When rolling out test process improvements, care is needed to ensure that the strategy is not too heavily biased toward quick wins. Even though the impact of these short-term gains on the change process is positive, a balance between short- and long-term gains is generally desirable. Some deep-seated issues may need time to take effect, especially where they affect working practices that have been in place for several years. Time is also required to establish a culture of improvement (see section 8.6.3). A strategy with too much emphasis on quick wins runs the risk that the change process loses momentum as the initial surge of activity and motivation drops off before long-term measures can take effect.

8.5 Making Change Happen

The principal activities in this phase of the fundamental change process are strongly focused in the people-related aspects of change. This is where many of the ideas introduced in the Satir model can be useful. The main activities are as follows:

- Communicating for buy-in and understanding
- Anticipating chaos
- Managing chaos
- Handling resistance
- Developing Transforming Ideas

Some of the issues we covered in chapter 6 (IDEAL model) will "ring a bell" in the following sections.

8.5.1 Communicating for Buy-In and Understanding

Communication is the key to minimizing the impact of the chaos that people go through after receiving a jolt (e.g., announcing that a new tool will be used for test management). Remember, chaos is a normal human response to a jolt they receive (see overview of the Satir model in section 8.2.2).

Good communication starts with informing people about what the improvement plan is and what the process of change will look (and feel) like. People need to be told how changes will affect them directly. Make presentations, hand out flyers, perform road shows, provide an access point where people can obtain information. This is the time to communicate the vision for the future that was agreed upon with sponsoring stakeholders (see section 8.4.1). The big picture needs to be explained in a clear and understandable way. What will future work practice be like? How will people benefit? Will there be winners and losers? How will you proceed (what is the strategy and the mix of long- and short-term improvement measures)?

This is also the stage to introduce the team of people who will be managing the test process improvement program and giving their support to making change happen. Introducing the key players who will be involved (connectors, oracles, salespeople, early adopters) can be a big step toward obtaining buy-in; people will feel more comfortable if they know that a particular, trusted person is involved in the change process. For example, if Harry (who is a great connector) is involved in spreading the word about improvements, people might say,

"If Harry is part of it, then so am I." (It will probably be more subtle than that, but you see our point.)

Obtaining buy-in and understanding is not a one-way street; people need the opportunity to give their feedback and ask questions. Giving a presentation and then leaving people to their "fates" is definitely not going to get their buy-in. Listen to them, learn from them, and if necessary, make adjustments to plans. It's important to be understanding but firm here, because the first signs of resistence will start to show even at this initial stage. The test improvement plan is not up for negotiation, but some constructive fine-tuning may be useful and help to build trust.

The practice of information-hiding should be avoided, unless it would mean distroying someone's trust (e.g., line management is planning to inform people about certain details next week and has asked you to not to say anything about it now), breaking some important rules or laws (e.g., established company policy regarding staff communications), or placing yourself, other people, or your company at risk (e.g., by revealing commercial secrets). Above all, keeping information away from people as an act of kindness (to spare them the jolt) or to avoid their reactions will backfire. Sooner or later people will find out the information one way or another. Rumors may spread and information will get transformed and distorted as people try to piece together the whole story. Naomi Karten is absolutely clear about information-hiding when she says "... such withholding is dishonest, thoughtless, and unkind. And withholding bad news because it just didn't occur to you that it would matter to others is a blatant sign of disrespect." Hiding information is about the best way possible to destroy the trust a test process improver needs when getting the ball rolling and making things happen.

8.5.2 Anticipating Chaos

We know that a state of chaos is going to occur when introducing change, so it's possible to take some measures to ease the impact. An important aspect is recognizing the factors and situations that can cause the jolt that leads to chaos. In section 8.3.1, the situations that can result in the need for test process improvement were listed. Each of these can represent a different level of severity when it comes to the "jolt" that occurs when necessary improvements are introduced. If improvement is introduced because it's company policy to improve continuously, the jolt is relatively mild. Improvements that result from disaster striking will probably result in a severe jolt. This has to be appreciated by the test process improver so that the severity of the chaos can be anticipated.

When individual improvements are proposed, a similar consideration should be made regarding the particular jolts that will result when they are introduced. Any proposal that involves changes to working practices, having to learn something new, the introduction of new technology (e.g., tools), or organizational restructuring should be considered by the test process improver as reasons to take precautions against the ensuing chaos.

What can the test improver do to reduce the effects of chaos? Naomi Karten sums this up neatly when she says, "What, when, and how you communicate with those affected influences the duration and intensity of the chaos" [Karten 2009]. Here are some helpful tips:

- Talk about the chaos that may happen before it happens; it may be difficult to recognize it when you're already in it.
- Let people know that experiencing chaos will be a normal reaction to the proposed changes and single out particular changes that are likely to have the biggest impact.
- Be aware that people often think they are immune to chaos and may respond with "I can handle it" if chaos is discussed. The problem is, often they can't handle it as well as they think.
- Get people to practice recognizing the signs of chaos so they can respond to it properly (refer to the following section).
- Anticipate a period of resistance; this is normal.
- Manage expectations by being clear about the main vision and objectives.

8.5.3 Managing the Chaos

The immediate impact of introducing "improvements" is a state of chaos in the people affected. The appropriate symbol for chaos, used by Naomi Karten, is shown in figure 8–2.

CHAOS

Figure 8–2   *How people experience chaos*

Here are some of the more common signs of chaos:

- People are more likely to react emotionally than in a reasoned, rational manner.
- People experience many emotions, such as stress, unease, and possibly also anger.
- People may feel a sense of loss and show signs of mourning for the way things used to be (i.e., the old status quo).
- People show resistance to the change (see section 8.5.4).
- Productivity drops (yes, it drops) as people try to adjust to change.

Test process improvers need to be aware of these signs and react in an appropriate manner. Here are some tips on managing chaos; they may apply to anyone who experiences change (including yourself):

- If you talk to someone in chaso rationally, they may not get your message because they are emotionally charged. Repeat your message or ask them if they have understood fully. Be patient if they reply no.
- Do not say, "You're in a state of chaos; it will get better." This can come across as patronizing. Remember, you are a test process improver, not a psychologist.
- Acknowledge the situation, be understanding, and offer support. The best thing to say is, "Let me know if I can do anything to help."
- When in a state of chaos, don't do or say anything you might regret later, (walk out, insult your customer, destroy your computer). The short-term "pleasure" of doing this will be replaced by long-term regret that could deepen the chaos.
- Manage expectations by making it known that productivity will initially drop. Be understanding about losses of productivity.
- Keep communication channels open and provide support where needed.

8.5.4 Handling Resistance to Change

Many test process improvers underestimate the phenomenon of resistance. When there is change, some people are simply *against* it. They have all kinds of reasons for not being keen on the process of change. Test process improvers must be able to cope with that and should be actively engaged in reducing resistance. That requires an understanding of how resistance is influenced by the test process improver's conduct over time. If that understanding exists, resistance becomes predictable and may be influenced.

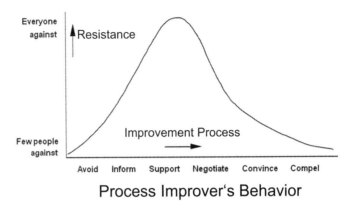

Figure 8–3   *Resistance is predictable and may be influenced.*

As shown in figure 8–3, at the start of the improvement process, few people will be aware of it. Resistance will not increase until more people have been informed about the changes and their impact. After the project has been announced, adequate support and tools should be available to help counter any resistance. Once it is put into practice and support is provided, test staff will suggest improvements. You should listen to them carefully, and the proposals should be discussed if necessary. A sensitive ear and acceptance of suggestions made will considerably reduce resistance. If support continues steadily, testers will become convinced, during this phase, of the benefits brought by the changes. They will carry doubting colleagues along with them and even compel them to join in. The resistance curve may be influenced by not delaying information, but more so by not providing it prematurely. Before wide-ranging information is provided, for example, support and tools should be available. If the kind of opposition likely to be aroused by a particular action is predicted, it will be possible to take precautionary measures to reduce it. Opposition can therefore be managed.

Virginia Satir notes that resistance is a natural response to change and can be experienced in a variety of forms:

- People make excuses regarding why they cannot implement the proposed changes. Especially common are excuses like "I don't have time" and "I'm too busy for these changes."
- People may get confrontational and challenge the wisdom of changes.
- People may use delaying tactics by saying things like, "I'll do this next week" (and next week they say the same).

To minimize resistance to change, the test process improver should understand the diagram shown in figure 8–3 and be able to apply the following recommendations:

- Do not try to pressure people who show signs of resistance by saying things like "Come on, just get on with it." The more people are pressured, the greater the resistance they build up against the person doing the pressuring. It distracts them from the change.
- Talk to people and listen carefully to their concerns. Where possible, try to find ways to address their concerns. If they say they are too busy, check on ways to free up some time for them, perhaps by talking to a project leader or line manager. Be politely persistent; use questions that start with *why*.
- Encourage the development of transforming ideas (see the next section).

Encouraging and motivating people who are resisting change takes time, patience, and energy. It's quite possible that the test improvement group and those people who support the rollout will not be able to convince all resistors to change. Provided the number of those who persistently resist change is comparatively small and their reasons for resistance have been reasonably considered, it may be necessary to reduce or even stop devoting further energy to these people. Many of them will change their ways when the changes have taken a strong foothold and their continued resistance becomes steadily more unreasonable, especially within their peer group.

8.5.5 Climbing Out of Chaos: Developing Transforming Ideas

At this stage many people are struggling with the chaos brought on by the introduction of improvements. The overall way forward will already have been laid out in the test improvement plan, but it cannot address all the specific needs of individuals.

Satir calls the ideas that help people implement changes and lift them out of their chaos *transforming ideas* [Satir, et al. 1991]. The test process improver can encourage the development of these ideas by helping to create the right environment. This means, above all, giving people support when they decide to try things out. The culture should be open and blame free and provide the space needed for people to experiment and find solutions. In this context, "failure" may be a good thing, if people can learn from it and create better alternatives. All concerned should remain open to ideas and should avoid rejecting them too quickly.

The test process improver can enable transforming ideas to be generated and to create the right environment. Here are some of the approaches that can be applied:

- Looking at things differently: Ask a person to take on the view of someone else with a different role or responsibility and then encourage them to walk through problems and proposed improvements from that point of view.
- Looking at things together: Groups may also perform the kind of perspective-based activity mentioned in the preceding point and generate ideas from the discussions that follow. A similar method may be to apply de Bono's principle of Six Thinking Hats, in which members of a group collectively consider a problem or idea according to six defined perspectives [de Bono 1999]. Other forms of group activity, such as workshops, brainstorming sessions, and walk-throughs, may also help to focus on specific topics.
- Explaining the problem: Ask people to explain step-by-step the problems they are facing. This often results in them finding solutions themselves. Ask them open questions like, What do you think about the improvements to …? Then practice active listening (see section 7.3.2) to focus on possible transforming ideas.
- Encouraging knowledge transfer: Where improvements are introduced in several areas of an organization at the same time (e.g., when the rollout takes place using a top-down strategy), the transfer of knowledge, experiences, and ideas can be a powerful motivator and source of inspiration. Encourage and enable groups from different projects or parts of an organization to come together regularly and even collaborate on implementing challenging improvements.

8.6 Making Change Stick

Perhaps the worst thing that can happen to a test process improver is to see proposed improvements successfully introduced but then, some time later, to find that practices have reverted to their "old status quo" ways. Making changes stick takes patience, a culture that supports and encourages improvement, and an "institutionalized" process that is part of a formal quality system and firmly establishes testing roles.

This phase includes the following principal activities:

- Roll out new ideas and practices.
- Provide lasting support.
- Create a new culture of improvement.
- Practice continuous improvement principles.

8.6.1 Rollout of New Ideas and Practices

When new practices are adopted, it takes time for them to become the "standard" way of doing things. Before a test improvement plan can be considered fully implemented, there will be successes and failures, each of which can provide a jolt to the people affected by the improvements. Some of the factors that can influence the speed and depth of adoption are discussed next.

Influence of Communication and Personality Types

Rolling out test process improvements and finding transforming ideas (see section 8.5.5) will be most effective and efficient if those affected have the ability to communicate well with each other. Workshops are more productive, the transfer of knowledge and experience is more focused, and problems can be more openly discussed if people are able to communicate well. The test process improver needs an appreciation of different people's ability to communicate to make the rollout as smooth as possible and to understand some of the issues that arise. One way to establish these abilities is to evaluate their particular personality type as proposed by Myers and Briggs [Briggs Myers and Myers 1995] in their classification scheme, the Myers-Briggs Type Indicator (also know simply as MBTI). Figure 8–4 shows the personality types.

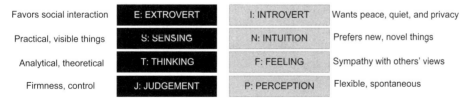

Figure 8–4 *Myers-Briggs personality types*

Note that the personality types are organized in four pairs. A person is assessed as having a personality that matches one of each pair (e.g., they are extrovert or introvert). Typically, the letters (*E* or *I*) are used to build a complete Myers-

Briggs Type Indicator covering all four attributes (e.g., ENFJ indicates that a person is an extrovert, intuitive, feeling, and applies judgment). The 16 possible MBTIs are shown in a matrix and individuals are positioned on the matrix according to their type. The example in figure 8–5 shows the MBTI personality types of four people (e.g., from a small project).

	TJ	TP	FJ	FP
ES	x	x	x	x
EN	x		x	x
IS	x	x	x	x
IN	x	x	x	x

Figure 8–5 *Myers-Briggs personality types (MBTI) example*

Here are some of the benefits to be gained from considering the MBTI personality types of people affected by change:

- You have a better understanding of how proposed changes will be adopted.
- You can predict whether change will likely be welcome (P: perception) or resisted (I: introvert).
- You can better determine if people will be prepared to experiment and accept some failure in the changes
  (E: extrovert, I: intuition) or if they would prefer to wait until a "perfect" solution is provided (T: thinking, J: judgment).
- You can better determine if people will communicate well with others or get on each others' nerves? Considering the matrix in figure 8–5, people whose MBTI are close to each other (e.g., ISTP and INTP) will tend to get along better than those who are far apart on the matrix (e.g., ESTJ and INFP).

Isabel Evans notes that people in IT are typically INTJ (introvert, intuition, thinking, judgment) but business owners are typically ESTJ (extrovert, sensing, thinking, judgment) [Evans 2004]. These positions, unfortunately, are not adjacent to each other on the MBTI matrix, which may explain some of the difficulties we in IT have in communicating with important stakeholders like business owners.

Influence of Different Learning Styles

There can be a considerable difference between different people's ability to learn new working practices and acquire new skills. These different styles are captured by a classification by Honey and Mumford that identifies four styles of learning, each with its advantages and disadvantages [Honey and Mumford 2002]. These are shown in figure 8–6.

REFLECTORS	
Good at collecting data and metrics Observant	Not spontaneous Need time
ACTIVISTS	
Like to try things Learn by doing Team workers	Not good at selfstudy
THEORISTS	
Like new ideas. Develop sound theories for reuse	Feel uncomfortable in unstructured situations
PRAGMATISTS	
Will follow a model that they can relate to	Quickly reject things they consider to be "just theory"

Figure 8–6   Honey and Mumford learning styles

The test process improver can use this information to adjust the amount and type of support provided to particular people during the rollout of improvements. Clearly, people who are activists will need more support, but they will be good early adopters of improvements and can benefit others by passing on their experiences. Pragmatists are likely to be good at adopting new work practices and giving appropriate feedback on whether these are well considered, practical, and not too theoretical.

Influence of the Test Improvement Team

The people involved in implementing test process improvements and the "champions of change" mentioned in section 8.2.3 are instrumental in rolling out new ideas and practices connected with test process improvements. They have a positive impact on making changes stick by communicating sucesses ("do good things and talk about them") and motivating others to implement improvements by encouraging them and giving them specific support. Overall control of the rollout remains with the Test Process Group (TPG), which follows the test improvement plan. The connectors, oracles, salespeople, and early adopters all play their respective roles in the spread of ideas and improvements, but care needs to be taken that the TPG coordinates its activities and ensures that the right messages are being communicated to the required people and projects; an overenthusiastic salesperson or a badly informed connector can undo much progress and prolong the rollout if the activities and statements made by these people are not coordinated correctly. Depending on the scale of the rollout and any challenges that may exist (e.g., strong resistance from particular people), it is advisable to regularly exchange information and feedback between everyone who is actively involved in implementing the rollout.

Use of social media can be helpful in spreading the word during the rollout. In particular, the use of tweets to feed people small items of information and news can be a powerful tool, especially if connectors are able to retweet (i.e., forward) messages to a large number of people. It's important, however, not to make this the only means of communication; not everyone uses social media.

8.6.2 Provide Lasting Support

As the rollout progresses, many people begin to see the light. They realize that their test process is improving and some of the early resistors to change become late adopters. Ensuring that changes stick involves providing all necessary support for questions and suggestions that may come up, even after the rollout of improvements is considered complete. People simply feel more secure knowing that someone will help them if needed, and the permanent nature of the Test Process Group (TPG) is a significant factor in ensuring that this support is available. The messages here from the TPG is clear:

- Reassurance: "We are in this together for the long term."
- Stability: "We are not going back" (to the old status quo).

The information channels set up for the rollout should be maintained where appropriate, and successfully implemented improvements should be built in to standard working practices, depending on the strategy adopted. If a top-down approach to improvement is being followed, updates should be made to items such as the overall process descriptions, general testing procedures, and company standards. These will provide the lasting support needed for others as the improvements are introduced across the organization.

The TPG may scale down the activities performed by the champions of change according to the test improvement plan and the achievement of specified improvement objectives. Particular people may be retained as oracles so that points of contact can be available for specific areas of testing, especially where these have involved learning new practices or techniques.

8.6.3 Create a New Culture of Improvement

A culture of improvement only develops over time. It's something that is practiced by the people within an organization as a matter of routine and is strongly linked to the overall company culture. *Culture* in the sense of test process improvement means many things, such as the ability to discuss problems in a blame-free environment, the encouragement of all stakeholders to suggest improvements, and the the practice of conducting project retrospectives. Testing knowledge is shared and transferred between different parts of an organization and people learn to share both their successes and their failures so that they and others may benefit.

Although surprises and setbacks can never be ruled out, a culture of improvement will make improvement a more routine activity that people expect to participate in. There are clear roles and responsibilities for managing the improvements (i.e., the TPG) and the company should have a stated policy on test process improvement.

The role of the test process improver is to help establish this culture by obtaining stakeholder backing for the specific measures needed. This may mean talking to line management about setting up company-wide "communities" for developing and taking responsibility for particular aspects of testing. It may also mean taking on the role of neutral moderator in discussions about successes ("Can we build on this?") and setbacks ("Can we learn from the root causes?").

The culture of improvement may be slow to develop, particularly when following a bottom-up strategy. Using this approach often means that certain parts of the organization remain relatively untouched by the improvements, which has the potential for discord between different groups or projects. In this sense, the use of top-down strategies has advantages regarding the establishment of a culture of improvement. The improvement culture is further discussed as a critical success factor in section 9.2.

8.6.4 Practice Continuous Improvement Principles

The IDEAL model described in chapter 6 is based on the principles of continuous improvement as initially discussed in chapter 2. Following this kind of process will cement the culture of improvement and support an incremental approach to rolling out changes. Please refer to chapter 6 for further details.

8.7 Data Privacy

When you evaluate people, you must take into account how the evaluation is conducted, how the results are used, and where resulting data is stored. In most cases you will need permission from line management and/or human resource departments before conducting such an evaluation. In some countries you will also need to involve local workers and councils, and obey legal requirements regarding data protection.

8.8 Exercises

The following multiple-choice questions will give you some feedback on your understanding of this chapter. Appendix F lists the answers.

8-1 Which step of the fundamental change process is missing from the following sequence: prepare for change, implement the changes, make the changes stick?

    A: Establish a test improvement plan

    B: Decide what to do

    C: Perform interviews

    D: Perform retrospectives

8-2 What is the step in the Satir model that follows a foreign element?

    A: Practice and integration

    B: Uncertainty

    C: Chaos

    D: Transforming ideas

8-3 Which of the following principles does *not* apply to the Tipping Point theory?

    A: Small changes to the way information is presented can make a big difference.

    B: Changes spread best within groups which do not exceed 150 people.

    C: Changes should be introduced gradually in a controlled step-by-step process.

    D: Creating many small changes can often enable larger changes to take place.

8-4 Which of the following can be used to show that there is a need for improving the test process?

A: Impact of past failures

B: Budget becomes available for improvement

C: Need to follow company policy

D: Realizing the need yourself and convincing stakeholders

E: A and D

8-5 Which of the following can be effective in making change happen?

A: Avoiding any form of chaos by good management practices

B: Handling resistance by setting milestones for specific changes

C: Increasing buy-in by communicating results, benefits, status, and progress

D: Ensuring that fast adopters of change are rewarded

8-6 What can the test improver do to reduce the effects of chaos?

A. Don't talk about it too much; it may make people nervous.

B. Plan a short period of resistance into the test improvement plan.

C. Convince people that they will have no difficulty taking on changes.

D. Let people know that experiencing chaos is normal.

8-7 Which of the following best describes how the test process improver should behave when resistance is experienced?

A. If some people are showing resistance after the majority of people have adopted the change, then the test process improver should try to convince them to follow the others.

B. If resistance is high, then the test process improver should focus on convincing them that the changes will be beneficial.

C. If only a few people are showing resistance before the change is introduced, then the test process improver should negotiate with them.

D. If very few people are still resisting change after the rest have adopted the changes, the test process improver should simply ignore them.

8-8 Which of the following is *not* a benefit to be gained from considering the MBTI personality type of people affected by change?

A. Better understanding of how proposed changes will be adopted

B. The ability to estimate the effort required to implement changes

C. The ability to estimate whether change will be welcomed or resisted

D. The ability to identify people who will be good communicators

8-9 What factors contribute to a culture of improvement?

A. Clear identification of roles and responsibilities so that mistakes can be more easily tracked

B. Strong leadership by the leader of the test improvement initiative so that too many conflicting ideas can be avoided

C. Performing assessments on a regular basis

D. People learning to share both their successes and their failures so that they and others may benefit

8-10 What are the qualities of a pragmatist according to the Honey and Mumford learning styles?

A. Develops sound theories for reuse

B. Observant and good at collecting metrics

C. Will follow a model they can relate to

D. Learns by doing

9 Critical Success Factors

Looking back at the chapters so far, you can readily identify several factors that could be called critical to the success of a test process improvement program. You have to choose the right improvement approach to achieve a particular goal, you need a solid process for implementing improvement, you need the skills and organization to implement improvements. And last but not least, you need to consider the process of change and what it means to those involved.

This chapter takes a look at those factors we consider critical to success. There will be some familiar factors mentioned, but some new aspects will also be discussed. The critical success factors are discussed in two distinct sets.

Section 9.1.1, "Getting Started," looks at the first set of success factors. They are primarily related to the initial phases of an improvement project and can be linked to the initiating and diagnosing phases from the IDEAL improvement framework (section 2.4.2).

Section 9.1.2, "Getting the Job Done," includes the second set of success factors, which are related to the implementation phases of an improvement project.

9.1 Critical Success Factors

Syllabus Learning Objectives

LO 9.1.1 (K2) Explain the risks behind not considering the critical success factors.

LO 9.1.2 (K5) Assess the critical success factors for a test improvement project.

LO 9.1.3 (K5) Recommend appropriate measures to mitigate the identified project risks.

9.1.1 Getting Started

Several factors are often found in the initial phases of an improvement program that can be considered critical to success [Broekman and van Veenendaal 2007]. Failure to recognize these key factors leads to an immediate and considerable risk for executing a planned improvement program. As indicated in the introduction to this chapter, the key factors are all related to activities in the initiating and diagnosing phases of the IDEAL model. Several key factors are described below:

- **Clear, Measurable, and Realistic Objectives for the Improvement Process**

It is necessary to clearly define and record the goals of an improvement program. Why do we improve our test process? As indicated in chapter 6, the goals of the change program are determined in the initiating phase and are subsequently developed or made concrete in the establishing phase. The goals must be known to everyone involved. What is the direction the organization wants to take and why? All this should be recorded in the test policy, which is derived from the quality policy and the organizational policy (section 6.1.2). The test policy globally describes the organization's philosophy about testing. In TMMi, the details of the test policy are elaborated upon within the process area Test Policy and Strategy.

We have unfortunately seen too many improvement initiatives run into problems because of inadequate goals. The problem is usually that inexperienced people simply want to get right on with the assessment task and don't want to "waste time" talking to stakeholders about goals. In this case, difficulties usually start to occur later in the improvement program when stakeholders need to be convinced of improvement recommendations. They will simply ask why, and more often than not, no convincing answer can be given—all that assessment work gone to waste; what a pity.

- **Management Commitment and Sponsorship Are Available**

Is quality important enough to the organization? How does the organization deal with a system of inferior quality at a milestone? Is the organization driven by budget, deadline, or quality? The answers to questions like these show the actual management commitment with regard to testing and quality. Without sufficient management commitment and an explicit sponsor at the management level, an improvement process is highly likely to fail. Acquiring management commitment is discussed in the "build sponsorship" activity in the initiating phase (section 6.2.4).

> **Critical success factor** An element necessary for an organization or project to achieve its mission. Critical success factors are the critical factors or activities required for ensuring success.

■ The Need to Improve

Before employees in an organization are willing to contribute to improvements, they must feel the need to improve (people frequently talk of "pain points" when referring to such needs). For example, this need can be to reduce the large number of defects when a system goes into production or to reduce the time required to run a test project. The need to improve must be clearly and frequently communicated, preferably by management. Improvement goals need to support the defined need to improve.

■ Test Improvement Organized as a Formal Project

During the "charter infrastructure" activity in the initiating phase, the organization that will support the improvement process is set up (section 6.2.5). It is highly recommended to choose a project structure with elements such as assignment, steering group, project lead, responsibilities, planning, milestones, deliverables, and reports. Change programs are often complex for several reasons. Our experience shows that creating an official project structure contributes to the change being taken seriously. As a defined project, the effort becomes visible in the organization, and it's clear that the employees who contribute to the improvement program don't just do it as an "extra" but rather as an assigned project.

■ People Involved Have Sufficient Time Scheduled for Participation

The recommendation is to discuss the resources available for the change during the "charter infrastructure" activity instead of delaying it until the "develop approach" activity in the establishing phase. It is important that management realizes that choices must be made. For example, allowing employees four working hours a week to spend on improvement may sound reasonable, but that often proves not to work in practice. When the employees working on the (test) project are pressed for time, they often do not have (or are not given) the extra four hours to spend. In addition, a small amount of time can easily become eaten up by the changes that occur between finishing one activity and starting another. It takes time to get back into the current improvement task; apart from the obvious loss of precious time, this can also result in repeating tasks by mistake or even losing momentum completely. An alternative can be to take a number of people off projects and assign them to the improvement program for a minimum of three days a week. This strategy leads to focus and progress and therefore to a timely delivery and measurable results.

- **Ambitions Mapped to the Maturity of the (Development) Organization**

In the "characterize current and desired states" activity of the diagnosing phase (section 6.3), it is important to look at the test processes as well as the other processes on which testing strongly depends. Without a minimum form of maturity in these processes, improving the test process will prove very difficult, although not impossible.

The principal areas of the development process to look at are project planning, configuration management, requirements development, requirements management, and the release process. Without a mature project planning process, establishing a thorough test planning process will be very difficult, due to the many dependencies between testing and development activities. When test design techniques are applied, the quality of the test basis (e.g., requirements) is of major importance. Any changes in the test basis must also be made known to the test team. Absence of configuration management often leads to nonreproducible findings or findings that "suddenly" reappear in a later release.

In our experience, one of the most common problems that influences testing relates to the process used to bring new releases of software into productive use. Typically, releases are scheduled on a quarterly or monthly basis and may be planned as a mix of major and minor releases. A common factor of many releases is failure to limit the number of new requirements and changes to an amount that can be developed and tested before the planned release milestone. We have noted a tendency to put too many new or changed requirements into a release, which then places strain on the development and testing process. Faced with oversized releases, corners are often cut in the test process such as, for example, reducing the time spent on test planning. A test process assessment may identify test planning as a weak point, but the problems cannot be solved in the test process; better release planning is required first.

9.1.2 Getting the Job Done

The previous section described how that important first hurdle of getting started must be overcome. For good results, momentum must be upheld in the program and everyone involved must stay focused. This section describes a number of important factors that help to determine the success of a test improvement program.

- **Clear time frames for improvements and length of feedback cycles are defined. These are not too large so that momentum can be maintained.**

Process improvement is in essence a long-term process. However, to retain motivation, it is important to score so-called quick wins early in the process. The supporters within senior management also want to be shown evidence of regular success to justify their support for the improvement team. Whenever success is achieved, for example during the pilot, this must be communicated clearly and repeatedly ("do good things and talk about them"). When you describe success using examples that are specific to the organization or its individual employees, the enthusiasm for the improvement program generally grows.

We have found regular project meetings to be a good opportunity to add an extra agenda item for reporting on test process improvement progress. Care has to be taken not to exaggerate successeses and to be honest; people will grow tired of success stories that have been polished up just so there is something positive to report.

- **Level of resistance will depend on the success or failure of previous improvement efforts. Manage resistance and perform marketing.**

Initially, most people naturally resist change. Trying to push through that resistance often has the opposite effect. It is better to try to convince them by marketing the improvement program and carefully noting the stages that people go through when they are affected by change (see chapter 8). For example, publish the achieved results or stories from people who have experienced the positive effects of the improvements in a regular newsletter. Whenever resistance is detected, it is advisable to talk about it with the employee concerned. In this conversation it is important that the person who is managing the change also listens to the objections of the employee. Resistance is often a result of uncertainty about the need and objectives of the change project, unfamiliarity with the approach of the change project, or uncertainty about the employee's own situation.

- **Use existing practices if they are already available; don't change for the sake of changing. If something that is available is not being used, first investigate the reasons.**

Even though it seems apparent that a lot needs improving, this does not mean everything is wrong. There have been many unsuccessful attempts to improve; sometimes some test projects are executed in a more controlled way than others are. It is likely that several employees have had good ideas, but they have not succeeded in deploying them for one reason or another, which may have been outside of their control. Involve those people and encourage them to have ideas. Resistance is less when changes are derived from one's own ranks.

During assessment interviews, we tend to ask people the question, "What do you think needs changing here?" Often you will get insight into why those good ideas sometimes fail.

Involve external consultants as needed for specific knowledge and skills, for example, but do not let them take full responsibility for the improvement project.

External consultants can positively add to a project with their knowledge and experience. When they are involved as a dedicated part of an improvement project, they can keep it going despite other activities being scheduled for the organization. However, the external consultants are there to advise, and they must not make decisions on company procedures; this must be decided by the employees of the organization. This is why in every improvement program internal employees should be the primary resources involved, supported as needed by external consultants. In addition, improvements must be anchored in the organization so the effort and momentum continues after the consultant leaves.

We have seen organizations become overdependent on external consultants. Remember, a good consultant puts customers into a position in which they can move forward and continue improving without external support. Consultants who make themselves indispensible might be popular with their employers, but frequently they are not providing long-term benefits to their customers.

- **Guard consistency**

Be sure to maintain consistency between the many individual parts of an improvement program. The total sum of all improvements must be integrated and work as one.

- **Other factors**

Of course, there are numerous other success factors based on many practical experiences (see the case study in section 9.1.3). Some of these are not described in detail here but are worth mentioning:

- Clear, measurable, and realistic improvement targets for every cycle
- Process ownership identified and organized
- Control and monitoring of all steps in the change management process (see chapter 8)
- Test professionals involved when defining and implementing the improvements
- Other stakeholders involved where problems lie outside the testing discipline (e.g., quality of specifications, change and release management processes)
- Stable project team that works well together and buys into the change/vision
- Tools to support and/or enable test improvements considered (see section 2.5.4)
- Available knowledge and skills of people involved considered. This covers not just testing in general but also areas related to the improvement process and skills for the improvement approach(es) to be used (e.g., specific model, analysis techniques).
- Human factors, such as learning styles, personality types, and attitudes considered
- Awareness of external standards, which may be mandatory (e.g., FDA for the medical industry)
- Overall process and terminology defined up front to ensure that the various components of the improvement strategy are aligned and part of an overall framework
- Relationships built with all affected stakeholders (e.g., software process improvement officers, quality assurance and human resources departments)
- Internal approval and/or regulatory processes obeyed
- Alignment with other improvement initiatives ensured

9.1.3 Critical Success Factors: A Case Study

One of the authors was doing a consultancy assignment a few years ago at an organization that developed highly complex multidisciplinary safety-critical systems. It was probably the most successful organization he had been involved in when it comes to setting up a test center of excellence and implementing test improvements. We tried to analyze what really made the difference. Many things came to mind, but there were some essential success factors that stand out:

- As always, trying to improve or manage an organization using just a top-down approach doesn't work.
- A combination of top-down and bottom-up is usually most successful.

During our analysis, we came up with two top-down and two bottom-up critical success factors.

Top-Down Approach: Test Policy

A test policy, if well written and with the right level of detail, provides direction on the improvements, states the values of the testing organization, shows how testing adds value to the overall business objectives, and defines some key test performance indicators. It is not without reason that the TMMi model has Test Policy and Strategy as one of its main process areas already at maturity level 2. At this company, the test policy was established in a way that added value (as it should do). It was written on one page only, well distributed, and displayed on walls near the coffee machine and copier to ensure that everyone was aware of it. The test policy was then re-discussed on a yearly basis in a brown paper session with managers and all test managers. Are the values still correct? What are the main problems we encounter? What should we focus on this year? How do we add business value? These are examples of questions that were discussed in the session, with the result being documented in an updated test policy.

Top-Down Approach: Leadership

Whenever we have been really successful in our careers, there has almost always been a manager that made the difference. Many managers immediately come to mind when we think of successful projects. Somehow it is sad that success should depend on one person only, but real leadership can make a difference. Leadership has been described as the "process in which one person can enlist the aid of others in the accomplishment of a common task." In this organization, a real leader was encountered. This was someone with a strong personality, who was there for his people when things got rough, was able to motivate them when needed, had a vision toward the future of the company and the role of testing, but also, and probably above all, was a pleasant, honest human being with integrity. Leadership is much more than providing resources. Real leaders just make the difference. Find them!

Bottom-Up Approach: The Test Managers' Meeting

One of the things we learned from Watts Humphrey many years ago is that critical stakeholders during change management are those directly responsible for the project, such as, for example, the project manager and test manager. They tend to be directly confronted with delays due to new and innovative processes, while their job is to deliver a quality product on time. Thus they are usually not too enthusiastic when it comes to process improvements to their projects. At this company, although a person was assigned as a process improvement facilitator, the test managers' meeting was the main driver of any improvement. At their weekly meeting, the managers would discuss, in addition to (test) project issues, improvement ideas, the status of improvement actions, and so on. They were the ones to decide whether an improvement had added value or not, thereby ensuring that the improvements were practical. In addition, using the test policy as their reference framework, they maintained a strong focus on the defined objectives. When a decision was made to define and implement an improvement action, a volunteer was sought among the test managers who would drive the specific action. Note that the improvement actions were not process oriented only but also concerned tasks like setting up and organizing a training session, tool selection, and developing a supporting spreadsheet template. As a result, little or no change management actions were required for the test managers, who are often "difficult" stakeholders. They were now in charge of doing things they perceived had added value to the projects, either short or long term.

Bottom-Up Approach: Everyone Involved

Although the test managers were driving the improvements, they would not necessarily do it all themselves. Normally they would take the action back to their team, discuss it, and make it a team assignment. In this way, all testers became involved in building a high-quality test organization and test process improvement. There was almost no need for change management; it was already part of their test process. Of course, implementation could still be difficult for many reasons, but at least there was little to no resistance and people had a positive mindset toward the changes. Important in this context was also a monthly test knowledge sharing meeting where testers and test managers would present their personal experiences regarding a new template, a test design technique, using a tool, and so on. Again, the test improvement coordinator was acting as a facilitator rather than a manager. A test process was being built that was already everyone's process.

You may notice that the critical success factors described earlier are strongly related to change management and people issues. We believe people do make the difference. Striving to become a testing center of excellence using just a process orientation will fail sooner or later. Real leadership, a clear policy, mission and direction, and a focus on change management and people issues can make it happen. But remember, changes do take time!

9.2 Setting a Culture for Improvement

Syllabus Learning Objectives

LO 9.2.1 (K2) Understand the factors involved in setting a culture for improvement.

LO 9.2.2 (K6) Create a test improvement plan considering cultural factors.

9.2.1 Defining "Improvement Culture"

When you start a new assignment at an organization, it doesn't take long to get a feel for their improvement culture. Are people open to the idea of improvement or is their enthusiasm somehow blunted? Do they respond to initial questions like, "Where do you see your test process two years from now?" with an enthusiastic flood of ideas and objectives, or do you see people simply shrugging their shoulders and being indifferent? Body language and responses given to general questions about the "way things are done here" are good "gut feeling" indicators for improvement culture.

When defining improvement culture, we often talk about this kind of "feeling," but there are also more specific aspects and factors to consider that influence an organization's overall approach and attitude regarding improvement. Understanding these aspects helps us to grasp the sometimes elusive concept of improvement culture and enables us to shed some light on possible problem areas. The following section describes these factors and their contribution to improvement culture.

9.2.2 Aspects of Improvement Culture

Six principal factors are identified in this section. Each of them can have a decisive influence on the culture of improvement and, ultimately, whether test process improvements will be successful.

Management Culture

How does management manage? The answer to this varies from company to company and even from country to country. Many organizations apply a "command and control" style of management where decisions are made at the top and handed down through the hierarchy of management until they reach the people who are instructed to perform specific tasks. In some countries, there could be several layers of management, with each layer having the freedom to decide on areas within their responsibility before handing over decisions to the next level down the hierarchy. In other countries and organizations, we may find a patriarchal style of management in place. The top boss decides what to do and the rest follow without changing or refining the decisions.

Management influences improvement culture by affecting the buy-in that people have with regard to suggested improvements. Achieving good buy-in generally means involving people at various stages in the decision making process and adopting a more consultative approach. Companies that practice strict command-and-control management styles often suffer from low levels of buy-in from the very people required to implement the changes. What could go wrong here? In our experience, the following situations can arise:

- People implement measures that they know are going to be ineffective "just because the boss says so."
- People become reluctant to show initiative.
- People avoid giving feedback to management, especially if it is not well received ("just do what I say").

Management can negatively influence improvement culture by introducing too many changes too quickly. Referring back to the Satir model we described in section 8.2.2, we find in some organizations that management sometimes has no real appreciation of the chaos phase that all people go through when affected by a change. Management wants to see results quickly when they instigate changes. If productivity falls temporarily as a result of a change (and we know it will), management may see this as sign of failure. Frequently, all that is needed is to give people some more time and support to help them out of their chaos (see chapter 8). Instead, some managers will introduce further changes to correct the previous "mistakes," which unfortunately only leads to an extension of the chaos and the potential for making bad "corrective" decisions.

A management culture that demands instant results is highly likely to create a negative improvement culture within an organization. It will be focused on short-term quick wins instead of long-term organization improvement and often sets targets that cannot realistically be achieved by staff within the time and budget made available. As test process improvers, we can sometimes recognize the signs of this when people say they are "tired of constant changes" or asked to "achieve the impossible." Recognizing this will help us understand situations (and maybe explain that shrug of the shoulders), but actually changing the situation may require management changes that are frequently beyond the scope of the test process improver. We should tactfully point out these issues to management stakeholders and ask them to consider their impact on the organization's culture of improvement.

Geographical Location

Sometimes geographical location can have an influence on the specific decisions made within a test improvement program. As test process improvers, we may hear statements like, "This is how we do things here" when, for example, referring to a particular analytical approach. The "here" part of such statements often refers not simply to the organization or project but to geographical location. For example, some software process improvement models are favored in certain countries (e.g., CMMI is used in the United States and Asian countries more than ISO/IEC 15504 is). If we ignore these aspects, we may be making proposals that go against the improvement culture in that country.

Attitude Toward Improvement

Test process improvement experiences within organizations and projects shape the goals, policies, and strategies that become ingrained into an improvement culture. This applies not only to positive experiences (a successful approach to rolling out changes to the test team) but also to negative experiences (inability to define realistic goals using a particular metric). Experiences gained by others (e.g., in a different department) may also influence attitudes toward improvement by way of anecdotes, tweets, and experience reports.

Our experience is, unfortunately, that the negative experiences tend to dominate the positive ones in shaping attitudes (bad news travels fast). It is also common to find that the views of one or two respected individuals can influence the attitudes adopted by whole project teams or even organizations. These are important people to identify if you want to understand or modify attitudes (the roles identified by Malcom Gladwell [Gladwell 2000] can be particularly useful in helping to identify them).

Organizational Relationships

Relationships between different parts of an organization can significantly influence improvement culture. These relationships may be formed either by spreading experiences via, for example, company-wide user groups or communities or by merging different companies into a larger whole. Generally speaking, the exchange of different experiences can (and should) have a positive influence on improvement culture by challenging old established practices and opening up different parts of an organization to fresh views and approaches. Skilled test process improvers can harness this positive cultural effect by encouraging cooperation between different organizational units.

Organizational relationships can also exert a negative influence on improvement culture if the so-called "not invented here" mentality is present. This kind of mentality can block good practices and ideas from being adopted from outside a project or department. The basic assumption behind this commonly found behavior is "if we didn't think of it, then it can't be any good." We have experienced this kind of protectionist behavior a number of times. Without wishing to take the role of psychologists, it would seem from our experiences that the effect is rooted in one or more of the following beliefs:

- Concern that another organization may be taking over
- Reluctance to admit that another organization has a better practice
- Belief that your own organization is so special that only the ideas developed within it can possibly work

The negative effects on improvement culture resulting from organizational relationships can be very subtle. Test process improvers must be aware that their recommended organizational process improvements may fail to spread due to these influences and, where possible, suggest measures to break down organizational barriers (e.g., establishing communities to consider organizational issues and exchange ideas).

Life Cycle Model

The life cycle model used within an organization or project can have a decisive influence on the way in which test process improvement is approached.

Take, for example, iterative or agile life cycle models (see chapter 10). The improvement culture here is closely aligned to the iterations and can be characterized as follows:

- Improvement is considered at frequent intervals (e.g., at the end of a sprint when using SCRUM).
- The scope of the improvement is often limited to the cycle (e.g., a sprint) that has just taken place, the aim being to improve a little but often.
- Improvements are closely coupled to the problem, and waiting times for improvements to be implemented are minimized.

Compare this with the improvement culture that develops when using a sequential life cycle model such as the V-model. This shows the following characteristics:

- Improvements generally are considered only occasionally, such as at the end of a software release cycle or at the end of the project itself.
- The scope of improvement is broader and there is more opportunity to address organizational improvements.
- The principal benefit is not focused on resolving issues in the current release or project, but for the next release (often with a different release manager) or the next project (often with a different project leader). So the culture is more attuned to making things better for your successors rather than for yourself (although it's of course possible that the same leader and team members will be in the next project).

Test Strategy

The test approach being used will influence the overall culture of improvement by making some kinds of improvements more acceptable than others. If your testing approach is strongly based on the use of tools and automation, for example, you are more likely to get improvements accepted that have a technical emphasis and improve the automation strategy (e.g., introducing data-driven approaches) than by improvements of a more procedural nature that affect mostly manual testing (e.g., a new checklist for reviewing requirements specifications). If the testing approach adopted tends to be repeated from project to project, an improvement culture will develop within the organization that reflects that type of approach. This development will be reinforced if project retrospectives are routinely practiced.

> **Project retrospective**   A structured way to capture lessons learned and to create specific action plans for improving on the next project or next project phase.

This is, of course, entirely logical, but inexperienced test process improvers who are unaware of the strong link between test approach and improvement culture must appreciate this to avoid making unacceptable proposals.

Summary

To appreciate the culture of improvement in a project or organization, you must understand people's attitudes in the context of that project or organization. Considering the preceding six factors is a key success factor in establishing good improvement recommendations and, particularly, in making them stick.

9.2.3   Test Process Improvement Manifesto

An example of an approach is the test process improvement manifesto [van Veenendaal 2008], which echoes the agile manifesto [URL: agile manifesto].

In addition to the improvement process as described in the IDEAL framework and the critical success factors that one needs to take into account during the implementation process, the test process improvement manifesto provides interesting recommendations and identifies several principles that can make a difference in a test process improvement project. These principles and recommendations are derived from an analysis of successful test improvement projects in various domains.

> **Test process improvement manifesto**   A statement that echoes the agile manifesto and defines the following values for improving the test process:
> – flexibility over detailed processes
> – best practices over templates
> – deployment orientation over process orientation
> – peer reviews over quality assurance (departments)
> – business-driven over model-driven. [van Veenendaal 2008]

Flexibility over Detailed Processes

In general, having defined processes supports an organization. Only something that is defined can be improved. It guides new engineers and acts as corporate memory. However, building processes that are too rigorous takes away the "people values." Good testers have the skills to act based on the context of a problem, and they perceive testing to be a challenging job. Supporting processes are needed, but the employed processes should provide enough flexibility and freedom to testers to allow them to think for themselves and find the best way forward. The ideal is "just enough process."

Best Practices over Templates

Templates are great, but it is even better to provide examples of how they should be used. What provides more support, a test plan template or three test plan best practices? Experienced testers will choose the latter. When doing test process improvement, it's important to focus on getting a library of best practices set up as soon as possible instead of overspending on defining templates. The best practices may not be the best in the industry, but they may be the best for your organization. If something better comes along, they can be replaced. This is what supports testing and makes process improvement work.

Deployment Orientation over Process Orientation

Building process is easy; it's been done many times and there are numerous examples to be found. However, getting the processes deployed and thereby changing someone's behavior is the hard part. Process improvement is all about change management. Test improvement plans sometimes erroneously focus almost entirely on defining the testing processes. In successful improvement projects, at least 70 percent of the improvement effort is spent on deployment—"getting the job done." Defining the processes is the easy part and should account for only a small percentage of the effort and focus.

Peer Reviews over Quality Assurance (Departments)

Communicating and providing feedback are essential to project success. It is exactly this that peer reviews, if applied well, do. In principle, quality assurance officers also evaluate documents and provide feedback to engineers, but they tend to focus on conformance to templates and defined processes, partly because they are somewhat distanced from the testing profession. This reduces the value they contribute. Peer reviews, when done by qualified peers, provide pertinent feedback and advice for the given application, which is generally more beneficial than just adherence to a template.

Business-Driven over Model-Driven

Just trying to get to a higher maturity level defined by a model (e.g., from TMMi level 2 to 3) without understanding the business context will sooner or later always fail. The improvement team must understand the business problem in order to determine how to address the improvements. Whatever you do, make sure you know why you are doing it. What is the business problem you are trying to address? What is the test policy supported by management? When addressing a certain practice from an improvement model, there are most often many different ways to comply. The business problem (poor product quality, long test execution lead time, costs, etc.) will determine which one to choose. Process improvement must be constantly reviewed against the business drivers and test policy to ensure compliance.

9.3 Exercises

The following multiple-choice questions will give you some feedback on your understanding of this chapter. Appendix F lists the answers.

9-1 Which key success factor can be achieved by a test policy?

    A: The test improvement is organized as a formal project.

    B: The ambitions of the improvement are mapped to the maturity of the development organization.

    C: Clear, measurable, and realistic objectives for the improvement process are set.

    D: Clear time frames for improvements and length of feedback cycles are defined.

9-2 Which activity can help to ensure that people involved in an improvement program have sufficient time scheduled for participation?

    A: Discuss within the team and allocate time to those who are not 100 percent scheduled to project work.

    B: Inform management of the choices that need to be made regarding more resources or reallocating tasks.

    C: Split scheduled work into regular, small chunks of time to ensure that other tasks can run in parallel.

    D: Ask for volunteers to work extra time.

9-3 Why is it recommended to use existing practices if already available?

   A: The team members may be offended.

   B: It is unlikely that everything needs improving.

   C: Employees may have had good ideas but have not succeeded in deploying them for one reason or another.

   D: Don't change for the sake of changing.

   E: B, C, and D are correct.

9-4 Which statement is *false* when considering management culture of improvement?

   A: Management culture may vary from country to country.

   B: Command-and-control styles involve decisions that are handed down through the hierarchy of management until they reach the people who perform specific tasks.

   C: Achieving good buy-in generally means involving people at various stages in the decision making process.

   D: Companies that practice strict command-and-control management styles usually benefit from high levels of buy-in.

9-5 Which of the following statements is true regarding the impact of external consultants on an improvement project?

   A: They can give advice based on their experienec and knowledge.

   B: They can make important decisions on the working procedures.

   C: Consultants who are "indispensible" to the project can provide long-term benefits to their customers.

   D: They must return to the project regularly to ensure that the momentum of improvements is maintained.

9-6 Which of the following factors is a critical success factor that is typically relevant while establishing improvements?

   A: Working on both long-term and short-term goals

   B: Management commitment

   C: The maturity of the development organization

   D: Organizing test improvement as a project

9-7 Which of the following factors is a critical success factor that is typically relevant while getting started on improvements?

A: Length of feedback cycles are defined; these are not too large so that momentum can be maintained.

B: Change management.

C: Existing practices used if already available.

D: Sufficient time is scheduled for those involved.

9-8 Which of the following statements is *not* part of the test process improvement manifesto?

A: Flexibility over detailed processes

B: Deployment orientation over process orientation

C: Responding to change over following a plan

D: Best practices over template

9-9 What is a major benefit for test improvement when SCRUM is being applied?

A: The scope of the improvement is usually the entire organization.

B: Improvements are considered at frequent intervals.

C: Improvements are decoupled from the problem.

D: Process orientation is strong.

9-10 Which of the following factors is *not* a principal factor that can have a decisive influence on the culture of improvement?

A: Test policy

B: Attitude toward improvement

C: Life cycle model

D: Geographical location

10 Adapting to Different Life Cycle Models

This chapter considers the principal issues relating to different life cycle models and their influence on test process improvement. Failing to understand these differences may result in inappropriate improvement recommendations being proposed and, ultimately, will damage the improvement culture within the project or organization. Those involved will simply lose faith in the value of improving the test process if proposals are "out of touch."

10.1 Test Process Improvement with Different Life Cycles

Syllabus Learning Objectives

LO 10.1.1 (K2) Understand the factors that influence the way improvement is organized and that this is always context dependent

LO 10.1.2 (K2) Summarize the test improvement approach in agile environments

LO 10.1.3 (K2) Summarize the test improvement approach in iterative environments

LO 10.1.4 (K2) Give examples of where test process improvement models need to be adapted to be suitable for agile and/or iterative life-cycles

In section 2.5.4 we looked at the way test process improvement is considered within different life cycles and how these models generally include activities related to learning and improvement as part of their life cycle definition. In section 9.2.2 we identified the life cycle model in use as one of the six factors that influence the culture of improvement within a project or organization.

> **Life cycle model**   A partitioning of the life of a product or project into phases. [Chrissis, Konrad, and Shrum 2004].

In the following sections, we draw on some of this material to show that the life cycle model used is a significant factor affecting the context within which test improvement takes place.

Influence of Iterative and Agile Life Cycle Models on Improvement Context

The principal aspects to consider here are as follows:

- Improvement of cycle frequency
- Organizational aspects
- Scope of improvement
- Source of improvements
- Level of (test) documentation
- Improvement methods
- Support from test process improvement models

Within projects that use these life cycle models, improvements generally take place in frequent feedback loops that enable test process improvements to be considered frequently. This will be the case, for example, where the iterative Rational Unified Process (RUP) is used or, when applying SCRUM, at the end of a sprint or even as part of a daily stand-up meeting.

Because the scope is often limited to the previous cycle or sprint, small but frequent improvements are made that focus mainly on solving specific project problems (see section 2.5.4 for an explanation of how retrospectives are used in agile development life cycle models such as SCRUM). The focus of these improvements is often not on cross-project learning and institutionalization of improvements.

Looking at the organization of test improvement, we find that there is likely to be less focus on Test Process Groups at an organizational level and more emphasis on the self-management of teams within the project. These teams generally have the mandate to change the testing process within the project

> **Rational Unified Process (RUP)**   A proprietary adaptable iterative software development process framework consisting of four project life cycle phases: inception, elaboration, construction, and transition.

> **SCRUM** An iterative incremental framework for managing projects commonly used with agile software development.

according to their needs, resulting in highly tailored processes. However, some organizations also use weekly test stand-up meetings to bring things to a higher and cross-project level.

Since there is a more project-specific focus on (test) process improvement, less emphasis is likely to be placed on broader issues affecting testing across the organization. This could mean, for example, that fundamental testing problems may not be fully addressed because they are beyond this project-centric context. A typical example here is the approach taken to testing certain quality attributes, such as performance and reliability. These issues may become deferred from iteration to iteration because they often require more skills and resources than the project team has available. It is hard in these areas to make a substantial next step without major investments. Solving problems only on a project level could also easily lead to suboptimization and losing touch with the bigger picture.

In agile and iterative contexts, the range and number of alternative improvement ideas to be considered may be considerably more than compared to the sequential life cycle models. Since most members have a part-time testing role within the project, these ideas can come from any project member. This places a stronger emphasis on evaluating and prioritizing improvement suggestions, which may be more of a team effort than a task assigned to a test process improver. Since this may require the specific testing knowledge of a test process improver, they can also act as a consultant to the team if requested to do so.

In projects using the agile methodology and practicing agile testing techniques such as extreme programming (XP), don't expect to find the level of test documentation you would expect from projects using a sequential life cycle.

There may be a single combined "test document" covering the essential elements of a test policy, test strategy, and even high-level test plan. Test process improvers should avoid making "improvement" suggestions that call for more rigorous and thorough test documentation. Like it or not, this isn't part of the

> **Agile testing** Testing practice for a project using agile software development methodologies, incorporating techniques and methods such as extreme programming (XP), treating development as the customer of testing and emphasizing the test-first design paradigm.

> **Extreme programming (XP)** A software engineering methodology used within agile software development whereby core practices are programming in pairs, doing extensive code review, unit testing of all code, and simplicity and clarity in code.

life cycle's approach. One of the main agile principles is that documentation is created only when there is a clear unambiguous need for it [URL: agile manifesto], [van Veenendaal 2008].

The methods used to propose test process improvements when using an agile or iterative life cycle will tend to be analytical methods for evaluating the root causes of problems, such as cause-effect diagrams. These are particularly useful methods for the problem-solving mindset that prevails at the end of an iteration or sprint. Note, however, that the life cycle used does not dictate the improvement method used.

As mentioned in chapter 5, analytical approaches go hand-in-hand with model-based approaches to test process improvement, and this is also true for projects that use an iterative or agile life cycle. However, more tailoring of the models is required. If a content-based model such as STEP or CTP is used (see sections 3.3.4 and 3.3.5), the amount of tailoring required will be substantial. The principal references to these models ([Black 2003], [Craig and Jaskiel 2002]) do not provide any explicit support for this tailoring and the model user is effectively on their own regarding the tailoring required. Basically, both STEP and CTP were developed in a period of time when agile and iterative development life cyles were almost nonexistant, and neither model has been updated since to adapt to today's context. Nevertheless, techniques and other tools that are very useful in agile and iterative environments can be found in both STEP and CTP.

When using a process improvement model such as TPI NEXT or TMMi, more help is available to make the necessary adjustments for agile and iterative life cycles.

The official TPI NEXT book [van Ewijk, et al. 2009] includes chapters that show how to use the model in agile and iterative projects. This includes, for example, a list of the principal key areas to be considered and how their checkpoints should be best tailored and interpreted. In addition, the TMap NEXT content-based methodology (which forms the methodological foundation for the TPI NEXT model) is tailored for SCRUM projects in *TMap NEXT in Scrum* [van der Aalst and Davis 2013] so that TMap can also be applied in agile and SCRUM contexts.

The TMMi website [URL: TMMi] provides case studies and other material on using TMMi in agile projects. One of the authors has provided consulting services to a small financial institution while achieving TMMi level 2 and to a medium-sized embedded software company while achieving TMMi level 3, both employing the agile (SCRUM) life cycle using the "standard" TMMi model. Note that within TMMi, only the goals are mandatory, not the practices.

With TMMi, a special project has been launched to develop a special derivate that focuses on TMMi in agile environments. The main underlying principle is that TMMi is a generic model applicable to various life cycle models and various environments. Most (specific) goals and (specific) practices as defined by TMMi have shown to be also applicable in agile environments. Remember, testing still needs to be done in a professional way. However, many of the sub-practices and examples, and their interpretation, are (very) different. As a result, the TMMi Foundation is not developing a new maturity model but will document the way TMMi can be applied in an agile environment. It will be determined whether each "standard" TMMi goal and practice is also applicable for testing in an agile life cycle. Some goals (or practices) may just not be. For each goal and practice that is applicable, typical lightweight agile sub-practices and examples will be defined. The latest updates and results of this project can be found on the TMMi website. [URL: TMMi]

Influence of Sequential Life Cycle Models on Improvement Context

When sequential life cycle models such as the V-model are used, test process improvement is generally considered at the end of a software release cycle, at the end of a phase, or at the end of the project itself. This is where, for example, milestone reviews can be a particularly useful method for performing causal analysis and identifying improvements (see section 4.2.6). The feedback loops for process improvement contained in sequential life cycles enable product and process conformance and suitability (verification and validation) to be checked at predefined points in the project.

Using sequential life cycle models, the scope of improvement is broader and there is more opportunity to address organizational improvements compared to the more project-centric approach in iterative and agile life cycles. However, the benefits of performing test process improvement often accrue only for other projects and may not have a direct impact on the current project.

Many of the improvement methods described in this book have been developed to support projects that apply sequential life cycles, projects for which "home-grown" approaches have been developed, or even projects for which no test process is defined. The process maturity concepts implemented in process reference models such as TMMi and TPI NEXT are well suited to sequential life cycles, and the stepwise approaches in content reference models such as CTP and STEP are also well aligned to projects using sequential life cycles. In general, however, the process reference models TPI NEXT and TMMi provide more support for both sequential and iterative/agile life cycle models and would need less tailoring if applied to the latter.

Other Factors That Influence the Context of Improvement

Apart from the life cycle model used, two other factors, management culture and test approach, have an influence on the acceptability of a suggested improvement approach.

Management Culture

As noted in section 9.2.2, management culture can have a decisive influence on the culture of improvement and, ultimately, on whether test process improvements will be successful. Management culture includes the following categories:

- Command and control: Decisions are made at the top and handed down through the hierarchy of management until they reach the people who are instructed to perform specific tasks.
- Consultative: Management involves people at various stages in the decision making process and adopts a more consultative approach to get good buy-in.
- Team driven: The team decides collectively on what is best in their project. This is typically found in projects using SCRUM.

Test Strategies Used and Their Influence on the Context of Improvement

Testing strategies may include one or more of the following:

- Automated (see section 2.5.4), often referred to as the regression-averse strategy
- Manual, including scripted (part of a methodical strategy), unscripted, and exploratory approaches (part of a dynamic strategy)

Clearly, the blend of approaches that are used within a project will influence the overall acceptability of the improvements proposed. Manual testing approaches may benefit from some automation, and the efficiency of automated approaches may be improved by introducing different techniques, such as keyword-driven.

An overview and description of the various test strategies is provided in *Foundations of Software Testing – ISTQB Certification* [Black, van Veenendaal, and Graham 2012].

Concluding Remarks

Adapting for different context factors is an essential element in creating acceptable improvement proposals. The test process improver must evaluate whether proposals "fit" the chosen life cycle model and propose only those recommendations that are appropriate.

10.2 Exercises

The following multiple-choice questions will give you some feedback on your understanding of this chapter. Appendix F lists the answers.

10-1 Which of the following aspects has an influence on improvement context when using an iterative or agile life cycle model?

   A: Test effectiveness metrics

   B: Improvement cycle frequency

   C: Time frames for reaching improvement milestones

   D: Availability of process improvement skills

10-2 What statement best reflects the involvement of the test process improver in projects using an agile life cycle?

   A: The test process improver has no direct involvement in agile projects. The team members take on testing tasks, including improvement.

   B: The role of test process improver is no different than in projects using sequential life cycle models.

   C: The test process improver may act as a consultant to the team on request.

   D: The test process improver performs mostly analytical tasks because test process improvement models are rarely used in agile projects.

10-3 Which of the following statements correctly reflects the influence of sequential life cycle models on improvement context?

A: Test process improvement models are intended for use with sequential life cycle models only.

B: The main opportunity for test process improvement is at the end of the project.

C: Improvement activities focus mostly on process conformance issues (not limited to just process conformance—e.g., product conformance, usability).

D: There is more opportunity to address organizational improvements.

10-4 If you are doing test improvement in a organization that is mainly applying agile development, which of the following methods would you most likely *not* use?

A: STEP

B: Causal analysis

C: TMMi

D: TPI NEXT

10-5 Which of the following management cultures would best fit the situation where agile (SCRUM) is being practiced?

A: Command and control

B: Exploratory

C: Team driven

D: Consultative

10-6 Which test strategy would support a test improvement approach centered around tools?

A: Dynamic

B: Methodical

C: Model-based

D: Regression averse

Appendix A: Glossary

This glossary provides a subset of software testing terms as defined by ISTQB [ISTQB-Glossary]. Only the terms used in the book are provided in this glossary. The ISTQB testing glossary is used as a reference document for the International Software Testing Qualification Board (ISTQB) software testing qualification scheme.

The terms in this glossary are in alphabetical order. Some terms are preferred to other, synonymous ones. In this case, the entry for the synonymous term will be a reference to the preferred term. For example, *completion criteria* and *exit criteria* are synonymous, but *exit criteria* is the preferred term. You will therefore find "See *exit criteria*" at the entry for *completion criteria*. You will also find cross-references that begin with "See also." These lead to terms that are related to the entry in some way, perhaps in a broader or narrower sense.

In this glossary, references are used in two ways.

- Square brackets without the addition of "after," e.g., [ISO 9126], mean that the exact text of the reference is used.

- In case a definition from a reference has been adapted to the context of the ISTQB Glossary by minor changes, the addition "after" is used, e.g., [After ISO 9126].

Finally, note that the terms that are underlined are those that are specifically identified by the "Improving the Test Process" syllabus [ISTQB-CTEL-ITP] as keywords. Definitions to these terms are also provided in the appropriate section of this book.

A

acceptance: See *acceptance testing*.

acceptance testing: Formal testing with respect to user needs, requirements, and business processes conducted to determine whether or not a system satisfies the acceptance criteria and to enable the user, customers or other authorized entity to determine whether or not to accept the system [After IEEE 610].

acting (IDEAL): The phase within the IDEAL model where the improvements are developed, put into practice, and deployed across the organization. The acting phase consists of the activities: create solution, pilot/test solution, refine solution, and implement solution. See also *IDEAL*.

agile manifesto: A statement on the values that underpin agile software development. The values are:
- individuals and interactions over processes and tools
- working software over comprehensive documentation
- customer collaboration over contract negotiation
- responding to change over following a plan

Agile software development: A group of software development methodologies based on iterative incremental development, where requirements and solutions evolve through collaboration between self-organizing cross-functional teams.

Agile testing: Testing practice for a project using agile software development methodologies, incorporating techniques and methods such as extreme programming (XP), treating development as the customer of testing and emphasizing the test-first design paradigm.

alpha testing: Simulated or actual operational testing by potential users/customers or an independent test team at the developer's site but outside the development organization. Alpha testing is often employed for off-the-shelf software as a form of internal acceptance testing.

analytical testing: Testing based on a systematic analysis of product risks or requirements for example.

anomaly: Any condition that deviates from expectation based on requirements specifications, design documents, user documents, standards, etc., or from someone's perception or experience. Anomalies may be found during, but not limited to, reviewing, testing, analysis, compilation, or use of software products or applicable documentation [IEEE 1044]. See also *bug, defect, deviation, error, fault, failure, incident*.

assessment report: A document summarizing the assessment results; e.g., conclusions, recommendations, and findings. See also *process assessment*.

assessor: A person who conducts an assessment; any member of an assessment team.

availability: The degree to which a component or system is operational and accessible when required for use. Often expressed as a percentage [IEEE 610].

B

balanced scorecard: A strategic tool for measuring whether the operational activities of a company are aligned with its objectives in terms of business vision and strategy. See also *corporate dashboard, scorecard*.

behavior: The response of a component or system to a set of input values and preconditions.

best practice: A superior method or innovative practice that contributes to the improved performance of an organization under a given context, usually recognized as "best" by other peer organizations.

beta testing: Operational testing by potential and/or existing users/customers at an external site not otherwise involved with the developers to determine whether or not a component or system satisfies the user/customer needs and fits within the business processes. Beta testing is often employed as a form of external acceptance testing for off-the-shelf software in order to acquire feedback from the market.

black-box test design technique: Procedure to derive and/or select test cases based on an analysis of the specification, either functional or non-functional, of a component or system without reference to its internal structure.

bug: See *defect*.

bug report: See *defect report*.

C

Capability Maturity Model Integration (CMMI): A framework that describes the key elements of an effective product development and maintenance process. The Capability Maturity Model Integration covers best practices for planning, engineering and managing product development and maintenance. [Chrissis, Konrad, and Shrum 2004]

CAST: Acronym for Computer Aided Software Testing. See also *test automation*.

causal analysis: The analysis of defects to determine their root cause. [Chrissis, Konrad, and Shrum 2004]

cause-effect analysis: See *cause-effect graphing*.

cause-effect diagram: A graphical representation used to organize and display the interrelationships of various possible root causes of a problem. Possible causes of a real or potential defect or failure are organized in categories and subcategories in a horizontal tree structure, with the (potential) defect or failure as the root node. [After Juran and Godfrey 2000]

cause-effect graph: A graphical representation of inputs and/or stimuli (causes) with their associated outputs (effects), which can be used to design test cases.

cause-effect graphing: A black-box test design technique in which test cases are designed from cause-effect graphs. [BS 7925-2]

certification: The process of confirming that a component, system, or person complies with its specified requirements, e.g., by passing an exam.

change management: (1) A structured approach to transitioning individuals and organizations from a current state to a desired future state. (2) Controlled way to effect a change, or a proposed change, to a product or service. See also *configuration management*.

CMMI: See *Capability Maturity Model Integration*.

code: Computer instructions and data definitions expressed in a programming language or in a form output by an assembler, compiler, or other translator. [IEEE 610]

code coverage: An analysis method that determines which parts of the software have been executed (covered) by the test suite and which parts have not been executed—for example, statement coverage, decision coverage, or condition coverage.

codependent behavior: Excessive emotional or psychological dependence on another person, specifically in trying to change that person's current (undesirable) behavior while supporting them in continuing that behavior. For example, in software testing, complaining about late delivery to test and yet enjoying the necessary "heroism" of working additional hours to make up time when delivery is running late, therefore reinforcing the lateness.

completion criteria: See *exit criteria*.

compliance: The capability of the software product to adhere to standards, conventions, or regulations in laws and similar prescriptions. [ISO 9126]

component: A minimal software item that can be tested in isolation.

component integration testing: Testing performed to expose defects in the interfaces and interaction between integrated components.

component testing: The testing of individual software components. [After IEEE 610]

configuration: The composition of a component or system as defined by the number, nature, and interconnections of its constituent parts.

configuration control: An element of configuration management consisting of the evaluation, coordination, approval or disapproval, and implementation of changes to configuration items after formal establishment of their configuration identification. [IEEE 610]

configuration item: An aggregation of hardware, software, or both that is designated for configuration management and treated as a single entity in the configuration management process. [IEEE 610]

configuration management: A discipline applying technical and administrative direction and surveillance to identify and document the functional and physical characteristics of a configuration item, control changes to those characteristics, record and report change processing and implementation status, and verify compliance with specified requirements. [IEEE 610]

consistency: The degree of uniformity, standardization, and freedom from contradiction among the documents or parts of a component or system. [IEEE 610]

<u>**content-based model**</u>**:** A process model providing a detailed description of good engineering practices, e.g., test practices.

<u>**continuous representation**</u>**:** A capability maturity model structure wherein capability levels provide a recommended order for approaching process improvement within specified process areas. [Chrissis, Konrad, and Shrum 2004]

<u>**corporate dashboard**</u>**:** A dashboard-style representation of the status of corporate performance data. See also *balanced scorecard, dashboard.*

cost of quality: The total costs incurred on quality activities and issues and often split into prevention costs, appraisal costs, internal failure costs, and external failure costs.

coverage: The degree, expressed as a percentage, to which a specified coverage item has been exercised by a test suite.

coverage tool: A tool that provides objective measures of what structural elements (e.g., statements, branches) have been exercised by a test suite.

<u>**critical success factor**</u>**:** An element necessary for an organization or project to achieve its mission. Critical success factors are the critical factors or activities required for ensuring the success.

<u>**Critical Testing Processes**</u> **(CTP):** A content-based model for test process improvement built around 12 critical processes. These include highly visible processes, by which peers and management judge competence, and mission-critical processes, in which performance affects the company's profits and reputation. See also *content-based model.*

<u>**CTP**</u>**:** See *Critical Testing Processes.*

D

dashboard: A representation of dynamic measurements of operational performance for some organization or activity, using metrics represented via metaphors such as visual dials, counters, and other devices resembling those on the dashboard of an automobile so that the effects of events or activities can be easily understood and related to operational goals. See also *corporate dashboard, scorecard*.

data-driven testing: A scripting technique that stores test input and expected results in a table or spreadsheet so that a single control script can execute all of the tests in the table. Data-driven testing is often used to support the application of test execution tools such as capture/playback tools. [Fewster and Graham] See also *keyword-driven testing*.

debugging: The process of finding, analyzing, and removing the causes of failures in software.

decision table: A table showing combinations of inputs and/or stimuli (causes) with their associated outputs and/or actions (effects), which can be used to design test cases.

defect: A flaw in a component or system that can cause the component or system to fail to perform its required function (e.g., an incorrect statement or data definition). A defect, if encountered during execution, may cause a failure of the component or system.

defect category: See *defect type*.

defect density: The number of defects identified in a component or system divided by the size of the component or system (expressed in standard measurement terms, e.g., lines of code, number of classes, or function points).

Defect Detection Percentage (DDP): The number of defects found by a test phase divided by the number found by that test phase and any other means afterward.

defect management: The process of recognizing, investigating, taking action and disposing of defects. It involves recording defects, classifying them, and identifying the impact. [After IEEE 1044]

defect management tool: A tool that facilitates the recording and status tracking of defects and changes. They often have workflow-oriented facilities to track and control the allocation, correction, and re-testing of defects and provide reporting facilities.

defect report: A document reporting on any flaw in a component or system that can cause the component or system to fail to perform its required function. [After IEEE 829]

defect tracking tool: See *defect management tool*.

defect type: An element in a taxonomy of defects. Defect taxonomies can be identified with respect to a variety of considerations, including, but not limited to, the following:

- Phase or development activity in which the defect is created (e.g., a specification error or a coding error)
- Characterization of defects (e.g., an "off-by-one" defect)
- Incorrectness (e.g., an incorrect relational operator, a programming language syntax error, or an invalid assumption)
- Performance issues (e.g., excessive execution time, insufficient availability)

deliverable: Any (work) product that must be delivered to someone other than the (work) product's author.

Deming cycle: An iterative four-step problem-solving process (Plan, Do, Check, Act) typically used in process improvement. [After Edwards 1986]

deviation: See *incident*.

diagnosing (IDEAL): The phase within the IDEAL model where it is determined where one is, relative to where one wants to be. The diagnosing phase consists of the following activities: characterize current and desired states and develop recommendations. See also *IDEAL*.

dynamic testing: Testing that involves the execution of the software of a component or system.

E

effectiveness: The capability of producing an intended result. See also *efficiency*.

efficiency: (1) The capability of the software product to provide appropriate performance, relative to the amount of resources used under stated conditions. [ISO 9126]
(2) The capability of a process to produce the intended outcome relative to the amount of resources used.

efficiency testing: The process of testing to determine the efficiency of a software product.

EFQM (European Foundation for Quality Management) Excellence Model: A non-prescriptive framework for an organization's quality management system, defined and owned by the European Foundation for Quality Management, based on five 'Enabling' criteria (covering what an organization does), and four 'Results' criteria (covering what an organization achieves).

emotional intelligence: The ability, capacity, and skill to identify, assess, and manage the emotions of one's self, of others, and of groups.

entry criteria: The set of generic and specific conditions for permitting a process to go forward with a defined task (e.g., test phase). The purpose of entry criteria is to prevent a task from starting that would entail more (wasted) effort compared to the effort needed to remove the failed entry criteria. [Gilb and Graham 1993]

equivalence class: See *equivalence partition*.

equivalence partition: A portion of an input or output domain for which the behavior of a component or system is assumed to be the same, based on the specification.

equivalence partitioning: A black-box test design technique in which test cases are designed to execute representatives from equivalence partitions. In principle, test cases are designed to cover each partition at least once.

error: A human action that produces an incorrect result. [After IEEE 610]

establishing (IDEAL): The phase within the IDEAL model where the specifics of how an organization will reach its destination are planned. The establishing phase consists of the activities: set priorities, develop approach, and plan actions. See also *IDEAL*.

evaluation: See *testing*.

exit criteria: The set of generic and specific conditions agreed upon with the stakeholders for permitting a process to be officially completed. The purpose of exit criteria is to prevent a task from being considered completed when there are still outstanding parts of the task that have not been finished. Exit criteria are used to report against and to plan when to stop testing. [After Gilb and Graham 1993]

expected result: The behavior predicted by the specification, or another source, of the component or system under specified conditions.

experience-based test design technique: Procedure to derive and/or select test cases based on the tester's experience, knowledge, and intuition.

experience-based testing: Testing based on the tester's experience, knowledge, and intuition.

exploratory testing: An informal test design technique where the tester actively controls the design of the tests as those tests are performed and uses information gained while testing to design new and better tests. [After Bach 2004]

extreme programming (XP): A software engineering methodology used within agile software development whereby core practices are programming in pairs, doing extensive code review, unit testing of all code, and simplicity and clarity in code. See also *agile software development*.

F

failure: Deviation of the component or system from its expected delivery, service, or result. [After Fenton 1991]

failure mode: The physical or functional manifestation of a failure. For example, a system in failure mode may be characterized by slow operation, incorrect outputs, or complete termination of execution. [IEEE 610]

Failure Mode and Effect Analysis (FMEA): A systematic approach to risk identification and analysis and of identifying possible modes of failure and attempting to prevent their occurrence. See also *Failure Mode, Effect and Criticality Analysis (FMECA)*.

Failure Mode, Effect and Criticality Analysis (FMECA): An extension of FMEA, as in addition to the basic FMEA, it includes a criticality analysis, which is used to chart the probability of failure modes against the severity of their consequences. The result highlights failure modes with relatively high probability and severity of consequences, allowing remedial effort to be directed where it will produce the greatest value. See also *Failure Mode and Effect Analysis (FMEA)*.

failure rate: The ratio of the number of failures of a given category to a given unit of measure, e.g., failures per unit of time, failures per number of transactions, failures per number of computer runs. [IEEE 610]

false-fail result: A test result in which a defect is reported although no such defect actually exists in the test object.

false-pass result: A test result that fails to identify the presence of a defect that is actually present in the test object.

false-positive result: See *false-fail result*.

false-negative result: See *false-pass result*.

fault: See *defect*.

Fault Tree Analysis (FTA): A technique used to analyze the causes of faults (defects). The technique visually models how logical relationships between failures, human errors, and external events can combine to cause specific faults to disclose.

fishbone diagram: See *cause-effect diagram*.

formal review: A review characterized by documented procedures and requirements, e.g., an inspection.

functional testing: Testing based on an analysis of the specification of the functionality of a component or system.

functionality: The capability of the software product to provide functions that meet stated and implied needs when the software is used under specified conditions. [ISO 9126]

G

Goal-Question-Metric: An approach to software measurement using a three-level model: conceptual level (goal), operational level (question), and quantitative level (metric).

GQM: See *Goal-Question-Metric*.

I

IDEAL: An organizational improvement model that serves as a roadmap for initiating, planning, and implementing improvement actions. The IDEAL model is named for the five phases it describes: initiating, diagnosing, establishing, acting, and learning.

impact analysis: The assessment of change to the layers of development documentation, test documentation, and components in order to implement a given change to specified requirements.

incident: Any event occurring that requires investigation. [After IEEE 1008]

incident management: The process of recognizing, investigating, taking action and disposing of incidents. It involves logging incidents, classifying them, and identifying the impact. [After IEEE 1044]

incident report: A document reporting on any event that occurred, e.g., during the testing, which requires investigation. [After IEEE 829]

independence of testing: Separation of responsibilities, which encourages the accomplishment of objective testing. [After DO-178B]

indicator: A measure that can be used to estimate or predict another measure. [ISO 14598]

initiating (IDEAL): The phase within the IDEAL model where the groundwork is laid for a successful improvement effort. The initiating phase consists of the activities: set context, build sponsorship, and charter infrastructure. See also *IDEAL*.

inspection: A type of peer review that relies on visual examination of documents to detect defects, e.g., violations of development standards and nonconformance to higher-level documentation. The most formal review technique and therefore always based on a documented procedure. [After IEEE 610, IEEE 1028] See also *peer review*.

inspection leader: See *moderator*.

intake test: A special instance of a smoke test used to decide if the component or system is ready for detailed and further testing. An intake test is typically carried out at the start of the test execution phase. See also *smoke test*.

integration: The process of combining components or systems into larger assemblies.

integration testing: Testing performed to expose defects in the interfaces and in the interactions between integrated components or systems. See also *component integration testing, system integration testing*.

interface testing: An integration test type that is concerned with testing the interfaces between components or systems.

interoperability: The capability of the software product to interact with one or more specified components or systems. [After ISO 9126] See also *functionality*.

Ishikawa diagram: See *cause-effect diagram*.

iterative development model: A development life cycle where a project is broken into a usually large number of iterations. An iteration is a complete development loop resulting in a release (internal or external) of an executable product, which is a subset of the final product under development and grows from iteration to iteration to become the final product.

K

key performance indicator: See *performance indicator*.

keyword-driven testing: A scripting technique that uses data files to contain not only test data and expected results but also keywords related to the application being tested. The keywords are interpreted by special supporting scripts that are called by the control script for the test. See also *data-driven testing*.

L

lead assessor: The person who leads an assessment. In some cases (for instance, with CMMI and TMMi) when formal assessments are conducted, the lead assessor must be accredited and formally trained.

learning (IDEAL): The phase within the IDEAL model where one learns from experiences and improves one's ability to adopt new processes and technologies in the future. The learning phase consists of the activities: analyze and validate, and propose future actions. See also *IDEAL*.

level test plan: A test plan that typically addresses one test level. See also *test plan*.

life cycle model: A partitioning of the life of a product or project into phases. [Chrissis, Konrad, and Shrum 2004] See also *software life cycle*.

M

maintainability: The ease with which a software product can be modified to correct defects, modified to meet new requirements, modified to make future maintenance easier, or adapted to a changed environment. [ISO 9126]

maintenance: Modification of a software product after delivery to correct defects, to improve performance or other attributes, or to adapt the product to a modified environment. [IEEE 1219]

management review: A systematic evaluation of software acquisition, supply, development, operation, or maintenance process performed by or on behalf of management that monitors progress, determines the status of plans and schedules, confirms requirements and their system allocation, or evaluates the effectiveness of management approaches to achieve fitness for purpose. [After IEEE 610, IEEE 1028]

manufacturing-based quality: A view of quality whereby quality is measured by the degree to which a product or service conforms to its intended design and requirements. Quality arises from the process(es) used. [After Garvin 1984] See also *product-based quality, transcendent-based quality, user-based quality, value-based quality*.

master test plan: A test plan that typically addresses multiple test levels. See also *test plan*.

maturity: (1) The capability of an organization with respect to the effectiveness and efficiency of its processes and work practices. See also *Capability Maturity Model Integration, Test Maturity Model integration*.
(2) The capability of the software product to avoid failure as a result of defects in the software. [ISO 9126] See also *reliability*.

maturity level: Degree of process improvement across a predefined set of process areas in which all goals in the set are attained. [van Veenendaal and Wells 2012]

maturity model: A structured collection of elements that describe certain aspects of maturity in an organization and aid in the definition and understanding of an organization's processes. A maturity model often provides a common language, shared vision, and framework for prioritizing improvement actions.

mean time between failures (MTBF): The arithmetic mean (average) time between failures of a system. The MTBF is typically part of a reliability growth model that assumes that the failed system is immediately repaired as a part of a defect.

mean time to repair (MTTR): The arithmetic mean (average) time a system will take to recover from any failure. This typically includes testing to ensure that the defect has been resolved.

measure: The number or category assigned to an attribute of an entity by making a measurement. [ISO 14598]

measurement: The process of assigning a number or category to an entity to describe an attribute of that entity. [ISO 14598]

measurement scale: A scale that constrains the type of data analysis that can be performed on it. [ISO 14598]

metric: A measurement scale and the method used for measurement. [ISO 14598]

milestone: A point in time in a project at which defined (intermediate) deliverables and results should be ready.

mind map: A diagram used to represent words, ideas, tasks, or other items linked to and arranged around a central keyword or idea. Mind maps are used to generate, visualize, structure, and classify ideas and as an aid in study, organization, problem solving, decision making, and writing.

mistake: See *error*.

model-based testing: Testing based on a model of the component or system under test, such as, for example, reliability growth models, usage models such as operational profiles, or behavioral models such as decision tables or state transition diagrams.

moderator: The leader and main person responsible for an inspection or other review process.

module: See *component*.

module testing: See *component testing*.

MTBF: See *mean time between failures*.

MTTR: See *mean time to repair*.

Myers-Briggs Type Indicator (MBTI): An indicator of psychological preference representing the different personalities and communication styles of people.

N

non-conformity: Non-fulfillment of a specified requirement. [ISO 9000]

non-functional testing: Testing the attributes of a component or system that do not relate to functionality, such as reliability, efficiency, usability, maintainability, and portability.

O

outsourced testing: Testing performed by people who are not co-located with the project team and are not fellow employees.

P

Pareto analysis: A statistical technique in decision-making that is used for selection of a limited number of factors that produce significant overall effect. In terms of quality improvement, a large majority of problems (80 percent) are produced by a few key causes (20 percent).

peer review: A review of a software work product by colleagues of the producer of the product for the purpose of identifying defects and improvements. Examples are inspection, technical review, and walk-through.

performance: The degree to which a system or component accomplishes its designated functions within given constraints regarding processing time and throughput rate. [After IEEE 610] See also *efficiency*.

performance indicator: A high-level metric of effectiveness and/or efficiency used to guide and control progressive development (e.g., lead-time slip for software development). [Chrissis, Konrad, and Shrum 2004]

performance testing: The process of testing to determine the performance of a software product. See also *efficiency testing*.

performance testing tool: A tool to support performance testing that usually has two main facilities: load generation and test transaction measurement. Load generation can simulate either multiple users or high volumes of input data. During execution, response time measurements are taken from selected transactions and these are logged. Performance testing tools normally provide reports based on test logs and graphs of load against response times.

portability: The ease with which the software product can be transferred from one hardware or software environment to another. [ISO 9126]

priority: The level of (business) importance assigned to an item, e.g., defect.

process: A set of interrelated activities that transform inputs into outputs. [ISO 12207]

process assessment: A disciplined evaluation of an organization's software processes against a reference model. [After ISO/IEC 15504]

process improvement: A program of activities designed to improve the performance and maturity of the organization's processes and the result of such a program. [Chrissis, Konrad, and Shrum 2004]

process-based model: A framework wherein processes of the same nature are classified into an overall model, e.g., a test improvement model.

product-based quality: A view of quality, wherein quality is based on a well-defined set of quality attributes. These attributes must be measured in an objective and quantitative way. Differences in the quality of products of the same type can be traced back to the way the specific quality attributes have been implemented. [After Garvin 1984] See also *manufacturing-based quality, quality attribute, transcendent-based quality, user-based quality, value-based quality.*

product risk: A risk directly related to the test object. See also *risk*.

project: A unique set of coordinated and controlled activities with start and finish dates undertaken to achieve an objective conforming to specific requirements, including the constraints of time, cost, and resources. [ISO 9000]

project retrospective: A structured way to capture lessons learned and to create specific action plans for improving on the next project or next project phase.

project risk: A risk related to management and control of the (test) project, e.g., lack of staffing, strict deadlines, changing requirements, etc. See also *risk*.

Q

quality: The degree to which a component, system or process meets specified requirements and/or user/customer needs and expectations. [After IEEE 610]

quality assurance: Part of quality management focused on providing confidence that quality requirements will be fulfilled. [ISO 9000]

quality attribute: A feature or characteristic that affects an item's quality. [IEEE 610]

quality characteristic: See *quality attribute.*

quality control: The operational techniques and activities, part of quality management, that are focused on fulfilling quality requirements. [After ISO 8402]

quality gate: A special milestone in a project. Quality gates are located between phases of a project that are strongly depending on the outcome of a previous phase. A quality gate includes a formal check of the documents of the previous phase.

quality management: Coordinated activities to direct and control an organization with regard to quality. Direction and control with regard to quality generally includes the establishment of the quality policy and quality objectives, quality planning, quality control, quality assurance, and quality improvement. [ISO 9000]

R

<u>**Rational Unified Process (RUP)**</u>: A proprietary adaptable iterative software development process framework consisting of four project life cycle phases: inception, elaboration, construction, and transition.

regression-averse testing: Testing using various techniques to manage the risk of regression—for example, by designing reusable testware and by extensive automation of testing at one or more test levels.

regression testing: Testing of a previously tested program following modification to ensure that defects have not been introduced or uncovered in unchanged areas of the software as a result of the changes made. It is performed when the software or its environment is changed.

reliability: The ability of the software product to perform its required functions under stated conditions for a specified period of time or for a specified number of operations. [ISO 9126]

requirement: A condition or capability needed by a user to solve a problem or achieve an objective that must be met or possessed by a system or system component to satisfy a contract, standard, specification, or other formally imposed document. [After IEEE 610]

requirements phase: The period of time in the software lifecycle during which the requirements for a software product are defined and documented. [IEEE 610]

retesting: Testing that runs test cases that failed the last time they were run in order to verify the success of corrective actions.

<u>**retrospective meeting**</u>: A meeting at the end of a project during which the project team members evaluate the project and learn lessons that can be applied to the next project.

review: An evaluation of a product or project status to ascertain discrepancies from planned results and to recommend improvements. Examples include management review, informal review, technical review, inspection, and walk-through. [After IEEE 1028]

reviewer: The person involved in a review who identifies and describes anomalies in the product or project under review. Reviewers can be chosen to represent different viewpoints and roles in the review process.

risk: A factor that could result in future negative consequences; usually expressed as impact and likelihood.

risk analysis: The process of assessing identified risks to estimate their impact and probability of occurrence (likelihood).

risk assessment: The process of assessing a given project or product to determine its level of risk, typically by assigning likelihood and impact ratings and then aggregating those ratings into a single risk priority rating. See also *product risk, project risk, risk, risk impact, risk level, risk likelihood.*

risk-based testing: An approach to testing to reduce the level of product risks and inform stakeholders of their status, starting in the initial stages of a project. It involves the identification of product risks and the use of risk levels to guide the test process.

risk category: See *risk type.*

risk identification: The process of identifying risks using techniques such as brainstorming, checklists, and failure history.

risk impact: The damage that will be caused if a risk becomes an actual outcome or event.

risk level: The importance of a risk as defined by its characteristics impact and likelihood. The level of risk can be used to determine the intensity of testing to be performed. A risk level can be expressed either qualitatively (e.g., high, medium, low) or quantitatively.

risk likelihood: The estimated probability that a risk will become an actual outcome or event.

risk management: Systematic application of procedures and practices to the tasks of identifying, analyzing, prioritizing, and controlling risk.

risk type: A set of risks grouped by one or more common factors, such as a quality attribute, cause, location, or potential effect. A specific set of product risk types is related to the type of testing that can mitigate (control) the risk type. For example, the risk of user interactions being misunderstood can be mitigated by usability testing.

root cause: A source of a defect such that if it is removed, the occurrence of the defect type is decreased or removed. [Chrissis, Konrad, and Shrum 2004]

root cause analysis: An analysis technique aimed at identifying the root causes of defects. By directing corrective measures at root causes, it is hoped that the likelihood of defect recurrence will be minimized.

RUP: See *Rational Unified Process.*

S

safety: The capability of the software product to achieve acceptable levels of risk of harm to people, business, software, property, or the environment in a specified context of use. [ISO 9126]

safety-critical system: A system whose failure or malfunction may result in death or serious injury to people, loss or severe damage to equipment, or environmental harm.

sanity test: See *smoke test*.

scenario testing: See *use case testing*.

scorecard: A representation of summarized performance measurements representing progress toward the implementation of long-term goals. A scorecard provides static measurements of performance over or at the end of a defined interval. See also *balanced scorecard, dashboard*.

SCRUM: An iterative incremental framework for managing projects commonly used with agile software development. See also *agile software development*.

security: Attributes of software products that bear on its ability to prevent unauthorized access, whether accidental or deliberate, to programs and data. [ISO 9126] See also *functionality*.

severity: The degree of impact that a defect has on the development or operation of a component or system. [After IEEE 610]

SMART goal methodology: A methodology whereby objectives are defined very specifically rather than generically. SMART is an acronym derived from the attributes of the objective to be defined: Specific, Measurable, Attainable, Relevant, and Timely.

smoke test: A subset of all defined/planned test cases that cover the main functionality of a component or system to ascertain that the most crucial functions of a program work but not bothering with finer details. A daily build and smoke test is among industry best practices. See also *intake test*.

software: Computer programs, procedures, and possibly associated documentation and data pertaining to the operation of a computer system. [IEEE 610]

software life cycle: The period of time that begins when a software product is conceived and ends when the software is no longer available for use. The software life cycle typically includes a concept phase, requirements phase, design phase, implementation phase, test phase, installation and checkout phase, operation and maintenance phase, and sometimes, retirement phase. Note that these phases may overlap or be performed iteratively.

Software Process Improvement (SPI): A program of activities designed to improve the performance and maturity of an organization's software processes and the results of such a program. [After Chrissis, Konrad, and Shrum 2004]

Software Usability Measurement Inventory (SUMI): A questionnaire-based usability test technique for measuring software quality from the end user's point of view. [van Veenendaal 2010]

software quality: The totality of functionality and features of a software product that bear on its ability to satisfy stated or implied needs. [After ISO 9126] See also *quality*.

specification-based test design technique: See *black-box test design technique*.

SPI: See *Software Process Improvement*.

stability: The capability of the software product to avoid unexpected effects from modifications in the software. [ISO 9126] See also *maintainability*.

staged representation: A model structure wherein attaining the goals of a set of process areas establishes a maturity level; each level builds a foundation for subsequent levels. [Chrissis, Konrad, and Shrum 2004]

standard: Formal, possibly mandatory, set of requirements developed and used to prescribe consistent approaches to the way of working or to provide guidelines (e.g., ISO/IEC standards, IEEE standards, and organizational standards). [After Chrissis, Konrad, and Shrum 2004]

state diagram: A diagram that depicts the states that a component or system can assume and shows the events or circumstances that cause and/or result from a change from one state to another. [IEEE 610]

statement: An entity in a programming language, which is typically the smallest indivisible unit of execution.

statement coverage: The percentage of executable statements that have been exercised by a test suite.

static analysis: Analysis of software development artifacts (e.g., requirements or code) carried out without execution of these software development artifacts. Static analysis is usually carried out by means of a supporting tool.

static testing: Testing of a software development artifact (e.g., requirements, design, or code) without execution of these artifacts (e.g., reviews or static analysis).

STEP: See *Systematic Test and Evaluation Process*.

structural coverage: Coverage measures based on the internal structure of a component or system.

SUMI: See *Software Usability Measurement Inventory*.

suitability: The capability of the software product to provide an appropriate set of functions for specified tasks and user objectives. [ISO 9126] See also *functionality*.

system: A collection of components organized to accomplish a specific function or set of functions. [IEEE 610]

system integration testing: Testing the integration of systems and packages; testing interfaces to external organizations (e.g., Electronic Data Interchange, Internet).

system of systems: Multiple heterogeneous, distributed systems that are embedded in networks at multiple levels and in multiple interconnected domains, addressing large-scale inter-disciplinary common problems and purposes, usually without a common management structure.

system testing: The process of testing an integrated system to verify that it meets specified requirements. [Hetzel]

Systematic Test and Evaluation Process: A structured testing methodology, also used as a content-based model for improving the test process. Systematic Test and Evaluation Process (STEP) does not require that improvements occur in a specific order. See also *content-based model*.

T

technical review: A peer group discussion activity that focuses on achieving consensus on the technical approach to be taken. [Gilb and Graham 1993], [IEEE 1028] See also *peer review*.

test: A set of one or more test cases. [IEEE 829]

test approach: The implementation of the test strategy for a specific project. It typically includes the decisions made based on the (test) project's goal and the risk assessment carried out, starting points regarding the test process, the test design techniques to be applied, exit criteria, and test types to be performed.

test automation: The use of software to perform or support test activities, e.g., test management, test design, test execution, and results checking.

test basis: All documents from which the requirements of a component or system can be inferred. The documentation on which the test cases are based. If a document can be amended only by way of formal amendment procedure, then the test basis is called a frozen test basis. [After Pol, Teunnissen, and van Veenendaal 2002]

test case: A set of input values, execution preconditions, expected results, and execution postconditions developed for a particular objective or test condition, such as to exercise a particular program path or to verify compliance with a specific requirement. [After IEEE 610]

test charter: A statement of test objectives, and possibly test ideas about how to test. Test charters are used in exploratory testing. See also *exploratory testing*.

test closure: During the test closure phase of a test process, data is collected from completed activities to consolidate experience, testware, facts, and numbers. The test closure phase consists of finalizing and archiving the testware and evaluating the test process, including preparation of a test evaluation report. See also *test process*.

test condition: An item or event of a component or system that could be verified by one or more test cases, e.g., a function, transaction, feature, quality attribute, or structural element.

test coverage: See *coverage*.

test cycle: Execution of the test process against a single identifiable release of the test object.

test data: Data that exists (for example, in a database) before a test is executed and that affects or is affected by the component or system under test.

test deliverable: Any test (work) product that must be delivered to someone other than the test (work) product's author. See also *deliverable*.

test design: (1) See *test design specification*.
(2) The process of transforming general testing objectives into tangible test conditions and test cases.

test design specification: A document specifying the test conditions (coverage items) for a test item, the detailed test approach, and identifying the associated high-level test cases. [After IEEE 829] See also *test specification*.

test design technique: Procedure used to derive and/or select test cases.

test design tool: A tool that supports the test design activity by generating test inputs from a specification that may be held in a CASE tool repository (e.g., requirements management tool), from specified test conditions held in the tool itself, or from code.

test environment: An environment containing hardware, instrumentation, simulators, software tools, and other support elements needed to conduct a test. [After IEEE 610]

test estimation: The calculated approximation of a result related to various aspects of testing (e.g., effort spent, completion date, costs involved, number of test cases, etc.), which is usable even if input data may be incomplete, uncertain, or noisy.

test execution: The process of running a test on the component or system under test, producing actual result(s).

test implementation: The process of developing and prioritizing test procedures, creating test data, and, optionally, preparing test harnesses and writing automated test scripts.

test improvement plan: A plan for achieving organizational test process improvement objectives based on a thorough understanding of the current strengths and weaknesses of the organization's test processes and test process assets. [After Chrissis, Konrad, and Shrum 2004]

test incident: See *incident*.

test incident report: See *incident report*.

test level: A group of test activities that are organized and managed together. A test level is linked to the responsibilities in a project. Examples of test levels are component test, integration test, system test, and acceptance test. [After Pol, Teunnissen, and van Veenendaal 2002]

test log: A chronological record of relevant details about the execution of tests. [IEEE 829]

test management: The planning, estimating, monitoring, and control of test activities, typically carried out by a test manager.

test management tool: A tool that provides support to the test management and control part of a test process. It often has several capabilities, such as testware management, scheduling of tests, the logging of results, progress tracking, incident management, and test reporting.

test manager: The person responsible for project management of testing activities and resources, and evaluation of a test object. The individual who directs, controls, administers, plans, and regulates the evaluation of a test object.

Test Maturity Model integration (TMMi): A five-level staged framework for test process improvement (related to the Capability Maturity Model Integration (CMMI) model) that describes the key elements of an effective test process.

test monitoring: A test management task that deals with the activities related to periodically checking the status of a test project. Reports are prepared that compare the actual activities to that which was planned. See also *test management*.

test object: The component or system to be tested.

test objective: A reason or purpose for designing and executing a test.

test oracle: A source to determine expected results to compare with the actual result of the software under test. An oracle may be the existing system (for a benchmark), other software, a user manual, or an individual's specialized knowledge, but it should not be the code. [After Adrion, Branstad, and Cherniabsky]

test performance indicator: A high-level metric of effectiveness and/or efficiency used to guide and control progressive test development. Defect Detection Percentage (DDP) is an example of a test performance indicator.

test phase: A distinct set of test activities (e.g., the execution activities of a test level) collected into a manageable phase of a project. [After Gerrard and Thompson 2002]

test plan: A document describing the scope, approach, resources, and schedule of intended test activities. It identifies, among other test items, the features to be tested, the testing tasks, who will do each task, degree of tester independence, the test environment, the test design techniques, the entry and exit criteria to be used and the rationale for their choice, and any risks requiring contingency planning. It is a record of the test planning process. [After IEEE 829]

test planning: The activity of establishing or updating a test plan.

test policy: A high-level document describing the principles, approach, and major objectives of the organization regarding testing.

test procedure: See *test procedure specification*.

test procedure specification: A document specifying a sequence of actions for the execution of a test. Also known as test script or manual test script. [After IEEE 829] See also *test specification*.

test process: The fundamental test process comprises test planning and control, test analysis and design, test implementation and execution, evaluating exit criteria and reporting, and test closure activities.

Test Process Group (TPG): A collection of (test) specialists who facilitate the definition, maintenance, and improvement of the test processes used by an organization. [After Chrissis, Konrad, and Shrum 2004]

test process improvement manifesto: A statement that echoes the agile manifesto and defines the following values for improving the test process:

- flexibility over detailed processes
- best practices over templates
- deployment orientation over process orientation
- peer reviews over quality assurance (departments)
- business-driven over model-driven. [van Veenendaal 2008]

test process improver: A person implementing improvements in the test process based on a test improvement plan.

test progress report: A document summarizing testing activities and results, produced at regular intervals, to report progress of testing activities against a baseline (such as the original test plan) and to communicate risks and alternatives requiring a decision to management.

test report: See *test summary report* and *test progress report*.

test script: Commonly used to refer to a test procedure specification, especially an automated one.

test session: An uninterrupted period of time spent in executing tests. In exploratory testing, each test session is focused on a charter, but testers can also explore new opportunities or issues during a session. The tester creates and executes test cases on the fly and records their progress. See also *exploratory testing*.

test set: See *test suite*.

test specification: A document that consists of a test design specification, test case specification, and/or test procedure specification.

test stage: See *test level*.

test strategy: A high-level description of the test levels to be performed and the testing within those levels for an organization or program (one or more projects).

test suite: A set of several test cases for a component or system under test, where the post-condition of one test is often used as the precondition for the next one.

test summary report: A document summarizing testing activities and results. It also contains an evaluation of the corresponding test items against exit criteria. [After IEEE 829]

test technique: See *test design technique*.

test tool: A software product that supports one or more test activities, such as planning and control, specification, building initial files and data, test execution, and test analysis. [Pol, Teunnissen, and van Veenendaal 2002] See also *CAST*.

test type: A group of test activities aimed at testing a component or system focused on a specific test objective, i.e., functional test, usability test, regression test, etc. A test type may take place on one or more test levels or test phases. [After Pol, Teunnissen, and van Veenendaal 2002]

testability: The capability of the software product to enable modified software to be tested. [ISO 9126] See also *maintainability*.

testability review: A detailed check of the test basis to determine whether the test basis is at an adequate quality level to act as an input document for the test process. [After Pol, Teunnissen, and van Veenendaal 2002]

tester: A skilled professional who is involved in the testing of a component or system.

testing: The process consisting of all life cycle activities, both static and dynamic, concerned with planning, preparation, and evaluation of software products and related work products to determine that they satisfy specified requirements, to demonstrate that they are fit for purpose, and to detect defects.

testware: Artifacts produced during the test process required to plan, design, and execute tests, such as documentation, scripts, inputs, expected results, set-up and clear-up procedures, files, databases, environment, and any additional software or utilities used in testing. [After Fewster and Graham 1999]

TMMi: See *Test Maturity Model integration*.

Total Quality Management (TQM): An organization-wide management approach centered on quality, based on the participation of all members of the organization, and aiming at long-term success through customer satisfaction and benefits to all members of the organization and to society. Total Quality Management consists of planning, organizing, directing, control, and assurance. [After ISO 8402]

TPI NEXT: A continuous business-driven framework for test process improvement that describes the key elements of an effective and efficient test process.

TPG: See *Test Process Group*.

TQM: See *Total Quality Management*.

traceability: The ability to identify related items in documentation and software, such as requirements with associated tests.

transactional analysis: The analysis of transactions between people and within people's minds; a transaction is defined as a stimulus plus a response. Transactions take place between people and between the ego states (personality segments) within one person's mind.

transcendent-based quality: A view of quality wherein quality cannot be precisely defined but we know it when we see it or are aware of its absence when it is missing. Quality depends on the perception and affective feelings of an individual or group of individuals toward a product. [After Garvin 1984] See also *manufacturing-based quality, product-based quality, user-based quality, value-based quality*.

U

unit: See *component*.

unit testing: See *component testing*.

use case testing: A black box test design technique in which test cases are designed to execute scenarios of use cases.

user acceptance testing: See *acceptance testing*.

user-based quality: A view of quality wherein quality is the capacity to satisfy needs, wants, and desires of the user(s). A product or service that does not fulfill user needs is unlikely to find any users. This is a context-dependent, contingent approach to quality since different business characteristics require different qualities of a product. [After Garvin 1984] See also *manufacturing-based quality, product-based quality, transcendent-based quality, value-based quality.*

V

V-model: A framework to describe the software development life cycle activities from requirements specification to maintenance. The V-model illustrates how testing activities can be integrated into each phase of the software development life cycle.

validation: Confirmation by examination and through provision of objective evidence that the requirements for a specific intended use or application have been fulfilled. [ISO 9000]

value-based quality: A view of quality wherein quality is defined by price. A quality product or service is one that provides desired performance at an acceptable cost. Quality is determined by means of a decision process with stakeholders on trade-offs between time, effort, and cost aspects. [After Garvin 1984] See also *manufacturing-based quality, product-based quality, transcendent-based quality, user-based quality.*

verification: Confirmation by examination and through provision of objective evidence that specified requirements have been fulfilled. [ISO 9000]

W

walk-through: A step-by-step presentation by the author of a document in order to gather information and to establish a common understanding of its content. [Freedman and Weinberg 1990], [IEEE 1028] See also *peer review.*

white-box test design technique: Procedure to derive and/or select test cases based on an analysis of the internal structure of a component or system.

Appendix B: Literature and References

B.1   Books/Journals

[Adrion, Branstad, and Cherniabsky 1982] Adrion, W., M. Branstad, and J. Cherniabsky. 1982. "Validation, Verification and Testing of Computer Software." *Computing Surveys*, Vol. 14, No 2.

[Anderson 2001] Anderson, L., and Krathwohl, D. A. 2001. *Taxonomy for Learning, Teaching and Assessing: A Revision of Bloom's Taxonomy of Educational Objectives*. New York: Longman.

[Bach 2004] Bach, J. "Exploratory Testing." 2004. In *The Testing Practitioner, 2nd Edition*, by E. van Veenendaal. UTN Publishing.

[Basili and Rombach 1988] Basili, V.R., and H.D. Rombach. 1988. "The TAME Project: Towards improvement oriented software environments." *IEEE Transactions on Software Engineering*, Vol. 14, No. 6.

[Basili and Weiss 1984] Basili, V.R., and D.M. Weiss. 1984. "A methodology for collecting valid software engineering data." *IEEE Transactions on Software Engineering*, Vol. 10, No. 4.

[Basili, Caldiera, and Rombach 1994] Basili, V.R., G. Caldiera, and H.D. Rombach. 1994. "GQM Paradigm." In *Encyclopaedia of Software Engineering," Volume 1*. John Wiley & Sons.

[Belbin 2010] Belbin, R. Meridith 2010. *Management Teams: Why They Succeed or Fail, Third Edition*. Butterworth Heinemann.

[Black 2003] Black, Rex. 2003. *Critical Testing Processes*. Addison-Wesley.

[Black 2009] Black, Rex. 2009. *Managing the Testing Process*. Wiley.

[Black, van Veenendaal, and Graham 2012] Black, R., E. van Veenendaal, and D. Graham. 2012. *Foundations of Software Testing – ISTQB Certification*, Third Edition. Cengage Learning.

[Briggs Myers and Myers 1995] Briggs Myers, I., and P. B. Myers. (1980) 1995. *Understanding Personality Type*. Mountain View, CA: Davies-Black Publishing.

[Broekman and van Veenendaal 2007] Broekman, B., and E. van Veenendaal. 2007. "Test Process Improvement" (in Dutch). In *Software Testen in Nederland; 10 jaar TESTNET*, edited by H. van Loenhout. Academic Service.

[Burnstein 2003]: Burnstein, I. 2003. *Practical Software Testing*. Springer.

[Buzan and Buzan 1995] Buzan, T., and B. Buzan. 1995. *The Mind Map Book: How to Use Radiant Thinking to Maximize Your Brain's Untapped Potential.* BBC-Books.

[Cannegieter 2003] Cannegieter, J.J. 2003. *Software Process Improvement* (in Dutch). SDU Publishing.

[Chrissis, Konrad, and Shrum 2004] Chrissis, M.B., M. Konrad, and S. Shrum. 2004. *CMMI, Guidelines for Process Integration and Product Improvement.* Addison-Wesley.

[Copeland 2003] Copeland, L. 2003. *A Practitioner's Guide to Software Test Design.* Artech House.

[Craig and Jaskiel 2002] Craig, R.D., and S.P. Jaskiel. 2002. *Systematic Software Testing.* Artech House.

[Curtis, Hefley, and Miller 2009] Curtis, B., W.E. Hefley, and S.A. Miller. 2009. *The People Capability Maturity Model (P-CMM), Version 2.* Software Engineering Institute.

[de Bono 1999] de Bono, E. 1999. *Six Thinking Hats.* MICA Management Resources Inc.

[Edwards 1986] Edwards, D. W. 1986. *Out of the Crisis.* MIT Center for Advanced Engineering Study.

[Evans 2004] Evans, I. 2004. *Achieving Software Quality through Teamwork.* Artech House.

[Fagan 1976] Fagan, M.E. 1976. "Design and Code Inspections to Reduce Errors in Program Development." *IBM Systems Journal* 15(3), 182–211.

[Fenton 1991] Fenton, N. 1991. *Software Metrics: A Rigorous Approach.* Chapman & Hall.

[Few 2006] Few, S. 2006. *Information Dashboard Design: The Effective Visual Communication of Data.* O'Reilly Media.

[Fewster and Graham 1999] Fewster, M., and D. Graham. 1999. *Software Test Automation, Effective Use of Test Execution Tools.* Addison-Wesley.

[Frank 1990] Frank, M. 1990. *How to Get Your Point Across in 30 Seconds or Less.* Simon & Schuster.

[Freedman and Weinberg 1990] Freedman, D., and G. Weinberg. 1990. *Walkthroughs, Inspections, and Technical Reviews.* Dorset House Publishing.

[Garvin 1984] Garvin, D.A. 1984. "What Does Product Quality Really Mean?" *Sloan Management Review* Vol. 26, No. 1 1984.

[Gerrard and Thompson 2002] Gerrard, P., and N. Thompson. 2002. *Risk-Based E-Business Testing.* Artech House Publishers.

[Gilb and Graham 1993] Gilb, T., and D. Graham. 1993. *Software Inspection.* Addison-Wesley.

[Gladwell 2000] Gladwell, M. 2000. *The Tipping Point: How Little Things Can Make a Big Difference.* Little, Brown and Company.

[Hetzel 1998] Hetzel, W. 1988. *The Complete Guide to Software Testing, Second Edition.* QED Information Sciences.

[Honey and Mumford 2002] Honey, P., and A. Mumford. 2002. *The Learning Styles Helper's Guide.* Peter Honey Publications. [URL: Honey]

[Humphrey 1997] Humphrey, W. 1997. *Introduction to the Personal Software Process.* Massachusetts: Software Engineering Institute.

[Humphrey 2000] Humphrey, W. 2000. *Introduction to the Team Software Process.* Massachusetts: Software Engineering Institute.

[ITIL 2002] ITIL. 2002. *Best Practice for Service Support*. Office of Government Commerce.

[Juran and Godfrey 2000] Juran, J., and A. Godfrey 2000. *Juran's Quality Handbook, Fifth Edition*. McGraw-Hill International Editions, Industrial Engineering Series.

[Kaplan and Norton 1996] Kaplan, R.S., and D.P. Norton. 1996. "Using the Balanced Scorecard as a Strategic Management System." *Harvard Business Review* January-February 1996.

[Karten 2009] Karten, N. 2009. *Changing How You Manage and Communicate Change: Focusing on the Human Side of Change*. IT Governance Publishing.

[Koomen and Pol 1999] Koomen, T., and M. Pol. 1999. *Test Process Improvement*. Addison-Wesley.

[Koomen et al. 2006] Koomen, T., L. van der Aalst, B. Broekman, and M. Vroon. 2006. *TMap Next for Result-Driven Testing*. UTN Publishers.

[Marselis and van der Ven 2009] Marselis, R., and R. van der Ven. 2009. "TPI NEXT clusters for CMMI." White paper, November 16. Sogeti Nederland B.V.

[Mayer 2004] Mayer, J.D. 2004. *Emotional Intelligence: Key Readings on the Mayer and Salovey Model*. National Professional Resources Inc.

[McFeeley 1996] McFeeley, B. 1996. *IDEAL: A User's Guide for Software Process Improvement*. Pittsburg: SEI. Handbook, CMU/SEI-96-HB-001.

[Pol, Teunnissen, and van Veenendaal 2002] Pol, M., R. Teunnissen, and E. van Veenendaal. 2002. *Software Testing: A Guide to the TMap Approach*. Addison-Wesley.

[Pulford, Kuntzmann-Combelles, and Shirlaw 1995] Pulford, K., A. Kuntzmann-Combelles, and S. Shirlaw. 1995. *A Quantitative Approach to Software Management – The AMI Handbook*. Addison-Wesley.

[Pyzdek and Keller 2009] Pyzdek, T., and P. Keller 2009. *The Six Sigma Handbook, Third Edition*. McGraw-Hill.

[Robson 1995] Robson, M. 1995. *Problem Solving in Groups*. Gower.

[Satir et al. 1991] Satir, V., J. Banmen, J. Gerber, and M. Gomori. 1991. *The Satir Model: Family Therapy and Beyond*. Science and Behavior Books, Inc.

[TMMi Foundation 2009] "TMMi Assessment Method Application Requirements (TAMAR), Version 2.0." 2009. Produced by the TMMi Foundation.

[Trienekens and van Veenendaal 1997] Trienekens, J., and E. van Veenendaal. 1997. *Software Quality from a Business Perspective*. Kluwer Bedrijfsinformaties.

[Tufte 1997] Tufte, E. 1997. *Envisioning Information*. Graphics Press.

[van der Aalst and Davis 2013] van der Aalst, L., and C. Davis. 2013. *TMap NEXT in SCRUM* (in Dutch). Line UP.

[van Ewijk, et al. 2009] van Ewijk, A., G. de Vries, B. Visser, L. Wilhelmus, M. van Oosterwijk, and B. Linker. 2009. *TPI NEXT – Business Driven Test Process Improvement*. UTN Publishing.

[van Loon 2007] van Loon, H. 2007. *Process Assessment and ISO/IEC 15504: A Reference Book, Second Edition*. Springer Verlag.

[Van Solingen 2000] Van Solingen, R., 2000. *Product Focused Software Process Improvement – SPI in the Embedded Software Domain*. BETA Research Institute, Eindhoven University Press.

[van Veenendaal 2008] van Veenendaal, E. 2008, "Test Process Improvement Manifesto." *Testing Experience*, Issue 04, December 2008.

[van Veenendaal 2010] van Veenendaal, E. 2010. *The Testing Practitioner*. UTN Publishers.

[van Veenendaal 2011] van Veenendaal, E. 2011. "Testing @ Domains, and the winner is ...." *Testing Experience*, Issue 01/11, March 2011.

[van Veenendaal 2012] van Veenendaal, E. 2012. *Practical Risk-Based Testing: The PRISMA Approach*. UTN Publishers.

[van Veenendaal and Cannegieter 2011] van Veenendaal, E., and J.J. Cannegieter. 2011. *The Little TMMi*. UTN Publishers.

[van Veenendaal and Cannegieter 2013] van Veenendaal, E., and J.J. Cannegieter. 2013. *Test Maturity Model integration (TMMi): Results of the First TMMi Benchmark - Where Are We Today?* EuroSTAR e-book.

[van Veenendaal and Wells 2012] van Veenendaal, E., and B. Wells. 2012. *Test Maturity Model integration (TMMi) – Guidelines for Test Process Improvement*. UTN Publishers.

[von Thun 2008] von Thun, Schulz. 2008. *Six Tools for Clear Communication*. Institut für Kommunikation (available from www.schulz-von-thun.de).

[Wagner 1996] Wagner, Abe. 1996. *The Transactional Manager*. Spiro Press.

[Weinberg 1992] Weinberg, G. 1992. *Quality Software Management, Volume 1*. Dorset House.

[Weska 2004] Weska, J. 2004. "Lockeed Martin Benefits Continue under CMMI." CMMI Technology Conference, November 2004.

[Zandhuis 2009] Zandhuis, J. 2009. "Improvement team relay, agile improvements" (in Dutch). SPIder Conference, October 6, 2009.

B.2   ISTQB Publications

The following ISTQB publications are mentioned in this book and may be obtained from the ISTQB website [URL: ISTQB]

[ISTQB-EL-EXAM] *ISTQB – Modularized Expert Level Exam Structure and Rules, Version 2.0*. April 12, 2013

[ISTQB_FL] *ISTQB Certified Tester Foundation Level Syllabus*. 2011.

[ISTQB-Glossary] *ISTQB Glossary of Terms Used in Software Testing, Version 2.2*. 2012.

[ISTQB-CTAL-TM] *ISTQB Certified Tester Advanced Level, Test Manager Syllabus, Version 2012*.

[ISTQB-CTEL-ITP] *ISTQB Certified Tester Expert Level Syllabus, Version 1.0.2*.

[ISTQB-CEP] *ISTQB Certified Tester Expert Level, Certification Extension Process, Version 1.0*. June 17, 2008.

[ISTQB-EL-OVIEW] *Certified Tester Expert Level, Modules Overview, Version 1.2*. August, 23, 2013.

B.3   Standards

[BS-7925-2] BS 7925-2 (1998) Software Component Testing.

[DO-178b] DO-178B (1992) Software Considerations in Airborne Systems and Equipment Certification, Requirements and Technical Concepts for Aviation (RTCA SC167).

[IEEE 610] IEEE 610.12™ (1990) Standard Glossary of Software Engineering Terminology.

[IEEE 829] IEEE Std 829™ (1998/2005) IEEE Standard for Software Test Documentation.

[IEEE829-08] IEEE Std 829™ (2008) IEEE Standard for Software Test Documentation.

[IEEE 1008] IEEE 1008™ (1993) Standard for Software Unit Testing.

[IEEE 1028] IEEE Std 1028™ (1997) IEEE Standard for Software Reviews.

[IEEE 1044] IEEE Std 1044™ (1993) IEEE Standard Classification for Software Anomalies.

[IEEE 1219] IEEE 1219™ (1998) Software Maintenance.

[ISO 8402] ISO 8402 (1994). Quality Management and Quality Assurance Vocabulary.

[ISO 9000] ISO 9000 (2005) Quality Management Systems – Fundamentals and Vocabulary.

[ISO 9126] ISO/IEC 9126-1 (2001) Software Engineering – Software Product Quality.

[ISO/IEC 12207] ISO/IEC 12207 (1995) Software Life Cycle Processes.

[ISO 14598] ISO/IEC 14598-1 (1999) Information Technology – Software Product Evaluation – Part 1: General Overview.

[ISO/IEC 15504] ISO/IEC 15504 (2004) Information technology – Process Assessment.

[ISO 25000] ISO/IEC 25000 (2005) Software Engineering – Software product Quality Requirements and Evaluation (SQuaRE).

B.4 Web References

The following references point to information available on the Internet. Although these references were checked at the time of publication of this book, the authors cannot be held responsible if the references are no longer available. Where references refer to tools, please check with the company for the latest tool information.

Reference tag	Short description	Internet address
[URL: Agile Manifesto]	Website of the Agile Manifesto	www.agilemanifesto.org
[URL: Baldrige]	Malcolm Baldrige Model	www.quality.nist.gov
[URL: EFQM]	Website of The European Foundation for Quality Management	www.efqm.org
[URL: SEI]	Website of the Software Engineering Institute	www.sei.cmu.edu
[URL: Honey]	Website of Peter Honey	www.peterhoney.com
[URL: Ishikawa]	Ishikawa on *Wikipedia*	http://en.wikipedia.org/wiki/Ishikawa_diagram
[URL: ISTQB]	Official website of ISTQB	www.istqb.org
[URL: Kirton]	Official website for KAI, the Kirton Adaption-Innovation Inventory	www.kaicentre.com
[URL: SUMI]	Software Usability Measurement Inventory	www.sumi.ucc.ie
[URL: TMMi]	Official website for the TMMi Foundation	www.tmmi.org
[URL: TPI NEXT]	Official website for the TPI NEXT model	www.tpinext.com
[URL: UML]	Resource page for UML	www.uml.org
[URL: MMP]	MindManager tool	www.mindjet.com

Appendix C: The Syllabus Parts

Table 13–1 and table 13–2 summarize the contents of part 1, "Assessing test processes," and part 2, "Implementing test process improvement," of the "Improving the Test Process" syllabus.

Part 1: Assessing test processes

Chapter	Section	Title
2	All	The context of improvement
3	All	Model-based improvement
4	All	Analytical-based improvement
5	All	Selecting test process improvement approaches
6	2	Initiating the improvement process
6	3	Diagnosing the current situation

Table 13–1 Part 1 contents

Part 2: Implementing test process improvement

Chapter	Section	Title
6	1	Process for improvement: introduction
6	4	Establishing a test improvement plan
6	5	Acting to implement improvement
6	6	Learning from the improvement program
7	All	Organization, roles, and skills
8	All	Managing change
9	All	Critical success factors
10	All	Adapting to different life cycle models

Table 13–2 Part 2 contents

Appendix D: The Exam

As mentioned in chapter 1, the "Improving the Test Process" syllabus consists of two parts, each with its own exam. Section 1.7 provided a general overview of the Expert Level exam. This appendix provides more details about the exam, including the general rules that govern it and the coverage of learning objectives in the exam for each syllabus part.

Essay questions have been introduced to the ISTQB Certified Tester Expert Level certification exams for the first time. We have provided some tips that will help candidates prepare for this part of the exam.

D.1 General Exam Aspects

Each exam is made up of two components:

- Multiple-choice question component
- Essay question component

Multiple-choice question component

- The duration of this component is 45 minutes.
- This component addresses the learning objectives shown in table D–3.

Table D-1 *Multiple-choice question component*

K-level	Points allocated	Time to answer question (guideline)
K2 "understand"	1	1 minute
K3 "apply"	2	3 minutes
K4 "analyze"	3	4 minutes

- Some questions may be more difficult than others. To reflect this, K3 questions may be set at 1, 2, or 3 points and K4 questions may be set at 2 or 3 points, at the discretion of the author of the question. The number of points allocated to a question is shown on the exam paper.
- Each multiple-choice question is expected to be associated with at least one learning objective.
- The allocation of the different K-levels of learning objectives (LOs) in the syllabus is reflected in the coverage of the learning objectives in the exam.
- The multiple-choice exam has 25 questions and is allocated 35 points.

Essay question component

- The duration is 90 minutes (see table D–2).
- An exam contains three essay questions, of which two must be answered. No extra credit is given for answering the third essay question. (Don't even consider it!)

Table D-2 Multiple-choice question component

K-Level	Time to answer question (guideline)
K5 "evaluate"	45 minutes
K6 "create"	45 minutes

- Each essay question is scenario based. The question starts with a descriptive scenario, and on the basis of this, one or more questions are asked.
- Each essay question covers at least two relevant business outcomes (see section 1.4 for a list).
- Essay questions are distributed according to the coverage of the business outcomes and K5 and K6 learning objectives. The required distribution for each specific syllabus part is provided in sections 14.2 and 14.3.
- It is not mandatory for exam participants to answer exam sections in a particular order. You are free to choose whether to answer the essay questions first and then the multiple-choice questions, to answer multi-choice questions first and then the essays, or even to mix them.
- The scoring of a candidate's answer to an essay question is marked according to a scoring guideline. This ensures the maximum possible objectivity in scoring questions.
- Each essay is allocated 50 points.

Rules affecting time available

- The total exam duration is 135 minutes, which is extended by 25 percent for those taking the exam in a language other than their own native language.
- There is no mandatory time limit assigned to each question. The 45 minutes per question is just a guideline. If, for example, a candidate completes an essay question in 40 minutes, they will have 50 minutes to complete another question.
- There is no mandatory time limit assigned to an exam component (multiple-choice and essay). If one component is completed in less time than indicated in the preceding tables, more time is available for the other component.

D.2 Part 1 Exam: "Assessing Test Processes"

The multiple-choice component

Coverage of learning objectives in the multiple-choice exam is shown in table D–3. Note that for certain learning objectives, a selection is given; for example, there will be a single question relating to learning objective 2.5.1 or 2.5.2.

Table D-3 Part 1 Exam multiple-choice questions

Learning objective	Number of questions
LO 4.4.1 (K2)	1
LO 6.3.4 (K2)	1
LO 3.3.8 (K3)	2
LO 3.3.9 (K3)	2
LO 4.2.5 (K3)	1
LO 4.2.7 (K4)	1
LO 4.3.2 (K3)	1
LO 4.3.3 (K3)	1
LO 6.2.2 (K4)	1
LO 2.1.1 (K2) LO 2.1.2 (K2) LO 2.2.1 (K2) LO 2.3.1 (K2) LO 2.3.2 (K2)	2

Learning objective	Number of questions
LO 2.4.1 (K2) LO 2.4.2 (K2) LO 2.4.3 (K2)	1
LO 2.5.1 (K2) LO 2.5.2 (K2)	1
LO 2.5.3 (K2) LO 2.5.4 (K2) LO 2.5.5 (K2)	2
LO 3.1.1 (K2) LO 3.1.2 (K2) LO 3.1.3 (K2) LO 3.1.4 (K2)	1
LO 3.2.1 (K2) LO 3.2.2 (K2) LO 3.3.1 (K2) LO 3.3.2 (K2) LO 3.3.3 (K2)	1
LO 3.3.4 (K2) LO 3.3.5 (K2) LO 3.3.6 (K2)	1
LO 3.4.1 (K2) LO 3.4.2 (K2) LO 3.4.3 (K2) LO 3.4.4 (K2) LO 3.4.5 (K2)	1
LO 3.4.6 (K2) LO 5.1.1 (K2)	1
LO 4.2.1 (K2) LO 4.2.2 (K2) LO 4.2.3 (K2) LO 4.2.4 (K2)	1
LO 4.3.1 (K2) LO 4.3.4 (K2) LO 4.3.5 (K2)	1
LO 6.2.1 (K2) LO 6.3.1 (K2)	1

The essay component

The following K5 and K6 learning objectives are covered in the essay component of the part 1 exam:

LO 2.1.3 (K6)
LO 3.3.7 (K5)
LO 3.3.10 (K5)
LO 4.2.6 (K5)
LO 4.4.2 (K5)
LO 5.1.2 (K5)
LO 6.2.3 (K6)
LO 6.3.2 (K6)
LO 6.3.3 (K6)*
LO 6.3.5 (K5)*

* The following two learning objectives are considered "high priority." It is recommended to include each of them as part of the essay questions:

LO 6.3.3 (K6) Create and present a summary of the conclusions (based on an analysis of the findings) and findings from an assessment.
LO 6.3.5 (K5) Recommend test process improvement actions on the basis of assessment results and the analysis performed.

Each essay question must cover a minimum of two business outcomes out of the four shown in section 1.4.

D.3 Part 2 Exam: "Implementing Test Process Improvement"

The multiple-choice component

Coverage of learning objectives in the multiple-choice exam is shown in table D–6. Note that certain learning objectives are grouped together for question selection. For example, there will be a single question which relates to either learning objective 6.4.1, 6.5.1 or 6.6.1.

Table D-4   Part 2 exam multiple-choice questions

Learning objective	Number of questions
LO 6.1.1 (K2)	1
LO 6.4.2 (K4)	2
LO 6.4.3 (K2)	1
LO 6.4.4 (K2)	1
LO 6.5.2 (K4)	1
LO 7.1.1 (K2)	1
LO 7.1.2 (K4)	1
LO 7.1.3 (K2)	1
LO 7.2.1 (K2)	1
LO 7.3.3 (K3)	2
LO 7.3.4 (K3)	1
LO 8.2.1 (K2)	1
LO 8.3.1 (K2)	1
LO 8.3.2 (K4)	1
LO 9.1.1 (K2)	1
LO 9.2.1 (K2)	1
LO 10.1.1 (K2)	1
LO 10.1.2 (K2)	2
LO 10.1.3 (K2)	1
LO 10.1.4 (K2)	1
LO 6.4.1 (K2) LO 6.5.1 (K2) LO 6.6.1 (K2)	1
LO 7.3.1 (K2) LO 7.3.5 (K2) LO 7.3.6 (K2)	1

The essay component

The following K5 and K6 learning objectives are covered in the essay component of the part 2 exam:

LO 6.1.2 (K6)
LO 6.4.5 (K6)*
LO 7.1.4 (K6)
LO 7.3.2 (K5)
LO 8.2.2 (K6)
LO 8.3.3 (K5)
LO 9.1.2 (K5)
LO 9.1.3 (K5)
LO 9.2.2 (K6)

* LO 6.4.5 (K6), "Create a test improvement plan," is considered "high priority." It is recommended to include this LO as part of the essay questions.
Each essay question must cover a minimum of two Business Outcomes taken from the list of four shown in section 1.4.

D.4   Tips

- Essay questions are marked using a predefined marking scheme that allocates points when specific content is included in the answer. You can't gain marks by showing knowledge in any area other than the one(s) asked for.
- An essay question frequently consists of different tasks. Always check the number of points allocated to a particular task and allocate a similarly proportional amount of time for your answer.
- Be sure that if the task asks for a specific number of items (e.g., "provide four reasons why <something> should be recommended"), you provide the requested number; no more and no less.
- Try to make your answers clear and to the point. Unless otherwise stated in the question, there are generally no extra points allocated for long explanations.
- Marks are allocated for content rather than writing style. It is, of course, important that you can be understood and make your point, but no extra marks are given for lengthy, verbose explanations (this should be an encouragement for anyone taking the exam in a language other than their own native language).

D.5 Common Problems

Candidates taking essay-type exams have tended to make similar mistakes, many of which are easily remedied with a little application. The most common problems are listed here for guidance:

- **Not answering the question set.** Examination questions usually incorporate a simple scenario that sets the context for the question. Candidates who do not pay enough attention to this information tend to answer the question in the style "write down all you know about…" rather than addressing the specific issue(s) raised by the question. While some of the candidate's answer may be relevant, there is a serious risk that much of it will not be and will earn no marks.
- **Not thinking through answers.** Candidates need to structure their response to a question to ensure that they impart the required information with minimum effort. With long and rambling answers, you run the risk of overlooking key information, and the relative importance of your ideas may be undermined by the lack of structure. Long answers also take longer to write down than a well structured but shorter response.
- **Answers are too superficial.** Questions are worded to indicate the level of response required. Sometimes a word count is included. If a question asks for a description of something, this will require more than simply identifying the "something" by name. Similarly, *justify* means provide some kind of evidence that your response is correct or appropriate. All information in an answer must be relevant; any irrelevant information will not earn marks. The candidate therefore wastes valuable time in writing down irrelevant information.
- **Addressing the scenario.** Where a scenario is provided (especially in double-length questions), there is an expectation that candidates will refer to the scenario in their answer, using it to identify specific examples of points raised or to illustrate issues. In an ISTQB Expert Level exam, it is important to demonstrate practical validity of answers wherever possible.
- **Running out of time.** The problems mentioned previously all contribute to wasted time. There is time to construct and write down good answers to the questions on the paper if time is not wasted. A good time plan is essential. It is a good idea to set out the key points of an answer in a bulleted list before starting to draft the text of the answer. At the end of the exam, further time should be allowed for checking through your answers to ensure that no major mistakes have been left uncorrected.

- **Illegible answers**. It is difficult to write both quickly and neatly. However, an illegible scrawl makes it very difficult for a script marker to read a candidate's response and important information may be unintelligible. Time planning should reduce the need to rush. Practice in writing at more than the usual speed would be sensible preparation for the examination, especially for candidates who do not normally communicate with pen and paper. You may find it helpful to highlight key points in your answer by underlining or writing in block capitals.

Appendix E: Summary of Cognitive Levels (K-Levels)

A K-level, or cognitive level, is used to classify learning objectives according to the revised taxonomy from Bloom [Anderson and Krathwohl 2001]. ISTQB uses this taxonomy to design its syllabi examinations.

Cognitive level / K-level	Meaning
K1 (Remember)	Remember or recognize a term or a concept.
K2 (Understand)	Select an explanation for a statement related to the question topic.
K3 (Apply)	Select the correct application of a concept or technique and apply it to a given context.
K4 (Analyze)	Separate information related to a procedure or technique into its constituent parts for better understanding and distinguish between facts and inferences.
K5 (Evaluate) (Expert Level only)	Make judgements based on criteria and standards. Detect inconsistencies or fallacies within a process or product, determine whether a process or product has internal consistency, and detect the effectiveness of a procedure as it is being implemented.
K6 (Create) (Expert Level only)	Put elements together to form a coherent or functional whole. A typical application is to reorganize elements into a new pattern or structure, devise a procedure for accomplishing some task, or invent a product.

Appendix F: Answers

The following table shows the correct answers to the questions for each chapter. Notes for some of these questions (<u>underlined</u>) are provided on the next page.

Chapter 2	Chapter 3	Chapter 4	Chapter 5	Chapter 6
2-1: D	<u>3-1: C</u>	4-1: B	5-1: A	6-1: D
2-2: A	<u>3-2: D</u>	4-2: A	5-2: C	6-2: B
2-3: A	3-3: A	4-3: D	5-3: D	6-3: B
2-4: B	3-4: B	4-4: C	5-4: D	6-4: D
2-5: A	3-5: B	4-5: C	5-5: E	6-5: D
2-6: C	3-6: A	4-6: A		6-6: A
2-7: B	3-7: C	4-7: D		6-7: C
2-8: D	<u>3-8: C</u>	4-8: B		6-8: A
2-9: C	3-9: D	4-9: B		6-9: D
2-10: A	3-10: B	4-10: D		6-10: B
	3-11: B			
	3-12: A			

Chapter 7	Chapter 8	Chapter 9	Chapter 10
<u>7-1: A</u>	8-1: B	9-1: C	10-1: B
7-2: A	8-2: C	<u>9-2: B</u>	10-2: C
7-3: C	<u>8-3: C</u>	<u>9-3: E</u>	10-3: D
<u>7-4: D</u>	8-4: D	9-4: D	10-4: A
7-5: C	<u>8-5: C</u>	<u>9-5: A</u>	10-5: C
<u>7-6: B</u>	<u>8-6: D</u>	9-6: A	10-6: D
<u>7-7: C</u>	<u>8-7: A</u>	9-7: D	
7-8: D	<u>8-8: B</u>	9-8: C	
7-9: C	<u>8-9: D</u>	9-9: B	
7-10: A	<u>8-10: C</u>	9-10: C	

When creating the exercises, we made notes about why certain answers were right or wrong in cases where a short explanation may be of help. The following list shows the notes we made (*in italics*) for selected questions.

3-1: Which of the following is *not* a desirable characteristic of models?

C: Gather test process metrics. *(This is not a desirable model characteristic. Metrics gathering can be supported by approaches like GQM, but models are not used for metrics gathering.)*

3-2: Which of the following is a benefit of using models?

A: Ability to capture project best practices *(No. Models are generally based on industry best practices.)*

B: Provide an industry benchmark *(No. This may arise if results from many projects are gathered by particular organizations, but it's not a benefit of using the model.)*

C: Show solutions to testing problems *(No. An analytical approach would be better for specific problems.)*

D: Compare the maturity status between projects *(Yes.)*

3-8: Which statement is true regarding the process dimension in ISO/IEC 15504 ?

A: The process dimension enables us to measure how well processes are being performed. *(No. That's the capability dimension.)*

B: The process dimension defines generic practices for each process. *(No. It defines base practices. Generic practices are in the capability dimension.)*

C: The process dimension identifies, describes, and organizes the individual processes within the overall software life cycle. *(Yes.)*

D: The process dimension provides indicators of process capability. *(No. Mix-up of capability and process dimensions.)*

7-1: What would you expect to find in the organization of a Test Process Group?

B: Lead Assessor Group *(not explicitly mentioned as part of a TPG.)*

C: Offshore Steering Group *(Not for offshore; Management Steering Group, yes.)*

D: Test Engineering Process Group *(Synonym for TPG, not a part of it.)*

7-4 Which of the following is a task typically performed by a lead assessor?

    A: Set the business goals. *(No. They are set by the organization.)*

    B: Check the assessment report written by the co-assessor. *(No. The co-assessor does not write the report.)*

7-5 Which of the following statements indicates *bad* interviewing skills?

    A: Asking open questions at the start of an interview *(Perfectly okay to do this.)*

    B: Asking "effective inner people" factual questions *(This is okay; you can expect to have difficulty in getting factual information from* ineffective *inner people.)*

    C: Ensuring that a codependent bond is established between interviewer and interviewee *(Yes, this is definitely something to avoid.)*

    D: Making notes *(This is a useful skill.)*

7-7 What is important for the assessor when practicing active listening during an interview?

    A: Give regular feedback to the interviewee on how well they are performing. *(Yes, give feedback, but not regarding their performance.)*

    B: Manage time to ensure that the discussion fits into the allocated time period *(Okay, but not part of active listening.)*

    D: Ask open questions *(Okay, but not part of active listening.)*

8-3 Which of the following principles does *not* apply to the Tipping Point theory?

    C: Changes should be introduced gradually in a controlled stepwise process. *(No. Tipping points are all about allowing change to spread like a virus.)*

8-5 Which of the following can be effective in making change happen?

    A: Avoiding any form of chaos by good management practices *(No. Chaos is going to happen. You can reduce its impact, but you can't avoid it completely.)*

    B: Handling resistance by setting milestones for specific changes *(Milestones may be a good thing, but they are not a good instrument for managing resistance.)*

D: Ensuring that fast adopters of change are rewarded *(No. This could be demotivating for those having trouble adapting to changes.)*

8-6 What can the test improver do to reduce the effects of chaos?

A. Don't talk about it too much; it may make people nervous. *(More communication is needed, not less.)*

B. Plan a short period of resistance into the test improvement plan. *(The period needs to be realistic, not short.)*

C. Convince people that they will have no difficulty taking on changes. *(Again, denial that chaos will have an impact.)*

8-7 Which of the following best describes how the test process improver should behave when resistance is experienced?

B. If resistance is high, then the test process improver should focus on convincing them that the changes will be beneficial. *(No. Provide support.)*

C. If only a few people are showing resistance before the change is introduced, then the test process improver should negotiate with them. *(No. The test process improver may avoid them and focus efforts on the majority.)*

D. If very few people are still resisting change after the rest have adopted the changes, the test process improver should simply ignore them. *(No. Measures should be taken to compel them to implement the change.)*

8-9 What factors contribute to a culture of improvement?

A. Clear identification of roles and responsibilities so that mistakes can be more easily tracked *(No. Ability to discuss problems in a blame-free environment is required.)*

B. Strong leadership by the leader of the test improvement initiative so that too many conflicting ideas can be avoided *(No. Encouraging all stakeholders to suggest improvements is good.)*

C. Performing assessments on a regular basis *(No. The conduct of project retrospectives is good, but regular assessments will not build improvement culture.)*

Appendix F: Answers   409

8-10 What are the qualities of a pragamatist according to the Honey and Mumford learning styles?

  A. Develops sound theories for reuse *(Theorist)*

  B. Is observant and good at collecting metrics *(Reflector)*

  D. Learns by doing *(Activist)*

9-2 Which activity can help to ensure that people involved in an improvement program have sufficient time scheduled for participation?

  A: Discuss within the team and allocate time to those who are not 100 percent scheduled to project work. *(No. This might be occasionally be okay for short-term planning or minor improvements, but management must approve resources available, not the project.)*

  C: Split scheduled work into regular, small chunks of time to ensure that other tasks can run in parallel. *(No. This will result in too many "context changes" and result in inefficiency.)*

  D: Ask for volunteers to work extra time. *(No. This will not work for anything other than minor improvements.)*

9-3 Why is it recommended to use existing practices if already available?

  A: The team members may be offended. *(No. This can be managed, but it is not a reason to keep existing practices; they may be the cause of problems.)*

9-5 Which of the following statements is true regarding the impact of external consultants on an improvement project?

  B: They can make important decisions on the working procedures. *(No. They can only give advice.)*

  C: Consultants who are "indispensible" to the project can provide long-term benefits to their customers. *(No. The primary people must be internal to the organization.)*

  D: They must return to the project regularly to ensure that the momentum of improvements is maintained. *(No. Improvements must be anchored in the organization so the effort and momentum continues after the consultant leaves.)*

Index

A
agile 344, 345, 352
all or nothing syndrome 219
analytical approaches 39, 212
analytical techniques 146, 243
analyzing
    messages 284
    results 243
assessment
    CMMI 82
    formal 241
    informal 241
    ISO/IEC15504 89
    plan 240
    preparation 241
    report 240, 248
    tasks 240
    TMMi 121

B
balanced scorecard 30, 235
balancing feedback loops 171
Belbin roles 287
benchmarks 244
bottom-up implementation 215, 251
brainstorming rules 163
broken windows concept 165
building sponsorship 237

C
career paths 8, 9
causal analysis 146, 212, 352
    cause-effect diagrams 155
    defect clusters 152
    formal reviews 171
    getting started 154
    identifying root causes 160
    IEEE 1044 151
    Ishikawa diagrams 155
    lessons learned 173
    organizing information 154
    responsibilities 160
    selecting items 148
    statistical distributions 152
    statistics 151
cause-effect diagrams 155
    basic form 155
    example 157
    standard categories 156
cause-effect fallacy 173
cause-effect graphing 168
champions of change 307
chaos
    anticipating 317
    managing 319
    signs 319
closed questions 275
CMMI 38, 71
    appraisal 82
    benefits 82
    capability levels 73
    causal analysis 216
    compared to ISO/IEC15504 90
    compared to TMMi 120
    constellations 74
    generic goals 76
    generic practices 76
    goals 76
    maturity levels 72
    practices 76
    process areas 73, 75, 76, 77, 79
    ratings 76
    SCAMPI assessment 82, 85
    specific goals 76
    specific practices 76
    structure 72, 77
CMMI testing specific 79
    other process areas 81
    process integration 81
    technical solution 81

412 Index

validation 80
verification 80
codependent behavior 280
content models 210
content reference models
    compared to process reference models 137
context of change 237
corporate dashboard 233
critical success factor 333
CTP
    critical testing processes 133
    metrics 136, 220
    principal steps 132
    structure 132
    using 137
culture of improvement 327

D

defect categorizations 149, 150
Defect classification
    IEE 1044 170
Deming cycle 25, 177, 224
DMAIC process 35

E

early adopters of change 312
EFQM excellence model 19
    defined 31
    enablers 33
    results 33
emotional intelligence 282
equivalence partitioning 149
exam
    components 10, 393
    entry conditions 10
    part 1 395
    part 2 397
    pass mark 11
expert
    business outcomes 6
    defined 5
expert level
    attributes 6
exploratory testing 50
external consultants 336

F

FDA 51
fishbone diagrams 155

fundamental change process 303
fundamental concepts of excellence 30

G

Generic improvement process
    Deming cycle 25
    IDEAL 29
GQM
    abstraction sheets 186
    analysis plan 181
    approach 39, 174, 214
    definition activities 182
    feedback sessions 188
    interpretation activities 183
    paradigm 176
    plan 179
    process steps 178
    tools and techniques 185

H

Honey and Mumford learning styles 325

I

IDEAL framework 28, 262
IDEAL phases
    acting 253
    diagnosing 239
    establishing 249
    initiating 229
    learning 255
implementation approaches
    big bang 255
    just in time 255
    one project at a time 255
improvement approach
    bottom-up 39
    different test approaches 47
    hybrid 39
    resources 54
    skills development 40
    standards 51
    tools 44
    top-down 39
improvement culture 215
indicator
    definition 192
information hiding 317
infrastructure 238
inspection 175
interviews 273, 279

feedback 243
  performing 242
Ishikawa diagrams 155
  generic tasks 161
  steps 161
ISO 9000 19
ISO/IEC 15504 20, 38
ISO/IEC15504 84
  assessments 89
  capability dimension 88
  capability levels 89
  compared to CMMI 90
  parts 84
  process assessment model 86
  process dimension 85
ISO/IEC15504 testing specific
  validation 88
  verification 87
ITIL 20

L

lifecycle model 343, 351

M

Malcolm Baldrige model 34
management culture 356
management steering group 263
measure
  definition 191
metrics 212
  coverage indicators 199
  defect detection percentage 193
  definition 192
  for quality attributes 197
  lead time 196
  predictability 197
  product quality 197
  test effectiveness 193
  test efficiency / cost 195
  test maturity 200
mind maps 158, 294
mixed approach 216
model benefits
  best practices 64
  comparability 65
  coverage 64
  objectivity 64
  structured approach 63
model risks
  lack of skills 67

model blindness 66
project context 65
wrong approach 67
models
  categories 67
  content reference 38, 68
  continuous representation 69, 70
  process reference 38, 68
  staged representation 69
models-desirable aspects
  content 61
  design 61
  formal 62
Myers-Briggs type indicator 288, 323

O

open questions 275
organizational relationships 343

P

Pareto rule 149, 166
People CMM 42
perspectives of an organization 235
pilot project 254
PRISMA method 51
process assessment 239
process models 206
process reference models
  compared to content reference models 137
product quality characteristics 22
PSP Personal Software Process 42

Q

QIP paradigm 177
quality view 20, 24
  manufacturing-based 22
  product-based 21
  transcendent 24
  user-based 22
  value-based 23
quick wins 315

R

RADAR improvement loop 34
recommendations 240, 247
reinforcing feedback loops 171, 201
reliability 371
resistance to change 319, 320, 335
retrospective meeting 49, 153

reverse quality push 18
risk-based testing 23, 50
roles
    co-assessor 271
    lead assessor 270
    test process improver 268
root causes 169, 213

S
Satir model 304, 316, 320
scope of improvement 237
SCRUM 49
Six Sigma 19, 35, 57, 58
skills 41, 273
    30-second message 295
    active listening 284
    analytical 292
    asking closed questions 275
    asking open questions 275
    interviewing 273
    listening 283
    management 297
    note-taking 293
    people 41
    persuasion 295
    persuasion by pull 297
    persuasion by push 296
    presentation 290
    reporting 291
    writing emails 292
software engineering process group 263
software lifecycle 48
    iterative 49
    sequential 48
    test closure 50
software process improvement 17
solution analysis 244
    approaches 245
SPI models 209, 216
    approach 140
    level of testing detail 139
    marketing considerations 140
    suitability for test improvement 138
SPICE 84
standards
    BS7925-2 53
    IEEE 1028 53
    IEEE 1044 151
    IEEE 829 52

ISO 25000 22
ISO 9126 22
ISO/IEC12207 87
ISO/IEC15504 84
STEP
    content 129
    metrics 220
    roles 131
    structure 128
    tasks and work products 130
    test level 129
stimulus for change 230
strategic action plan 252
structured testing 17
SUMI 293
syllabus 8
    parts 8, 9
system diagrams 170
system models 159
systems thinking 243, 245

T
tactical action plan 252
team and personal software process 20
technical working group 263
test approach 356
test assessment report 239
test career cube 40
test data 55
test environment 54
test improvement 17
    objectives 232
    plan 249
test policy 225, 226, 310, 332
Test Process Group 116, 206, 325, 326
    executive council 262
    for large organizations 262
    services 264
    skills 264
test process improvement
    context 18
    manifesto 345
    offshore organizations 266
    pre-conditions 17
tipping points 165, 244, 245, 306
TMap 93
TMap NEXT 93
TMMi 106, 207, 241
    alignment 107
    approach 123, 126

assessment scale 122
assessments 121
causal analysis 219
compared to CMMI 120
compared to TPI NEXT 124
generic goals 110
generic practices 111
main focus 125
maturity level 1 111
maturity level 2 111
maturity level 3 113
maturity level 4 114
maturity level 5 115
process areas 110
relationship to SPI 127
SCAMPI 122
specific goals 110
specific practices 110
structure 111, 117, 124
take-up 127
TAMAR 85
terminology 127
test methods 126
tool deployment 46
tool selection 46
top-down implementation 215, 251
total quality management 19
TPI 92
TPI NEXT 91
   approach 126
   business objectives 102

causal analysis 217
checkpoints 96
clusters 99
compared to TMMi 124
enablers 101
evaluating checkpoints 97
evaluating results 105
improvement suggestions 102
key areas 93
main focus 125
maturity levels 92
metrics 218
prioritizing key areas 103
relationship to SPI 127
setting priorities 106
structure 92, 125
take-up 127
terminology 127
test maturity matrix 98
test methods 126
transactional analysis 276
transforming ideas 321

V
vicious circle 171, 244, 245
virtuous circles 171
vision 231
V-model 355

W
Wagner's six inner people 276